First World War
and Army of Occupation
War Diary
France, Belgium and Germany

23 DIVISION
Headquarters, Branches and Services
Commander Royal Engineers,
Assistant Director Ordnance Services
and Assistant Director Veterinary Services
20 August 1915 - 31 October 1917

WO95/2174

The Naval & Military Press Ltd
www.nmarchive.com
Published in association with The National Archives

Published by

The Naval & Military Press Ltd

Unit 10 Ridgewood Industrial Park,
Uckfield, East Sussex,
TN22 5QE England
Tel: +44 (0) 1825 749494

www.naval-military-press.com
www.nmarchive.com

This diary has been reprinted in facsimile from the original. Any imperfections are inevitably reproduced and the quality may fall short of modern type and cartographic standards.

© Crown Copyright
Images reproduced by permission of The National Archives, London, England, 2015.

Contents

Document type	Place/Title	Date From	Date To
Miscellaneous			
Heading	23rd Division B.E.F. C.R.E. Aug 1915 To Oct		
Heading	23rd Division H.Q. 23rd Division C.R.E. Vol I Aug Of Sept 15		
War Diary	Bordon	20/08/1915	24/08/1915
War Diary	S' Hampton	24/08/1915	25/08/1915
War Diary	Havre	26/08/1915	27/08/1915
War Diary	St Omer	28/08/1915	28/08/1915
War Diary	Tilques	28/08/1915	28/08/1915
War Diary	Tilques	29/08/1915	06/09/1915
War Diary	Renescure	06/09/1915	07/09/1915
War Diary	Merris	08/09/1915	11/09/1915
War Diary	Croix Du Bac	12/09/1915	30/09/1915
Heading	H.Q. 23rd Division C.R.E. Vol 2 Oct 15		
War Diary	Croix Du Bac	01/10/1915	31/10/1915
Heading	H.Q. 23rd Division CRE Vol.3 Nov 15		
War Diary	Croix Du Bac	01/11/1915	30/11/1915
Heading	C.R.E. 23rd Division Vol:4		
War Diary	Croix Du Bac	01/12/1915	31/12/1915
Heading	C.R.E.23rd Division Vol :5		
War Diary	Croix Du Bac	01/01/1916	31/01/1916
Heading	C.R.E. 23rd Division Vol:6		
War Diary	Croix Du Bac	01/02/1916	29/02/1916
War Diary	Camblain Chatelain	01/03/1916	08/03/1916
War Diary	Chateau de-La Haie	09/03/1916	14/03/1916
War Diary	Ruitz	15/03/1916	22/03/1916
War Diary	Sains-en Gohelle	23/03/1916	19/04/1916
War Diary	Ruitz	20/04/1916	30/04/1916
Miscellaneous	Operation Order No. 6. By C.R.E. 23rd Division.	28/04/1916	28/04/1916
Heading	War Diary Of Head Quarters Royal Engineers 23rd Division From May 1st 1916 To May 31st 1916 Vol 9		
War Diary	Ruitz	01/05/1916	12/05/1916
War Diary	Sains En Gohelle	13/05/1916	31/05/1916
Miscellaneous	Officer Fear Office Base	03/07/1916	03/07/1916
War Diary	Sains-en Gohelle	01/06/1916	12/06/1916
War Diary	La-Thieuloye	13/06/1916	14/06/1916
War Diary	Verchin	15/06/1916	15/06/1916
War Diary	Matringhem	16/06/1916	29/06/1916
War Diary	Vaux-En Amienois	25/06/1916	30/06/1916
Heading	War Diary Of Headqrs. R.S. From 1st July 16 To 31st July 16 Vol 11		
War Diary	Vaux-En Amienois	01/07/1916	01/07/1916
War Diary	Baisieux.	02/07/1916	04/07/1916
War Diary	Dernancourt	05/07/1916	12/07/1916
War Diary	SI Gratien	13/07/1916	20/07/1916
War Diary	Henencourt	21/07/1916	25/07/1916
War Diary	Albert	26/07/1916	30/07/1916
War Diary	Albert W.27.c	31/07/1916	31/07/1916
Operation(al) Order(s)	23rd Division-C.R.E. Order No. S.7 Appendix I	06/07/1916	06/07/1916
Operation(al) Order(s)	23rd Division-C.R.E. Order No. S.8 Appendix 2	09/07/1916	09/07/1916

Operation(al) Order(s)	69th Infantry Brigade Order No. 55. Appendix.3	09/07/1916	09/07/1916
Heading	23rd Division Engineers C.R.E. 23rd Division August 1916		
Heading	War Diary Of H.Q. R.E. 23rd Division From 1st August To 31st August 1916 Vol 12		
War Diary	Albert	01/08/1916	08/08/1916
War Diary	Baizieux	09/08/1916	10/08/1916
War Diary	Ailly-In-Haut Clocher	11/08/1916	12/08/1916
War Diary	Fletre	13/08/1916	15/08/1916
War Diary	Steenwerck	16/08/1916	31/08/1916
Operation(al) Order(s)	C.R.E's Order No. S.10	06/08/1916	06/08/1916
War Diary	Camp W.26.c.o.4	01/10/1916	10/10/1916
War Diary	Montigny	11/10/1916	12/10/1916
War Diary	Ailly-Le-Haut Clocher	13/10/1916	13/10/1916
War Diary	St Riquier	14/10/1916	17/10/1916
War Diary	S.E. Poperinghe Camp	17/10/1916	20/10/1916
War Diary	Reninghelst.	21/10/1916	31/10/1916
Heading	War Diary of H.Q. Royal Engineers November Vol 15		
War Diary	Ypres	01/11/1916	15/11/1916
War Diary	Reninghelst	15/11/1916	30/11/1916
Heading	War Diary Of H.Q. R.E. For Month Of December Vol 16		
War Diary	Reninghelst	01/12/1916	31/12/1916
Heading	War Diary Of H.Q. R.E. 23 Div From January 1st To January 31st 1917 Vol 17		
War Diary	Reninghelst	01/01/1917	27/02/1917
Operation(al) Order(s)	23rd Divisional Engineers Operation Orders No. 1. Appendix A	22/02/1917	22/02/1917
Heading	War Diary Of Head Headquarters R.E. 23rd Division From 1st March To 31st March 1917 Vol 19		
War Diary	Arques	08/03/1917	20/03/1917
War Diary	Esquelbecq	20/03/1917	31/03/1917
Operation(al) Order(s)	23rd Division Engineers C.R.E's Orders No. 2. Appendix A	18/03/1917	18/03/1917
Heading	War Diary Headquarters R.E. 23rd Division Period April 1-April 30 inclusive 1917 Vol 20		
War Diary	Esquelbecq	01/04/1917	08/04/1917
War Diary	Busseboom G16.c.64 Sheet 28 N.W.	08/04/1917	08/04/1917
War Diary	Ypres Salient	06/04/1917	16/04/1917
War Diary	Busseboom	29/04/1917	30/04/1917
Operation(al) Order(s)	23rd Divisional Engineers. C.R.E's Order No. 3. Appendix A	03/04/1917	03/04/1917
Operation(al) Order(s)	23rd Divisional Engineers. Operation Order No. 4. Appendix B	04/04/1917	04/04/1917
Operation(al) Order(s)	23rd Divisional Engineers Operation Order No. 5. Appendix C	05/04/1917	05/04/1917
Operation(al) Order(s)	23rd Divisional Engineers Operation Order No. 5. Appendix E	13/04/1917	13/04/1917
Operation(al) Order(s)	23rd Divisional Engineers. Operation Order No. 6. Appendix D	14/04/1917	14/04/1917
Operation(al) Order(s)	23rd Divisional Engineers. Operation Order No. 8. Appendix F	30/04/1917	30/04/1917
Heading	War Diary Of H.Q. R.E. 23rd Division From May 1st 1917 To May 31st 1917 Vol 21		
War Diary	Busseboom	02/05/1917	02/05/1917
War Diary	Steenvoorde	02/05/1917	12/05/1917

War Diary	Busscboom	12/05/1917	31/05/1917
Operation(al) Order(s)	23rd Divisional Engineers Operation Order No. 9	09/05/1917	09/05/1917
Operation(al) Order(s)	23rd Divisional Engineers Operation Order No. 10 Appendix	14/05/1917	14/05/1917
Heading	23 Div. R.E. June 1917		
Miscellaneous	Cover for Branch Memoranda. Unregistered.		
Heading	War Diary Of Head Quarters R.E. 23rd Division From June 1st-June 30th Vol 22		
War Diary	Busseboom	03/06/1917	16/06/1917
War Diary	Berthen	16/06/1917	30/06/1917
Operation(al) Order(s)	23rd Division Engineers Operation Order No. 14. Appendix D	26/06/1917	26/06/1917
Operation(al) Order(s)	Operation Order No. 11. By Lieut Colonel E.H. Rooke R.E. C.R.E. 23rd Divisional Engineers. Appendix A		
Operation(al) Order(s)	Operation Order No. 12. By Lieut Colonel E.H. Rooke R.E. C.R.E. 23rd Divisional Engineers. Appendix B	14/06/1917	14/06/1917
Miscellaneous		04/06/1917	04/06/1917
Miscellaneous	Table Showing Concentration Of Troops From W To Z Day.		
Operation(al) Order(s)	23rd Divisional Engineers Operation Order No. 13. Appendix C	22/06/1917	22/06/1917
Heading	War Diary Of Headquarters R.E. 23rd Div From July 1st-July 31st Vol 23		
War Diary	Zevecoten	01/07/1917	23/07/1917
War Diary	Merris	23/07/1917	31/07/1917
Operation(al) Order(s)	23rd Divisional Engineers Operation Order No. 15 Appendix A	02/07/1917	02/07/1917
Operation(al) Order(s)	23rd Divisional Engineers Operation Order No. 16. Appendix B	11/07/1917	11/07/1917
Operation(al) Order(s)	23rd Divisional Engineers Operation Order No. 17. Appendix C	18/07/1917	18/07/1917
Operation(al) Order(s)	23rd Divisional Engineers Operation Order No. 18. Appendix D	19/07/1917	19/07/1917
Heading	War Diary Of Headquarters R.E. 23rd Div From August 1-August 31st Vol 24		
War Diary	Merris	05/08/1917	06/08/1917
War Diary	Wizernes	06/08/1917	09/08/1917
War Diary	Oosthoek	09/08/1917	26/08/1917
War Diary	Dickebusch	26/08/1917	30/08/1917
Operation(al) Order(s)	23rd Divisional Engineers Operation Order No. 27	30/08/1917	30/08/1917
Miscellaneous	A Form Messages And Signals		
Operation(al) Order(s)	23rd Divisional Engineers Operation Order No. 22	15/08/1917	15/08/1917
Operation(al) Order(s)	23rd Divisional Engineers Operation Order No. 23	18/08/1917	18/08/1917
Operation(al) Order(s)	23rd Divisional Engineers Operation Order No. 24	24/08/1917	24/08/1917
Operation(al) Order(s)	23rd Divisional Engineers Operation Order No. 25	25/08/1917	25/08/1917
Operation(al) Order(s)	To All Recipients Of 23rd Divisional Engineers Operation Order No. 24	25/08/1917	25/08/1917
Operation(al) Order(s)	23rd Divisional Engineers Operation Order No. 26	26/08/1917	26/08/1917
Heading	War Diary Of H.Q. R.E. 23 Div From Sept 1st-Sept 30 1917 Vol 25		
War Diary	Dickebusch	02/09/1917	04/09/1917
War Diary	Berthen	08/09/1917	14/09/1917
War Diary	Dickebusch	14/09/1917	25/09/1917
War Diary	Westoutre	25/09/1917	28/09/1917
Operation(al) Order(s)	23rd Divisional Engineers Operation Order No. 28 Appendix A	02/09/1917	02/09/1917

Operation(al) Order(s)	23rd Divisional Engineers Operation Order No. 29 Appendix B	06/09/1917	06/09/1917
Miscellaneous	23rd Divisional Engineers Operation Order No. 30 Appendix D	08/09/1917	08/09/1917
Operation(al) Order(s)	23rd Divisional Engineers Operation Order No. 32 Appendix E	09/09/1917	09/09/1917
Operation(al) Order(s)	23rd Divisional Engineers Operation Order No. 33 Appendix F	12/09/1917	12/09/1917
Operation(al) Order(s)	23rd Divisional Engineers Operation Order No. 32 Appendix I	11/09/1917	11/09/1917
Operation(al) Order(s)	23rd Divisional Engineers Operation Order No. 34. Appendix H	13/09/1917	13/09/1917
Operation(al) Order(s)	23rd Divisional Engineers Operation Order No. 35. Appendix I	14/09/1917	14/09/1917
Operation(al) Order(s)	23rd Divisional Engineers Operation Order No. 29. Appendix C	16/09/1917	16/09/1917
Operation(al) Order(s)	23rd Divisional Engineers Operation Order No. 36. Appendix K	18/09/1917	18/09/1917
Operation(al) Order(s)	23rd Divisional Engineers Operation Order No. 37. Appendix L	23/09/1917	23/09/1917
Heading	War Diary Of Headquarters R.E. 21 Division Oct 1 Of Oct 31 Vol 26		
War Diary	Millekruisse	01/10/1917	04/10/1917
War Diary	Meteren	04/10/1917	11/10/1917
War Diary	Cafe Belge	11/10/1917	22/10/1917
War Diary	Hestoutre	22/10/1917	31/10/1917
Operation(al) Order(s)	23rd Divisional Engineers. Operation Order 38. Appendix A	03/10/1917	03/10/1917
Operation(al) Order(s)	23rd Divisional Engineers. Operation Order 39. Appendix B	09/10/1917	09/10/1917
Operation(al) Order(s)	23rd Divisional Engineers. Operation Order 40. Appendix C		
Operation(al) Order(s)	23rd Divisional Engineers. Operation Order 40. Appendix C	21/10/1917	21/10/1917
Miscellaneous			
Heading	War Diary Of H.Q R.E. 23rd Division From Sept 1st 1916 To Sept 30th 1916 Vol 13		
War Diary	Baillevl	01/09/1916	06/09/1916
War Diary	Tilques	07/09/1916	10/09/1916
War Diary	Allonville	11/09/1916	11/09/1916
War Diary	Bresle	12/09/1916	19/09/1916
War Diary	Camp W.26c-0.4	20/09/1916	30/09/1916
Heading	23rd Division Dep. Asst Dir Ordnance Services Aug 1915-1917 Oct To Italy		
Heading	D.A.D.O.S. 23rd Division 23rd Oct to 31 Oct 1915 Vol I		
Heading	War Diary Of Major W.S.G Bishop D.A.D.S. 23rd Div. From 23.8.15 To 31st August 1915		
War Diary	Stomer	23/08/1915	25/08/1915
War Diary	Tilque	26/08/1915	31/08/1915
War Diary	War Diary Of Major W.S.L.S. Bishop D.A.O.S 23 Division From 1.9.15 To 30.9.15		
War Diary	Tilque	01/09/1915	05/09/1915
War Diary	Renescure	06/09/1915	06/09/1915
War Diary	Merris	07/09/1915	15/09/1915
War Diary	Croix Du Bac	16/09/1915	30/09/1915

War Diary	War Diary Of Major Bishop D.A.D.O.S. 23rd Div. 1st To 31st October 1915		
War Diary	Croix Du Bac	01/10/1915	31/10/1915
War Diary	H.Q 23rd Div D.A.D.O.S. Vol 2 Nov 15		
Heading	War Diary Of Major W.S.G. Bishop D.A.W.S. 23rd Div From 1st November 1915 To 30th November 1915		
War Diary	Croix Du Bac	01/11/1915	30/11/1915
Heading	D.A.D.O.S. 23rd Div Vol 3 Dec 15		
Heading	War Diary of Major W.S.G. Bishop A.O.D D.A.D.O.S. 23 Division From 1/12/15 To 31/12/15		
War Diary	Croix Du Bac	01/12/1915	31/12/1915
War Diary	D.A.O.S. 23rd Division Vol 4		
Heading	War Diary Of Major W.S.O.S. Bishop D.A.W.O.S. 23rd Division 1st To 31st January 1916		
War Diary	Croix Du Bac	01/01/1916	31/01/1916
Heading	D.A.D.O.S. 23rd Division Vol V		
War Diary	Croix Du Bac	01/02/1916	24/02/1916
War Diary	Estaires	24/02/1916	26/02/1916
War Diary	Blaringhem	26/02/1916	29/02/1916
War Diary	Bruay	29/02/1916	29/02/1916
Heading	War Diary Of Capt. J.B Oxenhem D.A.D.O.S. 23 Division 1st March To 31st March 1916 Vol 6		
War Diary	Bruay	01/03/1916	08/03/1916
War Diary	Maisnil Bouche	09/03/1916	16/03/1916
War Diary	Bruay	16/03/1916	22/03/1916
War Diary	Barlin	22/03/1916	31/03/1916
Heading	War Diary Of Capt. J.B. Oxenhem D.A.D.O.S. 23rd Division From 1st To 30th April 1916 Vol 7		
War Diary	Barlin	01/04/1916	18/04/1916
War Diary	Barlin Bruay	19/04/1916	19/04/1916
War Diary	Bruay	20/04/1916	30/04/1916
Heading	War Diary Of Capt J.B Oxenhem D.A.D.O.S. 23rd Div 1st To 31st May 1916 Vol 8		
War Diary	Bruay	01/05/1916	13/05/1916
War Diary	Barlin	13/05/1916	31/05/1916
Heading	War Diary Of Capt J.B. Oxenhem D.A.D.O.S. 23 Div From 1st To 30th June 1916 Vol 9		
War Diary	Barlin	01/06/1916	14/06/1916
War Diary	Bruay	14/06/1916	16/06/1916
War Diary	And Bomy	16/06/1916	24/06/1916
War Diary	Vaux	24/06/1916	30/06/1916
Heading	War Diary Of Capt. J.B Oxenhem D.A.D.O.S, 23rd Div 1st To 31st July 1916 Vol 10		
War Diary	Vaux & Baizieux	01/07/1916	04/07/1916
War Diary	Vaux & Baizieux & Dernancourt	04/07/1916	10/07/1916
War Diary	Dernancourt & Franvillers	11/07/1916	26/07/1916
War Diary	Franvillers & Albert	26/07/1916	31/07/1916
Heading	War Diary Of Capt J.B Oxenhem D.A.D.O.S. 23 Div 1st To 31st Aug 1916 Vol 11		
War Diary	Albert	01/08/1916	12/08/1916
War Diary	Ailly	12/08/1916	12/08/1916
War Diary	Fletre	13/08/1916	17/08/1916
War Diary	Steenwerck	17/08/1916	28/08/1916
War Diary	Steenwerck & Bailleul	29/08/1916	31/08/1916
Heading	War Diary Of Capt J.B. Oxenhem D.A.D.O.S. 23 Div 1st To 30th Sept 1916 Vol 12		

War Diary	Baillieul	01/09/1916	06/09/1916
War Diary	Baillieul & Watten	06/09/1916	10/09/1916
War Diary	Watten & Alonville	10/09/1916	10/09/1916
War Diary	Alonville	11/09/1916	11/09/1916
War Diary	Alonville & Bazieux	12/09/1916	19/09/1916
War Diary	Bazieux & Albert NS E-7-a	20/09/1916	30/09/1916
Heading	War Diary Of Capt I.B Oxenhem D.A.D.O.S. 23 Div 1-31 Oct 1916 Vol 13		
War Diary	Albert road E-7-a	01/10/1916	12/10/1916
War Diary	Albert road E-7-a & Ailly in Haut Clocher	12/10/1916	13/10/1916
War Diary	Ailly in Haut Clocher & St Ricquier	13/10/1916	15/10/1916
War Diary	Bailleul	15/10/1916	15/10/1916
War Diary	Poperinghe	16/10/1916	31/10/1916
Miscellaneous	23rd Division No. A. 802	19/12/1916	19/12/1916
Heading	War Diary Of Capt J.B. Oxenham D.A.D.O.S. 23 Div 1-30 Nov 1916 Vol 14		
War Diary	Poperinghe	01/11/1916	30/11/1916
Heading	War Diary Of Capt J.B. Oxenham D.A.D.O.S. 23 Div 1st To 31st Dec 1916 Vol 15		
War Diary	Poperinghe	01/12/1916	31/12/1916
Heading	War Diary Of Capt. J.B. Oxenham, D.A.D.O.S. 23 Div 1st To 31st Jany 1917 Vol 16		
War Diary	Poperinghe	01/01/1917	31/01/1917
Heading	War Diary Of Capt J.B. Oxenham D.A.D.O.S. 23rd Division 1-28 Feb 1917 Vol 17		
War Diary	Poperinghe	01/02/1916	27/02/1916
War Diary	Poperinghe & Watten	27/02/1917	28/02/1917
Heading	War Diary Of Capt J.B. Oxenham D.A.D.O.S. 23rd Div 1st-31st March 1917 Vol 18		
War Diary	Watten	01/03/1917	20/03/1917
War Diary	Esquelbecq	20/03/1917	10/04/1917
War Diary	Nr Poperinghe	11/04/1917	30/04/1917
Heading	War Diary Of Capt I.B Oxenhem D.A.D.O.S. 23rd Div 1-31 March 1917 Vol 20		
War Diary	No Poperinghe G. 14 B On	01/05/1917	01/05/1917
War Diary	Steenvorde	02/05/1917	12/05/1917
War Diary	G 14 B In	12/05/1917	13/05/1917
War Diary	G. 27 B 5.8	14/05/1917	31/05/1917
Heading	War Diary Of Capt J.B. Oxenhem D.A.D.O.S. 23 Div June 1917 Vol 21		
War Diary	Reninghelst G.27. B. 5.8	01/06/1917	13/06/1917
War Diary	Piebrouck R.21.c.5.0	13/06/1917	29/06/1917
War Diary	N.I.B.2.1	30/06/1917	30/06/1917
Heading	War Diary Of Capt. J.B. Oxenhem D.A.D.O.S. 23rd Div July 1917 Vol 22		
War Diary	N.1.B. 2.1 & Reninghelst	01/07/1917	17/07/1917
War Diary	Reninghelst	18/07/1917	23/07/1917
War Diary	Meteren	23/07/1917	31/07/1917
Heading	War Diary Of Capt I.B. Oxenhem D.A.D.O.S. 23rd Div Aug 1917 Vol 23		
War Diary	Meteren	01/08/1917	08/08/1917
War Diary	Eperlecques	09/08/1917	23/08/1917
War Diary	Reninghelst	24/08/1917	31/08/1917
Heading	War Diary Of Capt I.B Oxenhem D.A.D.O.S. 23 Div 1-30 Sept 1917 Vol 24		
War Diary	Reninghelst G.34.d.2.8	01/09/1917	04/09/1917

War Diary	Reninghelst G.34.d.2.8 & Lederzeele	04/09/1917	14/09/1917
War Diary	Reninghelst. G.34.d.in	17/09/1917	24/09/1917
War Diary	Westoutre	25/09/1917	28/09/1917
War Diary	Reninghelst G.34.d.on	29/09/1917	30/09/1917
Heading	War Diary Of Capt I.B. Oxenhem D.A.D.O.S. 23 Div Oct 1917 Vol 25		
War Diary	Reninghelst G.34.d.in	01/10/1917	01/10/1917
War Diary	Meteren	02/10/1917	10/10/1917
War Diary	H.30.c 28	11/10/1917	12/10/1917
War Diary	Sheet 28 H.30.c Angre Camp	13/10/1917	21/10/1917
War Diary	Wizernes	22/10/1917	31/10/1917
Heading	23rd Division Asst Dir. Vety Services Aug 1915-1917 Oct To Italy		
Heading	A.D.I.S. 23rd Division Vol: 1, 2, 3, 4, 5 Aug 15		
Heading	August 1915 War Diary of A.D.V.S 23rd Division		
War Diary	Bordon Southampton	24/08/1917	24/08/1917
War Diary	Havre	25/08/1917	26/08/1917
War Diary	Tilques	26/08/1917	31/08/1917
War Diary	September 1915 War Diary Of A.D.V.S. 23rd Division		
War Diary	Tilques	01/09/1915	06/09/1915
War Diary	Renescure	06/09/1915	07/09/1915
War Diary	Merris	07/09/1915	16/09/1915
War Diary	Croix Du Bac	16/09/1915	30/09/1915
Heading	October 1915 War Diary Of A.D.V.S. 23rd Division		
War Diary	Croix Du Bac	01/10/1915	31/10/1915
Heading	November 1915 War Diary Of A.D.V.S. 23rd Division		
War Diary	Croix Du Bac	01/11/1915	30/11/1915
Heading	December 1915 War Diary of A.D.V.S. 23rd Division.		
War Diary	Croix Du Bac	01/12/1915	31/12/1915
Heading	A.D.I.S. 23rd Division Vol:6		
War Diary	Croix Du Bac	01/01/1916	30/01/1916
Heading	A.D.I.S. 23rd Division Vol 7		
War Diary	Croix Du Bac	08/02/1916	23/02/1916
War Diary	Estaires	24/02/1916	25/02/1916
War Diary	Blaringhem.	26/02/1916	28/02/1916
War Diary	Bruay	29/02/1916	29/02/1916
Heading	War Diary March Vol 8 March.1916 ADVS 23rd Div		
War Diary	Bruay	01/03/1916	08/03/1916
War Diary	Caucourt	09/03/1916	16/03/1916
War Diary	Bruay	17/03/1916	22/03/1916
War Diary	Sains En Gohelle	23/03/1916	19/04/1916
War Diary	Bruay	20/04/1916	13/05/1916
War Diary	Sains En Gohelle	14/05/1916	24/05/1916
War Diary	Barlin	25/05/1916	14/06/1916
War Diary	Bruay	15/06/1916	24/06/1916
War Diary	Vaux-En-Amienoise	25/06/1916	30/06/1916
War Diary	Baizieux	01/09/1916	04/09/1916
War Diary	Dernancourt	05/07/1916	11/07/1916
War Diary	St Gratien	12/07/1916	21/07/1916
War Diary	Henencourt	22/07/1916	26/07/1916
War Diary	Albert	27/07/1916	07/08/1916
War Diary	Baizieux	08/08/1916	08/08/1916
War Diary	Querrieu and St Gratian	09/08/1916	10/08/1916
War Diary	Ailly Le Haut	11/08/1916	12/08/1916
War Diary	Fletre	12/08/1916	16/08/1916
War Diary	Steenwerck	17/08/1916	28/08/1916

War Diary	Bailleul	29/08/1916	31/08/1916
War Diary	Ribemont	01/08/1916	15/08/1916
War Diary	Nieppe	19/08/1916	31/08/1916
War Diary	Bailleul	01/09/1916	04/09/1916
War Diary	Tilques	05/09/1916	09/09/1916
War Diary	Allonville	10/09/1916	11/09/1916
War Diary	Baizieux	12/09/1916	18/09/1916
War Diary	Millencourt Albert Wood	19/09/1916	30/09/1916
War Diary	Albert	01/10/1916	08/10/1916
War Diary	Montigny	09/10/1916	11/10/1916
War Diary	Ailly Le Haut Clocher	12/10/1916	12/10/1916
War Diary	St Riquier	13/10/1916	15/10/1916
War Diary	Poperinghe	16/10/1916	19/10/1916
War Diary	Reninghelst	20/10/1916	31/01/1917
War Diary	Dieppe	30/01/1917	31/01/1917
War Diary	Reninghelst	01/02/1917	26/02/1917
War Diary	St. Omer	27/02/1917	19/03/1917
War Diary	Esquelbecq	20/03/1917	07/04/1917
War Diary	Busseboom	08/04/1917	01/05/1917
War Diary	Winnezeele	02/05/1917	11/05/1917
War Diary	Busseboom	12/05/1917	12/06/1917
War Diary	Berthen	13/06/1917	29/06/1917
War Diary	Zevecoten	30/06/1917	22/07/1917
War Diary	Merris	23/07/1917	05/08/1917
War Diary	Wizernes	06/08/1917	08/08/1917
War Diary	Eperlecques	09/08/1917	23/08/1917
War Diary	Reninghelst	24/08/1917	25/08/1917
War Diary	Dickebusch	26/08/1917	31/08/1917
Miscellaneous	23rd Division. Orders For Veterinary Officers Whilst Attached To This Division.	27/08/1917	27/08/1917
War Diary	Dickebusch	01/09/1917	01/09/1917
War Diary	Steenvoorde	02/09/1917	03/09/1917
War Diary	Lederzeele	04/09/1917	13/09/1917
War Diary	Laclytte Camp M.6.d.5.8. Sheet 28	14/09/1917	24/09/1917
War Diary	Westoutre	25/09/1917	27/09/1917
War Diary	Laclytte Camp M.6.d.5.8	28/09/1917	01/10/1917
War Diary	Berthen	02/10/1917	10/10/1917
War Diary	H.30.c.5.8. Sheet 28	11/10/1917	22/10/1917
War Diary	Wizernes	23/10/1917	31/10/1917

This item has been conserved as part of the WO95 Digitisation Project

Please keep this sheet at the front of the box

23RD DIVISION

BEF.

C. R. E.

AUG 1915-~~MAR 1919~~

TO 1917 OCT

23rd Division

121
7/21

H.Q. 23rd Division C.R.E.

Vol I

Aug & Sept. 15

Mar 19

Instructions regarding War Diaries and Intelligence Summaries are contained in F. S. Regs., Part II. and the Staff Manual respectively. Title pages will be prepared in manuscript.

Army Form C. 2118

WAR DIARY
or
INTELLIGENCE SUMMARY.
(Erase heading not required.)

Head Quarters R.E. 23rd Division

Place	Date	Hour	Summary of Events and Information	Remarks and references to Appendices
Bordon	20.8.15		Orders rec^d for move during ensuing week	
BORDON	21.8.15		Preparing for embarkation	
"	22.8.15		" " " Orders received for entrainment of 23rd Sig Co on 24/8/15	PM
"	23.8.15		Received orders to entrain at 3.30pm 24th inst. 101st + 102nd F. Cos to entrain on Wednesday evening. 128th F. Co to entrain on Friday morning	PM
BORDON	24.8.15	3.30 pm	Entrained at 3.30 PM	
S'HAMPTON	"	5.30 pm	Arrived at 38 birth	
			CRE 6 men and wagons and horses sailed from ~~embarked at~~ 38 birth	
"	25.8.15	4.30 pm		
"	"	6.30 p.m	Adjt, M.O. and 6 men sailed from 32 ~~birth~~ PM	
HAVRE	26.8.15	6.30 a.m.	Adjt's party disembarked	
"	"	3.30 pm	Disembarkation of CRE's party completed	
"	"	4.0 pm	Arrived at No 5 Rest Camp PM	
"	27.8.15	7.30 a.m.	Marched from No 5 Rest Camp to Gare des MARCHANDISES	
"	"	12.30 p.m.	Left Havre by train PM	
ST OMER	28/8/15	6.30 a.m.	Arrived St Omer	
[illegible]QUES	28/8/15	8.30	Arrived and took [illegible] Proprietor d'AMBI[illegible]URT TILQUES	PM

2353 Wt. W2544/1454 700,000 5/15 D. D. & L. A.D.S.S./Forms/C. 2118.

Instructions regarding War Diaries and Intelligence Summaries are contained in F. S. Regs., Part II. and the Staff Manual respectively. Title pages will be prepared in manuscript.

WAR DIARY
or
INTELLIGENCE SUMMARY.
(Erase heading not required.)

Army Form C. 2118.

Place	Date	Hour	Summary of Events and Information	Remarks and references to Appendices
TILQUES	29.8.15	11.a.m	Adjudant Marcel Vaussard 11 Regt d'Artillerie reported and took up duties of interpreter. RHP	
"	~~30.8.15~~ 31.8		101st & 102nd companies arrived RHP	
"	30.8.15		128th Fd Company arrived. Visiting companies. RHP	
"	31.8.15		Office work. Visiting companies RHP	
"	~~2.8.15~~ 1.9.		Divisional scheme in morning issued instructions for 101st to practice pontooning on 2.9.15 102nd on 3.9.15 and officers schemes. RHP	
"	2.9.15		Col. Edmonds arrived from G.H.Q. and pointed out defence line between CORMETTE and MOULE. Pontooning for 102nd F.Co cancelled In afternoon inspected pontoon bridges of 101st F. Co. wet afternoon RHP	
	3.9.15		102nd F.Co marked out ~~line~~ front line CORMETTE to MOULE. In afternoon details of work for the next day arranged and arrangements made for getting bricks at TILQUES and brushwood at Forêt d'EPERLECQUES. Rain nearly continuous all day. RHP	
"	4.9.15	7.a.m	345 Pioneers 1150 Infantry ½ 102nd F.Co. RE on front line CORMETTE to MOULE.	
		12.30 pm	Work stopped for heavy rain which continued with small intervals all day ~~with small intervals~~	

#353 Wt. W2544/1454 700,000 5/15 D. D. & L. A.D.S.S./Forms/C. 2118.

Army Form C. 2118.

Instructions regarding War Diaries and Intelligence Summaries are contained in F. S. Regs., Part II. and the Staff Manual respectively. Title pages will be prepared in manuscript.

WAR DIARY
or
INTELLIGENCE SUMMARY.
(Erase heading not required.)

Place	Date	Hour	Summary of Events and Information	Remarks and references to Appendices
TILQUES	4 9/15		101st Co. cutting Brushwood at Forêt d'EPERLECQUES.	
			Arranged for cutting Brushwood at Propriété d'AMBICOURT TILQUES fixed locality of Second line CORMETTE – MOULE PHP.	
		11pm	Orders that Division will move on 6/9/15 received all working parties cancelled PHP	
TILQUES	5 9/15		Detailed orders for move received PHP.	
"	6 9/15	9 a.m	Marched from TILQUES via S MARTIN S of St OMER to RENESCURE	
RENESCURE	"	3pm	Arrived RENESCURE and took up billets at the BRASSERIE a fine hot day. PHP	
RENESCURE	7 9/15	8.30am	marched out via HAZEBROUCK and STRAZEEL to MERRIS	
MERRIS		3pm	Arrived MERRIS Fine hot day. PHP	
MERRIS	8 9/15		101st Co left being attached to 20th Division at ESTAIRES and SAILLY from 8th to 14th inst.	
			102nd Co left being attached to 27th Division at ERQUINGHEM from 8th to Fine hot day HUB	
MERRIS	9 9/15		CRE visited 27th Divn HUB	

B353 Wt. W2544/1454 700,000 5/15 D. D. & L. A.D.S.S./Forms/C. 2118.

Army Form C. 2118.

Instructions regarding War Diaries and Intelligence Summaries are contained in F. S. Regs., Part II. and the Staff Manual respectively. Title pages will be prepared in manuscript.

WAR DIARY
or
INTELLIGENCE SUMMARY.
(Erase heading not required.)

Place	Date	Hour	Summary of Events and Information	Remarks and references to Appendices
MERRIS	10 9/15		2 Sections 128 Co cutting brushwood in Forest of NIEPPE CRE and 2 officers 128th Co visited 27th Division YHB Adjutant attached to 27th Division	
MERRIS	11 9/15		CRE visited 27th Division Fine hot day YHB	
CROIX du BAC	12 9/15		HQ took up temorary billets at CROIX du BAC 128th Co took up temporary billets at ERQUINGHAM 102 Co returned to 23rd Divisional Area. Fine Hot day YHB	
"	13 9/15		102 Co returned to temporary billets at ERQUINGHAM Taking over and learning work of 27th Division Fine Hot day 101 Co moved into ERQUINGHAM from 20th Divn Area. YHB	
"	14 9/15		Taking over work of 27th Division 128th Co took over billets & work of 17 Fd Co on night 14/15th Fine hot day YHB	
"	15 9/15		Taking over work of 27th Division 102nd Co took over billets & work of 1st Wessex Fd Co on night 15/16 Fine hot day YHB No 89387 128th Co wounded	
"	16 9/15	10 a.m.	Took over office & work from 27th Divn ~~at 10~~ 101st Co took over billets & work of 2nd Wessex Fd Co on night 16/17 Fine hot day YHB No 69339 128th Co Killed	
"	17 9/15		on taking over 128th Co were placed under orders of 70th Brigade 102nd Co were placed under orders of 69th Brigade 101st Co remained under CRE 2 Cos 9 S Staff Regt were placed under orders of CRE. YHB	

2353 Wt. W2544/1454 700,000 5/15 D. D. & L. A.D.S.S./Forms/C. 2118.

Army Form C. 2118.

Instructions regarding War Diaries and Intelligence Summaries are contained in F. S. Regs., Part II. and the Staff Manual respectively. Title pages will be prepared in manuscript.

WAR DIARY
or
INTELLIGENCE SUMMARY.
(Erase heading not required.)

Head Quarters RE 23rd Division

Place	Date	Hour	Summary of Events and Information	Remarks and references to Appendices
18/9/15 CROIX du BAC	18 9/15		Going over trenches and taking up work of 27th Division generally. Difficulty in obtaining transport. A quiet day. Fine and hot. YHB	
"	19 9/15		A quiet day. Adjutant to BERGUETTE, MERVILLE, ESTAIRES and BAILLEUL re stores, purchases and transport. A fine hot day. Three motor lorries supplied for first time. Fine and hot. YHB	
"	20 9/15		A quiet day	
		11 30pm	Operation Order No 5 received re attack by 8th division. 101st Field Co ~~are~~ to be attached to 68th Brigade from ~~day break~~ & ~~on~~ 12 30 p.m. Friday 24 9/15. Fine hot day cold night YHB	
"	21 9/15		Pushing on with dugouts and with issuing stores to ~~all~~ companies. experiments with searchlight and tin reflector ~~unsatisfactory~~.	
"	22 9/15		As on 21 9/15 large order of wood received from LUCHART-MALLET at MERVILLES. YHB Fine and hot. ~~Search~~ YHB	
"	23 9/15		As on 21 9/15 search light mirror unsatisfactory and discarded. Hot and cloudy. Heavy rain from 6.30 pm. YHB	

2353 Wt. W2544/1454 700,000 5/15 D. D. & L. A.D.S.S./Forms/C. 2118.

Army Form C. 2118

Instructions regarding War Diaries and Intelligence Summaries are contained in F. S. Regs., Part II. and the Staff Manual respectively. Title pages will be prepared in manuscript.

WAR DIARY
or
INTELLIGENCE SUMMARY.
(Erase heading not required.)

Place	Date	Hour	Summary of Events and Information	Remarks and references to Appendices
CROIX du BAC	24 9/15		Cloudy and foggy with some rain	
		3.30pm	CRE went into Advanced Headquarters at LA BOULAGERIE Farm. Pay of workmen HLB	
"	25 9/15		News of successful attacks to the South of here. In readiness awaiting orders. Increased difficulty in obtaining transport for stores only 2 lorries available. Wet day HLB	
			Work recommenced on BOIS GRENIER Line.	
"	26 9/15		68th Brigade left the division so no working parties on BOIS GRENIER LINE Standing by awaiting orders as on 25th. HLB.	
"	27 9/15		CRE returned from Advanced Headquarters. Ordinary work resumed HLB	
"	28 9/15		Carrying on with ordinary work HLB.	
"	29 9/15		Carrying on with ordinary work. ~~HLB~~ Major A G. Bremner RE arrived to take over the duties of CRE HLB	
"	30 9/15		Major A G. Bremner R.E took over and Lt Col P. G J Radcliffe left for. G.H.Q. HLB	
			CRE went round Right Section.	

H L Bulkeley Capt RE 23rd Division

8353 Wt. W2544/1454 700,000 5/15 D. D. & L. A.D.S.S./Forms/C. 2118.

121/7595.

HQ. 23rd Div: CRE.

Vol 2

Oct 15

2nd Aut[illegible]

Secret

Instructions regarding War Diaries and Intelligence Summaries are contained in F. S. Regs., Part II. and the Staff Manual respectively. Title pages will be prepared in manuscript.

WAR DIARY

or

~~INTELLIGENCE SUMMARY.~~ of

(*Erase heading not required.*)

Army Form C. 2118.

Head Quarter RE 23rd Division

From 1 10/15 to 31 10/15

Volume I

Place	Date	Hour	Summary of Events and Information	Remarks and references to Appendices
CROIX du BAC	1 10/15		CRE went round Left ~~Right~~ section.	
		6am	Orders received for 101st F. Co to march to BETHUNE and report to 1st Corps there.	
		10.15am	101st F. Co. left for BETHUNE HHB	
			Report received on suspected German mining operations against our line. HHB	
	2 10/15		Paid work men in morning. HHB 1 Section 180th Tunnelling Co arrived	
	3 10/15		CRE went round posts in morning. Meeting of O.C. Cos in afternoon HHB 1 Section 180th Tunnelling Co. arrived.	
	4 10/15		Paying bills all day. CRE in office HHB	
	5 10/15		Quiet day nothing to report. HHB	
	6 10/15		Nothing to report. CRE at conference of Brigadiers HHB	
	7 10/15		CRE at conference of C.R.E.s at SAILLY. Nothing to report HHB	
	8 10/15		Nothing to report HHB	
	9 10/15		Nothing to report HHB	

#353 Wt. W2544/1454 700,000 5/15 D. D. & L. A.D.S.S./Forms/C. 2118.

Instructions regarding War Diaries and Intelligence Summaries are contained in F. S. Regs., Part II. and the Staff Manual respectively. Title pages will be prepared in manuscript.

Army Form C. 2118.

WAR DIARY
or
INTELLIGENCE SUMMARY.
(Erase heading not required.)

H Q R.E. 23rd Divn

Place	Date	Hour	Summary of Events and Information	Remarks and references to Appendices
CROIX du BAC	10.10.15		Work generally construction breastwork communications, dugouts, subsidiary line, drainage of trenches and trenchboards and hutting. JCUB	
"	11.10.15		As on 10th nothing particular to report JCUB Paid bills in ARMENTIERES	
"	12.10.15		Work carried on nothing particular to report JCUB	
"	13.10.15		Work carried on nothing particular to report JCUB	
"	14.10.15		Work carried on nothing particular to report JCUB	
"	15.10.15		Cap Hoyle RE arrived to take over work of Roads Officer 3rd Corps from Lieut Ridgewell RE who is to be attached for work to 23rd Divn. Work as usual JCUB Paid workmen and bills ARMENTIERES	
"	16.10.15		Work as usual JCUB	
"	17.10.15		Lieut Ridgewell left in afternoon on week's leave prior to attachment to 23rd Division work as usual JCUB	
"	18.10.15		Lieut Gurney OC Section Bridging Train attached 23rd Divn ~~[illegible]~~ left on week's leave Work as usual JCUB.	
"	19.10.15		Work as usual. heard in evening that 101 Field Company were returning JCUB	
"	20.10.15		Work as usual	
		4.15PM	101st Co ~~went~~ arrived and went into billets at ERQUINGHEM	

2353 Wt. W2544/1454 700,000 5/15 D. D. & L. A.D.S.S./Forms/C. 2118.

Army Form C. 2118.

Instructions regarding War Diaries and Intelligence Summaries are contained in F. S. Regs., Part II. and the Staff Manual respectively. Title pages will be prepared in manuscript.

WAR DIARY

or

~~INTELLIGENCE SUMMARY.~~

(Erase heading not required.) H.Q. R.E. 23rd Divn

Place	Date	Hour	Summary of Events and Information	Remarks and references to Appendices
~~27~~ CROIX du BAC	21 10/15		Work as usual. Rain in night HLB	
"	22 10/15		Work as usual. Pay of workmen. Fine. HLB.	
"	23 10/15		Work as usual. Fine. HLB.	
"	24 10/15		Work as usual HLB	
"	25 10/15		Work as usual HLB	
"	26 10/15		Work as usual. Received orders for detachment 180th Tunnelling Co to rejoin their unit HLB	
"	27 10/15		Work as usual. HLB	
"	28 10/15	9.am	Detachment 180th Tunnelling Co. left to rejoin their unit. Work as usual HLB.	
"	29 10/15		Pay of workmen work as usual HLB	
"	30 10/15		Work as usual HLB	
"	31 10/15		Work as usual. The past week very bad weather HLB.	

H L Bulkeley Capt RE
Adjt RE 23rd Division
1/11/15

2353 Wt. W2544/1454 700,000 5/15 D. D. & L. A.D.S.S./Forms/C. 2118.

121
7624

HQ. 23rd Div:
CRE.

Vol: 3

Nov 15.

Secret

Instructions regarding War Diaries and Intelligence Summaries are contained in F. S. Regs., Part II. and the Staff Manual respectively. Title pages will be prepared in manuscript.

WAR DIARY

or

~~INTELLIGENCE~~ SUMMARY.

(*Erase heading not required.*) H Q ~~2~~R. E. 23rd Divn

Army Form C. 2118.

from 1-11 to 30.11.15

Place	Date	Hour	Summary of Events and Information	Remarks and references to Appendices
CROIX du BAC	1 11/15		Work as usual - Workshops, - dugouts - revetting - construction of Breastwork communications - Drainage - Hutting. very wet day JHB.	
"	2 11/15		Work as usual JHB	
"	3 11/15		Interpreter Adjt Marcel Vaussard left on transfer to G.H.Q. JHB	
"	4 11/15		Work as usual JHB.	
"	5 11/15		Work as usual. Pay of civilian workmen JHB.	
"	6 11/15		New Interpreter N.C.O. Octave Victor Goupil reported on transfer from 25th Divn work as usual. JHB	
"	7 11/15		Work as usual JHB.	
"	8 11/15		Work as usual JHB	
"	9 11/15		Directions received from IIIrd Corps Commander to concentrate work on communication trenches and front line during next 3 or 4 days. Work as usual. JHB	
"	10 11/15		Work as usual JHB	
"	11 11/15		Work as usual JHB	
"	12 11/15		Work as usual. Pay of civilian workmen.	

2353 Wt. W2544/1454 700,000 5/15 D. D. & L. A.D.S.S./Forms/C. 2118.

Army Form C. 2118.

Instructions regarding War Diaries and Intelligence Summaries are contained in F. S. Regs., Part II. and the Staff Manual respectively. Title pages will be prepared in manuscript.

WAR DIARY
or
~~INTELLIGENCE SUMMARY.~~

(Erase heading not required.) H.Q. R.E. 23rd Divn

Place	Date	Hour	Summary of Events and Information	Remarks and references to Appendices
CROIX du BAC	13/11/15		Work as usual - workshops - revetting - dugouts - Machine Gun Emplacements - conversion of Subsidiary Line - Drainage - Hutting. YUB	
	14/11/15		Fine day after very wet week. Work as usual YUB	
	15/11/15		Work as usual. YUB Frost at night	
	16/11/15		Work as usual. Paid bill at ESTAIRES. Interview re pumps & stovepiping at MERVILLE and re tripod Lewis gun mountings at LILLERS. Frost at night YUB	
	17/11/15		Work as usual. Very large quantities timber arriving at Station annexe ARMENTIERES during past 10 days. Difficulty in clearing though 6 lorries and 10 pontoon wagons employed daily. Frost in night YUB.	
	18/11/15		Work as usual. Black frost in night YUB.	
	19/11/15		Work as usual. Rain YUB Pay of civilian workmen increasing & shortage of change makes paying out difficult	
	20/11/15		Work as usual YUB	
	21/11/15		Work as usual YUB	

2353 Wt. W2544/1454 700,000 5/15 D. D. & L. A.D.S.S./Forms/C. 2118.

Secret

Instructions regarding War Diaries and Intelligence Summaries are contained in F. S. Regs., Part II. and the Staff Manual respectively. Title pages will be prepared in manuscript.

WAR DIARY
or
~~INTELLIGENCE SUMMARY.~~

Army Form C. 2118.

(Erase heading not required.) H Q R E 23rd Divn

Place	Date	Hour	~~From~~ Summary of Events and Information	Remarks and references to Appendices
~~22/11/15~~ CROIX DU BAC	22/11/15		Work as usual, workshops - SHAFTESBURY AVE - revetments - repairing front line - dugouts - Drainage - conversion of Subsidiary Line - ~~Drainage~~ - scheme for water supply of front line from BOIS GRENIER - Hutting - BOIS GRENIER line HMB	
	23/11/15		Work as usual HMB	
	24/11/15		Work as usual HMB	
	25/11/15		Work as usual. Field Companies come under the direct orders of the C.R.E. as far as regards work instead of being under the Brigadiers.	
	26/11/15		Work as usual. hard frost HMB	
	27/11/15		Work as usual. hard frost HMB	
	28/11/15		Work as usual. very cold ice nearly bearing HMB	
	29/11/15		Work as usual. frost broke - rain cold HMB	
	30/11/15		Work as usual very wet night HMB.	

1/12/15

H M Bulkeley
Capt RE
Adjt RE
23rd Divn

CRE. 23rd Div:
Vol: 4

121/7935

Secret

Instructions regarding War Diaries and Intelligence Summaries are contained in F. S. Regs., Part II. and the Staff Manual respectively. Title pages will be prepared in manuscript.

WAR DIARY
or
~~INTELLIGENCE SUMMARY.~~

(*Erase heading not required.*) H.Q. R.E. 23rd Division

Army Form C. 2118.

Place	Date	Hour	Summary of Events and Information	Remarks and references to Appendices
CROIX DU BAC	1 12/15		Work as usual i.e. Workshops - Hutting - Communication Trenches SHAFTESBURY AVENUE Jr QUEER ST - AVONDALE RD - WINE AVE - M.G. emplacements front and BOIS GRENIER Line - General repairs - reconstruction BOIS GRENIER Line and S Line - Drainage. River LAYES risen 10 ~~ft~~ inches in last 2 days height at ~~SHAFT~~ LONDON BRIDGE 3 feet 5 inches at I.C. 1 foot 1 inch. YLB	
	2 12/15		Work as usual. River LAYES 3 feet 8½ at LONDON BRIDGE YLB	
	3 12/15		Work as usual River LAYES 3 feet 9¾ at LONDON BRIDGE YLB	
	4 12/15		Work as usual River LAYES 4 feet 4 inches at LONDON BRIDGE YLB	
	5 12/15		Work as usual River LAYES 5 feet ½ inch at LONDON BRIDGE YLB	
	6 12/15		Work as usual River LAYES 5 feet 1 inch at LONDON BRIDGE YLB	
	7 12/15		Work as usual River LAYES 4 feet 11 inches at LONDON BRIDGE YLB	

8353 Wt. W2544/1454 700,000 5/15 D. D. & L. A.D.S.S./Forms/C. 2118.

Army Form C. 2118.

Instructions regarding War Diaries and Intelligence Summaries are contained in F. S. Regs., Part II. and the Staff Manual respectively. Title pages will be prepared in manuscript.

WAR DIARY
or
~~INTELLIGENCE SUMMARY.~~

(*Erase heading not required.*) H.Q. RE 23rd Division

Place	Date	Hour	Summary of Events and Information	Remarks and references to Appendices
CROIX DU BAC	7 12/15		Work as usual - Workshops - Hutting - on communication trenches SHAFTESBURY AVE, QUEER ST, AVONDALE RD, WINE AVE. Machine Gun emplacements Front line and BOIS GRENIER Line - raising front parapet - Dugouts in front parapet. - conversion of S Line and BOIS GRENIER Line. work on S line and drainage. Height of RIVER LAYES at LONDON BRIDGE 4 feet 11 inches at I.C. 1 foot 10½ in. JLB	
	8 12/15		Work as usual. River LAYES at LONDON BRIDGE 4 feet 11 inches JLB	
	9 12/15		Work as usual. River LAYES at LONDON BRIDGE 4 feet 9 inches JLB	
	10 12/15		Work as usual. River LAYES at LONDON BRIDGE 5 feet 4 inches JLB	
	11 12/15		Work as usual. River LAYES at LONDON BRIDGE 5 feet 9½ JLB	
	12 12/15		Work as usual River LAYES at LONDON BRIDGE 6 feet 1 inch. On this day the River LYS flood was reported to be the highest since 1894 and 2 feet higher than the maximum last winter. Trenches in the Right section badly flooded JLB	
	13 12/15		Work as usual. River LAYES 6 feet at SHAFTESBURY AVE JLB	

2353 Wt. W2544/1454 700,000 5/15 D. D. & L. A.D.S.S./Forms/C. 2118.

Army Form C. 2118.

Instructions regarding War Diaries and Intelligence Summaries are contained in F. S. Regs., Part II. and the Staff Manual respectively. Title pages will be prepared in manuscript.

WAR DIARY
or
~~INTELLIGENCE SUMMARY.~~

(Erase heading not required.) H.Q. R.E. 23rd Div.

Place	Date	Hour	Summary of Events and Information	Remarks and references to Appendices
CROIX DU BAC	14 12/15		Work as usual - Hutting - Workshops - Communication Trenches SHAFTESBURY AV^E, QUEER S^T, AVONDALE, WINE S^T, SALOP, PARK ROW - constructing TRAMWAY Post - Machine Gun emplacements Front and BOIS GRENIER Line underpinning front parapet - Reconstruction S line and BOIS GRENIER Line - Drainage. Height R LAIES LONDON BRIDGE 5 feet 9½ inches at 1 1c 2 feet HLB	
	15 12/15		Work as usual. R. LAIES. LONDON BRIDGE 5 feet 5 inches HLB	
	16 12/15		Work as usual. R LAIES LONDON BRIDGE 5 feet 1½ inches HLB	
	17 12/15		Work as usual. R. LAIES LONDON BRIDGE 4 feet 10 inches HLB	
	18 12/15		Work as usual. R. LAIES LONDON BRIDGE 4 feet 9 inches HLB	
	19 12/15		Work as usual. R. LAIES LONDON BRIDGE 5 feet. HLB	
	20 12/15		Work as usual. R LAIES LONDON BRIDGE 4 feet 10 inches HLB	

8353 Wt. W2544/1454 700,000 5/15 D. D. & L. A.D.S.S./Forms/C. 2118.

Instructions regarding War Diaries and Intelligence Summaries are contained in F. S. Regs., Part II. and the Staff Manual respectively. Title pages will be prepared in manuscript.

Army Form C. 2118.

WAR DIARY
or
~~INTELLIGENCE SUMMARY.~~
(Erase heading not required.) H.Q. R.E. 23rd Divn

Place	Date	Hour	Summary of Events and Information	Remarks and references to Appendices
~~21~~ CROIX DU BAC	21 12/15		Work as usual - Hutting - workshops - communication trenches SHAFTESBURY AVE, QUEER ST, WINE ST, WINE AVE, COWGATE, SAKOP, PARK ROW - Remodelling 10 bays front line and preparing with boxes for gas cylinders - M.G. emplacements Front and BOIS GRENIER Line - reconstruction S Line, SS Line, BOIS GRENIER Line - reconstruction AID POST PARK ROW - Drainage and ditching Height of River ~~LB~~ LAIES LONDON BRIDGE 4 feet 7½ inches, 11C 1 foot 8 inches YUB	
	22 12/15		Work as usual. River LAIES LONDON BRIDGE 5 feet 1 inch. YUB	
	23 12/15		Work as usual. River LAIES LONDON BRIDGE. 5 feet 3 inches YUB.	
	24 12/15		Work as usual. River LAIES LONDON BRIDGE 5 feet 11½ inches YUB	
	25 12/15		Work as usual. River LAIES LONDON BRIDGE 6 feet 2 inches YUB with the exception of no Infantry working parties no relaxation of work was allowed for Xmas	
	26 12/15		Work as usual. River LAIES LONDON BRIDGE 6 feet 4 inches YUB	
	27 12/15		Work as usual. River LAIES LONDON BRIDGE 6 feet 4½ inches YUB Though the flood is 3½ inches higher the condition of the front trenches is noticeably better than in the flood of the 12th inst. YUB	

8353 Wt. W2544/1454 700,000 5/15 D. D. & L. A.D.S.S./Forms/C. 2118.

Army Form C. 2118.

Instructions regarding War Diaries and Intelligence Summaries are contained in F. S. Regs., Part II. and the Staff Manual respectively. Title pages will be prepared in manuscript.

WAR DIARY
or
~~INTELLIGENCE SUMMARY.~~

(Erase heading not required.) H. Q. R E 23rd Divn

Place	Date	Hour	Summary of Events and Information	Remarks and references to Appendices
~~28~~ 12 CROIX DU BAC	28 12/15		Work as usual - Workshops - Hutting - Communication Trenches SHAFTESBURY AVE, QUEER ST, PARK ROW, WINE AVE, WINE ST, COWGATE - MG emplacements front and BOIS GRENIER Line - Reconstruction S Line SS Line & BOIS GRENIER Line - Firesteps and traverses in front line - AID post WINE AVE - Drainage and ditching.	
			Height R. LAIES LONDON BRIDGE 6 feet 4 inches, I C. 2 feet 8 inches HJB	
	29 12/15		Work as usual - River LAIES LONDON BRIDGE 6 feet 1 inch. HJB	
	30 12/15		Work as usual - River LAIES London Bridge 5 feet 10 inches HJB	
	31 12/15		Work as usual - River LAIES London Bridge 5 feet 6½ inches HJB	
			An accident happened about 6 pm resulting in the death of Lieut. E. W. Ruse RE 1 NCO and 3 Sappers and 4 Sappers & some RAMC & Infantry being wounded. This party were selected to make with Infantry a raid on the German lines this night. Lieut Ruse and the 4 men were apparently just completing making up the ~~Eight~~ charges of 20 lbs. when they exploded with above result. HJB	

A. G. Bremner
Lieut Col. R.E.
CRE 23/Divn

353 Wt. W2544/1454 700,000 5/15 D. D. & L. A.D.S.S./Forms/C. 2118.

CRE. 23rd Div:
Vol: 5

TAIV

Confidential

Instructions regarding War Diaries and Intelligence Summaries are contained in F. S. Regs., Part II. and the Staff Manual respectively. Title pages will be prepared in manuscript.

WAR DIARY
or
~~INTELLIGENCE SUMMARY.~~

Army Form C. 2118.

(Erase heading not required.) HQ RE 23rd Divn

Place	Date	Hour	Summary of Events and Information	Remarks and references to Appendices
CROIX DU BAC	1.1.16		Work as usual - Hutting, Workshops - Communication Trenches SHAFTESBURY AVE, QUEER ST, BAY AVE - S line - SS Line - BRIDOUX salient retrenchment, LONDON BRIDGE Post - MG Emplacements front and BOIS GRENIER Line - reconstruction BOIS GRENIER Line - Drainage - clearing debris of explosion at 128th Fd Co RE.	
			River LAIES depth at LONDON BRIDGE 5 feet 3 inches at 11C 2 feet 1 inch YHB	
	2.1.16		Work as usual River LAIES LONDON BRIDGE 5 feet 0¼ inches YHB.	
	3.1.16		Work as usual. River LAIES LONDON BRIDGE 4 feet 11½ inches YHB	
	4.1.16		Work as usual River LAIES LONDON BRIDGE 4 feet 10½ inches YHB	
	5.1.16		Work as usual. Lieut Ridgewell returned to HQ from loan to the 190th Drainage Co RE and commenced the duties of Officer i/c civilian labour.	
			River LAIES London Bridge 4 feet 9 inches. YHB	
	6.1.16		Work as usual River LAIES LONDON BRIDGE 4 feet 7½ inches YHB	
	7.1.16		Work as usual River LAIES LONDON BRIDGE 4 feet 7 inches	
			Work of HQ. during week much interfered with by break down of motor car. YHB.	

2353 Wt. W2544/1454 700,000 5/15 D. D. & L. A.D.S.S./Forms/C. 2118.

Army Form C. 2118.

Instructions regarding War Diaries and Intelligence Summaries are contained in F. S. Regs., Part II. and the Staff Manual respectively. Title pages will be prepared in manuscript.

WAR DIARY
or
~~INTELLIGENCE SUMMARY.~~

(*Erase heading not required.*) ~~[illegible]~~ H Q. R E 23rd Div

Place	Date	Hour	Summary of Events and Information	Remarks and references to Appendices
CROIX DU BAC	8 1/16		Work as usual - Workshops - Hutting - communication Trenches SHAFTESBURY AVE, QUEER ST, WINE AVE, WINE ST, SALOP, COWGATE - machine gun emplacements front and BOIS GRENIER Line - LONDON BRIDGE POST - repairs I 31.5 I31.3 I31.1 - S Line - Drainage - Aidpost WINE AVE - reconstruction BOISGRENIER Line work on salients & salient retrenchments River LAIES LONDON BRIDGE 4 feet 6 inches I C 1 foot 7 inches. HGS	
	9 1/16		Work as usual - Lieut Edglestone attached H.Q. from 102nd Fd Co RE to learn duties of adjutant. ~~X~~ River LAIES London Bridge 4 feet 5 1/2 inches HGS	
	10 1/16		Work as usual River LAIES London Bridge 4 ft 4 inches	HGE
	11 1/16		Work as usual River LAIES @ LONDON BRIDGE 4 ft - 2 inch	HGE
	12 1/16		Work as usual River LAIES @ LONDON BRIDGE 4 ft - 1 inch	HGE
	13 1/16		Work as usual River LAIES @ LONDON BRIDGE 4 ft - 4 1/2 ins	HGE
	14 1/16		Work as usual River LAIES @ LONDON BRIDGE 4 ft 2 inches	HGE

#353 Wt. W2544/1454 700,000 5/15 D. D. & L. A.D.S.S./Forms/C. 2118.

Instructions regarding War Diaries and Intelligence Summaries are contained in F. S. Regs., Part II. and the Staff Manual respectively. Title pages will be prepared in manuscript.

Army Form C. 2118.

WAR DIARY of H.Q R.E 23 Division
or
~~INTELLIGENCE SUMMARY.~~
(*Erase heading not required.*)

Place	Date	Hour	Summary of Events and Information	Remarks and references to Appendices
CROIX-DU-BAC	15/1/16		Work as usual - Workshops - Hutting - Communication trenches SHAFTESBURY AVE - QUEER ST. - WINE AVE - WINE ST - SALOP - COWGATE - Machine gun Emplacements front line and BOIS GRENIER line - LONDON BRIDGE POST HUDSON BAY - repairs on I 31.5 I 31.3, I 31.1 Cleaning, draining & revetting S line and S.S line - putting in foot boards & firing steps - Reconstruction BOIS GRENIER line, work on Salients & retrenchments. River LAIES @ LONDON BRIDGE 4 ft - 1 inch	HGE
	16/1/16		Work as usual River LAIES @ LONDON BRIDGE 4 ft - 0	HGE
	17/1/16		Work as usual River LAIES @ LONDON BRIDGE 3 ft - 11 inch	HGE
	18/1/16		Work as usual River LAIES at LONDON BRIDGE 3 ft - 11 in	YLB
	19/1/16		Work as usual River LAIES at LONDON BRIDGE 3 ft - 11 in	YLB
	20/1/16		Work as usual River LAIES at LONDON BRIDGE 4 ft - 1 in	YLB
	21/1/16		Work as usual River LAIES at LONDON BRIDGE 4 ft - 1 in	YLB

#353 Wt. W2544/1454 700,000 5/15 D. D. & L. A.D.S.S./Forms/C. 2118.

Army Form C. 2118.

Instructions regarding War Diaries and Intelligence Summaries are contained in F. S. Regs., Part II. and the Staff Manual respectively. Title pages will be prepared in manuscript.

WAR DIARY
or
~~INTELLIGENCE SUMMARY.~~

(*Erase heading not required.*) HQ RE 23rd Division

Place	Date	Hour	Summary of Events and Information	Remarks and references to Appendices
CROIX DU BAC	22 1/16		Work as usual - Workshops Hatting - Communication Trenches HAYMARKET, WHITE CITY, SHAFTESBURY AVE, MOAT FARM AVE, QUEER ST, PARK ROW, WINE AVE, SALOP, AVONDALE - Machine Gun Emplacements - Reconstruction ~~SS&B~~ 6 BRIDOUX Salient retrenchment, S line, SS line, BOIS GRENIER Line. River LAIES at LONDON BRIDGE ~~3~~ 4 ft 1½ in YLLB.	
	23 1/16		Work as usual. River LAIES at LONDON BRIDGE 4 ft 1 in. YLLB	
	24 1/16		Work as usual. River LAIES at LONDON BRIDGE 4 ft ½ in YLLB	
	25 1/16		Work as usual. River LAIES at LONDON BRIDGE 4 ft ½ in YLLB	
	26 1/16		Work as usual. 207th Fd Co RE 34th Divn attached 3 Sects 101st Fd Co 1 Sect to 128 Fd Co RE for instruction. River LAIES LONDON BRIDGE 3 ft 10¼ in. YLLB	
	27 1/16		Work as usual. River LAIES at LONDON BRIDGE 3 feet 9 in YLLB	
	28 1/16		Work as usual. River LAIES at LONDON BRIDGE 3 feet 9 in YLLB	

8353 Wt. W2544/1454 700,000 5/15 D. D. & L. A.D.S.S./Forms/C. 2118.

Instructions regarding War Diaries and Intelligence Summaries are contained in F. S. Regs., Part II. and the Staff Manual respectively. Title pages will be prepared in manuscript.

WAR DIARY
or
INTELLIGENCE SUMMARY.

(Erase heading not required.) H Q RE 23rd Divn

Army Form C. 2118.

Place	Date	Hour	Summary of Events and Information	Remarks and references to Appendices
CROIX DU BAC	29 1/16		Work as usual - ~~Shooting~~ Workshops - Ammunition Stores - Communication Trenches BAY AVENUE, SAFETY AVENUE, MOAT FARM AVENUE, HUDSONS BAY, QUEER ST, TORONTO ST, PARK ROW, WINE AVE - S line - SS line, BRIDOUX Salient, LONDON BRIDGE Post, BOIS GRENIER Line - machine Gun Emplacements - Water supply. River LAIES at LONDON BRIDGE 3 feet 7 inches YCLB.	
	30 1/16		Work as usual. River LAIES at LONDON BRIDGE 3 feet 5 inches YCLB	
	31 1/16		Work as usual. River LAIES at LONDON BRIDGE 3 feet 5 inches YCLB	

A.G. Bremner
Lt Col RE
CRE 23rd Divn.

2353 Wt. W2544/1454 700,000 5/15 D. D. & L. A.D.S.S./Forms/C. 2118.

CRE. 23rd Div:
VOL: 6

February ~~January~~ 1916

Instructions regarding War Diaries and Intelligence Summaries are contained in F. S. Regs., Part II. and the Staff Manual respectively. Title pages will be prepared in manuscript.

WAR DIARY
or
~~INTELLIGENCE SUMMARY.~~

(Erase heading not required.) HQ RE 23rd Div

Army Form C. 2118.

(1)

Place	Date	Hour	Summary of Events and Information	Remarks and references to Appendices
CROIX DU BAC	1.2/16		Work as usual Reconstruction BRIDOUX Salient and BOIS GRENIER Line - Work on communications SAFETY AVE, BAY AVE, MOAT FARM AVE, QUEER ST, PARK ROW WINE AVE & SALOP. Work on M.G. Emplacements fronts BOIS GRENIER Lines - Work on S Line SS Line, LONDON BRIDGE POST, HUDSON BAY - Water supply for BRIDOUX Salient - Hutting Drainage	
			Depth River LAIES at LONDON BRIDGE 3 feet 1½ inches YCM	
	2 2/16		Work as usual River LAIES at LONDON BRIDGE 3 feet 1½ inches YCM	
	3 2/16		Work as usual River LAIES at LONDON BRIDGE 3 feet 2 inches YCM	
	4 2/16		Work as usual River LAIES at LONDON BRIDGE 3 feet 1½ inches YCM	
	5 2/16		Work as usual River LAIES at LONDON BRIDGE 3 feet 2 inches YCM	
	6 2/16		Work as usual River LAIES at LONDON BRIDGE 3 feet 1 inches YCM	
	7 2/16		Work as usual River LAIES at LONDON Bridge 2 feet 11½ inches YCM	

2353 Wt. W2544/1454 700,000 5/15 D. D. & L. A.D.S.S./Forms/C. 2118.

Instructions regarding War Diaries and Intelligence Summaries are contained in F. S. Regs., Part II. and the Staff Manual respectively. Title pages will be prepared in manuscript.

WAR DIARY
or
~~INTELLIGENCE SUMMARY.~~

(*Erase heading not required.*) HQ RE 23rd Division

Army Form C. 2118.

(2)

Place	Date	Hour	Summary of Events and Information	Remarks and references to Appendices
CROIX DU BAC	8 2/16		208th Fd Co RE marched in from VIEUX BERQUIN and took up billets in RUE MARLE. They are attached to 128th Fd Co RE for instruction Work as usual – reconstruction BRIDOUX Salient and BOIS GREMER Line – Work on communications MOAT FARM AVE, BAY AVE, NEWGUFER ST, BREWERY to WHITE CITY, HUDSON BAY, PARK ROW. – M.G. Emplacements front and BOIS GREMER Lines. – S & SS Lines – BO LONDON BRIDGE POST – TRAMWAY POST – Wiring S Line – Water supply for BRIDOUX Salient – Salving tools – drainage – Hutting Depth of river LAIES at LONDON BRIDGE 3 feet HLB.	
	9 2/16		Work as usual. River LAIES at LONDON BRIDGE 3 feet 5 inches HLB	
	10 2/16		Work as usual. River LAIES at LONDON BRIDGE 3 feet 7 inches HLB	
	11 2/16		Work as usual. River LAIES at LONDON BRIDGE 3 feet 5¼ inches HLB	
	12 2/16		Work as usual. River LAIES at LONDON BRIDGE 4 feet 0¼ inches HLB	
	13 2/16		Work as usual. River LAIES at LONDON BRIDGE 4 feet 1 inch HLB	
	14 2/16		128th Fd Co RE marched out to VIEUX BERQUIN. 208th Fd Co RE took over Left Section of Line. Work as usual. River LAIES at LONDON BRIDGE 4 feet 1 inch HLB	

2353 Wt. W2544/1454 700,000 5/15 D. D. & L. A.D.S.S./Forms/C. 2118.

Instructions regarding War Diaries and Intelligence Summaries are contained in F. S. Regs., Part II. and the Staff Manual respectively. Title pages will be prepared in manuscript.

WAR DIARY
or
INTELLIGENCE SUMMARY.
(Erase heading not required.)

Army Form C. 2118.

HQ RE 23rd Division

Place	Date	Hour	Summary of Events and Information	Remarks and references to Appendices
CROIX DU BAC	15 2/16		Work as usual - Reconstruction BRIDOUX Salient, S & SS Line, BOIS GRENIER Line, Work on posts TRAMWAY, STANWAY and EMMA - Work on communications STANWAY AVE, MOATFARM AVE - NEW QUEER ST - SHAFTESBURY AVE, PARKROW - M. Gun Emplacements front and BOIS GRENIER Line - Water supply for BRIDOUX Salient - Construction of latrines - Drainage. River LAIES LONDON BRIDGE. 4 feet 6 inches YCUB	
	16 2/16		Work as usual. River LAIES LONDON BRIDGE 4 feet 1½ inches YCUB	
	17 2/16		Work as usual. River LAIES LONDON BRIDGE 4 feet 3 inches. CRE 34th Divn and HQRE 34th Divn arrived to take over work of area YCUB	
	18 2/16		Work as usual. River LAIES LONDON BRIDGE 5 feet. YCUB	
	19 2/16		Work as usual. River LAIES LONDON BRIDGE 4 feet 11½ inches YCUB	
	20 2/16		Work as usual. River LAIES LONDON BRIDGE 4 feet 11¼ inches YCUB	
	21 2/16		102nd Fd Co RE marched out to VIEUX BERQUIN. 207th Fd Co RE took over work of Right Section of Line River LAIES LONDON BRIDGE 4 feet 9 inches YCUB	

2353 Wt. W2544/1454 700,000 5/15 D. D. & L. A.D.S.S./Forms/C. 2118.

Instructions regarding War Diaries and Intelligence Summaries are contained in F. S. Regs., Part II. and the Staff Manual respectively. Title pages will be prepared in manuscript.

WAR DIARY
or
~~INTELLIGENCE SUMMARY.~~ HQ RE 23rd Divn
(Erase heading not required.)

Army Form C. 2118.

(4)

Place	Date	Hour	Summary of Events and Information	Remarks and references to Appendices
CROIX DU BAC	22.2/16		Work as usual. Handing over to 34th Division. Hard frost. JLUB	
	23 2/16		Work as usual. Handing over to 34th Division. Hard frost. 128th Field Company marched from STEENBEQUE to NEUF BERQUIN JLUB	
	24 2/16		marched out and took up billets in ESTAIRES. Preparing to take over line there.	
	25 2/16		Organising dumps and stores and work in new area we were about to enter. Orders received in evening cancelling and ordering us in GHQ reserve. 5 inches of snow. JLUB.	
	26 2/16		Marched to STEENBEQUE with 128th Fd Co RE. 102nd already there. 101 Fd Co RE still at NOUVEAU MONDE where they had gone on 25th JLUB	
	27 2/16		101st Fd Co RE joined us at STEENBEQUE. CRE Lt Col Bremner AG proceeded on 10 days leave. Major C B Bonham RE acting CRE JLUB	
	28 2/16		Orders received to march to BRUAY area. JLUB.	
	29 2/16		Marched to and took up billets in CAMBLAIN-CHÂTELAIN west of BRUAY JLUB Attached is tracing showing state of repair of front line trenches on handing over to 34th Division.	

C B Bonham ~~Major~~
Major RE
for CRE 23rd Divn

Army Form C. 2118.

Instructions regarding War Diaries and Intelligence Summaries are contained in F. S. Regs., Part II. and the Staff Manual respectively. Title pages will be prepared in manuscript.

WAR DIARY for month of March 1916.
or
INTELLIGENCE SUMMARY.
(Erase heading not required.)

H.Q. R.E 23rd Divn

(1)

Place	Date	Hour	Summary of Events and Information	Remarks and references to Appendices
CAMBLAIN CHATELAIN	1 3/16		Coys resting. Drill & discipline. Rifle exercises etc Cold. H.G.E.	
	2 3/16		Drill, rifle exercises etc — Snow & frost H.G.E	
	3 3/16		Drill etc — Snow & frost H.G.E	
	4 3/16		Short rifles and new pattern gas helmets issued to the companies. Lt-General Sir Henry Wilson commanding 4th Corps lectured to officers of 23rd Divn H.G.E	
	5 3/16		Capt & Adj. H. I. BULKELEY R E left Division to take command 81st Field Co. R.E. Lieut H.G. EDLESTON R E 102nd Field Coy took up duties as Adjutant R.E. H.G.E	
	6 3/16		Drill etc Thaw commenced. 2 sections 128th Field Co moved to GOUY-SERVINS	H.G.E
	7 3/16		101st & 102nd Field coys R.E moved to ABLAIN-ST-NAZAIRE Transport & H.Q to GOUY-SERVINS. ~~2 sections & H.Q~~ H.G.E	
	8 3/16		H.Q. R.E moved to CHATEAU-de-la-HAIE H.Q. & 2 sections 128th Field Co moved to VILLERS-au-BOIS. H.G.E Line taken over from French. 2nd Divn on our right.	
CHATEAU de-la-HAIE	9 3/16		101st Field Coys pumping out cellars & dug-outs in ABLAIN-ST-NAZAIRE. 128th Field Coy on repairs at CHATEAU-de-la-HAIE. C.R.E. returned from ENGLAND H.G.E	

H.G. Edleston Capt R.E
for Lt-Colonel,
Commanding Royal Engineers.
23rd Division.

2353 Wt. W2544/1454 700,000 5/15 D. D. & L. A.D.S.S./Forms/C. 2118.

Army Form C. 2118.

Instructions regarding War Diaries and Intelligence Summaries are contained in F. S. Regs., Part II. and the Staff Manual respectively. Title pages will be prepared in manuscript.

WAR DIARY
or
INTELLIGENCE SUMMARY.
(Erase heading not required.) H.Q. R.E 23rd Division

(2)

Place	Date	Hour	Summary of Events and Information	Remarks and references to Appendices
CHATEAU de-la-HAIE	10 3/16		Field coys on night work in the trenches 101st Field Co on right 102nd Field Co on left in front of SOUCHEZ. Trenches - very bad front line not continuous + inconceivably muddy. 128th Field Co working in reserve area. Work started improving trenches on NOTRE DAME de LORETTE.	H.G.E.
"	11 3/16		Work in trenches + Quarry retrenchment. making communications, draining etc	H.G.E.
"	12 3/16		Ditto H.G.E.	
"	13 3/16		Two sections of each field coy moved to RUITZ being relieved by two sections of the 4th LONDON 1/3 LONDON + 2/3 LONDON Field Coys R.E (47th Divn)	H.G.E.
"	14 3/16		H.Q. R.E 23rd Divn and remaining sections + H.Q. of field coys moved to RUITZ completing relief of R.E with (47th Divn) Bright sunny warm day. C.R.E discussed reliefs of Field Coys with C.R.E 2nd Divn	H.G.E.
RUITZ.	16 3/16		128th Field Coy moved to AIX-NOULETTE 101st + 102nd Field Coys overhauling stores + equipment H.G.E.	H.G. Eccleston Capt RE for Lt-Colonel, Commanding Royal Engineers. 23rd Division.
	18 3/16		101st Field Coy R.E moved to BULLY-GRENAY. 102nd Field Coy R.E. moved to FOSSE 10 sheet 36B pt R.8. All three field companies are now working under the orders of C.R.E 2nd Divn	H.G.E.

2353 Wt. W2544/1454 700,000 5/15 D. D. & L. A.D.S.S./Forms/C. 2118.

Army Form C. 2118.

Instructions regarding War Diaries and Intelligence Summaries are contained in F. S. Regs., Part II. and the Staff Manual respectively. Title pages will be prepared in manuscript.

WAR DIARY
or
INTELLIGENCE SUMMARY.
(Erase heading not required.)

H.Q. R.E 23rd Division. (3)

Place	Date	Hour	Summary of Events and Information	Remarks and references to Appendices
RUITZ	17 3/16		Field Coys working under C.R.E 2nd Division. C.R.E 23rd Division went over right sector H.G.E	
	18 3/16		Do Do C.R.E inspecting support & reserve lines. H.G.E	
	19 3/16		Do Do. C.R.E inspecting left sector. Adj to 1st Army Workshops at BETHUNE H.G.E	
	20 3/16		Do Do Adj to AIX-NOULETTE inspecting system of supply of R.E stores to trenches H.G.E	
	21 3/16		5th Field Coy R.E arrived from CALONNE area C.R.E H.G.E	
	22 3/16		H.Q. RE moved to SAINS-en-GOHELLE to relieve H.Q. R.E 2nd Div. C.R.E to hospital under doctors orders. Major C.B. BONHAM. 102nd Field Co R.E took over as a/ C.R.E. H.G.E.	
SAINS-en-GOHELLE	23 3/16		Five Field Coys in line, on left on CALONNE Sector are the 1/1 EAST ANGLIAN Field Coy and 101st Field Co R.E. In central or ANGRES sector is the 105th Field Co R.E On right on SOUCHEZ Sector are the 128th Field Co R.E and the 226th Field Co R.E. Lines in very bad condition on right, indifferent in centre and fairly good on left. Work proceeding mainly on Support lines a lot of wiring is being done also opening up of communication trenches 1st Division on left 47th on right. H.G.E	

H.G. Edleston Capt RE
for Lt-Colonel,
Commanding Royal Engineers
23rd Division.

2353 Wt. W2544/1454 700,000 5/15 D. D. & L. A.D.S.S./Forms/C. 2118.

Instructions regarding War Diaries and Intelligence Summaries are contained in F. S. Regs., Part II. and the Staff Manual respectively. Title pages will be prepared in manuscript.

WAR DIARY
or
INTELLIGENCE SUMMARY.

(*Erase heading not required.*)

Army Form C. 2118.

H.Q. R.E 23rd Division (4)

Place	Date	Hour	Summary of Events and Information	Remarks and references to Appendices
SAINS-en GOHELLE	24 3/16		Work contd Improving & laying trench boards on MAISTRE line CALONNE Sector Water supply system contd in this sector. Improving & wiring BAJOLLE line in centre sector also Trench O.P.s for artillery. On right clearing, deepening revetting & generally improving communication trenches & support lines. Arrangements discussed on recommendation of C.R.E for starting a Divl Dump & small workshop at SAINS-en-GOHELLE HGE	
	25 3/16		Work as above contd Difficulty experienced in obtaining stores for defence purposes particularly timber. HGE	
	26 3/16		Arrangements completed for Dump at SAINS-en-GOHELLE. Corps workshops report that delay is inevitable in supplying dug-out frames & revetment hurdles etc owing to lack of timber & pressure of other orders. Work contd on defences	HGE
	27 3/16		Lt-Col. A.G BREMNER returned from C.C.S. Stores commenced arriving at new Divl Dump. Fourth company of pioneers moved to NOULETTE wood from HERSIN area. Working in SOUCHEZ Sector with 128th Field Co R.E. Work rather held up owing to bad weather conditions. Raining hard.	HGE.

H.G. Edleston Capt RE
for Lt-Colonel,
Commanding Royal Engineers,
23rd Division.

2353 Wt. W2544/1454 700,000 5/15 D. D. & L. A.D.S.S./Forms/C. 2118.

Instructions regarding War Diaries and Intelligence Summaries are contained in F. S. Regs., Part II. and the Staff Manual respectively. Title pages will be prepared in manuscript.

WAR DIARY
or
INTELLIGENCE SUMMARY.
(Erase heading not required.)

Army Form C. 2118.

H.Q. R.E. 23rd Division (5)

Place	Date	Hour	Summary of Events and Information	Remarks and references to Appendices
SAINS-en-GOHELLE	28 3/16		Work contd Revetting, remodelling & wiring MAISTRE & BAJOLLE lines. Water supply systems contd. Pioneers & large parties of Inf. assisting at above. Weather still very bad. Work considerably hampered by state of the ground. HGE	
"	29 3/16		Work contd as above. 5th Field Co R.E relieved 226th Field Co R.E in right sector. 226th Field Co moved to RUITZ HGE	
"	30 3/16		Work contd as above. Improvement in weather. Large parties of Inf working on MAISTRE, BAJOLLE & Support lines. Demonstration of captured German Flammenwerfer apparatus with a flame projection of about 20 yds. Stores arriving rapidly at Div.l Dump. Small quantity of timber now available.	HGE
"	31 3/16		Work contd as above. Shelling by enemy heavies of Fosse 10 & Fosse 2. Fine sunny day. HGE	

H. G. Eddleston
for Lt.-Colonel, Capt R.E
Commanding Royal Engineers
23rd Division

2353 Wt. W2544/1454 700,000 5/15 D. D. & L. A.D.S.S./Forms/C. 2118.

Instructions regarding War Diaries and Intelligence Summaries are contained in F. S. Regs., Part II. and the Staff Manual respectively. Title pages will be prepared in manuscript.

WAR DIARY
or
INTELLIGENCE SUMMARY.
(Erase heading not required.)

Army Form C. 2118.

C.E. 23D Vol 8

H.Q. R E 23rd Div

Place	Date	Hour	Summary of Events and Information	Remarks and references to Appendices
SAINS-en-GOHELLE	1.4.16		Work continued on MAISTRE line, BAJOLLE line. Both lines are being remodelled, cleaned, drained revetted & wired. Trench boards are being laid and fire steps made. Water Supply System is being continued rapidly. Support line in SOUCHEZ is very bad & is being remodelled. Pioneers and infantry working parties are assisting under supervision of R.E. HGE	
	2.4.16		Work contd as usual. Warm clear day again. HGE	
	3.4.16		Work contd as usual. New system of supplying stores from Divl Dump at SAINS-en-GOHELLE commenced. Still short of timber generally – particularly planking. HGE	
	4.4.16		Work contd as usual. MAJOR M.S HAMNER RE 4/1st CHESHIRE Field Co WELSH DIVISIONAL ENGINEERS attached for duty for 3 days. HGE	
	5.4.16		Work contd as usual. HGE	
	6.4.16		Work contd as usual. HGE	
	7.4.16		Work contd as usual. MAJOR MS HAMNER RE returned to ENGLAND. HGE	

2353 Wt. W2544/1454 700,000 5/15 D. D. & L. A.D.S.S./Forms/C. 2118.

Army Form C. 2118.

WAR DIARY
or
INTELLIGENCE SUMMARY.
(Erase heading not required.)

Instructions regarding War Diaries and Intelligence Summaries are contained in F. S. Regs., Part II. and the Staff Manual respectively. Title pages will be prepared in manuscript.

H.Q. 23rd Div. R.E.

Place	Date	Hour	Summary of Events and Information	Remarks and references to Appendices
SAINS-en-GOHELLE	8/4/16		Work being contd on MAISTRE & BAJOLLE lines, remodelling, clearing, revetting, making firesteps, laying trench boards and wiring same. Work concentrated particularly on right (SOUCHEZ) section. Three sections of 101st Field Co R.E. are now working in this sector in addition to the 5th and 101st Field Co RE. Two companies pioneers & large infantry working parties are employed every night also. The commn trenches are being deepened & improved. M.G. Emplacements being constructed in support lines. O.P.s for the artillery. CHORD line BULLY CRATER 2" pipes being laid for water supply systems. HGE	
"	9/4/16		Work contd as above HGE	
"	10/4/16		Work contd as above HGE	
"	11/4/16		Work contd as above HGE	
"	12/4/16		Work contd as above. Orders recd from Corps that all leave is cancelled till further orders HGE	
	13/4/16		Work contd as above HGE	

2353 Wt. W2544/1454 700,000 5/15 D. D. & L. A.D.S.S./Forms/C. 2118.

Army Form C. 2118.

Instructions regarding War Diaries and Intelligence Summaries are contained in F. S. Regs., Part II. and the Staff Manual respectively. Title pages will be prepared in manuscript.

WAR DIARY
or
INTELLIGENCE SUMMARY.
(Erase heading not required.)

Place	Date	Hour	Summary of Events and Information	Remarks and references to Appendices
SAINS-en-GOHELLE	14 4/16		Work being continued improving MAISTRE & BAJOLLE lines, revetting laying trench boards making fire steps - traverses etc also revetting. Concrete M.G. Emplacements begun. Work proceeding on water supply system - Communications generally are being improved & new trenches constructed where necessary. A number of firesteps are being made in front line & concrete M.G. Emplacements are being constructed. One section 101st Field Co R E left for PERNES for duty at the Corps school	H.G.E
"	15 4/16		Work being contd as above. Fosse X heavily shelled in morning. H.G.E	
"	16 4/16		Work being contd as usual H.G.E	
"	17 4/16		Work being contd as usual H.G.E	
"	18 4/16		Work being contd as usual. Lt-Col A.G. BREMNER R.E down with fever	H.G.E
"	19 4/16		C.R.E 2nd Division took over from C.R.E 23rd Division. The 3 Field Coys of the 23rd Division are still remaining in the line under C.R.E 2nd Division. H.Q. R.E moved to rest billets at RUITZ. Lt-Col BREMNER C.R.E 23rd Division is rather worse	H.G.E

2353 Wt. W2544/1454 700,000 5/15 D. D. & L. A.D.S.S./Forms/C. 2118.

Instructions regarding War Diaries and Intelligence Summaries are contained in F. S. Regs., Part II. and the Staff Manual respectively. Title pages will be prepared in manuscript.

WAR DIARY
or
INTELLIGENCE SUMMARY.
(*Erase heading not required.*)

Army Form C. 2118.

Place	Date	Hour	Summary of Events and Information	Remarks and references to Appendices
RUITZ	20 4/16		Field Companies in line under C.R.E 2nd Division. H.Q.R.E in rest billets. Lt. Col. BREMNER R.E evacuated to Casualty Clearing Station.	H.G.E
"	21 4/16		MAJOR C.B. BONHAM R.E 102nd Field Coy R.E acting C.R.E 23rd Division	H.G.E
"	22 4/16		One section 102nd Field Co R.E moved to ABLAIN-ST-NAZAIRE for work under C.R.E 47th Div	
			" " 128th " " " " VILLERS-au-BOIS	H.G.E
"	23 4/16		101st Field Co. R.E moved from BULLY-GRENAY to rest billets at RUITZ	
	24 4/16		Capt. H.G. Eddleston Adjt. R.E. went on leave to England	
			Lieut. D. Baird R.E. acting adjutant.	D.B.
			101st Fd Co R.E. at work on No 22 C.C.S. BRUAY	D.B.
	25 4/16		Work as usual	D.B.
	26 4/16		Work as usual	D.B.
	27 4/16		Section of 101st Fd Co R.E. at PERNES relieved by another section of same company.	D.B.
	28 4/16		Work as usual	D.B.
	29 4/16		Work as usual	D.B.
	30 4/16		Work as usual.	D.B.

2353 Wt. W2544/1454 700,000 5/15 D. D. & L. A.D.S.S./Forms/C. 2118.

OPERATION ORDER NO.6. BY C.R.E. 23RD DIVISION.

B.109.

The following moves will take place on 1st May :-

a. 101st Field Company will proceed from RUITZ to BULLY.

b. 102nd Field Company will proceed from present billets to RUITZ.

One section 101st Coy. will proceed direct to VILLERS AU BOIS reporting to O.C. 2/3 London Field Company R.E. it will not be East of PETIT SERVINS before 7 p.m.

The section 102nd Field Company now at VILLERS AU BOIS will proceed to RUITZ starting after 7.30 p.m.

(2). On May 2nd one section 102nd Field Company will relieve one section 101st Field Company at PERNES.

The Section 101st Field Company will billet at RUITZ during night of 2/3 May, and proceed to BULLY on 3rd May.

The O. i/c Section 101st Field Company at PERNES will remain 24 hours to hand over the duties to the Officer relieving him.

(3). No movements between BULLY and FOSSE 10 will take place before 7 p.m.

(4). Cyclists billeting parties will be sent in advance.

(5). Rations. - Refilling Point (except for section at VILLERS) is at BARLIN. Rations for section at PERNES are sent direct by A.S.C. wagon on separate indent by unit concerned.

(sd) D.Hand, Lieut. R.E.
for Major R.E.
A/C.R.E., 23rd Division.

28/4/1916.

2.

"Q".

For information.

[signature] Major,
General Staff, 23rd Division.

Headquarters,
23rd Division.
29/4/1916.

RE. 23 Div
Vol 9

CONFIDENTIAL

WAR DIARY

OF

Head Quarters Royal Engineers 23rd DIVISION

from May 1st 1916 to May 31st 1916.

H.G. Ellerton
Capt RE
adj. RE 23 Div

Instructions regarding War Diaries and Intelligence Summaries are contained in F. S. Regs., Part II. and the Staff Manual respectively. Title pages will be prepared in manuscript.

WAR DIARY
or
~~INTELLIGENCE SUMMARY.~~
(Erase heading not required.)

MAY 1916

Army Form C. 2118.

H. Q. R.E. 23rd Divn

Place	Date	Hour	Summary of Events and Information	Remarks and references to Appendices
RUITZ	1/5/16		102nd Field Co. R.E. complete moved into rest billet at RUITZ	
			2 sections 101st Field Co R.E. moved from RUITZ to BULLY	
			1 " " " " " RUITZ to VILLERS au BOIS	DW
	2/5/16		1 section 102nd " " " " RUITZ to PERNES	
			1 " 101st " " " " PERNES to RUITZ	
			Work commenced on putting up 3 sheds 81' × 15' at HOUDAIN Station (Ammunition Railhead)	DW
			Taking down R.A. Hut at Chateau HOUDAIN (La VIELFORT)	DW
	3/5/16		1 section 101st Field Co R.E. moved from RUITZ to BULLY	
	4/5/16		Work as usual	DW
	5/5/16		Work as usual	DW.
	6/5/16		G.O.C inspected one section 102nd Fd Co R.E. ~~at~~ at PERNES at 10.15 am and remainder of coy at RUITZ at 3.30 pm.	DW.
"	7/5/16		Work as usual Capt H.G EDLESTON R.E. returned from ENGLAND	HGE
"	8/5/16		Work as usual Lt D BAIRD R.E returned to 101st Field Co R.E.	HGE
"	9/5/16		2 Section 102nd Field Co R.E moved from rest billets at RUITZ to FOSSE 10	
			128th Field Co R.E moved from AIX-NOULETTE to rest billets at RUITZ	HGE

C.B. Bonham
Major CRE 23 Div

Instructions regarding War Diaries and Intelligence Summaries are contained in F. S. Regs., Part II. and the Staff Manual respectively. Title pages will be prepared in manuscript.

WAR DIARY
or
INTELLIGENCE SUMMARY.
(Erase heading not required.)

MAY 1916

H.Q. R.E 23rd Division

Army Form C. 2118.

Place	Date	Hour	Summary of Events and Information	Remarks and references to Appendices
RUITZ	10.5.16		1 Section 102nd Field Co R.E moved from PERNES to rejoin company at Fosse 10 1 Section 128th Field Co R.E moved to PERNES in relief of above Remainder of 128th Field Co R.E. resting at RUITZ	H.G.E
	11.5.16		101st + 102nd Field Coys R.E. working in line under C.R.E 2nd Division 128th " " " working at Nozz C.C.S BRUAY	H.G.E
	12.5.16		Work as usual	H.G.E
SAINS-en-GOHELLE	13.5.16		H.Q. R.E moved to SAINS-en-GOHELLE + relieved C.R.E 2nd Division All 3 Field Coys of 2nd Division are at present working in line in addition to the 2 Field Coys of 23rd Division	H.G.E
	14.5.16		Work being concentrated as far as possible on SOUCHEZ (right) sector The trenches are still very poor + communication to front line difficult	H.G.E
	15.5.16		Work as usual. Large infantry working parties with each company every night. C.B. Binham Major CRE 23 D	H.G.E

2353 Wt. W2544/1454 700,000 5/15 D. D. & L. A.D.S.S./Forms/C. 2118.

Army Form C. 2118.

Instructions regarding War Diaries and Intelligence Summaries are contained in F. S. Regs., Part II. and the Staff Manual respectively. Title pages will be prepared in manuscript.

WAR DIARY
or
INTELLIGENCE SUMMARY.
(Erase heading not required.)

MAY 1916

H.Q. R.E 23rd Division

Place	Date	Hour	Summary of Events and Information	Remarks and references to Appendices
SAINS-en GOHELLE	16 5/16		Work being contd in front line & two reserve lines — MAISTRE and BAJOLLE lines. Orders recd from G.O.C. to construct deep dug-outs & complete wiring	HYE
	17 5/16		Work as usual	HYE
	18 5/16		Work being contd as far as possible in view of following moves. 128th Field Co R.E moved from RUITZ to their former billets AIX-NOULETTE 101st " " " BULLY-GRENAY to BOIS-du-BOUVIGNY 102 " " " Fosse 10 to BULLY-GRENAY Two field coys of 2nd Division moved back to rest billets The whole of the CALONNE (left) Sector was today handed over to 1st Division; and the whole of the spur NOTRE DAME de LORETTE was taken over by 23rd Division from 47th Division. In view of the importance of this spur the defence works will be taken in hand at once by 101st Field Co R.E. The 102nd Field Co R.E will work in the ANGRES Sector. This is now the left sector of this Division	HYE

C B Barker [illegible] 23 [illegible]

2353 Wt. W2544/1454 700,000 5/15 D. D. & L. A.D.S.S./Forms/C. 2118.

Army Form C. 2118.

Instructions regarding War Diaries and Intelligence Summaries are contained in F. S. Regs., Part II. and the Staff Manual respectively. Title pages will be prepared in manuscript.

WAR DIARY
or
INTELLIGENCE SUMMARY.

(Erase heading not required.)

MAY 1916

H.Q. R.E. 23rd Division

Place	Date	Hour	Summary of Events and Information	Remarks and references to Appendices
SAINS-en-GOHELLE.	19 5/16		Work being contd as usual. Very warm sunny day	HGE
	20 5/16		Work as usual	HGE
	21 5/16		Work as usual, being mainly concentrated on wiring and deep dug-outs.	HGE
	22 5/16		Work as usual. Considerable activity near SOUCHEZ, 5th Field Co R E 2nd Division under orders to move at 1 hours notice	HGE
	23 5/16		5th Field Coy RE moved from AIX-NOULETTE to 2nd Division area	HGE
	24 5/16		Work proceeding as usual. SAINS-en-GOHELLE heavily shelled during the morning. 2nd Division relieved 47th Division on our right.	HGE
	25 5/16		Work as usual. SAINS-en-GOHELLE shelled in the afternoon by 5" hows. Divl H.Q. cellars reinforced & outer walls being sandbagged.	HGE
	26 5/16		Work as usual. SAINS-en-GOHELLE shelled during afternoon	HGE
	27 5/16		Work as usual	HGE

C. B. Bonham
Maj. RE
a/CRE 23rd Div

HGE

2353 Wt. W2544/1454 700,000 5/15 D. D. & L. A.D.S.S./Forms/C. 2118.

Army Form C. 2118.

WAR DIARY
or
INTELLIGENCE SUMMARY.
(Erase heading not required.)

Instructions regarding War Diaries and Intelligence Summaries are contained in F. S. Regs., Part II. and the Staff Manual respectively. Title pages will be prepared in manuscript.

MAY 1916

H.Q. R.E 23rd Division

Place	Date	Hour	Summary of Events and Information	Remarks and references to Appendices
SAINS-en GOHELLE	28 5/16		Work as usual - a great deal of wiring is being done and a number of deep dug-outs are being constructed. Defences of NOTRE DAME being pushed ahead	HGE
" "	29 5/16		Work proceeding as usual. Horses & transport of Field Coys moved from Fosse 10 to BOIS-du-FROISSART	HGE
" "	30 5/16		Work proceeding as usual. The 101st Field Co. RE are now drawing stores from 2nd Divn Dump at GOUY in order to avoid the long haul from Coupigny to NOTRE DAME	HGE
" "	31 5/16		Work proceeding as usual. Very warm & sunny day.	HGE

C.B. Benham
Major RE
C.R.E. 23rd Div.

8353 Wt. W2544/1454 700,000 5/15 D. D. & L. A.D.S.S./Forms/C. 2118.

Officer i/c A.G.'s Office
BASE

Herewith War Diary of Headquarters R.E. 23rd Division for month of June 1916.

COMMANDING ROYAL ENGINEER
3 JUL. 1916
23RD DIVISION

3/7/16

H. G. Edleston
Captain, R.E.
Adjutant R.E.
23rd Division.

23 Div. RE

Army Form C. 2118.

Vol 10

Instructions regarding War Diaries and Intelligence Summaries are contained in F. S. Regs., Part II. and the Staff Manual respectively. Title pages will be prepared in manuscript.

WAR DIARY
or
INTELLIGENCE SUMMARY.
(Erase heading not required.)

JUNE (1)

H.Q. R.E. 23rd Division

COMMANDING ROYAL ENGINEER 3. JUL. 1916 23RD DIVISION

COMMANDING ROYAL ENGINEER 3. JUL. 1916 23RD DIVISION

Place	Date	Hour	Summary of Events and Information	Remarks and references to Appendices
SAINS-en GOHELLE	1 6/16		Work proceeding on NOTRE DAME de LORETTE defences & communications 1 coy of entrenching batt working on these in addition to 101st Field Co R.E. – 1 coy 9th S Staffs & large infantry working parties. Dug-outs are being made sufficient to accomodate the whole garrison a large amount of mining is being done on support & reserve lines. The water supply pipe is nearly completed in SOUCHEZ sector. Reserve lines are being cleared improved revetted & fire steps constructed in same.	HGE
" "	2 6/16		Work proceeding as above. Lt-Col A.G. BREMNER C.M.G. R.E. returned from hospital and resumed his duties as C.R.E. MAJOR C.B. BONHAM R.E returned to duty commanding 102nd Field Co R.E.	HGE
" "	3 6/16		Work proceeding as above, though the construction of deep dug-outs is being delayed owing to lack of mining frames. These are being turned out as quickly as possible by 25th A.T. Coy R.E. but the demand exceeds supply at present	H.G.E.
" "	4 6/16		Work proceeding as usual.	HGE

A.G. Bremner
Lt Col R.E.
C.R.E. 23rd Divn

2353 Wt. W2544/1454 700,000 5/15 D. D. & L. A.D.S.S./Forms/C. 2118.

Instructions regarding War Diaries and Intelligence Summaries are contained in F. S. Regs., Part II. and the Staff Manual respectively. Title pages will be prepared in manuscript.

Army Form C. 2118.

WAR DIARY
or
INTELLIGENCE SUMMARY.
(Erase heading not required.)

JUNE (2) H.Q. R.E 23rd Division

COMMANDING ROYAL ENGINEER 3 - JUL. 1916 23RD DIVISION

Place	Date	Hour	Summary of Events and Information	Remarks and references to Appendices
SAINS-en GOHELLE.	5 6/16		Work being continued as usual. Have now taken over a french civilian workshop complete with circular saw & band saw etc. This will enable much work to be done here which would otherwise have had to have been done by 25th A.T. Coy R.E. Find a Divisional workshop a necessity if the demands of field coys & infantry in line are to be satisfied.	HYE
" "	6 6/16		Work as usual. ~~Following~~ recd from 23 Division H.Q. The following appointment has been approved "Major C.B. BONHAM R.E (now commanding 102nd Field Co R.E), to command Royal Engineers 14th Division, and to be temp Lieut-Col, vice Major (temp Lieut. Colonel) F.M. CLOSE R.E. invalided". Major Bonham is now on leave in England	HYE
" "	7 6/16		Work as usual. Turning out a number of mining frames at Divl workshop	HYE
	8 6/16		Work as usual. Cold wet day.	HYE
	9 6/16		Work as usual.	HYE

A.G. Bremner
Lt Col R.E.
C.R.E. 23/Divn

2353 Wt. W2544/1454 700,000 5/15 D. D. & L. A.D.S.S./Forms/C. 2118.

Instructions regarding War Diaries and Intelligence Summaries are contained in F. S. Regs., Part II. and the Staff Manual respectively. Title pages will be prepared in manuscript.

WAR DIARY
or
INTELLIGENCE SUMMARY.
(Erase heading not required.)

Army Form C. 2118.

COMMANDING ROYAL ENGINEER 3 JUL. 1916 23RD DIVISION

JUNE (3) H.Q. R.E 23 Division

Place	Date	Hour	Summary of Events and Information	Remarks and references to Appendices
SAINS-en GOHELLE	10/6/16		Work as usual. Orders recd from Division for H.Q and all 3 field Coys to move to LA THIEULOYE on 12th inst. C.R.E 47th Div came in to discuss the handing over. Cold wet day again	H.Y.E
" "	11/6/16		One section of each Field Co R.E 47th Division relieved 1 section of each Field Co R.E 23rd Division. Relieved sections moved to billets at La THIEULOYE	H.Y.E
" "	12/6/16		Remaining sections of Field Coys R.E were relieved by remainder of corresponding Field Coys 47th Div. All 3 field coys are now in billets at La THIEULOYE	H.Y.E
LA THIEULOYE	13/6/16		H.Q. R.E moved to LA THIEULOYE	H.Y.E
	14/6/16		H.Q. R.E and all Field Coys resting at LA THIEULOYE.	H.Y.E
VERCHIN	15/6/16		H.Q. R.E and 3 Field Coys moved to billets at VERCHIN arriving about 4 P.M. Capt J.P.H OUCHTERLONEY R.E. reported his arrival having been appointed to command 102nd Field Co R.E. Major BONHAM returned from leave in England and immediately went off to 14th Division.	H.Y.E

A.G. Bremner Lieut Col R.E. C.R.E. 23/Divn

2353 Wt. W2544/1454 700,000 5/15 D. D. & L. A.D.S.S./Forms/C. 2118.

Instructions regarding War Diaries and Intelligence Summaries are contained in F. S. Regs., Part II. and the Staff Manual respectively. Title pages will be prepared in manuscript.

Army Form C. 2118.

WAR DIARY
or
INTELLIGENCE SUMMARY.
(Erase heading not required.)

JUNE (4) H.Q. R.E. 23 Division

COMMANDING ROYAL ENGINEERS 3 - JUL. 1916 23RD DIVISION

Place	Date	Hour	Summary of Events and Information	Remarks and references to Appendices
MATRINGHEM	16 6/16		H.Q. R.E and 3 Field Coys moved from VERCHIN to 1st Army Manoeuvre area All are now billeted at MATRINGHEM.	H.G.E.
" "	17 6/16		Field Coys. practising bridging with Weldon Trestles, overhauling kit etc.	H.G.E.
" "	18 6/16		Coys practising with Weldon Trestles also Extended Order Manoeuvres and Company Drill	H.G.E.
" "	19 6/16		Divnl Manoeuvres near Bomy 102nd & 128th Field Coys participated. One section of each Coy was attached to a Brigade for consolidation work. One ditto was told off for the construction of commn trenches. Remaining 2 sections of each Coy were held in reserve in the direct orders of C.R.E.	H.G.E.
" "	20 6/16		Field Coys practising company & extended order drill also overhauling equipment etc	H.G.E.
" "	21 6/16		Ditto Ditto	H.G.E.
" "	22 6/16		" "	H.G.E.

A.G. Bremner Lt Col R.E.
C.R.E. 23/Divn

Instructions regarding War Diaries and Intelligence Summaries are contained in F. S. Regs., Part II. and the Staff Manual respectively. Title pages will be prepared in manuscript.

Army Form C. 2118.

WAR DIARY
or
INTELLIGENCE SUMMARY.
(Erase heading not required.)

JUNE (5) H.Q. R.E 23rd Division

COMMANDING ROYAL ENGINEERS 3 JUL 1918 23RD DIVISION

Place	Date	Hour	Summary of Events and Information	Remarks and references to Appendices
MATRINGHEM	23/6/16		C.R.E inspected Field Companies in the morning. Remainder of the day the companies rested	H.G.E
" "	24/6/16		H.Q. R.E & Field Coys marched independently from MATRINGHEM to entraining stations ie 101st Field Co to LILLERS, H.Q. & 102nd Field Co to BERGUETTE 128th Field Co to AIRE. The pontoons & trestle wagons of each company entrained separately several hours later	H.G.E
VAUX-en AMIENOIS	25/6/16		H.Q. R.E & 3 Field Coys detrained at LONGEAU at hour intervals commencing at 7.30 AM. H.Q.R.E moved to VAUX-en-AMIENOIS via AMIENS. Field Coys to YZEUX via AMIENS	H.G.E
" "	26/6/16		Field Coys resting at YZEUX. The office baggage & kit of H.Q. has now been cut down to a minimum so as to enable everything to be carried on the baggage limber allowed. This is insufficient. A G.S. wagon in lieu would be more useful.	H.G.E
" "	27/6/16		Orders recd to move on 28th inst to ALLONVILLE	H.G.E

A.G. Bremner Lt Col R.E. C.R.E. 23/Divn

8353 Wt. W2544/1454 700,000 5/15 D. D. & L. A.D.S.S./Forms/C. 2118.

Army Form C. 2118.

Instructions regarding War Diaries and Intelligence Summaries are contained in F. S. Regs., Part II. and the Staff Manual respectively. Title pages will be prepared in manuscript.

WAR DIARY
or
INTELLIGENCE SUMMARY.
(*Erase heading not required.*)

JUNE (6) H.Q. R.E. 23rd Division

COMMANDING ROYAL ENGINEERS JUL 1916 23RD DIVISION

Place	Date	Hour	Summary of Events and Information	Remarks and references to Appendices
VAUX-en-AMIENOIS	28 6/16		Orders rec^d cancelling temporarily the move of Field Coys to ALLONVILLE. They are all still at YSEUX.	HQE
" "	29 6/16		Field Coys carrying on with any training possible. All 3 coys were inspected by C.E. II Corps.	HQE
" "	30 6/16		The 3 Field Coys moved from YSEUX to ALLONVILLE.	HQE

A.G. Bremner
Lieut.Col. R.E.
C.R.E. 23/Div^n

23 July

CRE 23 Div

Vol 11.

Confidential.

War Diary of Headqrs. R.E.

From 1st. July 16

To. 31st. July 16.

Army Form C. 2118.

WAR DIARY
or
INTELLIGENCE SUMMARY.
(Erase heading not required.)

Instructions regarding War Diaries and Intelligence Summaries are contained in F. S. Regs., Part II. and the Staff Manual respectively. Title pages will be prepared in manuscript.

JULY (1) H.Q. R.E 23rd Division

Place	Date	Hour	Summary of Events and Information	Remarks and references to Appendices
VAUX-en AMIENOIS	1 7/16		Orders recd in the morning for all units to stand by to move at short notice. H.Q.R.E started at 8.30 P.M + marched to BAISIEUX. All Field Coys moved from ALLONVILLE to LAHOUSSOYE by night. British attack commenced in early morning	H.G.E
BAISIEUX	2 7/16		Field Coys rested all day at LAHOUSSOYE. The 102nd Field Coy moved at night to HELLENCOURT. The 101st + 128th Field Coys moved at night to MILLENCOURT.	H.G.E
BAISIEUX	3 7/16		101st + 128th Field Coys moved to billets at ALBERT	H.G.E
BAISIEUX	4 7/16		Orders recd to take over from C.R.E 34th Div. H.Q.R.E moved to DERNANCOURT + 102nd followed to same place. Rained very heavily all afternoon. C.R.E to front line trenches on reconnaissance. We are now in III Corps.	H.G.E
DERNANCOURT	5 7/16		128th + 101st Field Coys R.E. consolidating strong points and wiring same. 102nd Field Coy R.E temporarily in reserve on tramway maintenance and digging of commn. trenches across original No-Man's land. MAJOR I.J. CONNOR R.E O.C 101st Field Co R.E and Major J.R.F. ARMSTRONG R.E. O.C 128th Field Co R.E were both killed in action. Lt. A.B. BEVAN R.E 128th Field Co RE wounded	H.G.E

A.G. Bremner Lt-Colonel
Commanding Royal Engineers 23rd Division

#353 Wt. W2544/1454 700,000 5/15 D. D. & L. A.D.S.S./Forms/C. 2118.

Instructions regarding War Diaries and Intelligence Summaries are contained in F. S. Regs., Part II. and the Staff Manual respectively. Title pages will be prepared in manuscript.

WAR DIARY
or
INTELLIGENCE SUMMARY.
(Erase heading not required.)

Army Form C. 2118.

JULY (2) — H.Q. 23rd Division R.E

Place	Date	Hour	Summary of Events and Information	Remarks and references to Appendices
DERNANCOURT	6.7.16		Orders rec^d that G.O.C. 23rd Division would attack CONTALMAISON on morning of 7th inst. It was therefore decided that 2 coys ie 101st & 128th Field Coys would rendez-vous as close up as possible consistent with safety and would be used for the purpose of consolidating the defences of CONTALMAISON as soon as this was firmly held by the infantry. Owing to the deaths, reported yesterday, of the O.C.'s these two coys. Capt J.P.H. OUCHTERLONY O.C. 102nd Field C R E was placed in command under the orders of C.R.E. (see CRE order No 7) The whole of latter Coy is working on comm^n trenches tonight and will be held in reserve tomorrow under the direct orders of C.R.E. Dumps of R.E material have been established well forward, these are being maintained + additional materials + tools sent up as reqd by means of Field Coy transport + other wagons from Div^l Train. Heavy rain at intervals.	APPENDIX 1 HGE
DERNANCOURT	7.7.16		Field Coys standing by as CONTALMAISON is not yet captured. 102nd Field Co R.E repairing roads close to our original front line. CAPT. P. de FONBLANQUE reported + assumed command of 128th Field Co R.E.	HGE
"	8.7.16		101st & 128th Field Coys moved up on it being reported that CONTALMAISON was in our hands. Later they came back as the report was inaccurate 102nd making good roads	HGE

A.G. Bremner Lt-Colonel, 23rd Division

2353 Wt. W2544/1454 700,000 5/15 D. D. & L. A.D.S.S./Forms/C. 2118.

Instructions regarding War Diaries and Intelligence Summaries are contained in F. S. Regs., Part II. and the Staff Manual respectively. Title pages will be prepared in manuscript.

Army Form C. 2118.

WAR DIARY
or
INTELLIGENCE SUMMARY.
(Erase heading not required.)

JULY (3) H.Q. R.E 23rd Division

Place	Date	Hour	Summary of Events and Information	Remarks and references to Appendices
DERNANCOURT	9.7.16		101st and 128th Field Coys R.E were ordered back to billets for a nights' rest in view of proposed operations tomorrow. They will move up again tomorrow in accordance with C.R.E's Order No S.8. (see APPENDIX 2) CONTALMAISON is again the objective. copy of 69th Brigade Order No 55 is attached. (see APPENDIX 3) 1 section of 102nd Field Co R.E was attached for special work to 10th WEST RIDING REGT under Corps orders. This section eventually returned not having been reqd. Remainder of this company is making roads in trench area and looking after tramway maintenance. H.G.E.	
"	10.7.16		101st and 128th Field Coys R.E. assembled at Rendez-vous at appointed time. CONTALMAISON having been taken, these Coys were ordered up but they were blocked by Infantry in the QUADRANGLE trench immediately under enemy's barrage and eventually had to withdraw over the open and make way for safety. It was now well on towards daylight 10th/11th. Following were the casualties incurred Killed:- 1 O.R. Wounded:- 1 off. (Lt ANDREWS 128th Field Co RE) and 16 O.R. 102nd Field Co R.E employed 1 section on roads, remainder stood by ready to move up quickly if required. H.G.E.	

A. Brown[?] Lt-Colonel, Commanding Royal Engineers, 23rd Division.

2353 Wt. W2544/1454 700,000 5/15 D. D. & L. A.D.S.S./Forms/C. 2118.

Instructions regarding War Diaries and Intelligence Summaries are contained in F. S. Regs., Part II. and the Staff Manual respectively. Title pages will be prepared in manuscript.

Army Form C. 2118.

WAR DIARY
or
INTELLIGENCE SUMMARY.

(Erase heading not required.)

JULY (9) H.Q. R.E 23rd Division

Place	Date	Hour	Summary of Events and Information	Remarks and references to Appendices
DERNANCOURT	11 7/16		101st, 128th + 2 sections of 102nd Field Co R.E. moved up to CONTALMAISON for consolidation work, arriving there about midday. Strong points were made where required, houses put in a state of defences covering approaches to the village and a number of open machine gun emplacements were constructed. All ranks worked with great vigour + the work was completed by 6 P.M at which hour the Coys returned. No casualties	
" "	12 7/16		1st Div relieved 23rd Division in the line. Field Coys of 1st Division relieved Field Coys of 23rd Division, companies moving to billets vacated by relieving company.	
			H.Q. R.E moved from DERNANCOURT to ST GRATIEN	
			101st Field Co R.E moved from ALBERT to FRANVILLERS	
			102nd " " " " DERNANCOURT to FRECHENCOURT	
			128th " " " ALBERT to BAISIEUX	
ST GRATIEN	13 7/16		101st Field Co R.E moved from FRANVILLERS to MOLLIENS-au-BOIS. Remainder of Divl R.E resting + overhauling equipment + wagons etc. Capt P.A. TURNER R.E arrived + assumed command of 101st Field Co R.E.	

A.W. Brennan[?]
Lt. Colonel,
Commanding Royal Engineers
23rd Division

2353 Wt. W2544/1454 700,000 5/15 D. D. & L. A.D.S.S./Forms/C. 2118.

WAR DIARY
or
INTELLIGENCE SUMMARY.

Army Form C. 2118.

Instructions regarding War Diaries and Intelligence Summaries are contained in F. S. Regs., Part II. and the Staff Manual respectively. Title pages will be prepared in manuscript.

JULY (5) (*Erase heading not required.*) H.Q. R.E 23rd Division

Place	Date	Hour	Summary of Events and Information	Remarks and references to Appendices
St GRATIEN	14 7/16		101st & 102nd Field Coys R.E working under C.E III Corps making hurdles, fascines etc 128th Field Co R.E. overhauling equipment etc	H.G.E
" "	15 7/16		As above B-General GODBY CE II Corps came over in the morning	H.G.E
" "	16 7/16		As above 128th Field Co R.E company drill etc.	H.G.E
" "	17 7/16		Pontoons of 128th Field Co R.E sent to 281st A.T. Coy in accordance with orders recd from C.E III Corps. 1 Section 128th Fd Coy mending road at St GRATIEN	H.G.E
" "	18 7/16		As above 101st & 102nd Field Coys making fascines etc, 1 section 128th Fd Coy repairing roads	H.G.E
" "	19 7/16		As above 128th Field Co R.E ordered to commence constructing trestles for rest station BAIZIEUX	H.G.E
" "	20 7/16		As above, orders recd to prepare to move tomorrow to HENENCOURT - BAIZIEUX area	H.G.E

A.G. Bremner Lt-Colonel,
Commanding Royal Engineers.
23rd Division

2353 Wt. W2544/1454 700,000 5/15 D. D. & L. A.D.S.S./Forms/C. 2118.

Army Form C. 2118.

Instructions regarding War Diaries and Intelligence Summaries are contained in F. S. Regs., Part II. and the Staff Manual respectively. Title pages will be prepared in manuscript.

WAR DIARY
or
INTELLIGENCE SUMMARY.
(*Erase heading not required.*)

JULY (6) H.Q. R.E 23rd Division.

Place	Date	Hour	Summary of Events and Information	Remarks and references to Appendices
HENENCOURT	21 7/16		101st Fd Co R.E moved from MOLLIENS-au-BOIS to MILLENCOURT. 102nd " " " " FRECHENCOURT to MILLENCOURT H.Q. R.E " " " ST GRATIEN to HENENCOURT.	H.G.E
" "	22 7/16		101st + 102nd Fd Coys R.E overhauling equipment etc, 128th working for 69th Field Amb. BAIZIEUX	H.G.E
" "	23 7/16		Do Do " " "	H.G.E
" "	24 7/16		In accordance with orders received from C.E III Corps 128th prepared project for repairs to BAIZIEUX – HENENCOURT road, 102nd prepared project for improvement of drainage at HENENCOURT wood camp.	H.G.E
" "	25 7/16		Orders received for RE 23rd Division to relieve R.E 1st Division.	H.G.E
ALBERT	26 7/16		H.Q. R.E moved from HENENCOURT to ALBERT 101st Fd Co R.E " MILLENCOURT to Bivouac BECOURT WOOD 102nd Fd Co R.E " " " " " 128th Fd Co R.E " BAZIEUX to " "	H.G.E

A.G. Bremner Lt-Colonel,
Commanding Royal Engineers.
23rd Division.

2353 Wt. W2544/1454 700,000 5/15 D. D. & L. A.D.S.S./Forms/C. 2118.

Instructions regarding War Diaries and Intelligence Summaries are contained in F. S. Regs., Part II. and the Staff Manual respectively. Title pages will be prepared in manuscript.

WAR DIARY
or
INTELLIGENCE SUMMARY.
(Erase heading not required.)

Army Form C. 2118.

JULY (7) H.Q. R.E 23rd Division.

Place	Date	Hour	Summary of Events and Information	Remarks and references to Appendices
ALBERT	27 7/16		101st Field Co R.E. is constructing new Brigade H.Q. for 70th Inf. Brigade and digging new front line at S.1.d 102nd Field Co R.E roads and strong points near front line 128th " " constructing roads up to CONTALMAISON	
" "	28 7/16		101st Field Co R.E constructing redoubt, making M.G. Emplacements & wiring same about S.2.c.4.7 102nd " " " strong points & wiring same, road FRICOURT FARM to CRUCIFIX 128th " " " roads as above & new Div H.Q W. of ALBERT.	H.G.E.
"	29 7/16		101st Field Co on H.Q. dug-outs for Brigade and wiring of front line about S.1.d 102nd " improving road from SHELTER WOOD towards CONTALMAISON. Improving trenches at Keep at CUTTING. Wiring round keep at CONTALMAISON VILLA. 128th Field Co roads as above & new Divl H.Q. W. of ALBERT.	H.G.E.
" "	30 7/16		Work of Field Coys as above	H.G.E.
ALBERT W.27.c	31 7/16		Work as above. ALBERT heavily shelled. H.Q. R.E moved from billets at ALBERT to new H.Q. bivouac at W.27.c.	H.G.E.

A.G. Bremner Lt-Colonel,
Commanding Royal Engineers.
23rd Division.

8353 Wt. W2544/1454 700,000 5/15 D. D. & L. A.D.S.S./Forms/C. 2118.

Appendix 1

23rd Division - C.R.E. Order No.S.7.

(1) The G.O.C. intends to attack CONTALMAISON and consolidate the line X.16.a.1.3. - X.16.b.2.3. Sheet 57D S.E.4. 1/10,000.

(2) The 101st and 128th Field Coys. R.E. each less 1 Officer and Coy. H.Q. will assemble in the cover of trenches about F.2.c.0.0. Sheet 62D S.E. 2 1/10,000 at 4.30 a.m. on 7.7.16.
Tool and water carts to be parked in this vicinity before above hour and teams sent back to Coy. Headquarters.

3. The Coys. will, primarily, be required for consolidation of the village of CONTALMAISON. The Infantry will consolidate line on Northern edge.

(4) The Coys. will be under the command of Captain Ouchterlony 102nd Field Coy. R.E. who will receive orders from C.R.E. at Divisional Headquarters.

(5) Orders will be sent through Signals at 24th Brigade H.Q. F.2.b.7.9. Sheet 62D N.E. 1/10,000 and for the delivery of messages 4 men from each Coy. (total 8) will be detailed to remain at 24th Brigade H.Q. <u>for this purpose only</u>.

(6) Two days' rations in addition to the iron ration to be carried by each man. Overcoats are not to be carried.

(7) Stores to be drawn from the Dump at BECOURT CHATEAU X.25.d.6.8 Sheet 57D S.E. 4 1/10,000.
The 34th Division will supply carrying parties.
The O.C. 102nd Field Coy. will detail an officer to take charge of this Dump who will reach the Dump not later than 4.30.a.m. on 7.7.16.
This officer will take earliest opportunity of ascertaining position of carrying parties 34th Division who have been ordered to rendezvous in BECOURT Wood.
He will obtain men from these carrying parties to remain with him to act as messengers between the Dump and carrying parties.

(8) Reports to C.R.E. at Divisional H.Q.

Sd. A.G.Bremner Lieut: Colonel R.E.

6.7.16. C.R.E. 23rd Division.

Issued at 4.00 p.m. by messenger.

Copy No.1 to O.C. 102nd Field Coy. R.E.
" 2 " 101st " "
" 3 " 128th " "
" 4 " 23rd Division.

appendix 2

23rd Division - C.R.E. Order No. S.8.

9.7.16.

(1) The 69th Infantry Brigade is to attack CONTALMAISON from the West tomorrow evening.

(2) One section of 128th Field Coy. R.E. will report to 9th YORKS Regt. at 3.30.p.m. on 10.7.16. at X.15.c.9.9. to assist in consolidation of a post at X.16.b.4.3. Route via. SAUSAGE Valley to X.20.b.4.3. and then up communication trench to above assembly point.

(3) The 101st Field Coy. less H.Q. and 128th Field Coy. less one section and H.Q. will assemble in trench at X.21.c.5.8 at 4.p.m. on 10.7.16. The 128th Field Coy. will leave one officer in billets to command the H.Q. of both Coys.

(4) On G.O.C. 69th Brigade informing Division when the Coys. are to move up, orders will be sent to them via 69th Bde. Advanced H.Qrs. at Scots Redoubt X.21.c.9.9.
The 128th Field Coy. will consolidate the Manor House buildings at X.17.c.2.8. and 101st Field Coy. will consolidate the vicinity of Cross Roads at X.16.d.8.4.
The Coys less one Section 128th Field Coy. will report to G.O.C. 69th Infantry Bde. at Scots Redoubt for orders as to route to be followed into CONTALMAISON.

(5) The R.E. working parties in (2) and (3) will be withdrawn before dawn.

(6) Instructions re material will be issued later.

(7) One day's rations in addition to the Iron Ration will be carried.
Overcoats will not be carried.

(8) Reports to C.R.E. at Divisional H.Q. via H.Q. 69th Infantry Brigade.

Sd. A.G.Bremner Lieut: Col. R.E.

C.R.E. 23rd Division.

Issued at 7.a.m. 10.7.16.
No.1 Copy to 101st Field Coy. R.E.
" 2 " 128th " "
" 3 " H.Q. 69th Brigade.
" 4 " H.Q. 23rd Division.

appendix 3 C. R. E.

SECRET.

69th Infantry Brigade
Order No.55.

Copy No. 9

9/7/16.

Ref.Map
57d.S.E.4
1/10,000.

1. The 69th Brigade will attack CONTALMAISON at 4.30p.m. on 10th inst.

2. The Artillery programme has been separately issued under No.B.M.S.236 dated 9/7/16.

3. Units will be formed up in trenches as follows:-

2 Coys.11th W.Yorkshire R.from about X.15.b.7.2. to X.15.d.9.7.

9th Yorkshire R. from about X.15.a.8.0. (exclusive) to about X.15.d.3.2.

8th Yorkshire R. from about X.15.d.3.2. to X.21.b.5.6.

2 Coys.11th W.Yorkshire R. in reserve between SCOTS REDOUBT and Point X.21.d.5.6.

The above will be in position at 3.30p.m.

4. The advance will be made in quick time in not less than four waves for each Company and will be followed by searching and consolidating parties in similar formation.

5. One days' rations and emergency ration will be carried on every man.
Assaulting troops and reserves will carry at least 4 bombs and 2 sandbags each.
Searching parties will carry at least 6 bombs and 4 sandbags each.
Consolidating parties will carry tools,4 sandbags each,wire and pickets.

6. The assault on BAILIFF Wood will be made by two Companies,11th West Yorkshire R.at 4.30p.m.
The barrage on BAILIFF Wood will lift at that hour.
The assault on trench X.16.b.8.5.to X.16.d.4.1.will be made by 9th Yorkshire R.on the left and 8th Yorkshire R.on the right at 4.50p.m.
The right of the 9th Yorkshire R. will direct:-
Point of direction CONTALMAISON Church.
True bearing from X.15.d.3.2.is 76 degrees.
The barrage on the front trench will lift at 5p.m.to a line from X.16.b.4.5.to X.16.d.6.3.,approximately following the line of the road running North through CONTALMAISON.
At 5.30p.m.the barrage will lift 200 yards to the line CHATEAU - OLD MANOR.
At 6.30p.m. till 7p.m. there will be a further lift of 200 yards.

7. All houses and cellars are to be searched by special parties.

8. The defensive front to be consolidated will face North, N.E. and East.

Strong points will be prepared under arrangements made by R.E. and by Battalion Commanders.

9. Signalling lamps will be taken and every effort made to maintain touch with Brigade H.Q. by this means.

10. A smoke barrage will be formed on the North West and South East of CONTALMAISON if wind is blowing from South West from 4.30p.m. to 6p.m.

11. 69th Machine Gun Company will place two guns in position to flank the left of the advance and two about X.15.d.7,0.

Four guns will be about X.22.d.0.2. 8 guns in reserve near WILLOW PATCH.

Three Machine guns of 6th Motor Machine Gun ~~Company~~ Battery are held in reserve at BECOURT Chateau.

12. O.C.69th Trench Mortar Battery will place four Stokes Mortars on left flank to co-operate with advance of 11th West Yorkshire R.

13. If any prisoners are taken they must be sent back with a very small escort and handed over for evacuation to the Brigade holding the lines.

14. Brigade Headquarters will be at BECOURT Chateau with advanced Brigade Headquarters at SCOTS REDOUBT.

Acknowledge.

C. P. Moore

Capt.,
Brigade Major, 69th Inf.Bde.

Issued at p.m.

Copy No.1. 11th W.Yorkshire R.
2. 8th Yorkshire R.
3. 9th Yorkshire R.
4. 10th W.Riding R.
5. 69th M.Gun Coy.
6. 69 T.M.Battery.
7. 23rd Division.
8. R.A.23rd Division.
9. C.R.E. do.
10. A.D.M.S. do.
11. 6th M.M.Gun Bty.
12. M.Sect.Special Bn.R.E.
13. 24th Inf.Bde.
14. 68th Inf.Bde.
15. 51st Inf.Bde.
16. Inf.Bde.
17. War Diary.
18. War Diary.
19. File.

23rd Divisional Engineers

C. R. E.

23rd DIVISION

AUGUST 1 9 1 6

CRE
Vol 12

War Diary
of
H. Q. R. E. 23rd Division

from

1st August to 31st August 1916.

Army Form C. 2118.

WAR DIARY
or
INTELLIGENCE SUMMARY.
(*Erase heading not required.*)

Instructions regarding War Diaries and Intelligence Summaries are contained in F. S. Regs., Part II. and the Staff Manual respectively. Title pages will be prepared in manuscript.

AUG. (1) H.Q. R.E 23rd Division.

Place	Date	Hour	Summary of Events and Information	Remarks and references to Appendices
ALBERT	1.8/16		101st Field Co R.E Bde. H.Q. dug-outs VILLA WOOD and improving front line system and excavating dug-outs 102nd Field Co R.E. constructing CONTALMAISON VILLA KEEP, – CUTTING KEEP, – road repairs FRICOURT FARM – CONTALMAISON, – repairs to motor pumps at well near PEAKE WOOD 128th Field Co R.E. is company in reserve doing road repairs, construction of Divn H.Q. Camp H.G.E.	
"	2 8/16		Work as above. Large demands for shrapnel proof dug-outs and mining cases from Brigades in front line. 1 complete section of 128th Field Co R.E has therefore been withdrawn and moved to DERNANCOURT where there are workshops circular saws etc. They are working two 8 hour shifts and turning out about 30 dug-out frames complete per day. H.G.E.	
"	3 8/16		as above. Workshops going full pressure. The two motor lorries attached to H.Q. R.E from Divn Sub-Park are proving invaluable and doing most excellent work. Large quantities of stores have been moved up to the Divn Dump at FRICOURT for use in forward area. H.G.E.	

Lt-Colonel,
Commanding Royal Engineers
23rd Division.

A.G. Bremner Lt Col R.E. C.B.E.

8353 Wt. W2544/1454 700,000 5/15 D. D. & L. A.D.S.S./Forms/C. 2118.

Instructions regarding War Diaries and Intelligence Summaries are contained in F. S. Regs., Part II. and the Staff Manual respectively. Title pages will be prepared in manuscript.

WAR DIARY
or
INTELLIGENCE SUMMARY.
(Erase heading not required.)

Army Form C. 2118.

AUG (2) H.Q. R.E 23rd Division

Place	Date	Hour	Summary of Events and Information	Remarks and references to Appendices
ALBERT	4.8.16		101st Field Co R.E making deep dug-outs in front trenches also Bde H.Q. dugouts	
			102nd " " wiring strong point at CUTTING, improvements & excavation of	
			BLACK WATCH ALLEY, strong point at CONTALMAISON VILLA. H.G.E	
" "			128th Field Co R.E making roads FRICOURT to CONTALMAISON and mining outskirts	
"	5.8.16		Work contd as above. Orders recd for relief of this Div by 15th Div on 8th	
			Albert heavily shelled at night H.G.E	
"	6.8.16		Work contd as above. H.G.E	
"	7.8.16		Field Coys are being relieved by Field Coys of 15th Division.	
			101st Field Co moved to FRANVILLERS H.G.E	
"	8.8.16		H.Q. R.E moved to BAIZIEUX	
			102nd Field Co R.E. moved to BEHENCOURT	
			128th Field Co R.E. moved to BRESLE H.G.E	

A.G. Bremner Lt Colonel, Commanding Royal Engineers. 23rd Division.

2353 Wt. W2544/1454 700,000 5/15 D. D. & L. A.D.S.S./Forms/C. 2118.

Army Form C. 2118.

WAR DIARY
or
INTELLIGENCE SUMMARY.
(*Erase heading not required.*)

Instructions regarding War Diaries and Intelligence Summaries are contained in F. S. Regs., Part II. and the Staff Manual respectively. Title pages will be prepared in manuscript.

AUG (3)

H.Q. R.E. 23rd Division

Place	Date	Hour	Summary of Events and Information	Remarks and references to Appendices
BAIZIEUX	9 8/16		Field Coys resting and overhauling equipment. H.G.E	
" "	10 8/16		As above H.G.E	
AILLY-le-HAUT CLOCHER	11 8/16		H.Q. R.E moved from BAIZIEUX + entrained at FRECHINCOURT for LONGPRÉ arriving 8 PM then marched to AILLY-le-HAUT-CLOCHER. Field Coys also entrained at FRECHINCOURT for LONGPRÉ + billeted in AILLY vicinity H.G.E	
" "	12 8/16		Field Coys resting H.G.E	
FLETRE	13 8/16		H.Q. R.E and 3 Field Coys entrained at LONGPRÉ for BAILLEUL and marched to billets in vicinity of FLETRE H.G.E	
" "	14 8/16		Preparations being made for taking over portion of line from 41st Division H.G.E	

A. G. Brewin [signature]
Lt-Colonel,
Commanding Royal Engineers,
23rd Division.

#353 Wt. W2544/1454 700,000 5/15 D. D. & L. A.D.S.S./Forms/C. 2118.

Instructions regarding War Diaries and Intelligence Summaries are contained in F. S. Regs., Part II. and the Staff Manual respectively. Title pages will be prepared in manuscript.

WAR DIARY
or
INTELLIGENCE SUMMARY.
(Erase heading not required.)

Army Form C. 2118.

AUG 4. H.Q. R.E. 23rd Division

Place	Date	Hour	Summary of Events and Information	Remarks and references to Appendices
FLETRE	15/8/16		101st Field Co R.E moved to LORIDAN FARM (T 29.d 9.5) and took over billets and work from 228th Field Co R.E.	
			102nd Field Co R.E moved to DOUDOU FARM (B.5.c.7.7) and took over billets and work from 237th Field Co R.E	
			128th Field Co R.E moved to PONT de NIEPPE (B.23.a.4.9) and took over billets and work from 233 Field Co R.E. H.G.E	
STEEVWERCK	16/8/16		C.R.E 23rd Division relieved C.R.E 41st Division. We are now in the IX Corps. The line is in exceptionally good condition on the left and fair in central & ~~right~~ poor in right sections. All Field Coys are working in front area, 101 on left, 102 in centre and 128 on right. There seems to be a good supply of stores & materials available. H.G.E	A.G. Brown Lt Colonel Commanding Royal Engineers 23rd Division
" "	17/8/16		Coys are all employed on construction work, a number of concrete T.M. emplacements are being made besides the ordinary trench work. A new front line is ~~to~~ under construction in parts.	H.G.E

Wt. W2544/1454 700,000 5/15 D. D. & L. A.D.S.S./Forms/C. 2118.

Army Form C. 2118.

Instructions regarding War Diaries and Intelligence Summaries are contained in F. S. Regs., Part II. and the Staff Manual respectively. Title pages will be prepared in manuscript.

WAR DIARY
or
INTELLIGENCE SUMMARY.
(*Erase heading not required.*)

AUG (5) H.Q. R.E. 23rd Divn

Place	Date	Hour	Summary of Events and Information	Remarks and references to Appendices
STEENWERCK	18 8/16 to 25 8/16		Field Coys are all employed on various works in front trench area principally the following Remodelling firetrenches, building up parapets, connecting up saps heads some distance in front of present front line in order to form a new advanced front line fire trench & straighten out line a little, wiring in front of this new trench (both the construction & wiring of this has been carried out with a minimum of casualties) – Constructing deep dugouts also reinforced ditto for Battn H.Q. – Construction & improvement of C Trenches – Preparation of defended localities in gaps front line in right sector.	
			A large quantity of huts have been constructed at the Divl workshop TROIS ARBRES and a number of same erected in rear area. Horse standings & shelters have also been taken in hand and a large number are now under construction. It is hoped to have all these completed before the wet weather comes on	
			H.Q.E.	

A.G. Bremner Lt Colonel, Commanding Royal Engineers 23rd Division

2353 Wt. W2544/1454 700,000 5/15 D. D. & L. A.D.S.S./Forms/C. 2118.

Army Form C. 2118.

Instructions regarding War Diaries and Intelligence Summaries are contained in F. S. Regs., Part II. and the Staff Manual respectively. Title pages will be prepared in manuscript.

WAR DIARY

or

INTELLIGENCE SUMMARY.

(Erase heading not required.)

AUG (6) H.Q. R.E 23rd Division

Place	Date	Hour	Summary of Events and Information	Remarks and references to Appendices
STEENWERCK	26 8/16		Work proceeding steadily on same lines as last week. There is no scarcity of materials but it is so scattered that a large quantity of transport is essential. Motor lorries are scarce for this work	H.G.E
"	27 8/16		Work as above. Orders recd from Div H.Q that H.Q would move to BAILLEUL on 29th inst. H.G.E	
"	28 8/16		Work as above H.G.E	
"	29 8/16		H.Q. R.E moved from STEENWERCK to billets at BAILLEUL, work proceeding as above H.G.E	
"	30 8/16		Work as above H.G.E	
"	31 8/16		Work as above H.G.E	

A.G. Bremner
Lt. Colonel,
Commanding Royal Engineers.
23rd Division.

2353 Wt. W2544/1454 700,000 5/15 D. D. & L. A.D.S.S./Forms/C. 2118.

C.R.E's Order No. S.10 COPY No. 7

The 23rd Division will be relieved by the 15th Division in Left Sector of 3rd Corps Front.

2. 101st Field Coy. R.E. will be relieved by 73rd Field Co. R.E. on 7th inst. and will then march to FRANVILLERS and take over billets vacated by relieving company.

102nd Field Coy. R.E. will be relieved by 91st Field Co. R.E. on 8th inst. and will then march to BEHENCOURT and take over billets vacated by relieving company.

128th Field Coy. R.E. will be relieved by 74th Field Coy. R.E. on morning of 8th instant and will then march to BRESLE and take over billets vacated by relieving company.

3. Coys will each send on in advance a small billeting party. to take over billets. The Town Majors concerned must be consulted and his concurrence obtained before billets are taken over. Times of marching out of coys. will be arranged by O's.C. Coys. Proposed times to be notified to this office.

4. All maps, plans and correspondense etc. relating to the present area will be handed over to relieving coys, also all tarpaulines and shelters etc. which were issued to or taken over by Coys. in present area.

5. H.Q.R.E. will open at BAIZIEUX at 6.p.m. on 8th inst.

6. Acknowledge.

H.G. Eddleston
Captain R.E.

6.8.16. Adjt. R.E. 23rd Division.

Copies to:-
1. 101st Fld. Coy.
2. 102nd " "
3. 128th " "
4. "G"
5. C.R.E. 15th Division.
6. File.
7)
8) War Diary.

Army Form C. 2118.

Vol 14

WAR DIARY
or
INTELLIGENCE SUMMARY.
(Erase heading not required.)

Instructions regarding War Diaries and Intelligence Summaries are contained in F. S. Regs., Part II. and the Staff Manual respectively. Title pages will be prepared in manuscript.

Oct (1) H.Q. R.E 23rd Divn

Place	Date	Hour	Summary of Events and Information	Remarks and references to Appendices
CAMP W.26.c.0.4	1.10.16 to 8.10.16		101st Fd Coy R.E working on roads CONTALMAISON - LA BOISSELLE and CONTALMAISON - MARTINPUICH. Work considerably hindered by wet weather. No infantry are now available for work on roads so the whole work is being carried on by Field Coys 102nd Fd Coy RE are working in forward area, laying out trenches in front of our lines, making strong points, wiring & supervising working parties. They have done most excellent work. Casualties not heavy in view of importance of work done 128th Fd Coy RE are laying light 60 c/m railway up to & West of MARTINPUICH. This work has progressed well until the supply of rails ran out on 6th inst Before the operations commenced which eventually led to the taking of LE SARS. Adv. Divnl H.Q were established near SHELTER WOOD. C.R.E moved up to Adv H.Q whilst Adjt remained to supervise supplies of stores etc.	

A.G. Bremner Lt Colonel, Commanding Royal Engineers, 23rd Division

Army Form C. 2118.

WAR DIARY
or
INTELLIGENCE SUMMARY.
(*Erase heading not required.*)

Instructions regarding War Diaries and Intelligence Summaries are contained in F. S. Regs., Part II. and the Staff Manual respectively. Title pages will be prepared in manuscript.

Oct (2) H.Q. R.E 23rd Divn

Place	Date	Hour	Summary of Events and Information	Remarks and references to Appendices
Camp W.26.C.0.4	9.10.16		Orders recd to hand over work etc to R.E. 15th Divn [initials]	
	10.10.16		C.R.E handed over to C.R.E 15th Divn	
			101st Fd Coy R.E handed over roads etc to 74th Fd Coy R.E	
			102nd " " " " work in forward area to 73rd Fd Coy R.E	
			128th " " " " light railway to 91st Fd Coy R.E	
			Transport of H.Q. and all Field Coys moved by road to ARGOEUVRES [initials]	
MONTIGNY	11.10.16		C.R.E moved to MONTIGNY	
			Dismounted personnel of 101st & 128th Fd Coys remained at present billets	
			" " 102nd entrained at ALBERT detrained at LONGPRÉ and marched to FAMECHON [initials]	
" "	12.10.16		Dismounted personnel of 101st & 128th Fd Coys entrained at ALBERT, detrained at LONGPRÉ & marched to COCQUEREL & COULONVILLERS respectively [initials]	

[signature] Lt Colonel, Commanding Royal Engineers. 23rd Division.

2353 Wt. W2544/1454 700,000 5/15 D. D. & L. A.D.S.S./Forms/C. 2118.

Army Form C. 2118.

WAR DIARY
or
INTELLIGENCE SUMMARY.

Instructions regarding War Diaries and Intelligence Summaries are contained in F. S. Regs., Part II. and the Staff Manual respectively. Title pages will be prepared in manuscript.

Oct (3) (*Erase heading not required.*) H.Q. R.E 23rd Div.

Place	Date	Hour	Summary of Events and Information	Remarks and references to Appendices
AILLY-LE-HAUT CLOCHER	13-10-16		H.Q. R.E moved to AILLY-LE-HAUT CLOCHER. Transport of Field Coys joined their coys at places named. WB	
ST RIQUIER	14 10/16		H.Q. R.E moved to ST RIQUIER. 101st Fd Coy R.E moved to MILLENCOURT 102nd " " " " ST RIQUIER WB	
" "	15-10/16		All Field Coys marched to CONTEVILLE & there entrained for the North. Station of detrainment HOUPOUTRE. WB	
" "	16 10/16		H.Q. R.E marched to CONTEVILLE & there entrained at 3 A.M for the North. Detrained at HOUPOUTRE and marched to temporary camp outside POPERINGHE. All Field Coys are in huts near BUSSEBOOM WB	

A.B. Brown[?] Colonel. Commanding Royal Engineers 23rd Division

8353 Wt. W2544/1454 700,000 5/15 D. D. & L. A.D.S.S./Forms/C. 2118.

Army Form C. 2118.

WAR DIARY
or
INTELLIGENCE SUMMARY.
(Erase heading not required.)

Instructions regarding War Diaries and Intelligence Summaries are contained in F. S. Regs., Part II. and the Staff Manual respectively. Title pages will be prepared in manuscript.

Oct (4) H.Q. R.E 23rd Divn

Place	Date	Hour	Summary of Events and Information	Remarks and references to Appendices
S.E. POPERINGHE CAMP	17 10/16		Recd orders to take over from C.R.E 2nd Australian Divn on 20th inst [initials]	
	18 10/16		101st Fd Coy R.E commenced taking over from 7th Aust. Fd Coy	
			102nd Fd ——— 5th ———	
			128th ——— 6th ——— [initials]	
	19 10/16		Reliefs of Fd Coys completed 101st Fd Coy & 128th Fd Coy are on front line work in left & right sectors respectively lying in YPRES 102nd Fd Coy R.E is in reserve doing work in rear of Divl area, hutting, light railway, workshops etc. [initials]	
	20 10/16		Took over from C.R.E 2nd Australian Divn and H.Q. R.E moved to RENINGHELST [initials]	

A. G. Bremner [signature] Colonel, Commanding Royal Engineers. 23rd Division

#353 Wt. W2544/1454 700,000 5/15 D. D. & L. A.D.S.S./Forms/C. 2118.

Army Form C. 2118.

WAR DIARY
or
INTELLIGENCE SUMMARY.
(Erase heading not required.)

Instructions regarding War Diaries and Intelligence Summaries are contained in F. S. Regs., Part II. and the Staff Manual respectively. Title pages will be prepared in manuscript.

Oct (5) H.Q. R.E 23rd Divn

Place	Date	Hour	Summary of Events and Information	Remarks and references to Appendices
RENINGHELST	21 10/16		Work proceeding on front line system reconstructing & improving front line trenches, revetting communications, making dugouts & shelters strong posts & new defence works. Present sector is in exceptionally bad condition & will require a great deal of work. The wet weather is delaying things.	
	to		The company in reserve (102nd) is working on hutting, horse standings Divl Baths, Workshops, light railway etc	
			Stores are coming in fairly well with the exception of cor iron & roofing material which is scarce	
	31 10/16.			

A. G. Bremner
Colonel,
Commanding Royal Engineers,
23rd Division

2353 Wt. W2544/1454 700,000 5/15 D. D. & L. A.D.S.S./Forms/C. 2118.

Vol 15

Secret

War Diary

of

H.Q. Royal Engineers

NOVEMBER.

Instructions regarding War Diaries and Intelligence Summaries are contained in F. S. Regs., Part II. and the Staff Manual respectively. Title pages will be prepared in manuscript.

Army Form C. 2118.

WAR DIARY or ~~INTELLIGENCE SUMMARY.~~ H.Q. R.E. 23rd Division

(Erase heading not required.)

November (1)

Place	Date	Hour	Summary of Events and Information	Remarks and references to Appendices
YPRES	1st to 15th November 1916		101st Field Co RE. repairing trenches, cleaning old trenches and revetting with U frames corrugated iron and XPM panels. Making bomb-stores and dug outs. Erecting small trench shelters. Thickening parapets and draining trenches. All this work in left Bde sector. 102nd Field Co RE at work in reserve Bde area. Erecting new Huts and stables. Repairing existing huts and stables by reroofing with tarred felt. Work is going on at about 30 different places. Labour is provided locally and this unit supervises the work. 128th Field Co RE. are working in right Bde sector of front line. Cleaning and revetting trenches with U frames, corrugated iron & panels. Reclaiming old trenches and draining same. Supervising improvement of Barracks in YPRES, and Bde HQ electric lighting.	[initials]
RENINGHELST	15 to 30th		Work proceeding as above	[initials]

[signature]
Captain, R.E.
Adjutant R.E.
23rd Division.

2353 Wt. W2544/1454 700,000 5/15 D. D. & L. A.D.S.S./Forms/C. 2118.

Vol 16

Confidential.

War Diary

of

H. Q. R. E

for month of DECEMBER.

Army Form C. 2118.

WAR DIARY
or
INTELLIGENCE SUMMARY.
(Erase heading not required.)

Instructions regarding War Diaries and Intelligence Summaries are contained in F. S. Regs., Part II. and the Staff Manual respectively. Title pages will be prepared in manuscript.

December

H.Q. R.E
23rd Divn

Place	Date	Hour	Summary of Events and Information	Remarks and references to Appendices
RENINGHELST				
1.12.16			Two Fd Coys in line (101st & 128th) and one Fd Coy (102nd) doing work in back area, hutting etc. Work of Fd Coys in line is being delayed owing to lack of materials. It is very difficult to obtain sufficient timber to make trench U frames and mining cases for deep dug-outs	WB
7.12.16			Work as usual. C.R.E went on leave to England. Major J.P.H. OUCHTERLONY RE O.C. 102nd Fd Coy RE took over in his absence.	WB
13.12.16			Scheme "X" recd	WB
21.12.16			C.R.E returned from England	WB
21.12.16 to 31.12.16			Work going on as usual, timber & other materials scarcer than ever, no stone for concrete at all & very little timber of any kind. Have commenced making trench frames out of angle iron. Work being delayed in the line.	WB

W. B[signature]
Captain, R.E.
Adjutant R.E.
23rd Division.

*353 Wt. W2544/1454 700,000 5/15 D. D. & L. A.D.S.S./Forms/C. 2118.

Vol 17

Confidential

War Diary

of

H.Q. R.E. 23rd Divn

from January 1st to January 31st 1917.

Army Form C. 2118.

Instructions regarding War Diaries and Intelligence Summaries are contained in F. S. Regs., Part II. and the Staff Manual respectively. Title pages will be prepared in manuscript.

WAR DIARY
or
INTELLIGENCE SUMMARY.
(Erase heading not required.)

JANUARY — H.Q. R.E. 23rd Div.

Place	Date	Hour	Summary of Events and Information	Remarks and references to Appendices
RENINGHELST	1.1.17 to 31.1.17		Disposition of Coys: Two in the line (101st & 128th) revetting & repairing trenches in front line area, constructing commn trenches building deep dug-outs, concrete M.G. emplacements etc. Defense work is considerably hampered by enemy artillery. trenches have been badly damaged necessitating considerable repair work. The third Coy (102nd) is employed in rear area principally hutting & making good cellars at KRUISSTRAAT. Severe frost has prevailed during the latter two weeks of this month. All work has been very much hindered in consequence. The ground is frozen 18" below the surface. Stores are still very scarce particularly timber of all kinds.	[signature] Captain, R.E. Adjutant R.E. 23rd Division

#353 Wt. W2544/1454 700,000 5/15 D. D. & L. A.D.S.S./Forms/C. 2118.

23

Vol 18 Army Form C. 2118.

(1)

Instructions regarding War Diaries and Intelligence Summaries are contained in F. S. Regs., Part II. and the Staff Manual respectively. Title pages will be prepared in manuscript.

WAR DIARY
or
INTELLIGENCE SUMMARY.
(Erase heading not required.)

February 1917. H.Q. R.E 23rd Divn

Place	Date	Hour	Summary of Events and Information	Remarks and references to Appendices
RENINGHELST	1.2.17 to 20.2.17		Two Field Coys working in front line area revetting & repairing trenches, making strong points, deep dug-outs, concrete M.G. emplacements etc. For detail see Diaries of Fd Coy concerned (101st & 128th)	
			102nd Fd Coy R.E are working in back area, hutting & constructing a new ammn refilling point H.14.b. Sheet 28 This latter was completed, except for the road passing through same, & handed over to R.A according to programme on 15th inst. No material is available for the roadway.	
			Lt Col A.G. Bremner C.M.G. R.E was appointed C.E XIX Corps on Feb 4th & left to take up his appointment on the 6th Feb. after handing over to Lt. Col. E.H. ROOKE R.E appointed C.R.E	WB
	20.2.17		Orders recd that this Divn would be relieved by 39th Divn. commencing 24th inst. Arrangements are now under way for this relief	WB

8353 Wt. W2544/1454 700,000 5/15 D. D. & L. A.D.S.S./Forms/C. 2118.

Instructions regarding War Diaries and Intelligence Summaries are contained in F. S. Regs., Part II. and the Staff Manual respectively. Title pages will be prepared in manuscript.

(2)

Army Form C. 2118.

WAR DIARY
or
INTELLIGENCE SUMMARY.
(Erase heading not required.)

H.Q. R.E.

Place	Date	Hour	Summary of Events and Information	Remarks and references to Appendices
RENINGHELST	27/2/17	11 a.m.	C.R.E. 23rd Division completed the handing over to C.R.E. 39th Division. AMC	
	–	4 p.m.	H.Q. R.E. Office opened at the Hotel de Ville ARQUES. AMC	
			Field Companies are located for training as follows:-	
			101st Field Coy R.E. VOLKERINCKHOVE	
			102 " " " TOURNEHEM	
			128 " " " WESTROVE AMS.	
			Stores for training very difficult to obtain, but C.R.E. obtained permission from C.E. Second Army to bring Stores for Field Coys' training from No. 3 RE Park Abeele. AMS.	Details of move Appendix A'
			Weather during last week good, and Field Coys moved into their new billets well up to time.	
			A. H. T. Saunders	

2353 Wt. W2544/1454 700,000 5/15 D. D. & L. A.D.S.S./Forms/C. 2118.

APPENDIX 'A'

23rd DIVISIONAL ENGINEERS

C.R.E.'s ORDERS No.1. COPY No.10

1. The 23rd Divisional R.E. will be relieved by the [illegible]th Divil. R.E. commencing on 24th inst.

2. The 101st Field Coy. R.E. will be relieved by the 287th Fld. Coy. R.E. at 9.0.p.m. on 26th inst.

An advance party of the latter company will arrive on the afternoon of the 25th inst. to take over work in hand and ensure continuity of same. Strength of this party to be arranged direct by O.C. Coys. concerned.

On completion of relief 101st Field Coy. R.E. will proceed by march route to billets at Divisional School C.10.c. reporting arrival and map reference to G.O.C. [illegible]. 68th Inf. Bde. and C.R.E. As much transport as possible and a small advance party will proceed to Divisional School on the afternoon of 26th inst. Horse lines to be clear for arrival of relieving unit by 2.p.m. on 26th inst.

Orders for subsequent moves will be issued by G.O.C. 68th Infantry Brigade Group.

3. The 102nd Field Coy. R.E. will be relieved by the 254th Field Coy. R.E. at 11.a.m. on the 24th inst. An advance party of 1 officer and [illegible] O.R. of the latter company will report at 9.a.m. on 23rd inst. to take over work in hand.

Dismounted personnel of 102nd Fld. Coy. will march to [illegible] on 24th and entrain for [illegible] between 12 and [illegible] p.m. Exact time of entraining will be notified later.

Horse transport will proceed by road on 24th inst. in accordance with orders issued by [illegible] Infantry Bde. Group (vide 23rd Division [illegible] [illegible]).

4. 128th Field Coy. R.E. will be relieved by the [illegible] Field Co. R.E. at [illegible].p.m. on 25th inst.

An advance party of the latter company will arrive on the evening of the 24th inst. to take over work in hand and ensure continuity of same. Strength of this party will be arranged direct

direct by O.C. Coys. concerned.

On completion of relief the 128th Field Coy. will proceed by march route to Divisional School (G.16.c.) reporting arrival and map reference to G.O.C. 69th Inf. Bde. and C.R.E. Transport and a small party to proceed to the Divisional School on the afternoon of 25th inst. Horse lines to be clear for arrival of relieving unit by 3.p.m.

All orders for subsequent moves will be issued by G.O.C. 69th Infantry Brigade Group.

5. All trench stores, maps, plans etc. dealing with work in hand are to be handed over to relieving unit and receipts obtained for same. These will be forwarded to this office.

6. Motor cycles are area stores and are to be handed ove to relieving company and receipts obtained as above.

7. H.Q.R.E. will close at RENINGHELST at 11 a.m. on 27th inst and will open at EPILECQUES at 6.p.m. same date.

8. Horse lines are to be disinfevted before leaving and all billets are to be left clean.

9. ACKNOWLEDGE.

Captain R.E.
Adjt. R.E.
23rd Division.

22.2.17.

Issued at 7.0.p.m.

Copy No. 1 to "Q"
2 101st Field Coy. R.E.
3 102nd " " "
4 128th " " "
5 68th Inf. Bde.
6 69th " "
7 70th " "
8 C.R.E. 39th Division.
9-10 War Diary.
11 File.

Vol 19

CONFIDENTIAL

WAR DIARY

of

HEAD QUARTERS R. E 23rd DIVISION

from 1st MARCH to 31st MARCH 1917

Original

Instructions regarding War Diaries and Intelligence Summaries are contained in F. S. Regs., Part II. and the Staff Manual respectively. Title pages will be prepared in manuscript.

WAR DIARY
or
~~INTELLIGENCE SUMMARY.~~
(Erase heading not required.)

(1)

Army Form C. 2118.

MARCH — H.Q. R.E. 23rd Division

Place	Date	Hour	Summary of Events and Information	Remarks and references to Appendices
ARQUES.	8/3/17	–	C.R.E. accompanied G.O.C. VIII Corps to the area N of YPRES to make a reconnaissance with a view to future operation if called on	SMS.
"	15 3/17	–	Orders received that Division would concentrate in BOLLEZEELE-HOUTKERQUE-PROVEN areas. Concentration to be completed by 20 3/17	SMS
	20 3/17	11.0a.m	H.Q R.E. Office at ARQUES closed at 11.0 a.m.	SMS
ESQUELBECQ	20 3/17	12.0a.m (midday)	H.Q. R.E. office opened at ESQUELBECQ. Map ref Sheet BELGIUM & FRANCE 1/40000 C.7.b.0.8.	SMS. Appendix A
	19 3/17 & 21 3/17	}	Field Coys. moving under Brigade orders to new areas.	
	21 3/17		Field Coys. are situated as follows. Map ref. Sheet 27 BELGIUM & FRANCE 1/40000 101st Field Coy R.E. E. 27. c. 53 102nd " " " D. 5. a. 9.9 128 " " " E. 25. b. 6.3.	SMS
	24 3/17		2 off & 40 O.R. from each of 101 & 102 Field Coys R.E. detached for work on defences N & N. of YPRES under orders of C.E. VIII Corps.	SMS
	24 3/17		D.R.O. 2523 repeats authority for 2/Lt. JM'I SAUNDERS R.E. (T.C.) 102nd Field Coy R.E. to be Adjutant R.E. 23rd Div. vice Capt. H.G. EDLESTON R.E. (S.R.) appointed S.O. R.E. XIX Corps. dated 21/3/17 Auth. VIII Corp. A/419/44 d/- 22/3/17.	SMS.

2353 Wt. W2544/1454 700,000 5/15 D. D. & L. A.D.S.S./Forms/C. 2118.

Instructions regarding War Diaries and Intelligence Summaries are contained in F. S. Regs., Part II. and the Staff Manual respectively. Title pages will be prepared in manuscript.

WAR DIARY
or
~~INTELLIGENCE SUMMARY.~~
(Erase heading not required.)

Army Form C. 2118.

(2)

MARCH — H.Q. R.E. 23rd Division

Place	Date	Hour	Summary of Events and Information	Remarks and references to Appendices
ESQUELBECQ	31/1/17	-	102nd Field Coy vacated their billets and proceeded to LEDRINGHAM on order of 70th Brigade. New billet Sheet 27 BELGIUM & FRANCE Square I. 2. b. 9.5	AMS
	21/1/17 to 31/1/17		General Field Coys during this period carried on their training in continuance of programme mapped out during early part of month.	SMS

S. McI. Lumsden

2353 Wt. W2544/1454 700,000 5/15 D. D. & L. A.D.S.S./Forms/C. 2118.

Copy.No. 8.

23rd DIVISIONAL ENGINEERS

C.R.E.'s Orders No.2.

Reference move of Division.

(1) Field Companies R.E. will move under Brigade orders to new areas.

101st Field Coy., R.E. on orders of G.O.C., 68th Brigade,
128th " " " " " " " 69th "
102nd " " " " " " " 70th "

(2) On completion of move Companies will report completion and Map reference of Company Offices to C.R.E.

(3) Headquarters R.E. will close at 11 a.m. at [illegible] and reopen at the same hour at [illegible], on 20th inst.

(4). Please acknowledge.

II Lieut. R.E.
a/Adjutant R.E.
23rd Division.

19th March, 1917.
Issued at 4.30 p.m.

Copy No.1 to 101st Field Coy. R.E.
2 102nd " " "
3 128th " " "
4 23rd Divn. "G"
5 68th Infty. Bde.
6 69th " "
7 70th " "
8-9 War Diary.
10 File.

CONFIDENTIAL Vol 20

WAR DIARY

Head Quarters R.E

23rd Division

Period April 1 – April 30 inclusive 1917

S M Hamden Lt
Adjutant R.E.
23rd Division

Original

Instructions regarding War Diaries and Intelligence Summaries are contained in F. S. Regs., Part II. and the Staff Manual respectively. Title pages will be prepared in manuscript.

APRIL 1917

WAR DIARY
or
~~INTELLIGENCE~~ SUMMARY.

(Erase heading not required.)

(1)

H.Q. R.E. 23rd Division

Army Form C. 2118.

Place	Date	Hour	Summary of Events and Information	Remarks and references to Appendices
ESQUELBECQ	1st to 5th	–	Training carried on as far as the restricted facilities would allow. SMS	Appendix A
"	4	–	Coys began move into forward area. as per C.R.E. O.O. 3. DM	
ESQUELBECQ	8	9.0am	C.R.E.'s office closed at ESQUELBECQ SMS	
BUSSEBOOM G16.C.6.4 Sheet 28 NW	8	4.0pm	C.R.E.'s office opened at BUSSEBOOM. 23rd Div. taking over a portion of the line from 39th Div. on the N + 47th Div. on the S. Boundaries of front line taken over from 39th Div. are I 24. d. 6½. 1 and I 29 b. 7. 0½. Boundaries on 47th Div area were I 29. b. 7. 0½ and I 34 b. 6½. 4½. Sheet 28 N.W. BELGIUM 1:20000 SMS	
YPRES SALIENT	6/7	–	On night of 6/7 – 128th Field Coy R.E. took over left subsector of new area from 39th Div. – 225th Field Coy. (I 24. d. 6½. 1 – I 29 b 7. 0½) SMS	
"	8/9		On night of 8/9 102nd Field Coy R.E. took over Right subsector of new area from 47th Div. – 518th Field Coy R.E. (I 29. b. 7. 0½ – I 34. 6½. 4½) SMS	Appendix C
"	6th		101st Field Coy took over Back area billets + horse lines at H13 d. 9.5 from 234th Field Coy R.E. SMS	Appendix B
	9th		Right Subsector (above named) was badly strafed by enemy ~~and~~ who practically obliterated the trenches (front line) SMS	

Original

Army Form C. 2118.

(2)

WAR DIARY
or
~~INTELLIGENCE SUMMARY.~~
(Erase heading not required.)

Instructions regarding War Diaries and Intelligence Summaries are contained in F. S. Regs., Part II. and the Staff Manual respectively. Title pages will be prepared in manuscript.

APRIL (cont) 1917

H.Q. R.E. 23rd Div.

Place	Date	Hour	Summary of Events and Information	Remarks and references to Appendices
YPRES Salient	9/15		During this period, the 39th Div. & 23rd Div both were using the R.E. Dump H13 d.9.2. pending such time that the 39th Div could find a new site. JMS	
"	15	Noon	23rd Div. took over the R.E. Dump ~~H~~13 d.9.2 in its entirety. JMS	APPENDIX D
"	15/16		On the night of the 15/16 the 23rd Div took over the HOOGE Sector of the Salient from the 39th Div to MENIN Road inclusive JMS	Appendix E
Busseboom	29		Orders received that the 23rd Div would be relieved by 19th Div. 23rd Div going back to STEENVOORDE area. Move commencing on the night of 30/1 JMS	APPENDIX F
"	30		Interpreter Sgt VARRIET McLeaves H.Q.R.E. and Interpreter Adj. de Flavis JMS	

J M S Saunders

Appendix A

SECRET

COPY NO. War Diary

23rd DIVISIONAL ENGINEERS.

C.R.E's ORDER No.3.

Map reference BELGIUM 28 N.W.

The following is the Programme of moves to be carried out by the Field Coys. R.E. 23rd Division.

	4th	5th	6th	7th	8th
101st Fld. Co. R.E.	-	-	Divisional Dump H.13.d.9.2.	-	-
102nd " " "	WATOU AREA	WATOU AREA	M.3.central	M.3.central	BELGIAN CHATEAU
128th " " "	-	M.3.central	KRUISSTRAAT	-	-

Companies will move under Company arrangements.

The O.C. 128th Field Coy. R.E. will keep in touch with G.O.C. 70th Infantry Brigade and arrange that his company gets away on the road in advance of the head of that Brigade Group.

Mounted portions of Companies will disengage and proceed to Billets at H.13.d.9.2. - when reaching billets in that area.

Arrangements for rations and refilling points are being made by "Q".

Please acknowledge.

[signature] IInd Lieut: R.E.
Adjt. R.E.
23rd Division.

3rd April 1917.

Issued at 10.p.m.

Copy No.1 to 101st Field Coy.R.E.
2 102nd " " "
3 128th " " "
4 23rd Division "Q"
5 " " "Q"
6 68th Infty. Bde.
7 69th " "
8 70th " "
9-10 War Diary.
11 File.

S E C R E T. Copy No. 5.

APPENDIX 'B'

23rd DIVISIONAL ENGINEERS.

OPERATION ORDER No. 4.

The 128th Field Coy., R.E. will take over the left subsector of the 23rd Divisional line from the 225th Field Coy., R.E. - 39th Division - on April 6th, sending an Officer to take over plans, notes of works in progress etc. on April 5th.

The 101st Field Coy., R.E. will take over the Divisional Dump, billets and horse lines from the 234th Field Coy., R.E. - 39th Division - on April 6th, sending an advanced party on April 5th.

Please acknowledge.

[signature]

Lieut: Colonel R.E.

4th April, 1917. C.R.E., 23rd Division.

Issued at 11.50 p.m.

Copy No. 1 to O.C. 101st Field Coy., R.E.
2 O.C. 128th " " "
3 23rd Division "G"
4 C.R.E., 39th Division.
5-6 War Diary.
7 File.

Appendix C

SECRET COPY NO. 10

23rd DIVISIONAL ENGINEERS

OPERATION ORDER No.5.

1. The 102nd Field Coy.R.E. will take over the right Sub-Sector of the 23rd Divisional new line from the 518th Field Coy.R.E. 47th Division on the night of the 8/9th April. Map reference of 518th Field Coy. R.E. - BELGIUM SHEET 28 N.W. H.20.d.3.2. - DICKEBUSCH HUTS - Telephone Call FIGURE.

2. O.C. 102nd Field Coy. R.E. will arrange direct with O.C. 518th Field Coy. R.E. for taking over all necessary plans, documents etc., and reconnoitring this sub sector and all works in progress prior to taking over the line.

3. The 102nd Field Coy. R.E. will be billetted in BELGIAN CHATEAU H.23.b.4.8. from 9.p.m. 8th April onwards.

PLEASE ACKNOWLEDGE.

[signature] Pryke

Lieut: Colonel R.E.

5.4.17. C.R.E. 23rd Division.

Issued at 11.10 p.m.

Copy No.1 to 101st Field Coy. R.E.
" 2 102nd " " "
" 3 128th " " "
" 4 C.R.E. 47th Division
" 5. 23rd Division "G"
" 6. " " "Q"
" 7. 68th Infty. Bde.
" 8. 69th " "
" 9. 70th " "
" 10-11 War Diary.
" 12. File.

S E C R E T   Appendix E   COPY No. 13

23rd DIVISIONAL ENGINEERS

OPERATION ORDER No.5.

1. The 23rd Division will take over the HOOGE SECTOR from the 39th Division on the night of the 15th/16th.

   Brigade Sub-Sectors will be as follows:-

   RIGHT BRIGADE GRAND FLEET STREET HENRY STREET inclusive - ZILLEBEKE STREET ST.PETERS STREET inclusive.

   LEFT BRIGADE ZILLEBEKE STREET ST.PETERS STREET exclusive - MENIN ROAD inclusive.

2. The 102nd Field Co. R.E. is allotted to the RIGHT SUB-SECTOR. The 128th Field Co. R.E. is allotted to the LEFT SUB-SECTOR.

3. The 102nd Field Co. R.E. will take over works in progress, plans etc. from 128th Field Co. R.E. by direct arrangement.

4. The 128th Field Co. R.E. will take over works in progress plans etc. and billets from the 227th and 234th Fld. Cos. R.E. by direct arrangement.

5. 9th Sth. Staffs. will be allotted as follows:-
   1½ (subsequently to be reduced to 1 Co.) coys to RIGHT SUB-SECTOR.
   1 Co. to LEFT SUB-SECTOR.
   1 Co. to TRAMWAYS.
   ½ (subsequently to be increased to 1 Co.) Co. to ROADS - CAMOUFLAGE.
   and will arrange direct for taking over works in progress, plans etc. in accordance with above distribution.

6. Completion of relief to be wired in code to H.Q.R.E.

   ACKNOWLEDGE.

PM Tooke

Lieut: Colonel R.E.
C.R.E. 23rd Division.

13th April 17.

Issued at 11.30 p.m.

Copy No.1 to H.Q. 23rd Division "G"
2 " " "Q"
3 C.R.E. 39th Division.
4. O.C. 101st Field Co. R.E.
5. " 102nd " " "
6. " 128th " " "
7. " 227th " " "
8. " 234th " " "
9. " 9th Sth. Staffs.
10. 68th Infty. Bde.
11. 69th " "
12. 70th " "
13-14. War Diary.
15. File.

S E C R E T

Appendix 'D' Copy No. 4

23rd DIVISIONAL ENGINEERS.

OPERATION ORDER No.6.

R.E.Dump H.15.d.9.2. Sheet 28 will be taken over by 23rd Division on 15th inst.

R.S.M. R.E. 23rd Division will assume control of the Dump as soon as receipts have been given to O. i/c Dump 39th Division

Report completion to this office.

Acknowledge.

14th April 17.

[signature] Lieut; R.E.
for Lt. Col. R.E.
C.R.E. 23rd Division.

Issued at 11.0.p.m.

Copy No. 1 to C.R.E. 39th Division.
" 2 O. i/c R.E.Dump.
3 File.
4.)
5.) War Diary.
6. R.S.M. 23rd Div. Engineers.

SECRET Appendix E COPY No. 13

23rd DIVISIONAL ENGINEERS

OPERATION ORDER No.8.

The following moves of Field Companies accompanied by attached Infantry will take place.

1. The 128th Field Coy. R.E. will hand over work in the line, maps, plans, documents etc. and forward billets to the 94th Field Coy. R.E. 19th Division on 30th April, and proceed by train from YPRES to GODEWAERSVELDE to be billetted in STEENVOORDE Area entraining at YPRES at 2.a.m. on 1st May.
This company will be affiliated to the 68th Brigade.

2. The 102nd Field Coy. R.E. will hand over work in the line, maps, plans, documents etc. and forward billets to the 82nd Field Coy. R.E. 19th Division on 1st May, and proceed by march route to WINNIPEG CAMP on night 1st/2nd May.
The Company will proceed from WINNIPEG CAMP to BOESCHEPE Area on May 2nd under company arrangements Mounted portion and transport will accompany the unit.
The O.C. Company will make his own arrangements for sending advance party to secure billets at WINNIPEG CAMP, MONTREAL EXTENSION and in BOESCHEPE Area.
This Company will be affiliated to the 70th Brigade.

3. The 101st Field Coy. R.E. will hand over the R.E. Dump, work in back area, and billets to the 81st Field Coy. R.E. 19th Division on May 2nd and proceed to billets in the STEENVOORDE area by march route under company arrangements.
On arrival in the STEENVOORDE Area this company will be affiliated to the 69th Brigade.

4. Completion of reliefs to be wired in code to this office.

5. ACKNOWLEDGE.

[signature]

Lieut: Colonel R.E.
C.R.E. 23rd Division.

30.4.17.
Issued at 4.30.p.m.

Copy No.1 to 23rd Division "G".
2. " " "Q"
3. C.R.E. 19th Division.
4. O.C. 101st Field Coy. R.E.
5. 102nd " "
6. 128th " "
7. 94th " "
8. 82nd " "
9. 81st " "
10. 68th Infty. Bde.
11. 69th " "
12. 70th " "
13 - 14 War Diary.
15. File.

Vol 21

CONFIDENTIAL

WAR DIARY

of

H. Q. R.E. 23rd DIVISION

from

MAY 1st 1917 to MAY 31st 1917

Original

Instructions regarding War Diaries and Intelligence Summaries are contained in F. S. Regs., Part II. and the Staff Manual respectively. Title pages will be prepared in manuscript.

MAY 1917

WAR DIARY
or
~~INTELLIGENCE SUMMARY.~~
(Erase heading not required.)

(1)

H.Q. R.E.
23rd Div.

Army Form C. 2118.

Place	Date	Hour	Summary of Events and Information	Remarks and references to Appendices
BUSSEBOOM	2	10am	Completing operation orders issued on 30 4/17 H.Q. R.E. handed over to C.R.E. 19th Div. and proceeded to STEENVOORDE. the office at BUSSEBOOM closed	
STEENVOORDE	2	12am	C.R.E's office re-opened at 8 Rue NEUVE	
"	3	-	G.O.C. Division inspected all Field Coys RE (101, 102, 128) and Pioneers (9th S. Staffs) G.O.C. quite satisfied with turnout	
"	4	.	101st Field Coy R.E. detailed to work under X Corps, forming a Dump at HEKSKEN.	
"	9	.	Orders issued for Division to go back into line & take over from 19th Div. (O.O. 9)	APPENDIX 'A'
.	12	9am	C.R.E's office in STEENVOORDE closed	
BUSSEBOOM	12	10am	C.R.E took over from C.R.E. 19th Division on exactly same front as previously C.R.E's office opened	
.	14	10am.	The HOOGE Sector as far South as St Peter St & ZILLEBEKE ST exclusive was handed over to 24th Div. O.O. 10	APPENDIX 'B'
	14 - end of month		Work on Div. front is being pushed forward so that position will be prepared for offensive ~~[illegible]~~ operations by 31st inst.	

Instructions regarding War Diaries and Intelligence Summaries are contained in F. S. Regs., Part II. and the Staff Manual respectively. Title pages will be prepared in manuscript.

MAY 1917

WAR DIARY
or
INTELLIGENCE SUMMARY.
(*Erase heading not required.*)

(2) H.Q. R.E. 23rd Div.

Army Form C. 2118.

Place	Date	Hour	Summary of Events and Information	Remarks and references to Appendices
Busseboom	31/5/17		All arrangements for offensive, so far as R.E. are concerned are practically complete. Right subsector quite complete Left Subsector almost. Forward Dumps are stocked with R.E. Stores and a Dump of Tramway material has been formed at I 23 c.1.5. R.E. Forward Dumps have been stocked at. I 22 c. 9.6 (Valley Cottages) I 30 a 1 8 (Armagh Wood) I 24 c 8 4, I 28 b 3.3 (Jacksons Dump) I 29 c 1 9 (Larch Wood) I 34 b. 4 9. & I 24 c.8.6	
			Transport on roads since 27/5/17 has been very difficult.	[initials]

2353 Wt. W2544/1454 700,000 5/15 D. D. & L. A.D.S.S./Forms/C. 2118.

SECRET. Copy No. 15.

23rd DIVISIONAL ENGINEERS

OPERATION ORDER No. 9.

The following moves of Field Companies accompanied by attached Infantry - and Pioneer Battalion will take place -

1. The 128th Field Coy. R.E. will proceed by March Route from present billets to R.E. Dump H.13.d.9.2. on 9th inst. under company arrangements, and take over billets, the Dump and work in progress from the 81st Coy. R.E. XIXth Division.
2 sections will be detailed to carry on the work at HEKSKEN Dump at present being carried out by the 101st Field Coy. R.E. from 10th instant, until completion.

2. 101st Field Coy. R.E. will proceed by March route from present billets to YPRES on the 10th relieving the 94th Field Co. R.E. XIXth Division in the line - HOOGE and MOUNT SORREL SECTORS.
Arrangements to be made direct between the companies concerned for taking over billets, trench plans, works in progress etc.
Lieut: GRIFFIN and the same N.C.O's and Sappers who when last in the line assisted the R.A. in the construction of gun positions etc. will be again detailed fro this work -
Lieut: GRIFFIN to get in touch with XIXth Division R.A. and take over work in progress etc.
Mounted portion of Coy. to H.13.d.9.2. R.E. Dump.

3. 102nd Field Coy. R.E. will proceed from present billets to YPRES by March route on 10th instant relieving the 82nd Field Coy. R.E. XIXth Division in the line - HILL 60 Sector.
Arrangements to be made direct between the companies concerned for taking over billets, trench plans, works in progress etc.
Mounted portion of Coy. to H.13.d.9.2. R.E. Dump.

4. The 9th South Staffs will proceed by March route from present billets to YPRES on the 10th instant relieving the Pioneer Battalion of the XIXth Division in the line.
Arrangements to be made between the battalions concerned for taking over billets, trench plans, works in progress etc.
1 N.C.O. and 15 Pioneers will be detailed to assist the T.M.B. in construction of Emplacements etc. as when last in the line.

5. Completion of reliefs to be wired in code to this office.

ACKNOWLEDGE.

[signature]
Lieut: Colonel R.E.
C.R.E., 23rd Division.

9.5.17.
Issued at 9.0 a.m.

Copy No. 1. to 23rd Division "G"
2. " " "Q"
3. C.R.E. 19th Division.
4. O.C. 101st Field Coy. R.E.
5. " 102nd " " "
6. " 128th " " "
7. " 9th South Staffs.
8. " 94th Field Coy. R.E.
9. " 82nd " " "
10. " 81st " " "
11. 68th Infantry Bde.
12. 69th " "
13. 70th " "
14 - 15. War Diary.
16. File.

Appendix B

S E C R E T COPY No. 13

23rd DIVISIONAL ENGINEERS

OPERATION ORDER No.10

101st will hand over work in HOOGE SECTOR and billets in YPRES to the 129th Field Coy. R.E. XXIVth Division on 14th instant and move into the TUNNELLED DUGOUTS - YPRES.
Arrangements to be made direct between Coys. concerned.

9th South Staffs. will hand over work in progress in HOOGE SECTOR on 14th to Pioneer Battn XXIVth Division and move into billets in TUNNELLED DUGOUTS- YPRES.
Arrangements to be made direct between Battns. concerned.

Acknowledge.

14.5.17.
Issued at 10.30a.m.

[signature]
Lieut: R.E.
for Lt. Col. R.E.
C.R.E. 23rd Division.

Copy No 1 to 23rd Div. "G"
2 23rd Div. "Q"
3 C.R.E. 24th Div.
4 O.C. 101st Field Co. R.E.
5 " 102nd " " "
6 " 128th " " "
7 " 9th Sth. Staffs.
8 " 129th Field Coy. R.E.
9 " Pioneer Battn. 24th Div.
10 68th Infty. Bde.
11 69th " "
12 70th " "
13-14 War Diaries.
15 File.

23 Div

R.E

June 1917

(23516.) Wt. W1119—W.P. 2160. 300m. 6/19. D & S. Est. 4930/1256.

COVER

FOR

BRANCH MEMORANDA.

Unregistered.

Referred to	Date	Referred to	Date

Vol 22

CONFIDENTIAL

WAR DIARY

of

HEAD QUARTERS R.E

23RD DIVISION

from

JUNE 1ST - JUNE 30TH

ORIGINAL

Instructions regarding War Diaries and Intelligence Summaries are contained in F. S. Regs., Part II. and the Staff Manual respectively. Title pages will be prepared in manuscript.

JUNE 1917

(1)

WAR DIARY
or
~~INTELLIGENCE SUMMARY.~~
(Erase heading not required.)

Army Form C. 2118.

H.Q. R.E. 23rd Div.

Place	Date	Hour	Summary of Events and Information	Remarks and references to Appendices
BUSSEBOOM	3	-	C.R.E. held a conference of Field Coy R.E. commanders & O.C. 9th South Staffs to discuss final details of work for operations in near future. JMS	
"	4		Operation orders issued detailing work to be done by units and giving disposition of Personnel. JMS	Appendix A
"	6	5.40	C.R.E., accompanied by Lt. R.G. Collingwood R.E., transferred his office for operations to Advanced Div. H.Q. situated at H.15. c.5.9 Map 28 NW BELGIUM. JMS	
			Lt. R.G. COLLINGWOOD R.E. is attached to H.Q. R.E. for operations	
"			All work in the line is completed and incidental repairs made good for tomorrow. JMS	
	7		Z Day. Operations commence Zero is 3.10 a.m. JMS	
"	7/8	-	In the afternoon Major J.P. OUCHTERLONY R.E. D.S.O., O.C. 102nd Field Coy R.E. killed in action. Capt. D.G. FARO R.E. assumed command of Coy.	
			During night the following works were carried out in Hill 60 Sector.	
			102nd Field Coy R.E. Strong Points – at junction of Impact Support & Impt Avenue; off Immovable Trench; S.E. of Caterpillar	
			Pioneers – Communication Trenches Swift Street to Immovable Trench	

8353 Wt. W2544/1454 700,000 5/15 D. D. & L. A.D.S.S./Forms/C. 2118.

Army Form C. 2118.

Instructions regarding War Diaries and Intelligence Summaries are contained in F. S. Regs., Part II. and the Staff Manual respectively. Title pages will be prepared in manuscript.

WAR DIARY
or
INTELLIGENCE SUMMARY.
(*Erase heading not required.*)

JUNE 1917 (2) H.Q. R.E. 23rd Div

Place	Date	Hour	Summary of Events and Information	Remarks and references to Appendices
Busseboom	7/8 incl		101st Field Coy R.E. Strong points I 30. c. 55, 85 " I 30 c 7, 6. Pioneer – Communication Trench I 30. a. 75.15. to I 30 a 7.0. " Old German front line & IMAGE Row to I 30 c 55, 85 cleared Tramway, N. of Zillebeke Lake kept in repair by Pioneer & practically all wounded evacuated thereby. Note Pioneer are 9th S. STAFFS	JMS
	8/9		Work in the newly captured was ~~consolidated~~ continued by R.E. as follows 101st Field Coy R.E. Support line from I 30 d 15.20 to IMAGE Avenue Started 102nd Field Coy R.E. Wired in part of IMMOVABLE Support	JMS
	12		Work on trenches & Strong points during last days has continued quite satisfactorily	JMS
	13		Division less Field Coys & Pioneers was relieved by 24th Div.	JMS
			23rd Div R.E. & Pioneers attached to 24th Div. to prepare for a minor operation	JMS
	14		On evening of 14th the 24th Div. in conjunction with 47th Div. successfully completed operation for capture of BATTLE WOOD. C.R.E. remained at Battle H.Q. at H15 c 4.9	
	15		with 24th Div. Staff until the afternoon of 15th	JMS

1353 Wt. W2544/1454 700,000 5/15 D. D. & L. A.D.S.S./Forms/C. 2118.

Instructions regarding War Diaries and Intelligence Summaries are contained in F. S. Regs., Part II. and the Staff Manual respectively. Title pages will be prepared in manuscript.

WAR DIARY
or
INTELLIGENCE SUMMARY.
(*Erase heading not required.*)

Army Form C. 2118.

JUNE 1917
3.

H.Q. R.E. 23rd Div

Place	Date	Hour	Summary of Events and Information	Remarks and references to Appendices
BUSSEBOOM	15/16		On night of 15/16 R.E. & Pioneer of 23rd Div were relieved by similar unit of 24th Div [illegible]	APPENDIX B
"	16	9am	C.R.E.'s office closed at BUSSEBOOM [illegible]	
BERTHEN	16	4pm	C.R.E.'s office opened at BERTHEN 128th Field Coy & 2 Coys Pioneer being left in line [illegible]	Appendix C
"	23		R.E. & Pioneer left in line rejoined the 23rd Div O.O. 13 [illegible]	
"	29		R.E. & proceeded to Salient again to relieve 24th Division [illegible]	Appendix D
"	30	8am	C.R.E.'s office closed at BERTHEN [illegible]	
		9am	C.R.E.'s office opened at ZEVECOTEN [illegible]	

2353 Wt. W2544/1454 700,000 5/15 D. D. & L. A.D.S.S./Forms/C. 2118.

SECRET APPENDIX D COPY No. 8

23rd DIVISIONAL ENGINEERS
OPERATION ORDER No.14.

1. The 23rd Division will relieve the 24th Division.

The following moves will be carried out by the Divisional R.Es and Pioneers.

The 101st, 102nd, and 128th Field Coys. R.E. 23rd Division will proceed from present billets on the 29th instant and take over work in the line from the 103rd, 104th and 129th Field Coys.R.E. 24th Division respectively by direct arrangement between the companies concerned - and work in the Back Area, Right Sector and Left Sector respectively.

Advanced Parties will be sent forward on the previous day.

2. Units will move independently under company arrangements.

3. Details as to location of billets, forward billets and horse lines will be issued separately.

4. The 9th South Staffs (Pioneers) will move from present billets on the 28th instant, and take over work in the line from the 12th Sherwood Foresters (Pioneers) 24th Division - in accordance with instructions contained in 24th Division G.Y.308/16 and 23rd Division G.O.475/11.

Advanced parties will be sent forward on the previous day.

5. Completion of moves to be wired to H.Q.R.E. which will close at present billet 9.a.m. 30th and re-open at MICMAC CAMP H.31.b.3.3. at the same time and date.

ACKNOWLEDGE.

26.6.17. Lieut: Colonel R.E.

Issued at 11 a.m. C.R.E. 23rd Division.

Copy No.1 to 101st Field Coy. R.E.
2 102nd " " "
3. 128th " " "
4. C.R.E. 24th Division
5. 23rd Division "G"
6. " " "
7. 9th Sth Staffs.
8-9 War Diary.
10. File
11. C.R.E. 23rd Division.

SECRET COPY No. 12

APPENDIX A

OPERATION ORDER NO. 11

BY

Lieut: Colonel E.H.ROOKE R.E.
C.R.E. 23rd DIVISIONAL ENGINEERS.

- - - - - - - - - - - -

Reference Trench Map HILL 60 and Sheets 28 N.W. 4 & 28 S.W.2 1/10000

- - - - - - - - - -

PLAN OF OPERATIONS. 1. The Second Army will attack the MESSINES - WYTSCHAETE Ridge and its extension northwards to KLEIN ZILLEBEKE on Z day.

This attack will be made by three Corps, of which the X Corps will be on the left.

The X Corps will attack between the DIEPENDAAL BEEK and OBSERVATORY RIDGE with 41st, 47th and 23rd Divisions in the order named from right to left.

The 24th Division (less Artillery and one Infantry Brigade will be employed in a subsequent attack on the OOSTAVERNE Line beyond the 41st Division's final objective.

The 142nd Infantry Brigade will be the Left Brigade of the 47th Division.

INFORMATION re ENEMY. 2. The 204th Division (WURTTEMBERG) consisting of 120, 413 and 414 Infantry Regiments holds the front from about opposite RAVINE WOOD (I.34.d) to opposite OBSERVATORY RIDGE.

TASK OF DIVISION 3. The task of the Division is:-

(a) To capture BATTLE WOOD and the KLEIN ZILLEBEKE SPUR.
(b) To cover the left flank of the Corps by forming a defensive flank facing East.

EMPLOYMENT OF R.E. & PIONEERS 4. The Divisional R.E. & Pioneers will carry out the following work in accordance with previous detailed Instructions.

(a) 69th INFANTRY BRIGADE AREA.

Strong Points.

D. I.30.a.4.1.
E. East end of THE CATERPILLAR.
F. I.29.d.5.4.

Communication Trenches.

No. 3. SWIFT STREET to IMMOVABLE ROW.
No. 4. ALLEN CRATER to I.24.d.2.5½.

70th INFANTRY BRIGADE AREA.

Strong Points.

H. I.30.c.60.35.
J. I.30.c.~~5.9~~. 8.8

Communication Trenches.

No. 5. I.30.c.4.9. to IMAGE ROW.
No. 6. From I.30.a.8.2.

General Officers Commanding concerned will be responsible for informing the parties when conditions admit of work being commenced.
On completion of task parties will return to billets, rest and stand by for further orders.

(b)

APPENDIX 'B'

SECRET COPY NO..11..

OPERATION ORDER No.12.

BY

Lieut: Colonel E.H.Rooke R.E.
C.R.E. 23rd DIVISIONAL ENGINEERS.

---

(1) The 23rd Divisional R.E. & Pioneers less one Coy. R.E. and 2 Coys. Pioneers will be relieved by R.E. and Pioneers of the 24th Division on night of 15th/16th June.

(2) Headquarters R.E. 23rd Division, 101st Field Coy. R.E., 102nd Field Coy. R.E. and Pioneers (less 2 Coys) will move into BERTHEN Area on 16th as follows:-

Headquarters R.E.	BERTHEN.
101st Field Coy. R.E.	X.10.b.3.9.
102nd " " "	R.33.a.2.4.

Sheet 27 1/40,000 BELGIUM & FRANCE.

Transport lines will be with Formation.

Units will move independently under their own arrangements. Completion of move to be wired to H.Q.R.E. at BERTHEN.

(3) Work in Progress, plans, papers etc. will be handed over to incoming units of 24th Division by direct arrangement with those units.

(4) 128th Field Coy. R.E. will arrange with 101st Field Coy. R.E. to take over their work in progress at MICMAC Camp and neighbourhood. 128th Field Coy. R.E. will carry on this work from the morning of 16th inclusive.

(5) The 128th Field Coy. R.E. and 2 Coys. 9th South Staffs. will remain and work under orders of C.R.E. 24th Division.

ACKNOWLEDGE.

14.6.17.

Issued at 2.30.p.m.

Lm Hamden Lieut: R.E.
Adjt. R.E.
23rd Division.

Copies to :-

No. 1. "G" 23rd Division.
2. A & Q " "
3. G 24th "
4 A & Q " "
5. 101st Field Coy. R.E.
6. 102nd " "
7. 128th " "
8. 9th Sth. Staffs. (P)
9. C.R.E. 24th Division.
10. " 23rd "
11. File.
12 - 13 War Diary.

(b) 2 Platoons Pioneers will be employed on maintenance of roads.

2 Platoons Pioneers will be employed on maintenance of Tramways.
The Pioneers will also be responsible for the operating of the tramway truck water supply.

<u>RESERVE</u> 5. 1 section of 101st Field Coy. R.E. and 1 Section 102nd Field Coy. R.E. will be held in Company Reserve.

128th Field Coy. R.E. & 1 Coy. 9th South Staffs. (P) will be held in C.R.E's Reserve.

<u>TIME OF ASSEMBLY Etc.</u> 6. Troops will be in position by 2.30.a.m. on Z day in accordance with Concentration Table issued separately Z day and Zero hour will be notified later.

<u>REPORTS etc.</u> 7. Advanced Divisional Headquarters will be at H.15.c.4.9. from 6.p.m. on Y day.
Full and clear reports of work done to be sent to H.Q.R.E. immediately on completion of work.

8. ACKNOWLEDGE.

[signature]

4th June 1917. Lieutenant Colonel R.E.

Issued at 3.30 p.m. Commanding Royal Engineer, 23rd DIV:

Copies to :-

No.1. G.
2. A & Q.
3. 68th Infty. Bde.
4. 69th " "
5. 70th " "
6. 101st Fld. Co. R.E.
7. 102nd " " "
8. 128th " " "
9. 9th South Staffs.
10. C.R.E.
11 - 12. War Diary.
13. File.

SECRET

Table shewing concentration of Troops from W to Z day.

UNIT	W day	W/X night	X/Y night	Y/Z night	ROUTE.
101st Fld. Co.R.E. & att. Infantry (101st & 128th)	YPRES	No change	No change	RITZ STREET NORTH OF DORMY HOUSE.	N. side of ZILLEBEKE LAKE.
102nd Fld. Co. R.E. & attd. Infantry.	YPRES	No change	No change	PROMENADE	
128th Field Coy. R.E.	Remain in present billets - prepared to move at 1 hours notice.				
9th Sth. Staffs. 12 Platoons.	YPRES	Camp "L" March when dark Camp "L" is next to Camp "M" in G.17.d. Route - VLAMERTINGHE H.7.c.3.6.	Camp "L"	X 6 Platoons PROMENADE	H.7.c.3.6. (9.45.p.m.) - H.13.d.9.1. - H.14.b.4.8 H.16.d.1.1. - KRUISSTRAAT - BRIDGE 14 - SHRAPNEL CORNER.
				X 2 Platoons RITZ STREET N. of DORMY HOUSE.	As above to BRIDGE 14.
				4 Platoons ESPLANADE DUGOUTS YPRES.	As above to KRUISSTRAAT.
4 Platoons	YPRES	No change, carrying on maintenance work on roads & Tramways.			

Routes - Starting Points and hour of passing must be strictly adhered to.
Units to be in position at ZERO - 30 minutes, and report to that effect sent to H.Q.R.E.

X to join R.E. and come under orders of Senior R.E. Officer.

SECRET.

APPENDIX C

Copy No. 6.

23rd DIVISIONAL ENGINEERS
OPERATION ORDER No.13.

(1) The 128th Field Coy., R.E. (less 1 section working under the orders of C.E. Xth Corps) and 2 Coys. 9th South Staffs (Pioneers) - will cease to come under the orders of the C.R.E., 24th Division from 6.30 a.m. 23rd instant, and will rejoin the 23rd Division in the BERTHEN AREA on that date.

(2) 5 lorries for the 128th Field Coy., R.E. and 15 for the 9th South Staffs. will be at their billets at 6.30 a.m. on the 23rd to convey the dismounted portions of those units to billets in the BERTHEN AREA.

(3) Completion of move to be wired to H.Q., R.E.

ACKNOWLEDGE.

22-6-17.

Issued at 10 p.m.

[signature] for Lieut: Colonel R.E.
C.R.E., 23rd Division.

Copy No.1 to 23rd Division "G".
2 " " "Q".
3 O.C. 128th Field Coy., R.E.
4 O.C. 9th South Staffords.
5 C.R.E., 24th Division.
6-7 War Diary.
8 File.

Vol 23

CONFIDENTIAL

WAR DIARY

of

HEADQUARTERS R.E 23rd DIV.

from

JULY 1st — JULY 31st

JULY 1917 (1)

Army Form C. 2118.

Instructions regarding War Diaries and Intelligence Summaries are contained in F. S. Regs., Part II. and the Staff Manual respectively. Title pages will be prepared in manuscript.

WAR DIARY
or
INTELLIGENCE SUMMARY.
(Erase heading not required.)

H.Q. R.E. 23rd Div

Place	Date	Hour	Summary of Events and Information	Remarks and references to Appendices
ZEVECOTEN	1	-	Field Coys + Pioneers commenced preparation of the Hill 60 + Mount Sorrel sector for Offensive Operation to be carried out by 24th Division. The 102nd Field Coy RE +128th Field Coy R.E. carrying out the work in the line + 101st Field Coy RE i[n] ~~Pioneers~~ working in back area. The Pioneers (9th S. Staffs) assisted the forward Field Coys + ~~also~~ worked on Tramways + Roads.	PM
	4	9.0am	23rd Div. ~~as~~ temporarily attached to II Corps, Fifth Army during preparation for offensive	APPENDIX A PM
	7.	-	A/Major PODMORE O.C. 128th Field Coy R.E. Wounded ([illegible])	
	12		104th Field Coy R.E + Pioneers (12th Sherwood Foresters) both of 24th Div. attached to 23rd Div. for work in preparation	APPENDIX B PM
	16		Capt Luby M., R.E. (Reg) from 2nd Field Coy R.E. assumed command of 128th Field Coy RE in place of A/Maj Podmore, wounded	PM
	23	10	C.R.E. handed over work in line + back area to C.R.E. 24th Div. which Division takes over from 23rd Div. + carries on work. C.R.E.'s office Closed at ZEVECOTEN. 101st Field Coy R.E. + 9th S Staffs remain in 24th Div Area to construct a road from CHESTER FARM to VERBRANDENMOLEN Road under direct orders of C.E. II Corps. Forward area practically complete + in readiness for offensive.	Appendices C+D PM

2353 Wt. W2544/1454 700,000 5/15 D. D. & L. A.D.S.S./Forms/C. 2118.

Army Form C. 2118.

Instructions regarding War Diaries and Intelligence Summaries are contained in F. S. Regs., Part II. and the Staff Manual respectively. Title pages will be prepared in manuscript.

WAR DIARY
or
INTELLIGENCE SUMMARY.
(*Erase heading not required.*)

Place	Date	Hour	Summary of Events and Information	Remarks and references to Appendices
MERRIS	23	12 noon	C.R.E. office opened. Div. comes under orders of X Corps Second Army. 102nd Field Coy + 128th Field Coy in BERTHEN Area	JMS
"	26	-	102nd Field Coy R.E. transferred to ZUTOVE, to work under Second Army at construction of a rifle range.	JMS
"	31st		Div still out of line. 101st Field Coy R.E. + 9th S. Staffs (Pioneers) still working on road under C.E. II Corps. 102nd Field Coy R.E. working under Second Army at Lumbres, & changed billets to that village. 128th Field Coy R.E. remain at FONTAINE HUICK, training + repairing rifle ranges.	JMS

8353 Wt. W2544/1454 700,000 5/15 D. D. & L. A.D.S.S./Forms/C. 2118.

S E C R E T

COPY No. 8

APPENDIX A

23rd DIVISIONAL ENGINEERS

OPERATION ORDER No.16.

1. The 23rd Division will be transferred to the IInd Corps from 9.a.m. on the 4th instant and the present Right Brigade sector will be handed over to the 47th Division on the night 3rd/4th. Relief to be completed by 9.a.m. on the 4th instant.

2. After transfer of the Division to the II.Corps, the southern boundary of the 23rd Division, which will also be the boundary between the II and X Corps, will be as follows:-

From I.36.a.06.42 (KLEIN ZILLEBEKE) - Railway at I.29.c.3.0 to junction of GRAND FLEET STREET with the old British front line - to point where stream crosses ZILLEBEKE ROAD at I.30.c.75.08 thence to CHESTER FARM (exclusive to 23rd Division) to I.32.d.3.3 thence by FRENCH TRENCH and CONVENT LANE TRENCH (both inclusive to 47th Division) to road junction at H.36.c.7.7. to WILTSHIRE FARM (inclusive to 47th Division) thence along light railway to CROSS COUNTRY TRACK at N.5.a.5.9., thence by track to the DICKEBUSCH - LA CLYTTE ROAD at N.33.a.0.6. (Tracks and light railway inclusive to Xth Corps) thence along S. edge of roads DICKEBUSCH - MILLEKRUISSE - LOCREHOF and thence as at present.

23rd and 47th Divisions will both have users rights over roads and tramways serving their sectors.

3. The 102nd Field Coy. R.E. will hand over forward billets, work in progress etc to the 518th Field Coy.R.E. 47th Division on the 3rd instant by direct arrangement between units concerned - information as to new forward billets of 102nd Field Coy. R.E. will be furnished later.
The 128th Field Coy. R.E. will vacate their forward billets in SPOIL BANK and proceed to LARCH WOOD on the 3rd instant.
Back billets will not be handed over.

4. 102nd Field Coy. R.E. will work in Right Sector of New Area.
128th " " " " " Left " " " "

Boundary - [illegible] ROW - [illegible] AVENUE to I.30.d.2.3. - front line at I.30.d.?.3. inclusive to 128th Field Coy. R.E.
O.C. 102nd Field Coy. R.E. will take over work in progress in Right Sector from O.C. 128th Field Coy. R.E. and commence work thereon on night 3/4th.

5. The 2 Companies 9th South Staffs. (Pioneers) working at present with the 102nd & 128th Field Coys. R.E. will work with these companies in the New Sectors.

6. Completion of relief to be wired to H.Q.R.E., 23rd Division.

ACKNOWLEDGE.

[signature]

Lieut: Colonel R.E.
C.R.E. 23rd Division.

2.7.17.
Issued at 7.30.p.m.

Copy No.1. to 23rd Division "G"
2. " " "Q"
3. C.R.E. 47th Division
4. 101st Field Coy. R.E.
5. 102nd " " "
6. 128th " " "
7. 9th Sth. Staffs.
8.-9. War Diary.
10. File.

SECRET

COPY No. 4

Appendix B

23rd DIVISIONAL ENGINEERS

C.R.E.'s ORDER No.16.

The following work will be carried out by 104th Field Coy. R.E. and 2 Coys. 12th Sherwood Foresters (Pioneers) 24th Division commencing on the 12th instant.

\- - - - - -

	104th Fld. Co. R.E.	12th Sher.Foresters
A.R.P. H.1.central / Bomb Store H.1.central.	2 sections	1 Company
A.R.P. HALLEBAST CORNER	1 section	-
TRACK. Map ref. H.34.c.3.3. H.4.a.5.0.	-	2 Platoons.
P. of War Cage. Map ref. H.36.b.1.9.	-	2 Platoons.

The O.C. 104th Field Coy. R.E. and O's.C.Companies 12th Sherwood Foresters will get in touch with the O.C. 101st Field Co. R.E. H.30.b.9.8. on the 11th instant when details of the work will be explained to them.

Daily Progress Reports will be forwarded to reach this office by 4.p.m.

ACKNOWLEDGE.

[signature]

11.7.17. Lieut; Colonel R.E.

Issued at 12 noon. C.R.E. 23rd Division.

Copy No.1 to 101st Field Co. R.E.
2. 104th " " "
3-4 Pioneers 24th Division.
5. C.R.E. 24th Division.
6-7 War Diary.
8. File
9. "G" 23rd Div. for information.

S E C R E T   COPY No. 10.

Appendix C

23rd DIVISIONAL ENGINEERS

OPERATION ORDER NO.17.

1. The 24th Division will relieve the 23rd Division in the line.

2. The 102nd and 128th Field Coys. R.E. will hand over work in the Line, plans, documents and forward billets to the 104th Field Coy. R.E. 24th Division on the 21st instant - by direct arrangement.
Forward sections will return to Back Area Billets on that evening after completion of day work.
These companies will proceed to the [illegible] AREA on the 22nd. Details as to hours of starting and route to be followed will be issued later. Advanced parties will be sent to report to the Area Commandant [illegible] for billets.

3. The 101st Field Coy. R.E. will hand over work in progress in Back Area to a Field Coy. R.E. 24th Division after work on the 23rd instant by direct arrangement and remain in present billets until further orders.

4. The 9th Sth. Staffs (pioneers) will hand over work in progress to the 12th Sherwood Foresters (Pioneers) 24th Division after day work on the 21st instant by direct arrangement and remain in present billets until further orders.

5. Headquarters R.E. will close at present billet at 10.0a.m. on 23rd instant and open at [illegible] at 11.0.a.m. on same date.

6. Completion of moves to be wired to H.Q.R.E.

ACKNOWLEDGE.

[signature]
Lieut: Colonel R.E.

18.7.17.   C.R.E. 23rd Division.

Copy No.1   to   23rd Division G
2   "   "   Q
3   C.R.E. 24th Div.
4.   101st Field Coy. R.E.
5   102nd   "   "
6   128th   "   "
7   104th   "   "
8   9th Sth. Staffs.
9   12th Sherwood Foresters.
10-11   War Diary.
12   File.

S E C R E T   COPY NO.

23rd DIVISIONAL ENGINEERS

OPERATION ORDER NO.18.

1. Operation Order No.17 is cancelled.

2. The 24th Division will relieve the 23rd Division in the line.

3. The 102nd and 128th Field Coys. R.E. will hand over work in the line, plans, documents and forward billets to the 103rd and 104th Field Coys. R.E. 24th Division respectively after day work on the 21st instant - by direct arrangement. Forward sections will return to Back Area Billets on that evening after completion of day work.
These companies will proceed to the [illegible] AREA on the 22nd. Details as to hours of starting and route to be followed will be issued later. Advanced parties will be sent to report to the Area Commandant [illegible] for billets.

4. The 101st Field Coy. R.E. will hand over work in progress in Back Area to the 129th Field Coy. R.E. 24th Division after work on the 22nd instant by direct arrangement, and remain in present billets until further orders.

5. The 9th Sth. Staffs. (Pioneers) will hand over work in progress to the 12th Sherwood Foresters (Pioneers) 24th Division after day work on the 21st instant by direct arrangement and remain in present billets until further orders.

6. Headquarters R.E. will close at present billets at 10.0 a.m. on 23rd instant and open at [illegible] at 11.0 a.m. on same date.

7. Completion of moves to be wired to [illegible].

ACKNOWLEDGE.

19.7.17.   Lieut. Colonel R.E.

Issued at 8.0 p.m.   C.R.E. 23rd Division.

Copy No.1 to 23rd Division G
2 " "
3 C.R.E. 24th Div.
4 101st Field Coy. R.E.
5 102nd " " "
6 128th " " "
7 [illegible] " " "
8 9th Sth. Staffs.
9 12th Sherwood Foresters.
10-11 War Diary.
12 File.

CONFIDENTIAL

Vol 24

WAR DIARY

of

Headquarters R.E. 23 Div

period

AUGUST 1 - AUGUST 31st

Instructions regarding War Diaries and Intelligence Summaries are contained in F. S. Regs., Part II. and the Staff Manual respectively. Title pages will be prepared in manuscript.

H.Q. R.E. 23rd Div

WAR DIARY or INTELLIGENCE SUMMARY.

(Erase heading not required.) (1)

August 1917.

Army Form C. 2118.

Place	Date	Hour	Summary of Events and Information	Remarks and references to Appendices
MERRIS	5		Received instruction that we are to move with D.H.Q. to WIZERNES	JMS
"	"	9.0pm	Received further instruction that 128th Field Coy also move into new area, final destination of this Coy is HAUT LOQUIN	JMS
"	6	9.0am	H.Q. R.E. Office closed in MERRIS + proceeded to WIZERNES	JMS
WIZERNES	6		Instruction received that all 3 Field Coys R.E. + 9th S.Staffs move into XVIII Corps area on 8th inst. C.R.E. also to go into that area on 9th	
"	8		C.R.E. Reported to C.E. XVIII Corps for instruction on the work of Field Coys R.E. + Pioneers and is told they will be employed on forward roads between Canal + Old British Front Line.	JMS
"	9	9.0am	C.R.E.'s Office Closed at WIZERNES	JMS
OOSTHOEK	9	3pm	C.R.E. Office opened. Office is situated at A. 23. c. 1.6 Sheet 28 N.W. 1/20000 The Coys are situated as follows. 101st Field Coy R.E. G 5 b. 1.9 102 " " H. 10 a. 5.5. 128 " " H. 10 b. 0.8. 9th S.Staffs H 4 c. 9.7.	JMS
"	10		Coys. start work on roads 102nd on BUFFS Road (C 21 c + d) 128th on BOUNDARY Road (C 27 a) 101 resting.	JMS Sheet 28

2353 Wt. W2544/1454 700,000 5/15 D. D. & L. A.D.S.S./Forms/C. 2118.

Army Form C. 2118.

Instructions regarding War Diaries and Intelligence Summaries are contained in F. S. Regs., Part II. and the Staff Manual respectively. Title pages will be prepared in manuscript.

H.Q. R.E.
23rd Div

WAR DIARY
or
INTELLIGENCE SUMMARY.
(Erase heading not required.)

August 1917

Place	Date	Hour	Summary of Events and Information		Remarks and references to Appendices
OOSTHOEK	11th – 15th		Work on roads continued.		
	16th		102 Fd. Co. & 1 Coy 9th S. Staffords responsible for BUFFS ROAD from ADMIRALS RD to ST JULIEN Road. ~~[illegible]~~		
			128 Fd Co + 1 Coy S. Staffs responsible for ADMIRALS RD from C.15.c.8.6 – C22c6.8.		
			Only urgent repairs and maintenance carried out today vide O.O. 22 attached.		O.O. 22 attached.
	21st		Companies heavily shelled on roads & had about 30 casualties (including S. Staffs).	SMS	O.O 23 attached
	22.		101st Field Coy R.E. took over work in the line		
	24		Adj returned from leave (Period 13–23 inclusive) Capt. Kyggel, 102nd Field Coy R.E having acted in his absence.	SMS	
	24		Instruction received that 23rd Div comes under orders of II Corps with effect from 10 am and that Field Coys R.E. + Pioneers will rejoin the Div at Reningelst	SMS	O.O 24 Attached
	25		Instruction received + orders issued that this Div. including R.Es. + Pioneers will take over from 14th Div.	SMS	O.O. 25 Attached
	26	9.0 am	C.R.E. office OOSTHOEK closed	SMS	
DICKEBUSCH	26	1.0 pm	C.R.E. office opened at H 27 b.7.7. and taking over from 14 Div. CRE completed	SMS	
			R.E Dumps are at DICKEBUSCH H27.d.5.1 and KRUISSTRAAT H18.d.2.2.		
	26	11.0 pm	Orders issued to Coys on the work to be done assuming an immediate offensive	SMS	O.O 26 Attached
			101st Field Coy R.E. + 128th Field Coy RE working in the line with 102nd Field Coy in reserve		
"	30	7.0	C.R.E. orders issued detailing work for offensive	SMS	O.O 27 Attached

2353 Wt. W2544/1454 700,000 5/15 D. D. & L. A.D.S.S./Forms/C. 2118.

S E C R E T. Copy No. 11

23rd DIVISIONAL ENGINEERS.

OPERATION ORDER No.27.

1. The 23rd Division in conjunction with the 47th Division on its left will attack on a date to be notified later.

2. The Divisional R.E. & Pioneers will carry out the following work:-

101st Field Coy., R.E. - 69th Brigade Area.(Right).

STRONG POINTS.

B - HERENTHAGE CHATEAU. J.20.b.2.8.

E - INVERNESS COPSE J.14.c.8.6.

1 Section R.E., 1 Platoon Pioneers and 2 Platoons attached Infantry (carrying party) will be detailed for each of the above.

128th Field Coy., R.E. - 68th Brigade Area (Left).

STRONG POINTS.

M - J.14.d.1.9.

N - L FARM J.14.b.2.4.

1 Section R.E., 1 Platoon Pioneers and 2 Platoons attached Infantry (carrying party) will be detailed for each of the above.

TRACKS.

In addition the following Infantry Tracks will be made, posted and notice boarded by the 9th South Staffs (Pioneers).

(a) MENIN ROAD about J.14.c.9.3. to HERENTHAGE CHATEAU - 1 Platoon

(b) CLAPHAM JUNCTION to S.P's M & N - 2 Platoons.

(c) J.14.a.3.2. to S.P. O at J.14.b.2.8. and on to S.P. L at J.14.b.8.6. - 2 Platoons.

The O.C 9th South Staffs will detail 5 Platoons for this work.

G.O's C. Brigades concerned will be responsible for informing the Parties when conditions admit of work being commenced.

The O's C. 101st and 128th Field Coys. R.E. and an Officer of the 9th South Staffs. will keep in close touch at Bde. H.Q. of the 69th and 68th Brigades - the Officer of the 9th S. Staffs. at Bde. H.Q. of the 68th Brigade.

On completion of task allotted parties will return to billet, rest and stand by for further orders.

3. 2 Sections 101st Field Coy., R.E. and 2 sections 128th Field Coy. R.E. will be held in Company Reserve.

102nd Field Coy., R.E. and 7 Platoons 9th S. Staffs)(Pioneers) will be held in C.R.E's Reserve.

4./

4. Place of Assembly will be as follows :-

Western end of RAILWAY DUG OUTS.

Troops will be in position at Zero - 1 hour.

5. Full and clear reports of work done will be sent to H.Q.R.E. immediately on completion of work.

6. Divisional H.Q. will remain at present location.

7. ACKNOWLEDGE.

Lieut: Colonel R.E.

C.R.E., 23rd Division.

30th August, 1917.
Issued at 7 p.m.

Copy No. 1 to 23rd Division "G"
2 " " "Q"
3 68th Infantry Brigade.
4 69th " "
5 70th " "
6 101st Field Coy., R.E.
7 102nd " " "
8 128th " " "
9 9th South Staffords.
10-11 War Diary.
12-13 File.

"A" Form.

MESSAGES AND SIGNALS.

Army Form C.2121 (in pads of 100.)

No. of Message ....

Prefix .... Code .... m.	Words	Charge	This message is on a/c of:	Recd. at .... m.
Office of Origin and Service Instructions.	Sent		.... Service.	Date ....
	At .... m.			From ....
	To			
	By		(Signature of "Franking Officer.")	By ....

TO { 23rd Bde R.[illegible]
" " [illegible]
" " Signals

Sender's Number.	Day of Month.	In reply to Number.	AAA
* B 227	30		

Map reference of 101st Field Coy R.E. is I.20.d.7.9.

4259

From C.R.E.

Place

Time 11.30 pm

The above may be forwarded as now corrected. (Z) [illegible] Capt. R.E.

Censor. Signature of Addressor or person authorised to telegraph in his name.

* This line should be erased if not required.

(7107) Wt. W12093/M1217 50,000 pads. 1/17. D. D. & L. (E764.) Forms C/2121/11.

SECRET & URGENT. COPY NO. 7.

23rd DIVISIONAL ENGINEERS

OPERATION ORDER No.22.

1. From Zero day inclusive onwards the 23rd Divisional R.E. and Pioneers will be responsible for the maintenance and repair of the following Roads and Tracks.

   (a) BUFF'S ROAD from ADMIRAL'S ROAD to ST JULIEN ROAD (C.25.a.4.5

   (b) ADMIRAL'S ROAD from Cross roads near Divisional boundry (C.18.c.8.6) to ST JULIEN ROAD (C.23.c.5.8.)

   (c) TRACK (BATH ROAD) from BOUNDARY ROAD to [illegible] FARM (C.16.b.5.3.)

2. 102nd Field Coy. R.E. with 1 Coy. 9th Sth. Staffs. will be responsible for (a) and the portion of (c) East of ADMIRAL'S ROAD.

   128th Field Coy. R.E. with 1 Coy. 9th Sth. Staffs. will be responsible for (b) and the portion of (c) WEST of ADMIRAL'S ROAD.

3. On Zero day urgent repairs and maintenance only will be carried out – 1 Sec. R.E. and 1 Platoon 9th Sth. Staffs. per company will be detailed for this work – these parties will not work on Z + 1 day.

4. After Zero day work must be pushed on as rapidly as possible.

5. Zero day will be notified later.

ACKNOWLEDGE.

[signature]

Lieut: Colonel R.E.
C.R.E., 23rd Division.

15.8.17.

Issued at 9.0 a.m.

Copy No.1 to 101st Fld. Co. R.E.
2 102nd " "
3. 128th " "
4. 9th Sth. Staffs.
5. "G" 23rd Division.
6-7 War Diary.
8. File.

SECRET. Copy No. 8.

23rd DIVISIONAL ENGINEERS

OPERATION ORDER No.23.

1. The 101st Field Coy., R.E. will take over work in the Line from the 128th Field Coy., R.E. on the 21st instant by direct arrangement.

   The 128th Field Coy., R.E. working in the line on 20th instant.

   The 101st Field Coy., R.E. from the 21st instant inclusive onwards.

2. Billets will be changed on the 20th instant, the 128th Field Coy., R.E. proceeding to those of 101st Field Coy., R.E. after work on that date.

3. Horse lines will be changed on the 20th instant unless companies mutually agree to retain their present lines - decision arrived at to be notified to this office.

4. ACKNOWLEDGE.

18th August, 1917. Lieut: Colonel R.E.

Issued at 8.15 p.m. C.R.E., 23rd Division.

Copy No.1 to 101st Field Coy., R.E.
2 102nd " " "
3 128th " " "
4 9th South Staffs.
5 C.E., XVIII Corps.
6 23rd Division "G".
7 " " "Q".
8-9 War Diary.
10 File.

SECRET. Copy No. 10.

23rd DIVISIONAL ENGINEERS

OPERATION ORDER No.[illegible].

1. 23rd Division (less Artillery) is transferred to II Corps with effect from 10 a.m. 24th August.

2. 23rd Divisional R.E. and Pioneers will move into II Corps Area on the 26th instant.
Billets as below :-

101st Field Coy., R.E. - [illegible] Camp (area). Exact location will be notified later.

102nd " " " - [illegible] Area. Billets [illegible]. Horse Lines [illegible].

128th " " " - [illegible] Area. Billets & Horse Lines [illegible]. (Note: 18 tents to be drawn from [illegible] Camp at [illegible]. Further information from Area Commandant).

9th S. Staffs (Pioneers) - [illegible] Camp. Any further information required by units in [illegible] Area will be obtained from Area Commandant at [illegible] [illegible] Road.

3. Units will march to new billets under their own arrangements, arranging for Advanced Parties, guides, etc.
Route via [illegible] Road.
Units to arrive at destination by [illegible].

4. The following intervals will be maintained on the march in II Corps Area.
(a) E. of [illegible] Road - [illegible] yards between Companies.
(b) W. of above road - [illegible] yards between Battalions.

5. Billets, work in the line, maps, plans, documents etc. to be handed over to incoming units of the [illegible] Divisional R.E. & Pioneers before leaving XVIII Corps Area.

6. H.Q., R.E. will close at present billets at [illegible] a.m. on 26th instant and open at [illegible] at 10 a.m. on the same date.

7. ACKNOWLEDGE.

[signature] Capt. R.E.
for Lieut: Colonel R.E.
C.R.E., 23rd Division.

24th August, 1917.
Issued at 7.45 p.m.

Copy No. 1 to C.E. XVIII Corps.
2 O.C. 101st Field Coy., R.E.
3 " 102nd " " "
4 " 128th " " "
5 " 9th South Staffords.
6 C.R.E., [illegible] Division.
7 23rd Division "G".
8 " " "Q".
9-10 War Diary.
11 File.
12. C.E. II Corps

SECRET. Copy No. 13.

23rd DIVISIONAL ENGINEERS

OPERATION ORDER No.25.

1. Paras. 2, 3 & 6 of Operation Order No.24 are cancelled.

2. 23rd Divisional R.E. & Pioneers will, on the 26th instant, take over billets, work in the line, plans, documents etc. from the 14th Divisional R.E. & Pioneers - who will leave behind the C.O. or 2nd in Command from each unit to hand over - and a liaison officer to remain up to 48 hours if required,
Commencing work on the 27th instant.

101st Fld. Coy., R.E. will take over from the 61st Fld. Coy. R.E., 14th Division, at H.30.a.2.8. - forward billets also to be taken over.

102nd Fld. Coy., R.E. will take over from the 89th Fld. Coy., R.E., 14th Division, at H.30.b.2.2. less work at HOOGE CRATER.

128th Fld. Coy., R.E. will take over from the 62nd Fld. Coy., R.E., 14th Division, at H.30.a.2.9. plus work at present being carried out at HOOGE CRATER BY the 89th Fld. Coy., R.E.

Horse Lines of all 3 Field Coys are at H.33.b.5.5.

9th South Staffs. (Pioneers) will take over from the 11th King's Liverpools (Pioneers), 14th Division, at H.23.d.5.5. Horse Lines at same place.

3. Units will march to new billets under their own arrangements and will arrive at their destination at 9 a.m.

4. Following intervals will be maintained on the march in II Corps Area.
(a) E. of RENINGHELST-POPERINGHE Road - 200 yards between companies.
(b) W. of above road - 500 yards between battalions.

5. H.Q., R.E. will close at present billets at 9 a.m. on the 26th instant and open at H.27.b.7.7. at 9.30 a.m. on the same date.

6. ACKNOWLEDGE.

25th August, 1917.
Issued at 4.30 p.m.

Lieut: Colonel R.E.
C.R.E., 23rd Division.

Copy No.1 to 101st Field Coy., R.E.
2 102nd " " "
3 128th " " "
4 9th South Staffords.
5 C.E. II Corps.
6 C.E. XVIII Corps.
7 C.R.E., 14th Division.
8 C.R.E., 58th Division.
9 23rd Division "G".
10 " " "Q".
11 " " Train.
12-13 War Diary.
14. File.

SECRET.

TO ALL RECIPIENTS OF 23rd DIVISIONAL ARTILLERY
OPERATION ORDER No. 14.

Para. 2   For DOMINION CAMP (area) read DEVONSHIRE CAMP (area).
G.22.b.central.

[illegible signature]

Lieut: Colonel R.A.
C.R.A., 23rd Division.

25th August, 1917.

SECRET.

Copy No. 13.

23rd DIVISIONAL ENGINEERS

OPERATION ORDER No.26.

1. The 101st Fld. Coy., R.E., "B" & "C" Coys. 9th South Staffs and ½ Coy. 56th Divisional Pioneers will work in the Right Brigade Area and carry out the following work :-
   (i) Infantry and Mule Track ZILLEBEKE to I.24.b.0.8. and continued firstly as Infantry Track, and subsequently improved to mule track - thence to CLAPHAM JUNCTION and STIRLING CASTLE.
   (ii) Improve and repair existing track from near TRANSPORT FARM to ZILLEBEKE.
   Above tracks to be well notice boarded throughout - order of precedence (i) (ii).
   (iii) Water points to take filled petrol tins to be made in slits with splinter proof protection at about J.19.b.2.9. and J.13.d.1.8. close to tracks and marked with notice boards - in consultation with 69th Brigade.
   (iv) Forward Dumps of R.E. Stores for consolidation purposes to be made in consultation with 69th Brigade.
   (v) Visual Stations to be made at I.24.d.8.4. and CLAPHAM JUNCTION.

2. The 128th Fld. Coy., R.E., "A" Coy., 9th South Staffs and ½ Coy. 56th Divisional Pioneers will work in the Left Brigade Area and carry out the following work :-
   (i) Infantry Track, subsequently to be improved to Mule Track round HOOGE CRATER and alternative route to above 100 to 150 yards SOUTH.
   (ii) Infantry Track, subsequently to be improved to Mule Track HOOGE to J.7.d.85.15. (marked to GLENCORSE WOOD).
   (iii) Mule Track past HALFWAY HOUSE to MENIN ROAD at a point E. of HOOGE.
   Above tracks to be well notice boarded where necessary - order of precedence (i) = (ii), (iii).
   (iv) Water points to take filled petrol tins to be made in slits with splinter proof protection at about J.13.a.4.8. - in consultation with 68th Brigade who will make another water point in tunnels under MENIN ROAD.
   (v) Forward Dumps of R.E. Stores for consolidation purposes to be made in consultation with 68th Brigade.
   (vi) Visual Signal Stations to be made at J.13.b.2.5. and J.13.a.85.30.

3. The 102nd Fld. Coy., R.E. and "D" Coy. 9th South Staffs will carry out all work in R.E. Dump and Back Area in accordance with special instructions already given.

4. ACKNOWLEDGE.

26th August, 1917.
Issued at 11 p.m.

Lieut: Colonel R.E.
C.R.E., 23rd Division.

Copy No. 1 to 101st Field Coy., R.E.
2 102nd " " "
3 128th " " "
4 9th South Staffords.
5 Detachment 56th Divnl. Pioneers.
6 23rd Division "G".
7 " " "Q".
8 " " Signals.
9 68th Infantry Bde.
10 69th " "
11 70th " "
12-13 War Diary.
14 File.

CONFIDENTIAL

Vol 25

WAR DIARY

of

HQRE 23 Div

from

Sept 1st - Sept 30 1917

Instructions regarding War Diaries and Intelligence Summaries are contained in F. S. Regs., Part II. and the Staff Manual respectively. Title pages will be prepared in manuscript.

Army Form C. 2118.

WAR DIARY or INTELLIGENCE SUMMARY.

(Erase heading not required.)

H.Q. R.E. 23rd DIV. SEPT. 1917 (1)

Place	Date	Hour	Summary of Events and Information	Remarks and references to Appendices
DICKEBUSCH	2	–	Div. less R.E. & Pioneers moved out to EPERLECQUES area. H.Q. R.E. moved to Cavalry Camp (near DICKEBUSCH). C.R.E. Handed over work in the line to C.R.E. 25th Div.	
"	3	–	Instruction received that R.E. + Pioneers move to BERTHEN area on 4th	Appendix A
	4	9.0 am	C.R.E. office in Cavalry Camp closed	
	4	12.0 noon	C.R.E. office opened in L'Ecole, BERTHEN	
BERTHEN	8	–	General instruction sent to Coys. R.E. + Pioneers as to work to be done with ref. to forthcoming offensive.	Appendix B + C
"	9	.	C.R.E. Proceeded to 24th Div. at ZEVECOTEN as Liason Officer for R.E. works	Appendix D
"	10		102nd Field Coy R.E. + 3 Coys 9th S. Staffs proceeded to 24th Div. Area to assist in R.E. preparation for coming Offensive	Appendix E
	13	[illegible]	101st and 128th Field Coys R.E. and remainder of 9th S. Staffs moved out of BERTHEN area into WESTOUTRE area	Appendix F + H
	14	9	C.R.E. office closed at BERTHEN	
DICKEBUSCH	14	12	C.R.E. office opened at DICKEBUSCH 28/H 34 a.5.5 and took over from C.R.E. 24th Div. 101 and 128 Field Coys moved into billets in DICKEBUSCH area.	Appendix G
	14		Adv. Div. H.Q. stationed at H 34. a.5.5. Rear D.H.Q. at La Clytte. G.O.C. 23 Div took over from G.O.C. 24th	

8353 Wt. W2544/1454 700,000 5/15 D. D. & L. A.D.S.S./Forms/C. 2118.

Instructions regarding War Diaries and Intelligence Summaries are contained in F. S. Regs., Part II. and the Staff Manual respectively. Title pages will be prepared in manuscript.

Army Form C. 2118.

WAR DIARY
or
INTELLIGENCE SUMMARY.
(Erase heading not required.)

H.Q. R.E. 22nd Div — Sept. (contd) 2

Place	Date	Hour	Summary of Events and Information	Remarks and references to Appendices
DICKEBUSCH	14	–	Assembly position for offensive altered. MS	Appendix I
"	15		Capt. KIGGELL of 102nd Field Coy R.E. attached to H.Q. R.E. as Operation Officer MS	
			Capt BRAMWELL MO i/c R.E. attached (temporarily) to 69th Fld Amb.	
	18		Forward billets of Field Coys R.E. vacated in favour of 1st Australian Div. until Attack day. MS	Appendix K
DICKEBUSCH	20	5.40am	Attack day, and Attack launched	
		7.0am	Parties of 101st Field Coy R.E. and 128th Field Coy R.E. and 9th S. Staffs Regt (Pioneers) in assembly trenches and dugouts, R.Y. Dugouts.	
		11.0am	Parties of 101st Field Coy R.E. left assembly position to carry out their task	
		11.20am	68th Bde report Ground round DUMBARTON LAKES muddy but passable. BASSEVILLE BEEK very swampy – passable in places	
		12.45	Message from Major Turner (101st Fld Coy RE) All Brigade objectives taken – R.E. + Pioneers passed I. 18. d. 5. 1. at 12.30 pm on way to work.	
		1.45	S.P. "G" and track thereto commenced	
		3.0pm	S.P. "G" going strong. Track from STIRLING CASTLE to "G" marked with posts and notice boards throughout.	
		3.45pm	Parties ~~from~~ of 128th Field Coy left R.Y. Dugouts to commence work.	
		6.50pm	Col. Stephenson (9th S. Staffs) reports that Capt Cullen has returned with his party, and that S.P. "G" & "I" and tracks thereto are finished MS	

2353 Wt. W2544/1454 700,000 5/15 D. D. & L. A.D.S.S./Forms/C. 2118.

Instructions regarding War Diaries and Intelligence Summaries are contained in F. S. Regs., Part II. and the Staff Manual respectively. Title pages will be prepared in manuscript.

H.Q. R.E. 23rd Div

WAR DIARY or INTELLIGENCE SUMMARY.

(Erase heading not required.)

Sept. (Contd) (3)

Army Form C. 2118.

Place	Date	Hour	Summary of Events and Information	Remarks and references to Appendices
DICKEBUSCH	20	5.45	Report from 9th S Staffs timed 5.45 "Owing to TOWER HAMLETS not being taken we cannot start work on S.P. 'D' but are marking track to S.P. 'A' up to 6.15 am then take cover during attack and start again	
		6.0pm	Report from S. Staffs "3 Platoons now at work and doing well – Ground through DUMBARTON ~~LAKES~~ WOOD is very bad, most places appear ankle deep in mud	
		9.0pm	Lt WILSON (128th F.C.R.E.) reported in person. Bridge made across DUMBARTON LAKES and BASSEVILLE BEEK.	
	21	–	Works continued + improved	
"	23	–	Orders issued to the effect that R.E. + Pioneers will work under orders of C.E. X' Corps from 25th inst	Appendix L
	25	7.0	H.Q. R.E. closed at DICKEBUSCH	
WESTOUTRE	25	10.0	H.Q. R.E. opened at WESTOUTRE	
	26	–	Instruction from C.E. X' Corps that C.R.E. takes charge of completion of PLUMER DRIVE (between Observatory Ridge Road + Menin Road) on 27th	
"	28	10	H.Q. R.E. office closed at WESTOUTRE. C.R.E. 37th Div. carrying on until 23 Div.	
	28	11.	H.Q. R.E. office opened at MILLEKRUISE.	

[signature] Capt & Adj RE 23rd Div

#353 Wt. W2544/1454 700,000 5/15 D. D. & L. A.D.S.S./Forms/C. 2118.

SECRET [illegible] Copy No. 9.

Appendix A.

[illegible]

[illegible]

1. The [illegible] Divisional [illegible] will move into the [illegible] area on the [illegible] instant, and will move under their own arrangements.

2. All movements [illegible] - [illegible] to be by Companies at [illegible] paces distance.

3. Billeting parties should be sent today to report to Town Commandant [illegible] for billets for their units.

4. Completion of move and map reference of units to be notified by wire to [illegible].

5. [illegible] will close at present billets at [illegible] on [illegible] and open at [illegible] at 12 noon on the same date - map reference will be issued later.

6. ACKNOWLEDGE.

[illegible]

Issued at [illegible]. [illegible] Colonel, [illegible]

[illegible] [illegible] Division.

Copy No. 1 to [illegible]
2 [illegible]
3. [illegible]
4. [illegible]
5. [illegible]
6 [illegible]
7. [illegible]
8-9. [illegible]
10. File.

S E C R E T

COPY No. 10

Appendix B

23rd DIVISIONAL ENGINEERS

[illegible] No.89.

1. (a) The [illegible] Corps is to be prepared to take part in an attack by the Second Army - Preparations for this attack are to be completed by 10th September.

(b) The 23rd Division will be the left division of the attack.

2. The 68th Infantry Brigade will attack on the front from [illegible] (J.19.b.[illegible]) to junction [illegible] (J.19.a.7.7.) and 69th Infantry Brigade will attack on the [illegible] J.19.b.7.7. to [illegible] (J.14.c.2.9.)

The 70th Infantry Brigade will be in Divisional reserve.

3. The Divisional [illegible] Pioneers will carry out the following work.

128th Field Coy. R.E. - 68th Brigade Area [illegible]

[illegible]

1. Corner of Wood J.2[illegible].
2. Strongpoint J.20.a.6.3.
1 section R.E. + 1 platoon Pioneers + 1 platoon attached Infantry (carrying party) will be detailed for each of the above.

102nd Field Coy. R.E. - 69th Brigade Area - (Right)

[illegible]

3. Strongpoint [illegible]
4. Strongpoint [illegible]
1 section R.E. + 1 Platoon Pioneers + 1 platoon attached Infantry (carrying party) will be detailed for each of the above.

TRACKS

In addition the following [illegible], routes [illegible] by the [illegible].

(a) [illegible]

(b) TRACK [illegible] Junction of [illegible]

(c) TRACK [illegible]

(d) TRACK [illegible]

[illegible]

[illegible] the action [illegible]
[illegible]
On completion of [illegible] - rest and stand by [illegible].

5. 2 Sections 101st Field Coy. R.E. and 2 Sections 128th Field Coy. R.E. will be held in Company Reserve.

[illegible] Field Coy. R.E. and 2 Coys. 9th Bn. Staffs. (Pioneers) will be held in C.R.E.'s Reserve.

6. Place of Assembly -

[illegible] Western end of [illegible].

Troops will be in position at ZERO - 1 hour.

7. [illegible] reports of work done will be sent to [illegible] immediately on completion of task.

8. [illegible] will be at [illegible].

9. ACKNOWLEDGE.

[illegible signature]

8.9.17. Lieut. Colonel R.E.

Issued at 12.[illegible] p.m. C.R.E. 23rd Division.

Copy No.1 to 23rd Division "G".
2. " " "Q"
3. 68th Infantry Brigade.
4. 69th " "
5. 70th " "
6. 101st Field Coy. R.E.
7. 102nd " " "
8. 128th " " "
9. 9th South Staffs.
10-11. War Diary.
12-13. File.

SECRET. COPY NO. 9.

Appendix D

23rd DIVISIONAL ENGINEERS.

OPERATION ORDER No.30

The C.R.E. 23rd Division will proceed to the H.Q. 24th Division on the 9th instant and will remain there until the 23rd Division comes into the line - His office will remain at BERTHEN and all routine correspondence will be dealt with there.

Issued at 4.0.p.m.

8.9.17.

[signature]
Captain R.E.
for Lieut: Colonel R.E.
C.R.E. 23rd Division.

Copy No.1 to O.C. 101st Field Coy. R.E.
2. " 102nd " " "
3. " 128th " " "
4. " 9th Sth. Staffs.
5. 23rd Division "G"
6. " " "Q".
7. C.R.E. 24th Division.
8&9. War Diary.
10. File.

SECRET. COPY No. 13

23rd DIVISIONAL ENGINEERS.

OPERATION ORDER No. [illegible]

1. The 102nd Field Coy. R.E. and 3 Coys. 9th Sth. Staffs. will proceed to the 24th Division area on the 10th instant to work under the orders of the C.R.E. 24th Division on preparation for the coming offensive.

2. Location of Billets will be as follows:-

   102nd Field Coy. R.E. - H.36.c.8.4.

   2 Coys. 9th Sth. Staffs. - RAILWAY DUGOUTS (103rd Field Co. R.E. 24th Div. at Rly. Dugouts will point out billets).

   1 Coy. 9th Sth. Staffs. - [illegible] Huts. H.3.central.

   (129th Field Co. R.E. 24th Division at H.33.d.3.2. will point out billets).

   Horse lines H.34.d.3.2.

3. Units will move under their own arrangements, sending an officer to H.Q. C.R.E. 24th Division ([illegible]) in advance on the 10th instant to receive instructions as to work to be carried out commencing on the 11th instant.

4. Work must be pushed on as rapidly as possible.

5. Completion of move to be wired to Hd. Qrs. C.R.E. 23rd & 24th Divisions.

6. ACKNOWLEDGE.

[signature]

Lieut. Colonel R.E.

C.R.E. 23rd Division.

9.9.17.

Issued at 10.0 a.m.

Copy No.1 to 23rd Division "G"
2 " " " "
3 C.R.E. 24th Division.
4. O.C. 101st Field Coy. R.E.
5. " 102nd " " "
6. " 128th " " "
7. " 103rd " " " 24th Division.
8. " 129th " " " " "
9. " 9th Sth. Staffs.
10. " 23rd Divisional Train.
11-12. War Diary.
13-14 File.

SECRET. COPY No. 8.

[illegible] DIVISIONAL ENGINEERS

OPERATION ORDER No.[illegible].

1. [illegible] Field Coy. R.E. and [illegible] Field Coy. R.E. will march out independently from their present billets in the [illegible] AREA at [illegible] a.m. on the [illegible] instant - and march to the [illegible] AREA - via [illegible].

2. They will, on passing through [illegible], report to the [illegible], and be informed as to the location of their billets for the 13th and night 13/14th.

3. On the 14th instant, after noon, they will proceed to take over billets of the Field Companies [illegible] Division as previously instructed.

4. Completion of move to be wired to [illegible] Division.

ACKNOWLEDGE.

Issued at [illegible] p.m.

12.9.17.

Captain R.E.
for Lieut-Col. R.E.
C.R.E. [illegible] Division.

Copy No. 1 to [illegible] Division [illegible].
2 [illegible]
3 [illegible] Field Coy. [illegible]
4. [illegible]
5. [illegible]
6. [illegible]
7-8 War Diary.
9. File.

S E C R E T   COPY No. 16

23rd DIVISIONAL ENGINEERS.

OPERATION ORDER No.32.

1. 121st Field Coy. & 128th Field Coy. R.E. - H.Q. and B. Coy. 9th Sth. Staffs. will move into the line - 24th Division Area on the 14th instant.
Units will move under their own arrangements, but will not arrive at billets before 12 noon.

2. Billets will be as follows-

121st Field Coy. R.E.

Billets of 129th Fld. Coy. R.E. H.30.d.8.2. H.Q. & 2 Sections.
Railway Dugouts 2 Sections.

1 Officer & Billeting Party to report at H.30.d.8.2. on afternoon of 12th inst. and go round the line on 13th.

128th Field Coy. R.E.

Billets of 104th Field Coy. R.E. * H.34.c.4.4. H.Q. & 2 Sects
Railway Dugouts 2 Sections.

* On 14th this Coy. will go into billets vacated by 103rd Fld. Coy. R.E. at [illegible] FARM until departure of 104th Fld. Coy. R.E. at noon on 15th.
1 Officer and billeting party will report at H.34.c.4.4. on afternoon of 12th and go round the line on the 13th.

9th Sth. Staffs.

H.Q. & B. Coy. to billets of 12th Sherwood Foresters (Pioneers) H.32.c.5.8.
1 Officer and billeting party to be sent in advance.
C Company will move from present billet in [illegible] to H.[illegible].8 on the afternoon of the 14th instant.

Horse Lines of all above units are near the billets.

3. Instructions as to work to be carried out will be issued separately.

4. Work will be commenced on 15th instant and be pushed on as rapidly as possible.

5. Attached Infantry will report by mid-day 14th instant to each of the 3 Field Coys. - C.R.E. will arrange with [illegible] Brigades.

6.

6. H.Q.R.E. will close at BERTHEN at 10.0.a.m. on 14th instant and open at BURGOMASTER FARM at 11.a.m. on the same date.

7. ACKNOWLEDGE.

11.9.17.

Issued at 9.p.m.

Lieut: Colonel R.E.

C.R.E. 23rd Division.

Copy No.		
1	to	23rd Division "G"
2		" " "Q"
3.		" " Train.
4.		C.R.E. 24th Division.
5.		101st Field Coy. R.E.
6.		102nd " " "
7.		128th " " "
8.		103rd " " " 24th Division.
9.		104th " " " " "
10.		129th " " " " "
11.		9th Sth. Staffs. (P).
12.		12th Sherwood Foresters (P) 24th "
13.		24th Division "G"
14.		" " "Q"
15-16		War Diary.
17-18.		File.

S E C R E T   COPY No. 8.

23rd DIVISIONAL ENGINEERS

OPERATION ORDER No. 34.

1. 101st & 128th Field Coys.R.E. - H.Q. & 1 Coy. 9th Sth. Staffs. (Pioneers) will march out of present billets billets in BERTHEN AREA at 8.a.m. on 13th instant to WESTOUTRE AREA.
Billets will be allotted by Area Commandant WESTOUTRE AREA - (in WESTOUTRE).

2. Units will march from WESTOUTRE AREA on the 14th instant to billets in 24th Division Area in accordance with instructions contained in Operation Order No.33.

3. Completion of move and Map reference to be wired to H.Q.R.E. at BERTHEN and to C.R.E. 23rd Division care of C.R.E. 24th Division.

4. ACKNOWLEDGE.

Issued at 1.a.m.
13.9.17.

Captain R.E.
for Lt. Colonel R.E.
C.R.E. 23rd Division.

Copy No.1. to 23rd Div. "G".
2. " " "Q".
3. 101st Fld. Co. R.E.
4. 102nd " " "
5. 128th " " "
6. 9th Sth. Staffs.
7-8. War Diary.
9. File.
10. 23rd Divisional Train.

SECRET.   COPY No. 11

23rd DIVISIONAL ENGINEERS.

OPERATION ORDER No.35.

1. Ref. my Operation Order No.29 para 6.

Place of Assembly will be Western end of RAILWAY DUG-OUTS and not Western end of PROMENADE.

2. ACKNOWLEGE.

Lieut.Colonel R.E.
C.R.E. 23rd Division.

14/9/17.

Copy No. 1.to 23rd Division "G".
2. " " "Q".
3. 68th Infantry Brigade.
4. 69th " "
5. 70th " "
6. 101st Field Coy.R.E.
7. 102nd " " "
8. 128th " " "
9. 9th S.Staffords.
10-11. War Diary.
12-13. File.

SECRET COPY No. 11

Appendix C

23rd DIVISIONAL ENGINEERS

Amendments to OPERATION ORDER No.29.

(1) The following will be added to para. 3 Operation Order No.29.

SWAMP CROSSINGS.

4 Mat crossings will be laid across the swamp between the Lakes in J.20.a.
1 Section 128th Field Co. R.E. will be detailed for this work, and will be billetted in a forward dugout, location of which will be notified direct by 68th Infantry Brigade to O.C. 128th Field Co. R.E. - 68th Infantry Bde. will provide assistance in carrying material and laying mats.

DEMOLITIONS.

A party of 1 N.C.O. and 3 sappers with 8 mobile charges will be detailed by O.C. 101st Field Co. R.E. for demolition of dugout doors, they will be billetted in a forward dugout, location of which will be notified direct by 69th Infantry Bde. to O.C. 101st Field Coy. R.E.

TRAMWAYS.

That portion of tramway system between VALLEY COTTAGES and TOR TOP, switch to 41st Divisional line, and siding at Divisional Collecting Station will be maintained by the 9th Sth. Staffs - 2 Platoons 9th Sth. Staffs will be detailed for this work.

(2) Para. 5 will be amended to read.

2 Sections 101st Field Coy. R.E. and 1 Section 128th Field Coy. R.E. will be held in Company Reserve.

102nd Field Coy. R.E. and 6 Platoons 9th Sth. Staffs (Pioneers will be held in C.R.E's Reserve.

ACKNOWLEDGE.

[signature]
Lieut; Colonel R.E.
C.R.E. 23rd Division.

16.9.17.

Issued at 5.p.m.

Copy No.		
1	to	23rd Division "G".
2		" " "Q".
3		68th Infantry Bde.
4		69th " "
5		70th " "
6		101st Field Coy. R.E.
7		102nd " "
8		128th " "
9		9th Sth. Staffs.
10-11.		War Diary.
12-13.		File.

SECRET & URGENT COPY No. 19

23rd DIVISIONAL ENGINEERS.

OPERATION ORDER NO.36.

1. All billets occupied by R.E. & Pioneers in RAILWAY DUGOUTS West of Cutting at I.20.d.8.9. will be vacated before 2.p.m. today 18th instant - for temporary occupation by 1st ANZAC Division.

2. Forward Sections of 101st & 128th Field Coys. R.E., D Coy. and that portion of A.Coy. (if any) of 9th Sth. Staffs. billetted West of I.20.d.8.9. will march to Back Area billets of their units after work today - clearing RAILWAY DUGOUTS before 2.p.m. - arrangements have been made for additional accommodation in Back Area Billets.

3. Barrage rations will be left at RAILWAY DUGOUTS under charge of 9th Sth. Staffs.
Any further Barrage rations received today will also be sent up to RAILWAY DUGOUTS and placed under charge of 9th Sth. Staffs.

4. Party of 9th Sth. Staffs. billetted in TOR TOP for forward Area work, will on completion of work, return to Back Area Billets.

5. Work in forward area on 19th AND onwards will be carried out from Back Area billets.

6. No wheeled traffic will be allowed EAST of KRUISSTRAATHOEK VIERSTRAAT ROAD after night of September 19th except water carts and ambulances.
Any transport proceeding North of Canal will return by the MIDDLESEX ROAD.
Pack transport may accompany units.

7. Place of Assembly on "ATTACK DAY" will be Western end of RAILWAY DUGOUTS as previously ordered.
Units to be in position at ZERO + 1 hour and 40 minutes.

8. ACKNOWLEDGE.

Captain R.E.
For Lieut: Colonel R.E.
C.R.E. 23rd Division.

Issued at 7.30.a.m.

18.9.1917.

Copy No. 1 to 23rd Division "G"
2 " " "Q"
3 101st Field Co. R.E.
4 102nd " " "
5 128th " " "
6 9th Sth. Staffs.
7 68th Infantry Bde.
8 69th " "
9 70th " "
10 23rd Divisional Train.
11-12 War Diary.
13-14. File.

SECRET   COPY NO. ~~15~~ 14

23rd DIVISIONAL ENGINEERS

OPERATION ORDER 37.

(1) 23rd Divisional R.E. & Pioneers will come under the orders of the Xth Corps on the 25th instant.

Instructions as to work to be carried out will be communicated direct to units by the C.E. Xth Corps & C.R.E. Xth Corps Troops.

(2) Units will proceed to billets in the following areas on the 24th instant - Advanced parties will be sent today to arrange with Area Commandants for accommodation.

101st Field Coy. R.E.	BOESCHEPE AREA.
102nd " " "	MILLEKRUISSE AREA.
128th " " "	WESTOUTRE "

Units will march under their own arrangements but must be clear of their billets before 10.0.a.m.
9th Sth Staffs. will remain in present billets.
Completion of moves to be wired to H.Q.R.E.

(3) 101st, 102nd & 128th Field Coys. R.E. will hand over work in the line, maps, documents, billets etc. to the 11th, 212th & Field Coys. R.E. 33rd Division respectively.

9th Sth. Staffs. (P) will hand over work, plans & documents to 19th Middlesex (P).

(4) H.Q.R.E. will close at present billets at 7.a.m. on the 25th instant, and open at WESTOUTRE at 8.0.a.m. on the same date.

(5) ACKNOWLEDGE.

Issued at 7.30.p.m.   Lieut: Colonel R.E.

23rd Sept. 1917.   C.R.E. 23rd Division.

Copy No.1 to 23rd Division "G"
2 " " "Q"
3 C.R.E. 33rd Division.
4 O.C. 101st Fiel Coy. R.E.
5 " 102nd " " "
6 " 128th " " "
7 " 11th " " ")
8 " 212th " " ") 33rd Division.
9 " 222nd " " ")
10 " 9th Sth. Staffs.
11 " 18th Middlesex Regt. " "
12 " 23rd Divisional Train.
13 - 14 War Diary.
15 File.
16 C.E. Xth. Corps.
17 C.R.E. " " Troops.

Vol 26

CONFIDENTIAL

WAR DIARY

of

HEADQUARTERS R.E 23rd DW

OCT. 1

to

OCT 31

Instructions regarding War Diaries and Intelligence Summaries are contained in F. S. Regs., Part II. and the Staff Manual respectively. Title pages will be prepared in manuscript.

H.Q. R.E. 23rd Div

WAR DIARY or INTELLIGENCE SUMMARY.

(Erase heading not required.)

OCTOBER 1917 ①

Army Form C. 2118.

Place	Date	Hour	Summary of Events and Information	Remarks and references to Appendices
MILLEKRUISSE	1	–	Work on PLUMER DRIVE in hand	SMS
"	3	–	Instruction received that C.R.E. 33rd Div will take over work on PLUMER DRIVE	Mm
"	4	12 noon	C.R.E. 33rd Div took over work + billets from CRE 23rd Div. Office closed at MILLEKRUISE	MM
METEREN	4	4 pm	C.R.E. office opened at METEREN.	MM Appendix A.
"	5	–	9th S Staff relieved and withdrawn to rest to enable them to send away a draft of about 400, and absorb a draft of 400 Sappers. 101, 102 & 128 Field Coys remain under C.R.E. X Corps Troops for work	MM Appendix B
"	9	–	Instruction issued for relief of 7th Div. by 23rd Div.	MM
"	11	9.30	C.R.E.s office Closed Meteren instead of on 12th	MM
Café Belge	11	12.0	C.R.E.s Office opened ANZAC CAMP – Café Belge	
"	12	–	Field Coys employed as follows. 102 + 128 Field Coy RE on forward tracks 101 Field Coy RE on dugout accomodation in HOOGE & ZILLEBEKE BUND and general work on D.H.Q.	MM
"	13-21		Work carried on as described above	MM
"	22		Field Coys R.E. and Pioneers moved to BERTHEN area. R.E. to work on hutments and Pioneers to reorganise. C.R.E. received instruction to report to E in C for a conference	Appendix C MM

2353 Wt. W2544/1454 700,000 5/15 D. D. & L. A.D.S.S./Forms/C. 2118.

Army Form C. 2118.

Instructions regarding War Diaries and Intelligence Summaries are contained in F. S. Regs., Part II. and the Staff Manual respectively. Title pages will be prepared in manuscript.

H.Q. R.E. 23rd Div

WAR DIARY
or
INTELLIGENCE SUMMARY.
(Erase heading not required.)

OCTOBER 1917

(2)

Place	Date	Hour	Summary of Events and Information	Remarks and references to Appendices
HESTOUTRE	22	12.0	H.Q. R.E. opened at M.8 c.o.u. (ARAGON CAMP)	[initials]
"	23	9.0am	C.R.E. (Lt/Col Rooke) proceeded to E.i.C. office G.H.Q.	[initials]
"	26		Wire received that Lt/Col. Rooke R.E. had been admitted to Hospital sick	[initials]
	30		Wire received that Bt Lt Col (T/Lt Col) C.E.P. SANKEY. D.S.O. R.E. appointed C.R.E. 23rd Div.	[initials]
	28	12.30	Instructions received for Field Coy R.E. & Pioneers, 23rd Div. to hold themselves in readiness to move at short notice, destination unknown	[initials]
	31	5.0pm	Bt Lt Col (T/Lt Col) C.E.P. SANKEY D.S.O., R.E. arrived H.Q. R.E.	
	"		Wire received from Lt. Col E.H. ROOKE. R.E. stating he was rejoining on 1st Nov.	[initials]

[signature] Capt. & Adjt. R.E.
C.R.E. 23rd Div.

S E C R E T COPY No. 17

Appendix A

23rd DIVISIONAL ENGINEERS.

OPERATION ORDER 38.

C.R.E. 33rd Division will take over billets and work on PLUMER DRIVE from C.R.E. 23rd Division on 4th October at 12.0. noon.

C.R.E. 33rd Division and H.Q.R.E. will move on that date to METEREN AREA.

3.10.17.

Issued at 8.0.p.m.

[signature] Lieut: Colonel R.E.

C.R.E. 23rd Division.

Copy No.1 to C.E. Xth Corps.
2 23rd Division G.
3. " " Q.
4 " " Sigs.
5 S.S.O. 23rd Division.
6 3rd Canadian Tunnelling Coy.
7 175th Tunnelling Coy. R.E.
8 101st Field Coy. R.E.
9 102nd " " "
10 128th " " "
11 222nd " " "
12 9th Sth. Staffs.
13 18th Middlesex.
14 1/6th Argyll & Sutherland Highlanders.
15 Lieut: Sainsbury c/o 6th Monmouths.
16-17 War Diary.
18. File.

S E C R E T   COPY NO. 12

Appendix 13

23rd DIVISIONAL ENGINEERS.

OPERATION ORDER 39.

(1) 23rd Division will relieve the 7th Division in the line night 11th/12th.

(2) 23rd Divisional R.E. will cease to work under Xth Corps after work on 10th and take over billets from the Field Coys. R.E. WORKING in 7th Divisional Area on 11th instant, and work in the line from 12th instant inclusive. 102nd Field Coy. R.E. will work in Right Sub-sector.-
128th Field Coy. R.E. will work in Left Sub-sector.
101st Field Coy. R.E. will work in Back Area.

(3) Coys. will send advanced parties to reconnoitre billets and work on the 10th instant - reporting to C.R.E's Office 7th Division at H.30.a.5.0. (near CHATEAU SEGARD) for information. as to Map Locations of their opposite numbers.

(4) 9th Sth. Staffs. will remain out of the line until its re-organisation is complete.

(5) H.Q.R.E. will move from present billets to vicinity of CHATEAU SEGARD on morning of 12th October.

(6) ACKNOWLEDGE.

9.10.17.

Issued at 11.15.p.m.

J M Hamden Capt RE
for Lieut. Colonel R.E.
C.R.E. 23rd Division.

Copy No.	to	
1		O.C. 101st Field Coy. R.E.
2		" 102nd " " "
3		" 128th " " "
4		" 9th Sth. Staffs.
5.		C.R.E.Xth Corps Troops.
6		C.E. " "
7		C.R.E. 7th Division.
8		Headquarters "G" 23rd Division.
9.		" "Q" " "
10.		23rd Div. Train.
11-12		War Diary.
13.		File.

Appendix C

SECRET COPY NO. 11.

23rd DIVISIONAL ENGINEERS.

AMENDMENTS TO OPERATION ORDER NO.40.

Reference O.O.40 para. 4.

H.Q.R.E. 23rd Division will close at ANZAC CAMP on 22nd instant at 9.0.a.m. and reopen at WESTOUTRE same date.

21.10.17.

Issued at 3.45.p.m.

Lieut: Colonel R.E.

C.R.E. 23rd Division.

To recipients of O.O.40.

Appendix [illegible]

SECRET. COPY NO. 12

23rd DIVISIONAL ENGINEERS.

OPERATION ORDER NO.4[illegible].

1. 23rd Divisional R.E. will come under the orders of C.R.E. Xth Corps Troops on the 23rd inst.
Instructions as to work to be carried out will be communicated direct to units by C.R.E. Xth Corps Troops.

2. Units will cease work in the line after work on 21st instant.

3. Units will march under their own arrangements to billets in following areas on the 22nd instant, but must be clear of their billets before 10.0 a.m. Advance parties will be sent on 21st instant to arrange billets.

101st Field Coy. R.E.	Remain as at present.
102nd " " "	Xth Corps Signal School M.14.b.7.0. Horselines M.15.d.7.1. (Take over from 95th Fld. Co)
128th " " "	[illegible] Area. Q.24.[illegible].3.8. 5 Off. 120 o.rs ~~& Horselines~~. Q.24.d.3.9. 2 Off. 100 o.r. & Horselines.
9th Bn. S.Staffs.	To MICMAC Camp on 22nd. To [illegible] Camp on 23rd in accordance with instructions already wired.

Completion of move to be wired [illegible].

4. Move of [illegible] will be notified later.

5. ACKNOWLEDGE.

[signature]

21.10.17. Lieut.-Colonel R.E.

Issued at [illegible] C.R.E. 23rd Division.

Copy No.1 to O.C. 101st Field Coy. R.E.
2. " 102nd " "
3 " 128th " "
4 [illegible]
5 O.C. Xth Corps Signal[illegible].
6 C.R.E. Xth Corps Troops.
7 23rd Division.
8 [illegible]
9 [illegible]
10. [illegible]
11-12. War Diary.
13 File.
14. C.R.E. [illegible] Division.

2.(a) 101st, 102nd, 128th Field Coys. R.E. & 9th Sth. Staffs. will hand over work in the line, maps & documents to 98th, 126th, 97th Field Coys. R.E. and 14th N.F. respectively on 22nd.
102nd & 128th Field Coys. R.E. will hand over billets to 97th & 98th Field Coys. respectively on 22nd inst.

Secret

Vol 13

War Diary

of

H.Q. R.E. 23rd Division

from Sept 1st 1916 to Sept 30th 1916.

Army Form C. 2118.

WAR DIARY
or
INTELLIGENCE SUMMARY.
(*Erase heading not required.*)

Instructions regarding War Diaries and Intelligence Summaries are contained in F. S. Regs., Part II. and the Staff Manual respectively. Title pages will be prepared in manuscript.

Sept (1) H.Q. R.E 23rd Division

Place	Date	Hour	Summary of Events and Information	Remarks and references to Appendices
BAILLEUL	1/9/16 to 3/9/16		Field Coys still employed on front line system, remodelling firetrenches, building up parapets. Constructing deep dug-outs and reinforced concrete ditto for Battn H.Q etc. A number of concrete T.M. positions are also under construction. Comm: trenches are being improved & drained. The hutting programme is being carried on with rapidly also the horse standings & shelters. HJ3	
"	4/9/16		Orders recd that C.R.E 19th Divn would take over from us on 6th inst. 101st Fd Co R.E was relieved by part of 82nd Fd Co RE & marched to LA BOURSE. 102nd Fd Co RE was relieved by part of 82nd Fd Co RE & marched to FLETRE area. 128th Fd Co RE was relieved by 94th Fd Co RE & also moved to FLETRE area HJ3	

A.H. Bremner [signature]
Lt. Colonel.
Commanding Royal Engineers.
23rd Division

2353 Wt. W2544/1454 700,000 5/15 D. D. & L. A.D.S.S./Forms/C. 2118.

Army Form C. 2118.

WAR DIARY
or
INTELLIGENCE SUMMARY.
(*Erase heading not required.*)

Instructions regarding War Diaries and Intelligence Summaries are contained in F. S. Regs., Part II. and the Staff Manual respectively. Title pages will be prepared in manuscript.

Sept (2) H.Q. R.E 23rd Divn

Place	Date	Hour	Summary of Events and Information	Remarks and references to Appendices
BAILLEUL	5/9/16		Dismounted personnel of Field Coys entrained at BAILLEUL for S.T OMER thence marched to BLEU MAISON area. The transport of all Field Coys & H.Q. RE under the command of Capt D. BAIRD RE 101st F.C. C RE proceeded by road staying the night at HONDEGHEM from thence to billets on 6th inst. HGE	
"	6/9/16		Handing over to C.R.E 19th Divn completed. H.Q. R.E moved to TILQUES HGE	
TILQUES	7/9/16		H.Q. R.E & all Field Coys resting. HGE	
" "	8/9/16		H.Q. R.E & all Field Coys resting, overhauling kit equipment etc. Orders recd for Divn to entrain at ARQUES on 10th for the SOMME area HGE	

A.G. Bremner Lt-Colonel, Commanding Royal Engineers, 23rd Division

2353 Wt. W2544/1454 700,000 5/15 D. D. & L. A.D.S.S./Forms/C. 2118.

Army Form C. 2118.

WAR DIARY
or
INTELLIGENCE SUMMARY.
(*Erase heading not required.*)

Instructions regarding War Diaries and Intelligence Summaries are contained in F. S. Regs., Part II. and the Staff Manual respectively. Title pages will be prepared in manuscript.

Sept (3) H.Q. R.E 23rd Division

Place	Date	Hour	Summary of Events and Information	Remarks and references to Appendices
TILQUES	9/9/16		C.R.E proceeded to SOMME area by motor in advance. Advance billeting parties were also sent ahead by train HGE	
" "	10/9/16		H.Q. R.E and all Field Coys marched to ARQUES and entrained with all horses & transport. H.Q. R.E detrained SALEUX at 11 P.M and marched to ALLONVILLE HGE	
ALLONVILLE	11/9/16		H.Q. R.E and all 3 Field Coys are billeted at ALLONVILLE. Orders rec^d to move to BRESLE on 12th	
BRESLE	12/9/16		H.Q. R.E and 3 Field Coys marched to BRESLE. No billets available so coys slept out. HGE	
" "	13/9/16		128th Fd Co R.E moved up to BECOURT wood, 1/2 Coy is attached to 15th Divn for work on light railways & 1/2 Coy is attached to 50th Divn also for work on tramways. 101st & 102nd Fd Coys erecting shelters. HGE	

A.G. Bremner Lt Colonel Commanding Royal Engineers 23rd Division

8353 Wt. W2544/1454 700,000 5/15 D. D. & L. A.D.S.S./Forms/C. 2118.

Army Form C. 2118.

Instructions regarding War Diaries and Intelligence Summaries are contained in F. S. Regs., Part II. and the Staff Manual respectively. Title pages will be prepared in manuscript.

WAR DIARY
or
INTELLIGENCE SUMMARY.
(Erase heading not required.)

Sept (4) H.Q. R.E 23rd Divn

Place	Date	Hour	Summary of Events and Information	Remarks and references to Appendices
BRESLE	14 9/16		H.Q. R.E & 2 Field Coys standing by under orders to move at 2 hrs notice. A few hut shelters have been erected for men of Field Coys H9E	
BRESLE	15 9/16 to 18 9/16		Field Coys standing by waiting to move. The hut shelters have been completed and a number of deep latrines dug throughout the village H9E	
"	19 9/16		R.E relieved R.E of 15th Divn in accordance with C.R.E's Order No S.D. 14 (see Appendix 1) H.Q. R.E moved to camp on MILLENCOURT – ALBERT road 101st Fd Co R.E is at BECOURT WOOD 102 " " " " SHELTER WOOD	

A.G. Bremner Lt Colonel,
Commanding Royal Engineers
23rd Division

H9E

Instructions regarding War Diaries and Intelligence Summaries are contained in F. S. Regs., Part II. and the Staff Manual respectively. Title pages will be prepared in manuscript.

WAR DIARY
or
INTELLIGENCE SUMMARY.
(*Erase heading not required.*)

Army Form C. 2118.

Sept (5) H.Q. R.E 23rd Divn

Place	Date	Hour	Summary of Events and Information	Remarks and references to Appendices
CAMP W.26.c.0.4	20 9/16 to 30 9/16		Field Coys taking over, + carrying on work of 7th Coy 15th Divn. 101st Fd Coy RE are working on improvement of roads CONTALMAISON - LABOISSELLE and CONTALMAISON MARTINPUICH. 102nd Fd Coy R.E are doing defence works in forward area principally strong posts in front of MARTINPUICH, wiring of same + wiring trenches on each flank. 128th Fd Coy R.E are laying light trench railway up to MARTINPUICH via CONTALMAISON. This is progressing well. Sidings are being put in. and the whole line ballasted, and graded. The Divnl Dump for R.E materials is at the CUTTING CONTALMAISON stores are being sent up daily. Operations hampered by wet weather.	

A G Brennan Lt-Colonel,
Commanding Royal Engineers.
23rd Division.

€353 Wt. W2544/1454 700,000 5/15 D. D. & L. A.D.S.S./Forms/C. 2118.

23RD DIVISION

DEP. ASST DIR. ORDNANCE SERVICES

AUG 1915 - ~~FEB 1919~~ 1917 OCT

TO ITALY

121/7595.

Q

D.A.D.O.S. 23rd Divn.

23rd Aug. to 31 Oct 1915

Vol. I

Feb '19

Nil Appx

Confidential

War Diary
of

Major W.L.G. Bishop DADOS 23rd Divn

From 23·8·15 to 31st August 1915

Instructions regarding War Diaries and Intelligence Summaries are contained in F. S. Regs., Part II. and the Staff Manual respectively. Title pages will be prepared in manuscript.

WAR DIARY

or

~~INTELLIGENCE SUMMARY.~~

(*Erase heading not required.*)

Army Form C. 2118.

Place	Date	Hour	Summary of Events and Information	Remarks and references to Appendices
St Omer	23 8/15	12.30 pm	Landed at Boulogne from Folkestone Boat & proceeded direct to St Omer Reporting arrival to DDOS GHQ same evening.	
	24th } 25th }		Remained in St Omer awaiting arrival of Division, time occupied by receiving, taking down, & reading up, various orders & instructions relating to duties, also reported to Ordnance Communications, by instruction, how Division stood with regard to Smoke Helmets	
Tilque	26th		Left St Omer for H.Q. Offices at Tilque, Offices started same evening. Indents commenced to be received from Units.	
	27th		Ordinary duties at H.Q. Furnished various reports as to description of Arms & Equipment in Divn	
	28th		Visited A.O.D. Calais, drew urgent Stores & made certain arrangements regarding despatch &c	
	29th		Ordinary duties in connection with indents &c St Omer made Railhead.	
	30th		Instructed to proceed to Hazebrouck & report to DDOS 2nd Army with a view to obtaining permission to visit the refilling point of one of the D.O.O.s of 2nd Army in order to see the actual working of the system of stores sent up to Railhead from Base & distribution to Troops. The D.O.O. I visited was attached to the 49th Division. Much useful information is gained from these visits. I returned to Tilque the same day.	
	31st		Amongst other stores arriving from Base today, were the first portion of the Divisional Reserve of Smoke Helmets, 11000 were received & stored in one of the stables attached to the building used as Divisional Head Quarters.	

[signature] Major
DDOS
23 Division

2353 Wt. W2544/1454 700,000 5/15 D. D. & L. A.D.S.S./Forms/C. 2118.

Confidential

War Diary

of

Major W.L.G. Bishop DADOS 23 Division

From 1. 9. 15. To 30. 9. 15.

Instructions regarding War Diaries and Intelligence Summaries are contained in F. S. Regs., Part II. and the Staff Manual respectively. Title pages will be prepared in manuscript.

WAR DIARY

~~or~~

~~INTELLIGENCE SUMMARY.~~

(*Erase heading not required.*)

Army Form C. 2118.

Place	Date	Hour	Summary of Events and Information	Remarks and references to Appendices
Tilque	1.9.15		Placed first order for Breech rifle Covers at St Omer. 8 Bomb Guns & 8 Catapults received for the Division.	
	2.9.15 3.9.15 4.9.15 5.9.15		Ordinary duties in connection with the supply of stores. Small consignment of stores coming up each day	
Renescure	6.9.15		Division left for Renescure, arrived the same evening.	
Merris	7.9.15		Left Renescure for Merris, arrived the same evening with a large consignment of stores which could not be disposed of to the Troops on the march. Took over a Shed to store them in until Troops were able to draw.	
	8.9.15		Hazebrouck Garage appointed Railhead	
	9.9.15		Stores coming up from Base Regularly. 22000 Respirators were received today for issue to the Troops as a second anti gas appliance, until sufficient Tube [?] Helmets become available. Wired for Blankets for the Division	
	10.9.15		Ordinary duties	
	11.9.15		4th Lewis machine gun for each Battalion of Division received & issued.	
	12.9.15		Ordinary duties	
	13.9.15		Blankets for Division arrived in 6 trucks at Hazebrouck Station. Wire received from D.A.C. that a G.S. Wagon containing 4.5" Ammunition had fallen into Canal. Ammunition recovered & sent to Base for examination. The wagon was rendered unserviceable & also sent to Base. A new wagon being supplied.	

Army Form C. 2118.

WAR DIARY

or

~~INTELLIGENCE SUMMARY.~~

(Erase heading not required.)

Instructions regarding War Diaries and Intelligence Summaries are contained in F. S. Regs., Part II. and the Staff Manual respectively. Title pages will be prepared in manuscript.

Place	Date	Hour	Summary of Events and Information	Remarks and references to Appendices
Merris	14.9.15		First Consignment of Tube helmets received.	
	15.9.15		Conveyed tube helmets to Rolanderie & Rue Marle for 69th and 70th Infantry Brigades.	
Croix du Bac	16.9.15		Left Merris for Croix du Bac, visited Ordnance Travelling Workshops and arranged programme with the D.O.M. regarding the Conversion of the Water Carts in possession of units of the Division.	
	17.9.15 18.9.15		Bac St Maur appointed Railhead. The 4 Lorries were ~~[illegible]~~ taxed to their utmost, owing to the large quantity of stores, blankets &c as well as the Divisional Reserve of Smoke helmets having to be brought up from Merris.	
	19.9.15		Took over 3 small stables at L'Epinette to be used for keeping out stores for issue.	
	20.9.15 21.9.15		Ordinary duties, Large Consignments of stores, clothing were received during these 2 days	
	22.9.15		Proceeded to Bethune & placed order for 208 Trench Stretchers.	
	23.9.15		Divisional Armourers shops started at Erquinghem Lys.	
	24.9.15 25.9.15 26.9.15		Tube helmets having been provided for every officer & man in the Division, the respirators are being withdrawn & will be sent to the Base.	
	27.9.15		Purchased first lot of Bomb carriers at Estaires.	
	28.9.15		The Armourers shop started a few days ago is doing excellent work. 7 Armourer Sergts are working continuously in the repair of rifles. The long rifles with which the Infantry Bns are armed require a lot of attention & cases of bursts have already occurred.	
	29.9.15		Obtained from St Omer the balance of the Breech rifle covers due.	
	30.9.15		Ordinary duties, Stores coming up from Base regularly.	

[illegible] Bishop Major
DADOS
23 Div

2353 Wt. W2544/1454 700,000 5/15 D. D. & L. A.D.S.S./Forms/C. 2118.

CONFIDENAL

WAR DIARY

OF

MAJOR BISHOP

DADOS 23RD DIVN

1ST TO 31ST OCTOBER 1915

Army Form C. 2118.

Instructions regarding War Diaries and Intelligence Summaries are contained in F. S. Regs., Part II. and the Staff Manual respectively. Title pages will be prepared in manuscript.

WAR DIARY
~~or~~
~~INTELLIGENCE SUMMARY.~~
(Erase heading not required.)

Place	Date	Hour	Summary of Events and Information	Remarks and references to Appendices
Croix Du Bac	1/10/15. 2/10.		Ordinary duties in connection with supply of stores	
	3/10		As Braziers were not forthcoming from the Base, a number of paint & oil drums were collected & in this manner about 150 were improvised.	
	4/10		Many of the long rifles in use of the Infantry are being brought to the armoury for repair, bolts loose causing in some instances miss fires.	
	5/10		Divisional Baths being fitted out with Shirts, Socks, drawers & Vests in order to supply each man bathing with a clean shift.	
	6/10 7/10 8/10		Nothing of importance, stores coming up very well from the Base, usually 1 truck per day arrives occasionally there are 2 or 3 trucks.	
	9/10 10/10 11/10		Short rifles in possession of RA, ASC, AOC, AVC, Divisional Supply column and other small Units, withdrawn & handed over to Infantry Bns: a similar number of long rifles being withdrawn, the necessary bayonets suitable for the short rifle being sent up from the Base.	
	12/10 13/10		The long rifles withdrawn from the Infantry have been reissued to RA. &c as a temporary measure until such time as the old rifles eventually to be supplied to these units are received.	
	14/10		Ordinary duties, nothing of importance.	
	15/10		Helmets of Tube [illegible], suitable for practice purposes are to be collected from Railheads & marked D.P. First consignment of Thigh [illegible] boots received & issued to 68 & 69 Infantry Brigades.	
	16/10		Nothing of importance.	
	17/10		One hundred Steel trench helmets were received & issued to 68 & 69 Infantry Brigades on trial.	
	18/10 19/10		Nothing of importance, stores still coming up from Base regularly & in good quantities.	
	20/10		The long rifles taken from 1st Lorry Drivers, clerks &c sent to Base.	

2353 Wt. W2544/1454 700,000 5/15 D. D. & L. A.D.S.S./Forms/C. 2118.

Army Form C. 2118.

WAR DIARY

~~or~~

~~INTELLIGENCE SUMMARY.~~

(*Erase heading not required.*)

Instructions regarding War Diaries and Intelligence Summaries are contained in F. S. Regs., Part II. and the Staff Manual respectively. Title pages will be prepared in manuscript.

Place	Date.	Hour	Summary of Events and Information	Remarks and references to Appendices
Croix Du Bac	21/10		101st Fd Co R.E. temporarily attached to 28th Division, rejoins.	
	22/10 – 23/10		Nothing of importance, Stores are coming up from the Base regularly & Everything is working smoothly.	
	24/10		A certain number of P. Tube Helmets being available for Drill Purposes, first issue is made to Infantry Bns.	
	25/10		The rifles withdrawn from Stretcher Bearers were sent to Base today	
	26/10 – 27/10		Further supplies of Thigh Gum Boots were received & distributed to Battalions. These boots appear to be a great boon to the men, judging by the number of applications made for them.	
	28/10		Special Bulk indent for winter clothing sent to Base	
	29/10		Third distribution of Thigh Gum boots made to Infantry Brigades.	
	30/10		Reported to Advance Base that I could deal with 24 tons clothing & stores per day, in order to push out the winter clothing.	
	31/10		200 Suits C.S.L. received for issue to units requiring them. 300 sets of bottoms are notified as coming up also.	
			L. Bishop Major DADOS 23 Div.	

2353 Wt. W2544/1454 700,000 5/15 D. D. & L. A.D.S.S./Forms/C. 2118.

H.Q. 23rd Div:
D.A.D.O.S.
Vol: 2

121/7678

P

Nov 15.

Confidential

War Diary

of

Major W.S.C.G. Bishop D.A.D.O.S. 28th Div

From 1st November 1915 To 30th November 1915

Forwarded to D.A.G.
Base.

Instructions regarding War Diaries and Intelligence Summaries are contained in F. S. Regs., Part II. and the Staff Manual respectively. Title pages will be prepared in manuscript.

WAR DIARY

~~or~~

~~INTELLIGENCE SUMMARY.~~

(Erase heading not required.)

Army Form C. 2118.

Place	Date	Hour	Summary of Events and Information	Remarks and references to Appendices
Croix Du Bac	1/11/15 & 2/11/15	-	Various reports received regarding the misfires with the long rifle. Letter respecting complete exchange of these rifles for short rifles sent forward.	
	3/11.	-	200 Traversor mats for use with barbed wire received & issued	
	4/11	-	400 Pairs F.S. Boots arrived	
	5/11	-	300 Sets of Tent Bottoms arrived & were off loaded on banks of the River Lys, arranged for their transport to a safer place. Sent an Armourer Staff Sergt to Aire with samples of the defective rifle	
	6/11		1000 pairs of thigh gum boots arrived & were issued.	
	7/11		334 pairs of Shoepacks arrived & were issued. Armourers report on long rifles forwarded	
	8/11		33 Sets of Salvus Breathing apparatus received. Instructions received to select any Infantry Battalion & have the whole of the long rifles examined & gauged.	
	9/11		Nothing of importance. Inspection of long rifles proceeding.	
	10/11		Conference at H.Q. 3rd Corps	
	11/11		Inspection of long rifles of Bn selected completed & report sent to Aire. Large consignment of fur undercoats arrived.	
	12/11		305 Pairs of thigh gum boots, also 1 Shield Parapet Machine Gun for trial arrived.	
	13/11		Instructions received to have all long rifles in which bolt closes over ·074 gauge exchanged.	
	14/11		12 Catapults received & were issued.	

2353 Wt. W2544/1454 700,000 5/15 D. D. & L. A.D.S.S./Forms/C. 2118.

Instructions regarding War Diaries and Intelligence Summaries are contained in F. S. Regs., Part II. and the Staff Manual respectively. Title pages will be prepared in manuscript.

WAR DIARY

~~or~~

~~INTELLIGENCE SUMMARY.~~

(Erase heading not required.)

Army Form C. 2118.

Place	Date	Hour	Summary of Events and Information	Remarks and references to Appendices
Divn. Ord. Dep.	15/11/15		5 – 9.5 m/m Mortars received from 1st Corps for conversion to 4 pdrs.	
	16/11	–	Nothing of importance.	
	17/11	–	400 Lanterns tent folding received, also 2 sets of 5 Baths with 2 heaters, as gifts.	
	18/11	–	2 – 9.5 m/m Mortars received from Bomb School Bethune for conversion to 4 pdrs.	
	19/11	–	Nothing of importance	
	20/11	–	1362 Magazines for Lewis Guns received, this completes Division to Authorized Scale	
	21/11	–	Winter clothing still coming up from Base.	
	22/11	–	Nothing of importance	
	23/11	–	2 Hand Carts drawn from 1st Army Heavy Mobile Shop & issued to 12 Trench Mortar Battery.	
	24/11	–	Nothing of importance	
	25/11	–	1996 pairs of thigh gum boots taken over from 8th Division.	
	26/11	–	Nothing of importance	
	27/11	–		
	28/11	–	6 West Spring guns received & issued to 68 & 24th Infantry Brigades.	
	29/11	–	Nothing of importance	
	30/11	–	Demanded 200 long rifles to replace those which failed the test of examination	

[signature] Lieut. D.A.D.O.S. 23 Div.

2353 Wt. W2544/1454 700,000 5/15 D. D. & L. A.D.S.S./Forms/C. 2118.

D.A.D.O.S. 23rd Div:

Vol: 3

121
7809.

Dec. 15

Confidential

23rd DIVISIONAL HEADQUARTERS
A 802
1. 1. 16

War Diary

of

Major W. L. G. Bishop A.O.D. DADOS 23 Division

From 1/12/15 to 31/12/15.

Instructions regarding War Diaries and Intelligence Summaries are contained in F. S. Regs., Part II. and the Staff Manual respectively. Title pages will be prepared in manuscript.

Army Form C. 2118.

WAR DIARY of Major W.S.G. Bishop A.O.D. ~~or INTELLIGENCE SUMMARY~~. D.A.D.O.S. 23rd Division

(Erase heading not required.)

Place	Date	Hour	Summary of Events and Information	Remarks and references to Appendices
Croix Du Bac	1/12/15	–	Nothing of importance.	
	2/12	–	A large consignment of General Stores, & Boots arrived, also 22 Sappers Stores.	
	3/12		Truck 6313 failed to arrive with convoy today, reported non arrival to Base.	
	4/12		Wire received truck 6313 derailed, will be sent as early as possible.	
	5/12		Truck 6313 arrived	
	6/12		Report on examination of rifles of 4 Battalions forwarded.	
	7/12		2 Limbers G.S. 18 pr Carriage arrived for D/104 Bde R.F.A. & were issued.	
	8/12		1122 Pairs thigh gum boots received.	
	9/12		Obtained pattern of suitable clog, submitted it for approval.	
	10/12		Gave an order for the manufacture of 400 prs of clogs at 4 Frs per pair, to a firm at Laventie.	
	11/12		Nothing of importance	
	12/12		19600 Tube helmets arrived, towards the requirements of 2nd tube helmet per officer & man. Chemical Adviser 1st Army inspected Salvus sets before issue & found 7 sets requiring adjustment.	
	13/12		130 Pairs short gum boots received for issue to those working in horse lines &c. 200 Lugs[illegible] arrived.	
	14/12		D.D.O.S. 1st Army inspected a number of long rifles received yesterday & found 11 unserviceable.	
	15/12		R.A. completed with 2nd Tube helmet, also 6 Battalions.	

2353 Wt. W2544/1454 700,000 5/15 D. D. & L. A.D.S.S./Forms/C. 2118.

Army Form C. 2118.

Instructions regarding War Diaries and Intelligence Summaries are contained in F. S. Regs., Part II. and the Staff Manual respectively. Title pages will be prepared in manuscript.

WAR DIARY
~~or~~
~~INTELLIGENCE SUMMARY.~~
(Erase heading not required.)

Place	Date	Hour	Summary of Events and Information	Remarks and references to Appendices
Croix Du Bac	16/12	–	Nothing of Importance	
	17/12	–	Urged Base urging supply of parts of Lewis Machine Guns due to Units, especially Piston rods & Return Spring.	
	18/12	–	General Routine duties.	
	19/12	–	Staff Sergt J. F. Hennion AOC reported arrival, for training as Bde Warrant Officer.	
	20/12	–	General Routine duties	
	21/12	–	1 Water Cart, 1 Cooks Cart, 4 G.S. Limbered wagons, & 1 G.S. wagon arrived for 24th Brigade Machine Gun Company.	
	22/12	–	General Routine duties.	
	23/12	–	All spare parts of guns due to Units on indents, hastened from Base.	
	24/12	–	2 - 18 pr Guns & Carriages belonging to C/102 Bty, damaged by Shell fire, Demands to Base to replace. 400 pairs of Clogs authorized per Division, were obtained from A Leroy Fentrie, at Laventie at 4 Francs per pair	
	25/12	–	Base notifies shortage of No 200a wheels, asks if No 200 can be accepted in lieu, Reply sent yes. No 1 Section Armoured Car Bty, No 1 Section Bridging Train; No 6 Motor Machine Gun Bty, transferred to 3rd Corps Troops. 2nd East Lancaster Regt, reports 1 Maxim Gun rendered unserviceable by hostile rifle fire, wire to Base to replace	
	26/12	–	General Routine duties	
	27/12	–	2 - 18 pr Guns & Carriages received to replace those damaged by Shell fire (C/102 Battery) Issue completed of 2nd Tube helmet on the man. Demanded D.P. helmets to complete each Unit to scale of 10 %.	

2353 Wt. W2544/1454 700,000 5/15 D. D. & L. A.D.S.S./Forms/C. 2118.

Instructions regarding War Diaries and Intelligence Summaries are contained in F. S. Regs., Part II. and the Staff Manual respectively. Title pages will be prepared in manuscript.

WAR DIARY

~~or~~

~~INTELLIGENCE SUMMARY.~~

(Erase heading not required.)

Army Form C. 2118.

Place	Date	Hour	Summary of Events and Information	Remarks and references to Appendices
Croix du Bac	27/12	-	63 Food Carriers received for the Division.	
	28/12	-	1 - 4·5" Howitzer & carriage damaged by hostile shell fire. (A/105 Bty) Wired to Base to replace	
	29/12	-	2245 Hypo Smoke helmets despatched to 38th Division	
	30/12	-	1 - 4·5" Howitzer & carriage received for A/105 Battery.	
	31/12	-	Lt J. B. Oxenham arrived for instruction in duties of Divisional Ordnance Officer.	

[illegible] Major
DADOS
23 Div.

S.A.D.D. 23rd Div:
Vol: 4

TAW

Original

Confidential

War Diary

of

Major W.S.G. Bishop

D.A.D.O.S

23rd Division

1st to 31st January 1916

Army Form C. 2118.

Instructions regarding War Diaries and Intelligence Summaries are contained in F. S. Regs., Part II. and the Staff Manual respectively. Title pages will be prepared in manuscript.

WAR DIARY
~~or~~
~~INTELLIGENCE SUMMARY.~~
(*Erase heading not required.*)

Place	Date	Hour	Summary of Events and Information	Remarks and references to Appendices
Croix Du Bac	1/1/16		Ordinary Routine Duties	
	2/1/16		Divisional Chaff Cutter established, at Farm near Head Quarters.	
	3/1/16		Ordinary Routine Duties.	
	4/1/16		A consignment of F.S. Boots received today for Troops in trench Lines.	
	5/1/16		Conference at office of A.D.O.S. 3rd Corps.	
	6/1/16		One 18 pdr Gun and Carriage in possession of D/102 Bde R.F.A. rendered unserviceable by hostile shell fire. Wired Base for Gun & Carriage to replace.	
	7/1/16		Wired for 1 Lewis Gun for 11th West Yorks, to replace one beyond local repair.	
	8/1/16		18 pdr Gun and Carriage, also ~~[illegible]~~ Lewis Gun wired for on 6th & 7th received & issued.	
	9/1/16		Sixteen Lewis Machine Guns arrived for issue to Battalions 24th Infantry Brigade, to replace their Maxims & Vickers Guns to be transferred to 24th Bde Machine Gun Company when formed.	
	10/1 11/1		} Ordinary Routine duties.	
	12/1		Office and Store inspected by A.D.O.S. 3rd Corps, 10 Hand carts manufactured in Heavy Mobile Shops, for Trench Mortar Batteries received.	
	13/1		A further consignment of 6 hand carts arrived.	
	14/1		750 pairs thigh gum boots, 20 Telescopic Rifles received & issued. 9 Shovel Shields also received for trial purposes.	

2353 Wt. W2544/1454 700,000 5/15 D. D. & L. A.D.S.S./Forms/C. 2118.

Instructions regarding War Diaries and Intelligence Summaries are contained in F. S. Regs., Part II. and the Staff Manual respectively. Title pages will be prepared in manuscript.

WAR DIARY

~~or~~

~~INTELLIGENCE SUMMARY.~~

(Erase heading not required.)

Army Form C. 2118.

Place	Date	Hour	Summary of Events and Information	Remarks and references to Appendices
Croix Du Bac	15/1		Further consignment of 6 hand carts received for Trench Batteries.	
	16/1		Ordinary Routine Duties.	
	17/1		A Consignment of 16 Briefs received for Batteries RFA in replacement for 1 set of Saddlery per Battery.	
	18/1		1200 Capes Mackintosh received. Saddlery withdrawn from Batteries yesterday returned to Base.	
	19/1		DDOS 1st Army and ADOS 3rd Corps, paid visit of inspection	
	20/1		Wired for 1 Lewis Machine Gun for 9 Yorkshire Regiment; to replace one damaged beyond local repair.	
	21/1		Ordinary Routine duties.	
	22/1		Lewis M Gun wired for on 20th, also 1 Water Cart for DAC and 1 Mess Cart for D/105 Bde. Received.	
	23/1 24/1		} Ordinary Routine Duties.	
	25/1		The 16 Lewis M Guns received on the 9th issued to Battalions 24th Bde, and 11 Maxims, 5 Vickers Machine Guns transferred to 24th Infantry Brigade Machine Gun Company.	
	26/1		Private Dalton AOC arrived to give instruction in Gun boot repairing, Classes are to be formed at once	
	27/1		Ordinary Routine Duties.	
	28/1		Two Vesta Pattern Forges for trial purposes, received & issued 1 to DLOY and 1 to Divisional Train. Lieut Wooding arrived to give advice regarding management of Divl: Shoemakers Shop.	
	29/1		5000 Tube helmets received for Divisional Reserve in replacement of Hypo [illegible]	
	30/1		Wired for Maxim Gun for 24th Bde M Gun Company, to replace 1 beyond local repair	
	31/1		Ordinary Routine duties.	

[illegible] Major
DADOS
23 Division

2353 Wt. W2544/1454 700,000 5/15 D. D. & L. A.D.S.S./Forms/C. 2118.

D.A. O.V.S

2nd Division

Vol V

Instructions regarding War Diaries and Intelligence Summaries are contained in F. S. Regs., Part II. and the Staff Manual respectively. Title pages will be prepared in manuscript.

WAR DIARY
or
INTELLIGENCE SUMMARY.
(Erase heading not required.)

Army Form C. 2118.

Place	Date	Hour	Summary of Events and Information	Remarks and references to Appendices
Croix Du Bac	1/2/16		One Maxim Gun received for 24th Brigade Machine Gun Company, to replace 1 unserviceable.	
	2/2		Orders received to call for indents for short rifles to rearm those units of the Division who are still in possession of the long rifle	
	3/2		Orders received to proceed to 56 Division to take over the duties of D.A.D.O.S.	
	4/2		1 Maltese Cart received for 1st Sherwood Foresters, to replace unserviceable.	

[illegible] Major
D.A.D.O.S.
23 Div:

2353 Wt. W2544/1454 700,000 5/15 D. D. & L. A.D.S.S./Forms/C. 2118.

Instructions regarding War Diaries and Intelligence Summaries are contained in F. S. Regs., Part II. and the Staff Manual respectively. Title pages will be prepared in manuscript.

WAR DIARY
or
~~INTELLIGENCE SUMMARY.~~
(Erase heading not required.)

Army Form C. 2118.

Place	Date	Hour	Summary of Events and Information	Remarks and references to Appendices
Croix du Bac	5/2/16		Maj Bishop, D.A.D.O.S. 23rd Divn, left station to take over 56th Divn. Took over duties of D.A.D.O.S. 23rd Divn. Pursuant to arrangement between G.O.C. & D.A.D.O.S. wired for 4500 tube helmets in anticipation of gas practise. Issued 3 telescopes for snipers, purchased in Boulogne, to Infy. Bges. Visited D.O.O. 8th Divn.	
— " —	6/2/16		Conference with A.D.O.S. 3rd Corps at his office: system of receipts discussed. Took D.O.O. 34th Divn round 23rd Divn area. Practise gas alarm — issued tube helmets indented for from reserve & demanded from Base to replace.	
— " —	7/2/16		Routine duties. Visited Armoury & D.O.O. 8th Divn.	
— " —	8/2/16		With A.D.O.S. 3rd Corps visited new area & site for dump, with office adjacent in Morbecque. Inspected 34th Divn dump & offices — dump will do for armourers.	
— " —	9/2/16		G.O.C's conference. Routine duties. Informed by Q new office must be at H.Q.	
— " —	10/2/16		With Camp Comdt. visited new area & arranged for new office at H.Q.	
— " —	11/2/16		Routine duties. Visited armourers shop & inspected damage done by shell fire; roof affected, no loss of material, & no casualties A.O.C.	
— " —	12/2/16		No car available — visited new area on lorry, taking Ar. S. Sgt. to inspect site for armoury.	
— " —	13/2/16		Routine duties.	
— " —	14/2/16		Received notification of rifles sent to rearm 68th Bge. Arranged for issue.	
— " —	15/2/16		Sent 69th Bge W.O. with 2 lorries of stores to new area. Arranged with Q. to notify formations of new dump & issue arrangements. Visited workshops.	
— " —	16/2/16		69th Bge. stores being issued from new dump in back area. 865 short rifles & 809 bayonets received for 68th Bge. Further consignment notified for 69th Bge — asked Abbeville to divert to new railhead. G.O.C's Conference.	
— " —	17/2/16		Drew 7 tents from 8th Divn for issue to 68 Bge. Visited 8th Divn & arranged for issues to R.A. 102 Bge, D/104 & C/105 temporarily attached, to be made through 8th Divn after 23rd move back. Surplus winter clothing transferred from 1st Notts & Derbys to 24th N.F. (34th Divn.)	

2353 Wt. W2544/1454 700,000 5/15 D. D. & L. A.D.S.S./Forms/C. 2118.

Army Form C. 2118

Instructions regarding War Diaries and Intelligence Summaries are contained in F. S. Regs., Part II. and the Staff Manual respectively. Title Pages will be prepared in manuscript.

WAR DIARY

~~or~~

~~INTELLIGENCE SUMMARY~~

~~(Erase heading not required.)~~

Place	Date	Hour	Summary of Events and Information	Remarks and references to Appendices
Croix du Bac	18/2/16		Received 1470 short rifles & 1575 bayonets for 69th Bge. Reconsigned one truck to new area railhead; Sent 2 lorries to new area with rifles bayonets & stores for 69th Bge. Wired 11th W. Yorks to ~~do~~ exchange rifles at new dump	
— " —	19/2/16		Visited new area. Issued 201 short rifles & bayonets to 11th W. Yorks. Called Bailleul re delivery of collar chains ordered.	
— " —	20/2/16		Two lorries to new area, with stores for 69th & 70th Bges. Bought 348 collar chains.	
— " —	21/2/16		Visited new area. Notified by Q that armourers shop site is required for Signals. Inspected new sites, found one suitable. Rifles from Base offloaded at new railhead	
— " —	22/2/16		Short rifles & bayonets issued to 68th Bge. in exchange for long. Arranged for 69th Bge to draw tomorrow at new dump before marching back	
— " —	23/2/16		857 rifles & bayonets issued to 69th Bge. passing Morbecque dump. Notified D.H.Q. moving to Estaires tomorrow – searched Estaires for dump. Armourers shop Erquinghem handed over to 34th Divn, – Armourers move to back area	
— " — Estaires	24/2/16		D.H.Q. move to Estaires. A few stores 68th Bge. left at old dump. Issues now proceeding at back area to 24th Bge & most of the artillery. One Bge (69th) in Estaires, no dump available. One Bge R.F.A. & 2 batteries attached 8th Divn. R.E. Units & F. Amb. scattered. Supply difficult. Very cold – severe frosts. Frost nails available, more demanded.	
— " —	25/2/16		Railhead Lestrem. Back area railhead closed. Q finding dump.	
— " — Blaringhem	26/2/16		D HQ move to Blaringhem. Units moving to back area. Reconsigned 4 trucks to new railhead, Steenbecque (open 28th). Frost.	

1875 Wt. W593/826 1,000,000 4/15 J.B.C. & A. A.D.S.S./Forms/C. 2118.

Instructions regarding War Diaries and Intelligence Summaries are contained in F. S. Regs., Part II. and the Staff Manual respectively. Title pages will be prepared in manuscript.

WAR DIARY
or
~~INTELLIGENCE SUMMARY.~~
(Erase heading not required.)

Army Form C. 2118.

Place	Date	Hour	Summary of Events and Information	Remarks and references to Appendices
~~27/2/16~~ Blaringhem	27/2/16		Conference ADOS 10. No car until 10.30. Thaw road regulations to operate – lorry movements restricted. Arranged for 2 horsed wagons to report at dump. G.O.C. wants rifles issued at once to infantry. Wired base for 500 rifles & 1500 bayonets to complete Division.	
—"—	28/2/16		Warned to prepare for move. Arranged for offloading 4 trucks & distributing rifles & bayonets to ~~a.s~~ complete infantry. No car available until 2.30. ADOS called, requiring Corps stores to be called in from Units. Visited dump, armoury, railhead. Arranged for trucks with rifles & P.H. helmets to be reconsigned to new railhead, unknown yet, in view of immediate move. Q. & ADOS concurring. Other stores to be issued as quickly as possible. DOO 39th Divn called for information re area. Q. notified Units to return Corps stores including light mortars & carts before entraining.	
—"— & Bruay	29/2/16		Moved to Bruay with Division. Left some stores at Morbecque – including Corps stores returned by Units. Searched for dump at Bruay, found one suitable for ordinary stores. Notified by 4th Corps ADOS that trench stores had been demanded for 23rd Divn. from Base. Q. suggest reconsigning to final railhead. 6 trucks sent.	
Bruay			Base ~~H~~ not to send further trucks until notified. Wired due, & [illegible] the railhead 10 miles back. 9 being already	

[signature] Lt
D.A.D.O.S.
23rd Divn.

2353 Wt. W2544/1454 700,000 5/15 D. D. & L. A.D.S.S./Forms/C. 2118.

Confidential

War Diary

of

Capt. J. B. [illegible]

D.A.D.O.S.

23. Division

1st March to 31st March

1916

Instructions regarding War Diaries and Intelligence Summaries are contained in F. S. Regs., Part II. and the Staff Manual respectively. Title pages will be prepared in manuscript.

(1)

Army Form C. 2118.

WAR DIARY
or
~~INTELLIGENCE SUMMARY.~~
(Erase heading not required.)

Place	Date	Hour	Summary of Events and Information	Remarks and references to Appendices
Bruay	1/3/16		A.D.O.S. 4th Corps called. Trench stores must be taken here. Found a second dump in town to use as Armoury & for trench stores in bulk, & P.H. helmets; other stores can be dealt with at dump found yesterday. Wired 4th Corps for 10 extra lorries for tomorrow & fatigue parties. Wired Base now prepared to receive further trucks (beyond 9 due). A.D.O.S. 3rd Corps called – does not now require stores left for him at Morbecque. Arrange to go back early tomorrow & clear old dump at Morbecque, sending 2 lorries.	
— " —	2/3/16		To old dump at Morbecque. Met A.D.O.S. 3rd Corps & D.O.O. 39th Div. Handed over tents, fire extinguishers & 8 trench carts to 39th Div. 8 trench carts at railhead reconsigned to Bruay; 5 others to be brought on lorry – these with 3 in the Div. should complete 16, for 2 batteries. Found 2 u/s 3.7 mortars at dump; returned to Base. Bought paint at Hazebrouck for treating helmets against "shine". To Bailleul, paying for collar chains & bringing back 60. Visited D.O.O.s 8th & 34th Divs. – nothing outstanding. Collected 6 [illegible] sets Bethune. Returned to Bruay where ADOS 4th Corps had inspected sites for permanent dumps. Wired units to return accumulated stores, & Signal Co. to exchange rifles. Still waiting for long bayonets.	
— " —	3/3/16		Units of 24th & 69th Bdes drew P.H. helmets, 1 per man. Searched town for dump sites; found 2 suitable, now occupied by troops.	
— " —	4/3/16		Rifles & bayonets received – issued to complete Div. with short rifles. G.O.C.'s conference. With ADOS to new area; found possible dump at Hermin. Three trucks. Much trench & other stores. Heavy snow & roads bad. Lorries running well.	

2353 Wt. W2544/1454 700,000 5/15 D. D. & L. A.D.S.S./Forms/C. 2118.

Instructions regarding War Diaries and Intelligence Summaries are contained in F. S. Regs., Part II. and the Staff Manual respectively. Title Pages will be prepared in manuscript.

(2)

Army Form C. 2118

WAR DIARY
or
~~INTELLIGENCE SUMMARY~~
(Erase heading not required.)

Place	Date	Hour	Summary of Events and Information	Remarks and references to Appendices
Bruay	5/3/16		No truck. Lorry rifles returned to Base. Saw Staff Capt. 69th Bde. re drawing trench stores tomorrow. P.H. helmet issue continued.	
— " —	6/3/16		To new area, selected hut for dump in Fresnicourt, more accessible than Hersin. Site of office allotted by HQ – 2 miles from HQ & 4 from dump – cars not readily available. Instructed by DA & QMG to buy stoves chairs & tables for HQ offices – new site very bare & R.Es. unable to supply in time. Sent 3 Stretcher lorries (by order) to 69th Bde. who are going into new line & had failed to draw.	
— " —	7/3/16		Bought stoves, chairs & tables at Bruay & Bethune. One truck of stores & tubs. Visited A.D.O.S. re tents urgently required for new area.	
— " —	8/3/16		Moved to new area – Souchez district. One lorry broken down on road out. Moved HQ, ordnance stores & 40 tents & bottoms with remaining three. A difficult day. Unable to visit points when necessary, no car.	
and Maisnil Bouché	9/3/16		Railhead still Lillers – a long run; one lorry still out of action. Visited dumps & ammunition at Bruay & Fresnicourt – former not yet cleared as trench stores still on hand. Visited Q & HQ.	
— " —	10/3/16		Lorry to Bethune to collect Salvus sets used by class. Trucks with 3 days stores cleared (these stores had been held up during moves). Collected 4 2" mortars from St Venant for 2/23. Instructed by Q to wire for 5000 shirts, drawers & vests as Divn. reserve. New railhead Hersin	
— " —	11/3/16		Visited HQ – also ammunition & stores at Bruay. Cleared Bruay dumps. Collected 3.7 mortar from OZ. Visited new A.O.D. workshop at Oldhain, No 8	

1875 Wt. W593/826 1,000,000 4/15 J.B.C. & A. A.D.S.S./Forms/C. 2118.

(3)

Army Form C. 2118

WAR DIARY
or
~~INTELLIGENCE SUMMARY~~
(Erase heading not required.)

Instructions regarding War Diaries and Intelligence Summaries are contained in F. S. Regs., Part II. and the Staff Manual respectively. Title Pages will be prepared in manuscript.

Place	Date	Hour	Summary of Events and Information	Remarks and references to Appendices
Marœuil Bouche	12/3/16		Further issues of trench stores stopped by Q – Division to move back to Bruay & then into 2nd Div. area. Visited 2nd Div. dump at Hersin, & railhead. Visited 47th Div in Bruay & arranged for transfer of fuel stores on 15th & 16th.	
— " —	13/3/16		D.O.O. 47th Div visited area. Visited H.Q. – informed that medium trench hows. will not be taken back.	
— " —	14/3/16		No car available in the morning. Visited railhead, dump, 2nd & 47th Divs. Baths will be opened shortly – instructed by Q to wire for 5000 prs drawers similar numbers of vests & shirts to be included in bulk wires	
— " —	15/3/16		To dump, railhead, No 8 Workshops & Bruay. Wired for 2000 blankets, reserve for disinfection.	
— " — & Bruay	16/3/16		Moved back to Bruay. Found 47th Div. armoury not moved – put my armoury in sheds adjoining reserve store. Visited ADOS.	
— " —	17/3/16		No car until afternoon. Visited 2nd Div & arranged to take over all their store houses & billets. Units not drawing freely from Bruay – wired Bgs to draw. Q state that 15000 vests, drawers & shirts will be required eventually as baths reserve: include gradually in bulk wires.	
— " —	18/3/16		D.O.O. 2nd Div visited area. New sites for dumps, two sheds near station. Drew ~~4~~ 3" Stokes mortars from 24th Bge HQ – to be kept here for 2nd Div. Two 2" Trench Hows. sent to 69th Bge. to replace u/s in front line, leaving 2 only to be handed to 2nd Div. – Q's instructions.	
— " —	19/3/16		Visited new front area. Second P.H. helmet arrived. Barlin dump being used by 2nd & 23rd Divs during move. No further space available, arranged to store at Hersin shed, & issue by lorry tomorrow. Stores accumulate during move when central store system operates	
— " —	20/3/16		To Barlin & Hersin – 2 trucks. Left Baths reserve clothing at Hersin. Goc stated that he wished Division to be smartly dressed & that indents should be expedited.	

1875 Wt. W593/826 1,000,000 4/15 J.B.C. & A. A.D.S.S./Forms/C. 2118.

(4)

Army Form C. 2118

Instructions regarding War Diaries and Intelligence Summaries are contained in F. S. Regs., Part II. and the Staff Manual respectively. Title Pages will be prepared in manuscript.

WAR DIARY
or
~~INTELLIGENCE SUMMARY~~
(Erase heading not required.)

Place	Date	Hour	Summary of Events and Information	Remarks and references to Appendices
Bruay	21/3/16		To new area dump & railhead. No truck. 2nd Div. cleared from Barlin dump – 23rd Div stores cleared from Bruay. Barlin railhead tomorrow. Purchased stores – pails, brooms, cotton &c, – urgently required for baths. Bought 3 long baths in Bethune for special skin cases. Instructed by Q to buy mangles. Drawers for baths not yet received – hastened	
— " — & Barlin	22/3/16		Moved to Barlin. Div. HQ are 3¼ miles on. G.O.C's conference. Rocket covers are wanted, 5-signal rockets being now used	
— " —	23/3/16		To 24th Bge re rocket covers – 50 a minimum per Bge; also re boots, adverse reports having been sent in. Boots refused to not forthcoming. Visited No 8 Workshop re marking of stores sent in for repair, trench stores being sometimes brought in by a Unit when in one section of trench & removed by them when in another. To Bethune – bought a wringer for baths, & aprons for cooks, &a. G.S require telescopes for Intelligence Officer.	
— " —	24/3/16		ADOS called: reported local purchases for baths & offices & raised question of transport for Lewis guns – no carts available yet. Rocket covers demanded. No authority yet received for Trench mortar by W/23, or 23 Div Tunnelling Co – detail indents cannot proceed. 2 Lewis guns addl. per Bn arrived.	
— " —	25/3/16		To Bethune on local purchase of urgent items. 2nd Div OO called – re fixing new sites for dumps at back area, Bruay.	
— " —	26/3/16		To Hersin, where P.H. helmets are being issued to complete 2 per man. About 15000 issued; only 400 P. yet returned. Inspected Salvage Corps dump, & Baths stores.	
— " —	27/3/16		ADOS called re vehicle wrecks	
— " —	28/3/16		General routine.	
— " —	29/3/16		Raised question of equipment of Trench mortar batteries, no authorised scale. – unit not to be self contained. G.O.C's conference – paint for vehicles to be hastened	

1875 Wt. W593/826 1,000,000 4/15 J.B.C. & A. A.D.S.S./Forms/C. 2118.

Army Form C. 2118

(5)

Instructions regarding War Diaries and Intelligence Summaries are contained in F. S. Regs., Part II. and the Staff Manual respectively. Title Pages will be prepared in manuscript.

WAR DIARY

or

~~INTELLIGENCE SUMMARY~~

(Erase heading not required.)

Place	Date	Hour	Summary of Events and Information	Remarks and references to Appendices
Barlin	30/3/16		Collected 2 West Spring guns from Corps. Issue of second P.H. helmets nearly completed. To Noeux les Mines re local purchase. Arranges for medical inspection & baths for A.O.C. New accounting bulk system discussed with ADOS who agrees that our present system embodies all points raised.	
— " —	31/3/16		Routine duties. Purchased lamps in Bethune. Still continuing daily visits to HQ – 4 miles distant	

[illegible] Capt.
DADOS
23rd Div.

1875 Wt. W593/826 1,000,000 4/15 J.B.C. & A. A.D.S.S./Forms/C. 2118.

DADOS 23 DIV VOL 1

Confidential

War diary of

Capt. J. B. Oxenham

D.A.D.O.S. 23rd Division

From 1st to 30th April 1916.

Confidential

Instructions regarding War Diaries and Intelligence Summaries are contained in F. S. Regs., Part II. and the Staff Manual respectively. Title Pages will be prepared in manuscript.

WAR DIARY
or
~~INTELLIGENCE SUMMARY~~
(Erase heading not required.)

(1)

Army Form C. 2118

Place	Date	Hour	Summary of Events and Information	Remarks and references to Appendices
Barlin	1/4/16		Visited dump at Hersin – temporarily closed, shell fire. To Lapugnoy re estimates for helmet covers. A.O.C. individually examined, all fit. Bought stoves & pails for 69th F.A., used as special hospital for quick treatment of abdominal wounds	
–"–	2/4/16		Bought sample helmet covers; also 3 D.C.M. ribbons for presentation. Collected 20 rocket [illegible] from Merville Heavy shops. 13 Sprayers delivered by 2nd Div., 12 demanded from Base (all for R.A)	
–"–	3/4/16		8 trench carts received from 3rd Corps (left in old area). P.H. 2nd helmet issues complete 10000 "P" returned. Bought collar chains Bailleul. Visited Heavy Shop Merville – 3 carts will be ready next week for mortars. Saw R.O.O. ~~Barlin~~ Bruay – winter clothing will be returned to Bruay; daily truck accommodation to be sent to me & passed on to Units.	
–"–	4/4/16		To Corps HQ – Saw ADOS re need for experienced clerk for Indents, to relieve C.C. of such routine – all my staff of W.O.s & N.C.O.s are N.F. except the C.C. Cycles for interpreters have arrived. H.Q. state no saddlery to return, only 13 horses in use, & only 9 more cycles required.	
–"–	5/4/16		Issued 4 2" mortars complete to D.A.C. for X/23 – carts not yet drawn. Div HQ re claim for hire of armourers shop at [illegible], paid amount to claims officer. Visited No 2 Workshop. DOCs conference.	
–"–	6/4/16		Collected repairs from No 2 Shop. Arranged to send 12 breech parts for mortars – 10M will cut down u/s rifles. Visited by D.D.O.S 1st Army – approved systems working	
–"–	7/4/16		Supplied rifles with defective barrels to 10M No 2 Shop, for cutting out breech mechanism for use with mortars. 100 tubs washing to 4th Corps. Returned bugles & rifles surplus to Base.	
–"–	8/4/16		Visited special HQ (69th F. Amb.) Hersin. O/C states refrigerator & ~~[illegible]~~ sterilizer demanded not really necessary – cancelled. Bombers shields arrived & taken to H.Q. for inspection – also sample helmet covers & bomb buckets.	

1875 Wt. W593/826 1,000,000 4/15 J.B.C. & A. A.D.S.S./Forms/C. 2118.

Instructions regarding War Diaries and Intelligence Summaries are contained in F. S. Regs., Part II. and the Staff Manual respectively. Title pages will be prepared in manuscript.

(2)

Army Form C. 2118.

WAR DIARY
or
~~INTELLIGENCE SUMMARY~~.

(*Erase heading not required.*)

Place	Date	Hour	Summary of Events and Information	Remarks and references to Appendices
Barlin	9/4/16		General routine. Arranged with RA to draw 4 2" mortars. Samples of helmet covers & bomb buckets to HQ for inspection – Instructed to buy.	
– " –	10/4/16		Arranged for 3 Bges to return jerkins & undercoats to railhead – DRO re return ~~of the~~ from remaining units. Visited workshops. Saw DDOS 2nd Div re transfers on relief of Division – only one shed available for use at Bruay. Ordered 1500 helmet covers, also bomb buckets.	
– " –	11/4/16		Bethune – purchased flags for DHQ & cars – also sample set of shoemakers tools. Certain units complained of lack of stores – DHQ informed that all stores demanded & authorised had been issued, save those demanded within a week.	
– " –	12/4/16		Lapugnoy re purchase of bomb buckets. Cancelled order, 400 recd from Base. Saw 2nd Div & arranged for them to hand over 4000 marked P helmets for drill on 20/4/16. Arranged for K2 Ship 10M. to demand spare water cart for issue during repairs. Visited Meuville Heavy shops re handcarts & rocket covers. To Barlheim for collar chains, still required in lieu of ropes which are destroyed by horses. Winter clothing being handed in – arranged dates for jerkins & undercoats. G.O.C's conference.	
– " –	13/4/16		General routine. Winter clothing being returned.	
– " –	14/4/16		Purchased paint. Ordered aprons & towels for Special HP.	
– " –	15/4/16		5 Bomb throwers from Base. To be handed to 2nd Div, our Bges now being relieved. 1 Bathing apparatus from IV Corps. 4 carts from Meuville for 68/1 T.M.B. – Bought boot repairing tools.	
– " –	16/4/16		1. Bn. now supplied by lorry at Pernes. Demanded box respirators & PHG helmets on new scale.	
– " –	17/4/16		Arranged with 2nd Div re transfer of stores on move back. Brass band [illegible] for Division. R.O.O. re winter clothing returns.	
– " –	18/4/16		Visited workshops. Arranged for issues at new refilling points. Issued to 69th Bge / fresh meat by lorry.	

(3)

Army Form C. 2118.

Instructions regarding War Diaries and Intelligence Summaries are contained in F. S. Regs., Part II. and the Staff Manual respectively. Title pages will be prepared in manuscript.

WAR DIARY
or
~~INTELLIGENCE SUMMARY.~~
(Erase heading not required.)

Place	Date	Hour	Summary of Events and Information	Remarks and references to Appendices
Barlin / Bruay	19/4/16		Moved to Bruay, took over 2nd Div quarters. Left 5 West guns, 20 food carriers, tubs & braziers for ingoing Divn — also 20000 helmets tube. Truck not detached at Bruay as requested — stores transferred from Barlin.	
Bruay	20/4/16		Two Bges. to refilling points early; 2 for railhead; One later to Bge in Monceaux area. Found several units prefer to come in to Bruay to draw rather than pick up at refilling points. Brought towels & aprons from ~~Belt~~ Lafougnay. Complaints of quality of sleevers still coming in — hardening at shops not successful.	
— " —	21/4/16		Issuing at refilling points — several units short of transport for stores. To Merville Heavy Shop re Mills grenade cups & rocket ...	
— " —	22/4/16		Delivered 69th Bge stores — Bge in Monceaux area. 32 wheels arrived from Base. Units come in to draw stores — refilling point system abandoned except for 69th Bge.	
— " —	23/4/16		Ordnance lorry detailed by Q. for Baths work. Demanded stores for repair of trench helmets in armoury.	
— " —	24/4/16		Armourer sent to 2nd Div. for instruction in Vermorel sprayer repair work. P. helmet reserve at Hersin slightly damaged by shell fire. Saw ADOS re storage of u/s clothing — he will see R.E. re shed, if arrangement is to be made for storage at all. Baths now issue all underclothing & shirts. Bought paint & flags for Monceaux area troops.	
— " —	25/4/16		P.H. helmets for Div reserve to 1 per man received: 4000 sent 2nd Divn. in lieu of 4000 left here by them.	
— " —	26/4/16		4 T.M.B. carts arrived from shop for 24/2. Buying paint & collar chains, Base not supplying.	
— " —	27/4/16		Lafougnay re canvas for water troughs. Bethune re chains & paint: collecting tins for paint bought locally. To No2 shop for breech mechanisms. Visited Bges, who have practically no u/s winter clothing — all serviceable returned.	
— " —	28/4/16		To Bailleul to settle collar chains account. Merville re chains. Still buying paint.	

2353 Wt. W2544/1454 700,000 5/15 D. D. & L. A.D.S.S./Forms/C. 2118.

(4)

Army Form C. 2118.

WAR DIARY

or

~~INTELLIGENCE SUMMARY.~~

(*Erase heading not required.*)

Instructions regarding War Diaries and Intelligence Summaries are contained in F. S. Regs., Part II. and the Staff Manual respectively. Title pages will be prepared in manuscript.

Place	Date	Hour	Summary of Events and Information	Remarks and references to Appendices
Bruay	29/4/16		Visited 69th Bge re trench carts & winter clothing – latter all returned. Bought canvas at Bethune for water troughs. Visited workshops.	
– " –	30/4/16		Routine. Bought paint & arranged for supply of tins from Salvage Corps.	

[illegible] Capt.
D.A.D.O.S.
23. Div.

2353 Wt. W2544/1454 700,000 5/15 D. D. & L. A.D.S.S./Forms/C. 2118.

DADOS 23 Div 8

Confidential

War Diary of

Capt. J. A. Oxenham

D.A.D.O.S 23rd Divn.

1st to 31st May 1916

Instructions regarding War Diaries and Intelligence Summaries are contained in F. S. Regs., Part II. and the Staff Manual respectively. Title pages will be prepared in manuscript.

(1)

Army Form C. 2118.

WAR DIARY
~~or~~
~~INTELLIGENCE SUMMARY.~~
(Erase heading not required.)

Place	Date	Hour	Summary of Events and Information	Remarks and references to Appendices
Bruay	1/5/16		26 Lewis guns received for 13 Bns. Paint received from Base, & L.P. 1050 trench helmets received	
— " —	2/5/16		No truck. D.A.D.O.S. on leave. Canvas for troughs purchased	
— " —	3/5/16		Wired for Sprayers & box respirators. Rendered return of handcarts for mortars.	
— " —	4/5/16		Kitchens received for 10th W Ridings, 11th N.F. & 2 E. Lancs. Rendered return of gas cylinders. Drew gum boots from Corps Troops for Tunnelling Co. Board held on n/s winter clothing: very little doubtful clothing sent in, majority returned to railhead serviceable.	
— " —	5/5/16		Drew gum boots from R.O.O. for Tunnelling Co.	
— " —	6/5/16		Dummy grenades, 1 & 5, 8 each received for each Bn., also 64 wire cutters. Two armourers 24th Bge exchanged in shop.	
— " —	7/5/16		4 Knapsack sprayers & 6 box respirators received from Base. Q. asked for distribution	
— " —	8/5/16		Lorry to Merville Heavy shops for handcarts; 69/2 = 2. 2/23 = 5.	
— " —	9/5/16		Stokes mortars not yet available	
— " —	10/5/16		Stokes mortar asked for by 12th — wired ADOS 23rd Div. & 4th Corps. 2000, & 876, helmet covers from	
— " —	11/5/16		42 bicycles received from Base — no authority received for issue. 6 more handcarts received from Merville shops, also 354 dust excluders [illegible], & 340 fore Wired 7/23 & 2/23 to remove 3 handcarts each.	
— " —	12/5/16		1100 magazines Lewis gun received. 2043 helmet covers from 4th Corps. Armourers shop & part stores moved to Barlin. Demanded 110 tents C.S.L. for units	
& Barlin	13/5/16		D.A.D.O.S. rejoined from leave. Moved to Barlin. Wired for 1 armourer for 24th Bge. M.G. Co.	
— " —	14/5/16		To HQ re scheme for abolition of Bge Am. columns & surplus vehicles & harness. No truck. Visited R.O.O. & 2nd Div.	
— " —	15/5/16		Three trucks, one with mess cart & 2 kitchens. Arrange with Q. & R.A. re disposal of surplus vehicles & harness under R.A. ammunition scheme, & for [illegible] cycles & Maltese cart required. No information yet as to equipment stores for new D.A.C. Base returned B.A.C. indents "Unit abolished".	

Instructions regarding War Diaries and Intelligence Summaries are contained in F. S. Regs., Part II. and the Staff Manual respectively. Title pages will be prepared in manuscript.

(2)

Army Form C. 2118.

WAR DIARY
~~or~~
~~INTELLIGENCE SUMMARY.~~
(Erase heading not required.)

Place	Date	Hour	Summary of Events and Information	Remarks and references to Appendices
Barlin	16/5/16		Bought lamps at Bethune – delivered to 24th Bge. Visited No 2 Shops. To Q re disposal of 98 tents received & re storage of old clothing: latter to wait over. Wired Gas School to remove bulbs – cannot deliver by lorry.	
—"—	17/5/16		18 pr. damaged by shell fire – asked I.O.M. for report – wired for new gun. More tents required – asked ADOS if provision could be made for marquees also. Bicycles being issued to R.A. in exchange for saddlery (2 per Bty). No tents with 1st & 2nd Dns.	
—"—	18/5/16		To Hersin railhead for blankets, & H.Q. re tents required. G.O.C. conference. Bells required, also hooks & muslin for meat safes. Samples of trench helmets, 2 colours, inspected – to be issued for trial.	
—"—	19/5/16		18 pr. arrived from Base for D/104. Batteries now renamed, on reorganisation of DAC & formation of mixed Bges. Second satchel for tube helmets coming up from Base	
—"—	20/5/16		Visited Bge. HQs. Tents required for a battn in reserve. A.D.O.S. says no marquees allowed. Bought tables & chairs for offices. Made up specimen meat safes in Armoury from hay bale wire, string & muslin. No instructions yet re muslin from Base: I could supply this & hooks, – Units making up. Bought handbells required by GOC for gas alarms – instructed to buy all now available, 48. Attended conference GOC. Gas helmets worn 2 nights not to be changed.	
—"—	21/5/16		Visited Workshops. Leave still very slow for personnel. To Bethune re bells for gas alarm. Gas alert on.	
—"—	22/5/16		Units indenting for tube helmets. HQ decide no need to supply, gas shells only having been used. 18 pr. reported damaged	
—"—	23/5/16		Another 18 pr reported out of action – hasten IOM for reports on both guns. Visited No 2 Shops, & Hersin railhead (re return of 1st blanket). A.D.O.S. says buy muslin locally, Base not supplying yet. Fly season advancing. Bought tools for OC Baths. Arranging for trench helmets to be painted by Armourers – half helmets already have covers. 10 trench carts from Heavy Shops.	
—"—	24/5/16		H.Q. & roads shelled. Prepared to move but Div decided to remain. 4.5 how reported out of action. To A.D.O.S. re 18 pr not yet reported upon – told not to indent for gun until damaged gun is dug out. GOC's conference. Bought muslin material for safes. Parker shelter received for 4th Corps. Visited No 2 Shops, & Corps Troops.	

2353 Wt. W2544/1454 700,000 5/15 D. D. & L. A.D.S.S./Forms/C. 2118.

Instructions regarding War Diaries and Intelligence Summaries are contained in F. S. Regs., Part II. and the Staff Manual respectively. Title pages will be prepared in manuscript.

3

WAR DIARY
or
~~INTELLIGENCE SUMMARY.~~
(Erase heading not required.)

Army Form C. 2118.

Place	Date	Hour	Summary of Events and Information	Remarks and references to Appendices
Barlin	25/5/16		Another 4.5 out of action. Received reports on both 4.5in & demanded new guns. No report yet on the 18 pr of C/102. Visited No 2 & No 8 shops, Bruay & Hersin. Railheads re trench helmets & return of surplus artillery equipment. Notes on excess issues April received. This Divn keen on appearance of men – HQ office notified that issues are heavy. Drew 10 tents from Corps for R.A. Units.	
–"–	26/5/16		18 pr reported damaged. One Av. Lt. Gun sent to IV Corps Instruction School. Ordered 30000 safety pins for use with smoke helmets.	
–"–	27/5/16		No car available. Sample meat safes issued, Ordnance supplying hooks & muslin & Units finding hay bale wire & string. 4 2" mortars issued to replace others ~~lent~~ lost by another Divn. 2 4.5" Hows. received & sent to Ord shops for fitting	
–"–	28/5/16		Shields for A/105 received. No car available.	
–"–	29/5/16		To Merville re handcarts. Tent bottoms issued to Vendred camp. Gun received for A/104. Q branch moved to Barlin, Div HQ shelled.	
–"–	30/5/16		Car breakdown. Tubs & tent bottoms issued to Vendred camp. C.I.O.M. inspected defective Lewis gun magazines reported by me; spring appears to be badly constructed.	
–"–	31/5/16		Visited No 2 Shop. Bought lamps at Bethune. Visited Baths re return of clothing. GOC's conference. Large clothing issues referred to. GOC anxious that men should be smartly dressed – moral effect considerable.	

[signature] Capt
DADOS
23. Divn

2353 Wt. W2544/1454 700,000 5/15 D. D. & L. A.D.S.S./Forms/C. 2118.

D.A.D.O.S. 23 Div
Vol 9

Confidential

War Diary of

Capt. J. B. [illegible]

D.A.D.O.S. 23 Div.

From 1st to 30th June 1916

Confidential

Instructions regarding War Diaries and Intelligence Summaries are contained in F. S. Regs., Part II. and the Staff Manual respectively. Title pages will be prepared in manuscript.

(1)

~~WAR DIARY~~

~~or~~

INTELLIGENCE SUMMARY.

(Erase heading not required.)

Army Form C. 2118.

Place	Date	Hour	Summary of Events and Information	Remarks and references to Appendices
Barlin	1/6/16		No car available. Visited railhead. General routine.	
"	2/6/16		Units complaining of "unnecessary correspondence" over indents for Lewis gun parts. Q. investigated, & satisfied that action by D.O.O. is necessary to prevent duplication & confusion. Visited No 8 Stop & railheads re blankets required. Two Bns. of R.N. Divn. in district & requiring stores.	
"	3/6/16		Saw Staff Capt., 3rd Naval Bge, & passed indents for certain special stores required by 2 Bns under G.R. Orders. Other Bns. dealt with by Corps Troops pending arrival of D.O.O. of the Divn. Bulk not required.	
"	4/6/16		Demanded trench helmets for R.N.D. Bns. D.O.O. wired that he had demanded them, so cancelled indent. No further demands from Naval Bns. Collected trench helmets (18) from railhead: also blankets; latter not always clean, shall indent direct in future.	
"	5/6/16		Have returned defective magazines Lewis guns – springs are weak & a big percentage of last new pattern issue have gone back.	
"	6/6/16		Experimenting in painting trench helmets with paint supplied from Calais – cannot get proper shade.	
"	7/6/16		D.O.Os. conference. Question of strengthening rifles for grenade use raised. Bought watering cans (for Cresol) in Bethune. 68/2 drew 4 Stokes guns.	
"	8/6/16		60 tents drawn from 4th Corps.	
"	9/6/16		Bethune re safety pins – delivery in a few days. Bought lamps & aprons. Instructed to issue 40 tents to Vendrel camp, ~~[illegible]~~ & 18 to other units: am still retaining band instruments for Divl. band partly formed. Naval Divn. Bns. using store temporarily – have issued on their demands. Visited railheads Barlin & Bruay – am acting pro. tem. for R.O.O. on leave.	
"	10/6/16		Hours foreshadowed. Getting rid of stores to units & railheads. A.D.O.S. called – 18 more handcarts shortly available for mortars, to complete establishment. 4.5. How. demanded to replace one burst.	

2353 Wt. W2544/1454 700,000 5/15 D. D. & L. A.D.S.S./Forms/C. 2118.

Instructions regarding War Diaries and Intelligence Summaries are contained in F. S. Regs., Part II. and the Staff Manual respectively. Title pages will be prepared in manuscript.

~~WAR DIARY~~

~~or~~

INTELLIGENCE SUMMARY.

(Erase heading not required.)

(2)

Army Form C. 2118.

Place	Date	Hour	Summary of Events and Information	Remarks and references to Appendices
Barlin	11/6/16		No car available. 47th Div. O.O. called re forthcoming moves. Visited Bruay railhead. A.D.O.S. called – examined new pattern nosebag intended for H.D. horses – Base nosebags last 10–14 days only.	
– " –	12/6/16		Visited probable new area, Busnes & district. Saw D.O.O. [illegible] Div. & arranged for transfer of stores. Collected 30000 safety pins, Bethune.	
– " –	13/6/16		To Div. H.Q. re moves. Visited railheads & 47th D.O.O. Armourers shop moved to Bruay. A.D.O.S. called re dumps here.	
– " – & Bruay	14/6/16		Moved to Bruay. Instructed by Q. to [illegible] stores, Divn moving.	
– " –	15/6/16		Armourers Shop moved to training area – P.H. helmet reserve & other stores taken over to new dump. [illegible] instructed me to procure signalling discs [illegible] & machines for aircraft use. 8 Stokes guns advised. Wired re carts for Lewis guns – "not available" – 1st Army.	
– " – and Busnes	16/6/16		Moved to Busnes. Office & stores at [illegible], 3 miles from H.Q. To Lapugnoy re making of aircraft signalling signs ordered by G.S. To Aire, saw D.D.O.S. re making of signalling shutters required, & to Merville Heavy shops. Shutters can be made – required by 18th inst. Instructed armourers to return to units – 2 only retained for [illegible], & one cycle fitter.	
– " –	17/6/16		Collected portions of signalling signs completed. Stokes guns issued. To Bruay, Lillers & Aire re return of stores to railheads. Arranged for stores to be accepted at Lillers. Am taking in stores at dump for return to railhead for units who are distant. Armourers returned to units, as above, including one for [illegible] by [illegible]. All kits to be cut down & surplus stores returned.	
– " –	18/6/16		To Lapugnoy for balance of signalling signs. To Merville Shops for shutters – not ready, 2 on 19th, & remaining 14 on 20th – paint difficulty. 8 carts, to complete mortar batteries, promised today. 5 3.7" guns returned by units & sent to Heavy shops.	
– " –	19/6/16		No truck. To Merville 7 a.m. for shutters. One completed. [illegible] requires modification. No further information re next move.	

2353 Wt. W2544/1454 700,000 5/15 D. D. & L. A.D.S.S./Forms/C. 2118.

Army Form C. 2118.

(3)

WAR DIARY
or
~~INTELLIGENCE SUMMARY.~~
(Erase heading not required.)

Instructions regarding War Diaries and Intelligence Summaries are contained in F. S. Regs., Part II. and the Staff Manual respectively. Title pages will be prepared in manuscript.

Place	Date	Hour	Summary of Events and Information	Remarks and references to Appendices
Borny	20/6/16		To Lafugnay & Bunny re bills. Also to R.O.O. re receipt of returned stores & for news of truck notified. 4 shutters, & 4 carts from Ikeville shops.	
— " —	21/6/16		Move will be on 24/25. My lorries to go by road independently. Asked DDOS to sanction issue of 5150 helmet covers to complete Div. Maj Symthe called from DDOS — covers due 23rd. Suggested stopping truck 23rd – 24th – wired Base accordingly. Six more shutters delivered.	
— " —	22/6/16		No truck. Visited railhead Ain & arranged for reconsignment of trucks tomorrow after withdrawal of urgent stores: also for empty trucks to be available for tube helmets & surplus stores for new railhead (25th). To Lillers railhead, where about 1 truck of old stores per day has been returned from 23rd Div. during the week.	
— " —	23/6/16		Attended Court Martial on an Ar. S. Sgt. lately of Div. Ammn. Shop, for absence with 'faked' pass. Collected remaining shutters from Heavy Shops & issued. Reconsigned trucks & sent reserve of tube helmets, less 1200 by hand, to new railhead.	
— " — & Vaux	24/6/16		Moved to Vaux by train. Lorries by road, arriving first. Found dump selected too small — took another. Visited II Corps — A.D.O.S. on sick leave.	
— " —	25/6/16		One truck only. Units should complete move today & draw from dump tomorrow. Considering method of issues in event of forward move: central dump, refilling point, & Brigade group dumps all with disadvantages. G.S. anxious to obtain signalling lamps for day work with aeroplanes — asked IV Army for instructions & informed no lamps available for issue; G.S. may be able to arrange transfers from units in possession.	
— " —	26/6/16		Reconsigned trucks not available yet. To Amiens, ordered brassards, & bought fire	
— " —	27/6/16		To next area. Saw DADOS 17th Div, & arranged to take over his dump, 28th.	
— " —	28/6/16		Reconsigned trucks arrived. Sent 4 lorry loads, including some helmet reserves, to new area dump. Move cancelled 2 pm — brought back stores & instructed units to draw from old dump. Visited O.O. Corps Troops — ADOS still away sick. Visited Workshop re Lewis gun repairs & water carts	

2353 Wt. W2544/1454 700,000 5/15 D. D. & L. A.D.S.S./Forms/C. 2118.

(4)

Instructions regarding War Diaries and Intelligence Summaries are contained in F. S. Regs., Part II. and the Staff Manual respectively. Title pages will be prepared in manuscript.

~~WAR DIARY~~
~~or~~
INTELLIGENCE SUMMARY.
(Erase heading not required.)

Army Form C. 2118.

Place	Date	Hour	Summary of Events and Information	Remarks and references to Appendices
Vaux	29/6/16.		No truck early. To Amiens for brassards &c. No new orders yet re move. Truck arrived afternoon. Visited refilling of D.S.C. at railhead.	
— " —	30/6/16		To Ord. Workshop re. water cart repairs, & manufacture of wagon parts. To Amiens to arrange for sewing work. Bdes. to move today, Div HQ remains; some dump, being abreast as central in new areas. Units draw well, except when moving, when I have nearly one day's stores in hand. As moves cannot be foreseen & trucks stopped, this temporary accumulation is unavoidable.	

[signature] Capt.
D.A.D.O.S.
23 Divn

2353 Wt. W2544/1454 700,000 5/15 D. D. & L. A.D.S.S./Forms/C. 2118.

July

23

D.A.D.O.S. 23rd Di. Vol 10

Confidential

War Diary of

Capt. J. B. Oxenham

D.A.D.O.S, 23rd Divn

1st to 31st July 1916.

Confidential

Instructions regarding War Diaries and Intelligence Summaries are contained in F. S. Regs., Part II. and the Staff Manual respectively. Title pages will be prepared in manuscript.

WAR DIARY

or

~~INTELLIGENCE SUMMARY.~~

(~~Erase heading not required.~~)

(1)

Army Form C. 2118.

Place	Date	Hour	Summary of Events and Information	Remarks and references to Appendices
Vaux & Bazieux	1/7/16		Moved to new area at 2 hrs. notice. Arrived 11 pm & selected dump. Lorries arriving midnight found dump occupied.	
	2/7/16		Found dump & offloaded lorries. Railhead still Vignacourt, 15 miles. Cleared trucks & moved part of reserve helmets &c from Vaux. To railhead — arranged with Q. &c for collection of 99 Lewis gun carts by the Sub Park.	
— " —	3/7/16		Issues from dump. Consigned trucks to new area. Cleared Vaux dump. To Dernancourt, selected site for dump: visited 34th Dn now in tents there.	
— " — & Dernancourt	4/7/16		No car early. To A.D.O.S. office, 3rd Corps. Moved to new front area, Dernancourt. Several lorry journeys necessary. New railhead.	
— " —	5/7/16		Cleared truck — issues from store. Received sundry stores e.g. waterbags from 34th Dvn. Ammn. wagon arrived for D.A.C. Visited Corps shops.	
— " —	6/7/16		Visited Salvage dump, & railheads for stores required. Collected trench helmets & Lewis gun magazines. Took stores to reinforcement camp. Railhead now here, clearing 2 am. Division in action — formal "returns" not obtainable. Received tents for Div H.Q. & ambulance work.	
— " —	7/7/16		To Amiens for stores. Visited Workshops — 22 & 31. Heavy Art. Units attached for Ordnance. Units drawing from dump.	
— " —	8/7/16		Visited railheads & Salvage 34th Dvn. Collected tin helmets — also part for Lewis gun which was completed & issued by our Armourer staff attached.	
— " —	9/7/16		A.D.O.S. re gun demands — also to shops. Guns must go to shops if possible. Heavy Batteries now with Corps Troops — also Amn. Sub Park. 6 Trench mortar batteries indenting — no detail re attachment, but am passing indents. X, Y & Z/23 still away but not transferred. Visited next area. H.Q. St Gratien, too far for dump, which will be at Franvillers. Collected Lewis gun from Salvage. Wired for 4000 socks.	

2353 Wt. W2544/1454 700,000 5/15 D. D. & L. A.D.S.S./Forms/C. 2118.

(2)

Army Form C. 2118.

WAR DIARY
or
~~INTELLIGENCE SUMMARY.~~
(~~Erase heading not required.~~)

Instructions regarding War Diaries and Intelligence Summaries are contained in F. S. Regs., Part II. and the Staff Manual respectively. Title pages will be prepared in manuscript.

Place	Date	Hour	Summary of Events and Information	Remarks and references to Appendices
Dernancourt	10/7		Visited 23rd Salvage dump & railhead. Collected one Lewis gun & some magazines. Units attached for few days only to one Div. must find difficulty in getting bulk stores during moves. Mineral oil short – wired Base. Took tents from Camp to Corps Troops – ordered to reverse proceedings 2 hours afterwards. Sending one lorry load to our dump. Collected oil from 19th Div.	
— " — & Franvillers	11/7		Div. HQ moved to St Gratien. Dump at Franvillers. Saw HQ RA re dump for stores while arty. is still in line; also Salvage officer re retention of equipment – any urgent issues by him to be reported to me. Collected trench mortar parts from Heavy Shop Beauval. To Amiens re brassards & [illegible]. To Q – instructed to demand more socks, 9000 already due.	
— " —	12/7		No car available. 6 cars in Div. { 1. GOC 2 G car (refitting) 3 Q car (away) 4 – CRE 5 – refitting 6 – Mails & Staff }. Clothing arriving for partial re-equipment – 4000 suits, 4000 shirts, 4000 drawers.	
— " —	13/7		Demanded 6 Lewis guns in replacement, & Standards (4) for 8. Tanks. Collected Stokes mortar from Heavy Shops. Visited dumps & railheads.	
— " —	14/7		Visited dump & railhead. Re-equipment proceeding. Items of equipment being issued direct to Units from Salvage dump, details being sent to me & passed through books.	
— " —	15/7		To Amiens for bowls & sign sheets (aircraft) – also paint. Visited Salvage dumps, railheads, & 19th D.O.O.	
— " —	16/7		To ADOS & 3rd Corps Troops. Also to railheads & Salvage dumps. Made urgent issue of oil to Workshops. Visited 24th Bge stores, – Bge being transferred to [illegible] Div. Large Div. dump would be useful for storage of surplus kits of Div. & any surplus stores, e.g. tube helmets. This Div. has spread out system of Bge. dumps at present.	

2353 Wt. W2544/1454 700,000 5/15 D. D. & L. A.D.S.S./Forms/C. 2118.

(3)

Army Form C. 2118.

Instructions regarding War Diaries and Intelligence Summaries are contained in F. S. Regs., Part II. and the Staff Manual respectively. Title pages will be prepared in manuscript.

WAR DIARY
or
~~INTELLIGENCE SUMMARY.~~

(Erase heading not required.)

Place	Date	Hour	Summary of Events and Information	Remarks and references to Appendices
Franvillers	17/7/16		Nine lorry loads of stores. Clothing estimates of Q were excessive – 3 times quantity on hand. Railhead shelled again. To Amiens for medal brooches & signalling discs. Wired for trench helmets 70th Bde.	
— " —	18/7/16		To Heavy shops for T.M. stores – also Amiens for brooches to 70th Bde drawing clothing. Demanded Vickers gun for 68 M.G. Co. Receipts from Salvage &c. Urgent issue of oil to No 31 Shop.	
— " —	19/7/16		Visited H.Q., also 70th Bde re refitting. To Salvage dump Albert – still shelled – & Shops re 18 pr demanded. A.D.O.S. states gun available, & only demand carriage, C/103	
— " —	20/7/16		With A.D.O.S. to H.Q. re tents & shelters. To Frechencourt railhead for steel helmets – these now difficult to obtain in any numbers through Salvage – 3000 coming up from Base. H.Q. borrowing lorries for move tomorrow – Ordnance lorries much employed lately – H.Q. also requires one to transport tents. Ordnance stores & office to remain Franvillers – H.Q. going to Henencourt & Bdes moving round.	
— " —	21/7/16		Two trucks – steel helmets & horseshoes. To Amiens purchasing, also Shops, Salvage dumps, & railheads. Collected a few helmets. 600 for me at Heilly. Collected 100 shelters, III Corps Troops. Saw ADOS at No 22 Shop – will move P.H. helmets from Frechencourt to Franvillers tomorrow. Conference at Div. H.Q. No car called – could not attend. Sent lorry to Div H.Q.	
— " —	22/7/16		Div H.Q. Visited Salvage & Shops re gun damaged. R.A. continue to demand wholesale before I.O.M.'s inspection – am awaiting I.O.M.'s report in this case, B/103. Collected steel helmets – received another 1000 from Base. To Amiens on purchase. Sent lorry to move 31 Shop to Albert.	
— " —	23/7/16		Traffic congested at dump – issued regulating orders. Brought mortar stores from Heavy shop. Transferred "loaned" mortar batteries back to their Divisions. Visited shops, & 19th Div. 8th Div stores arrived for 70th Bde recently transferred. Wired for two 18 pr guns.	
— " —	24/7/16		Visited Workshops, & Salvage dump; also A.D.O.S. Arranged for Police to control traffic here.	

2353 Wt. W2544/1454 700,000 5/15 D. D. & L. A.D.S.S./Forms/C. 2118.

Instructions regarding War Diaries and Intelligence Summaries are contained in F. S. Regs., Part II. and the Staff Manual respectively. Title pages will be prepared in manuscript.

(4)

WAR DIARY

~~or INTELLIGENCE SUMMARY.~~

(Erase heading not required.)

Army Form C. 2118.

Place	Date	Hour	Summary of Events and Information	Remarks and references to Appendices
Franvillers	25/7/16		Visited Heavy Shops for TM parts. 700 grenade carriers from Base. Collected others from Salvage &c.	
— " — & Albert	26/7/16		Moved to camp on Amiens road. Left 14000 PH helmets in shed at Franvillers. Camp store 30x20 on marquee poles. Office in C.S.L. tents. To Beauval for Stokes gun, 70th I.A.B. Visited 5th Div, handed over Stokes mortar from Salvage.	
— " —	27/7/16		42 bicycles drawn for artillery transfers. A.D.O.S. re tents for Div HQ moving to canvas. Bought signalling sheets. Lewis gun carts not good — handle weak & low, tyres come off — trying to refix tyres here. Visited railhead 1 am to 4 am — 3 trucks off track — supply getting difficult.	
— " —	28/7/16		Salvage at new dump — arranged to store spare stores there if necessary. Visited site for Div H.Q. forward. Collected marquees from 22 Shop. Mule shoes with frost cogs arrived on VAS & Bde's requisition; not required at the moment. Paint up for tents. Bought cables for 69th Ambulance. Six AOC arrived without definite orders — wired A.D.O.S. for instructions.	
— " —	29/7/16		Salvage dump — found some Lewis guns & mortars. Visited site for Div HQ camp — issued stores tents & paint. To 69th Amb. with cables required. No 31 Shops for gun parts. No truck. Railhead AOC. Cpl. killed by shell yesterday. 8th Div. not yet received truck with stores for 24 Bgde despatched 16th. Base queried demand for 12000 pr socks — based on previous requirements after action — reduced to 4000 on the indent.	
— " —	30/7/16		No truck. Albert re 8th Div truck — traced despatch on 16/7/16. Conference at A.D.O.S. Sent 6 AOC to railhead, reinforcements sent to me in error.	
— " —	31/7/16		FOC anxious to acquire more water carts. No spares allowed in IV Army — not even in shop. Saw I.O.M. re condemnations. Vermorel sprayers required — ours left in last trench area: drew 8 from Corps Troops & wired Base for more.	

[signature] Capt.
D.A.D.O.S.
23rd Div.

D.A.D.O.S. VOL 11

Confidential

War Diary of

Capt. J. B. Oxenham

D.A.D.O.S.

23. Div.

1st to 31st Aug. 1916

Confidential

Instructions regarding War Diaries and Intelligence Summaries are contained in F. S. Regs., Part II. and the Staff Manual respectively. Title pages will be prepared in manuscript.

WAR DIARY

or

~~INTELLIGENCE SUMMARY.~~

(*Erase heading not required.*)

Army Form C. 2118.

(1)

Place	Date	Hour	Summary of Events and Information	Remarks and references to Appendices
Albert	1/8/16		Drew more stripes from Corps Troops & issued to units. To Amiens for 70th Bgd flags, & for letter signs required for air signals. Bought butter muslin. Issued remaining tents. No truck.	
– " –	2/8/16		Two trucks on late supply train. Reserve clothing arrived + 800 blankets for Ambulances. Hastened manufacture of letter signs. Some stores in 19th Div truck – asked Rosecamp R.S. to send to me before reconsigning to 19th north.	
– " –	3/8/16		Visited Salvage, shops, railheads. One truck. Visited Bgd transport lines. Sent lorry to Amiens for signs (aircraft) – not ready. Bought stores in Amiens. Visited III Corps Troops – drew 50 tents from 22 Shop.	
– " –	4/8/16		To Amiens re signs – sent lorry to collect. Bought wire & cord. To Albert railhead re 19th Div reconsigned truck, & RFO re stores from Calais.	
– " –	5/8/16		Salvage & railheads. Bought staples to repair Lewis gun carts – handles are constantly breaking. Trucks at Heilly, not advised until 4 pm. To Corps Troops re return of Corps stores on move. Issued letter signs & strips.	
– " –	6/8/16		Conference A.D.O.S. On moving from Corps all tents & shelters to be handed in – also Corps stores. Dump will not move with Div's first move back, site convenient as at present. Wired for Lewis gun, 10th W. Ridings. With one Armourer I have been able to repair & fit up several Lewis guns. Q. will not order return of Trench carts, these were brought into the area & will be taken back by units. Gas shell effects felt here. Wired to additional clothing to refit.	
– " –	7/8/16		70th Bgd. move back. No car available in the morning.	
– " –	8/8/16		Remainder of Divn, ex Arty, moving. My dump to remain on Albert Rd, – 15th Div Ordnance moved up alongside dump. To ADOS & railhead re move north.	
– " –	9/8/16		No car until 3 pm. ADOS called re return of tentage. Corps satisfied. Saw 3rd Corps Troops OO re urgent Arty. indents – he will deal with stores arriving between 11th & 14th.	

(2)

Army Form C. 2118.

Instructions regarding War Diaries and Intelligence Summaries are contained in F. S. Regs., Part II. and the Staff Manual respectively. Title pages will be prepared in manuscript.

WAR DIARY
~~or~~
~~INTELLIGENCE SUMMARY.~~

(Erase heading not required.)

Place	Date	Hour	Summary of Events and Information	Remarks and references to Appendices
Albert	10/8/16		Cleared truck of Art. stores only: reconsigned remainder. Filled 2 trucks with helmets & all other stores & sent to new railhead with 3 men on train. No car available for me. Transferring tents & stores not required, to 15th Div, or 3rd Corps Troops.	
—"—	11/8/16		Handed over stores tents &c. to 15th Div. Lorries & staff moved to Ailly — no car available for me. ADOS asked re Corps stores — these now handed over to III Corps Troops. DSC to be transferred to a X Corps Division later	
—"— & Ailly	12/8/16		To Shops & Corps Troops re 4.5 How. damaged. Artillery stores to go to III Corps Troops pending move north — also wheels for HQ Coy. Train.	
& Flêtre	13/8/16		By car to Bailleul: saw V Corp ADOS, & fixed dump at Flêtre. Staff & office arrived by rail, 9 pm Flêtre.	
—"—	14/8/16		Three trucks at Castre railhead — cleared by 3 lorries borrowed from Corps. To 41st Div OO re taking over Steenwerck stores on reliefs in line — will transfer helmets reserve. DDOS & ADOS visited dump. Units drawing slowly — moving up	
—"—	15/8/16		Trucks from Calais cleared at Castre. Certificates received from IOM 3rd Corps condemning certain guns & cys of batteries of Div Art. still remaining in Somme area. Wired III Corps for consignment instructions — told to consign III Corp railhead. Indented accordingly.	
—"—	16/8/16		Units moving to Steenwerck area. Visited IX Corps (relieved V Corps) & 41st DOO. Transferring stores &c. tomorrow. Saw B/RA re guns — he requires guns here — wired ADOS III Corps to confirm his order to consign III Corps railhead. Wired Calais to stop consignment — Calais already consigned.	
—"— & Steenwerck	17/8/16		ADOS III Corps writes artillery procedure uncertain — arrange with IOM for guns to be reconsigned here if required. Asked HQ RA for details of guns left in Shops. Div HQ want tents &c. for Div School: wired ADOS for instructions — tents not allowed. Moved to Steenwerck. Issued fire orders. Four lorries lent to me from 41st DSC pending allotment. III Corps wire that guns will be reconsigned to 15th Corps for issue to Divn. arriving south.	

2353 Wt. W2544/1454 700,000 5/15 D. D. & L. A.D.S.S./Forms/C. 2118.

(3)

Army Form C. 2118.

Instructions regarding War Diaries and Intelligence Summaries are contained in F. S. Regs., Part II. and the Staff Manual respectively. Title pages will be prepared in manuscript.

WAR DIARY

~~or~~

~~INTELLIGENCE SUMMARY.~~

(Erase heading not required.)

Place	Date	Hour	Summary of Events and Information	Remarks and references to Appendices
Steenwerck	18/8/16		Three trucks. Dump rather full, artillery being still or more in back area. RA demand 2" hose & rifle mechs. – not available at Calais or shops. Visited ADOS & 41st Div.	
— " —	19/8/16		Bought soda & paint. Visited Heavy shop at Hazebrouck & light shop Bailleul. To 36th Div dump with DAQMG re new scheme for running siding up to ordnance dumps: not practicable at this site but might be arranged on new ground if ramps & covered stores could be built & traffic roads made. Saving in lorry journeys to railhead would hardly warrant expense. Found possible dump on Nieppe road, – Division likely to move from Steenwerck	
— " —	20/8/16		ADOS re 2nd Army returns & systems of indents for guns. Visited shops & Div. Rest station. Sent P.H. helmets to new dump. Artillery now in, & drawing	
— " —	21/8/16		No car available in morning. Inspected 41st Div. Salvage dump. (to be taken over by 23rd). Conference, FOC	
— " —	22/8/16		Bought stores in Hazebrouck. Moved stores to new dump, office remaining here for time. Asked HQ. for Armourers & P.B. men	
— " —	23/8/16		To new dump where issues are now being made. Visited Baths with soda, – & DOO 51st re taking over my old dump, now vacant. HQ asking for bells & telephones – passed to ADOS	
— " —	24/8/16		New dump in working order. Armourers asked for – not yet sent in by Div. To A.D.O.S. – also shops for meat safe wire	
— " —	25/8/16		Several West guns & rifle batteries from Salvage. Bought lamps & ordered covers for sprayers, Estaires. Made enquiries for hose for water carts, – slow from Base. No butter muslin yet from Base	
— " —	26/8/16		To Hazebrouck re paint. Saw I.O.M. re water cart hose. Issued tents to Rimfat Camp.	
— " —	27/8/16		New scheme for bulk books – 3 groups only. Visited Baths & ADOS	
— " —	28/8/16		Hazebrouck & Estaires re purchases. Handed over old dump Steenwerck to 51st Div.	
Bailleul	29/8/16		Moved to Bailleul, dump still at Nieppe. Armourers & cycle shops now running	
— " —	30/8/16		Visited Div School & Baths. Service paint still wanted.	
— " —	31/8/16		ADOS wants stoves for ironing – this is R.E. service – I will buy irons. To 68th Bge for details of drawing sets required.	

[signature] Capt
DADOS
23 Div

2353 Wt. W2544/1454 700,000 5/15 D. D. & L. A.D.S.S./Forms/C. 2118.

Vol 12

War Diary of

Capt. J. B. Oxenham

DADOS 23 Divn

1st to 30th Sept. 1916.

(1)

Confidential

Instructions regarding War Diaries and Intelligence Summaries are contained in F. S. Regs., Part II. and the Staff Manual respectively. Title pages will be prepared in manuscript.

WAR DIARY

or

~~INTELLIGENCE SUMMARY.~~

(Erase heading not required.)

Army Form C. 2118.

Place	Date	Hour	Summary of Events and Information	Remarks and references to Appendices
Bailleul	1 Sept		Arranged for issue of tents to camp forming. To Calais depôt, saw OC Indents & Group offices re sundry supplies. Notified that Div is likely to move again shortly – paint, blankets, &c not likely to be required.	
— " —	2 "		Tents being brought in 70th Bde moving back. Q. ordered tent bags & pins of tents left standing to be handed in to Dump.	
— " —	3 "		No car in morning. Saw 19th DOO re transfer of dump &c. Artillery being reorganised. Saw ADOS re trench helmets, Lewis carts, & breech mechanisms.	
— " —	4 "		To new area. Stores are fixed by Q. at Watten, not a central position but near railhead – dumps will be necessary. No information yet re new artillery numbering. ADOS re tentage &c to be left here. Stores to move tomorrow, after issues; offices on 6th	
— " —	5 "		Sent stores for 70th Bde to new area. 19th Divn. coming in to old dump. Issued paint to 19th Divn from stock not now required by me.	
& Watten	6 "		Moved to new area. Arranged to issue from 3 dumps. Artillery remaining in front area.	
— " —	7 "		To front area. Arranged for artillery dump tomorrow, & for bringing away helmet issue from Westoutre. Saw ADOS & DOO 19th & 10th. Opened Armourers shop. Orders for move switch on 10th	
— " —	8 "		Sent lorries for helmets, Westoutre & to issue to artillery. Issued from dumps in this area. Units not drawing well & demanding irregularly. No car all day. Arranged for trucks for remaining stores	
— " —	9 "		No car all day. Arranged with OC Baths for trucks for his clothing. One lorry to Westoutre for remainder of tube helmets. Issued early from dumps – 13th DLI declined to accept – reported. Q. produced bleat from 70th Bde units re clothing; all quite regular here, units figures incorrect & indents submitted late, reported. Armourers to units to alter Lewis guns – all returned after completing. Loaded trucks – 2½.	
— " — & Alonville	10 "		Personnel, Baths personnel & few stores by lorry to new area. Found dump &c at Alonville. Visited ADOS III Corps re Lewis carts, tents, &c. No trucks ~~today~~ tomorrow – hope to clear tomorrow into new dump near Bazieux, if I can find one	

2353 Wt. W2544/1454 700,000 5/15 D. D. & L. A.D.S.S./Forms/C. 2118.

Instructions regarding War Diaries and Intelligence Summaries are contained in F. S. Regs., Part II. and the Staff Manual respectively. Title pages will be prepared in manuscript.

(2)

WAR DIARY

~~or~~

~~INTELLIGENCE SUMMARY.~~

~~(Erase heading not required.)~~

Army Form C. 2118.

Place	Date	Hour	Summary of Events and Information	Remarks and references to Appendices
Allonville	11/9/16		Saw B.Q. 70th Bge. re clothing issues & explained bulk system, imperfectly understood by Bns. With O.C. Baths in search of dumps & laundries. Found Ord. dump at Bazieux & sent stores over.	
— " — & Bazieux	12/9/16		Demanded sundry stores authorised for 4th Army. R.O. springs to be held by me for issue to Shops only. Have an oil reserve for buffers – also V. Springs. Baths clothing arrived late – trucks cleaned & helmet reserve dumped near station with clothing & covered by tarpaulins.	
— " —	13/9/16		Indent received for rifles telescopic – Had arranged with Q re these in 2nd Army area when they were becoming available when Div. left – demand later, as such stores would only have to be dumped during 4th Army operations.	
— " —	14/9/16		~~Trucks coming~~ in at all hours. G. require infantry position screens. Signalling sheets & letters, also stretcher handles for ground sheets, – all required from Amiens. Saw ADOS re Lewis gun parts – Units will duplicate indents in spite of warnings.	
— " —	15/9/16		Examined roads for new dump sites. Visited Corps Salvage dumps. Also Shops for T.M. parts – Stokes parts no longer held by Shops. Saw R.A. re out dump. Amiens re screens.	
— " —	16/9/16		Front area re dumps for 68th & 70th Bge & 2 Bges R.A. 1st Div. re letter engines not handed over. R.A. require dial sights – visited H.Q. to find out requirements to put guns in action. Amiens for stores.	
— " —	17/9/16		Shops & R.A. re dial sights. Trucks too late for dump. C.C. awarded Military Medal, seems a good man. Orders for move 18th or 19th. Demanded an 18 pr gun & a Lewis gun.	
— " —	18/9/16		Saw 15th D.O.O. re exchange of dumps. Agreed to take his standing on 20th & issue 2 store & 11 C.S.L. tents to him to form his dump elsewhere. 1st Div. not moving dump yet. Q not yet clear about laundry clothing but instructed me to issue underclothing to laundry only. Indent from V/23 Heavy T.M.B. an unknown unit – Q. state personnel only, so cannot pass detail indents. 20 Amiens for screens & sheets. Units moving, & few drawing from dumps. Demanded 3000 chargers – weather cold & wet.	
— " —	19/9/16		H.Q. of Div. exchanging with 15th Div. Sent much stores with cogs & nails to forward Div. dump. Dial sights arriving for R.A. – three still outstanding. Sent in qualification report re A/S.C. Sims, C.C.	

Instructions regarding War Diaries and Intelligence Summaries are contained in F. S. Regs., Part II. and the Staff Manual respectively. Title pages will be prepared in manuscript.

(3)

~~WAR DIARY~~ ~~or~~

INTELLIGENCE SUMMARY.

(~~Erase heading not required.~~)

Army Form C. 2118.

Place	Date	Hour	Summary of Events and Information	Remarks and references to Appendices
Bazieux & Albert Rd E-7-a	20/9/16		Moved to Albert road site - took over 15th Div. camp standing. Issued dial sights & carriers to complete Div. Art. To Amiens for tape & staples required by H.Q. for forward area	
— " —	21/9/16		M.G. demanded for 69th Bde. Bought oil stoves in Amiens on H.Q. orders. 18 pr. gun & eq. up for B/103.	
— " —	22/9/16		Demanded 9000 jerkins for infantry. Demanded 6000 cardigans, - troops deficient not having refitted during hot weather. Issuing tents, shelters & tarpaulins as stock allows. Visited Salvage - not many items worth having - it is no use collecting stuff at any dump unless it is required at once. Tin helmets, gun magazines, Very pistols always wanted	
— " —	23/9/16		Demanded Lewis gun for 13 DLI. Laundry clothing taken to site in Albert where issues will be made. Saw ADOS re V/23 T.M.B. - until guns are demanded & received I am not to obtain equipment beyond that for personnel. Collected handles &c. for improvised ground sheet stretchers - scale of issue required seems high but ADOS requires Corps scale of 2 per [illegible] to be met. Brought instruments for repair from forward dump. Visited 47th Div. Ordce. & cycle shops working well - tin hats being repaired. Armourers	
— " —	24/9/16		Sent one lorry for old clothing &c. to be taken to Amiens laundry. No car in morning - did not attend conference ADOS	
— " —	25/9/16		Artillery want refilling point forward: arranged. Clothing now being obtained from Rouen. Winter clothing demanded - weather now warm again. Butter muslin (for flies) first received, off summer indents. Blankets not to be demanded yet for units - transport difficulty.	
— " —	26/9/16		Wrote Q. to Amiens district re washing. Small contracts only possible, except at Cagny where several divisions wash; about 500 sets is an average issue to each daily. Not enough for Division - 1000-1500 sets would be desirable. Demanded new identity discs.	
— " —	27/9/16		No car this morning. Cardigans coming up & jerkins arranged. How will new discs be marked? ADOS wants [illegible] samples - collected some from Martinpuich	
— " —	28/9/16		Visited ADOS & DDOS. Demanded 2 Lewis guns for 10 N.F. Jerkins arrived. Q. say winter clothing not to be demanded yet. R.A. not drawing from special dump.	
— " —	29/9/16		Reported to R.A. H.Q. re drawing stores by batteries from here & not from forward dump. To Amiens for muzzle covers. Trench covers issued - wet.	
— " —	30/9/16		Shops, & ADOS. Also to Amiens re muzzle covers & water ladles. Very Pistols allowed for Arty. groups - drawn by 15th Div. & not handed over, ADOS enquiring. Issued to artillery at dump.	

[signature] Capt.
DADOS
23rd Div.

2353 Wt. W2544/1454 700,000 5/15 D. D. & L. A.D.S.S./Forms/C. 2118.

Vol 13

Cr. Spinks

War Diary of

Capt. J.B. Oxenham
DADOS
23 Div.

1 – 31 Oct 1916

Instructions regarding War Diaries and Intelligence Summaries are contained in F. S. Regs., Part II. and the Staff Manual respectively. Title pages will be prepared in manuscript.

(1)

Army Form C. 2118.

~~WAR DIARY~~ or INTELLIGENCE SUMMARY.

(Erase heading not required.)

Place	Date	Hour	Summary of Events and Information	Remarks and references to Appendices
Albert 1/40 000 E-7-a	1/10/16		Conference, ADOS. Discussed ordnance arrangements in event of artillery being separated from Div. – suggested Bge. staff & lorry be left. Very pistols 15 Div. Art. not handed over to 23rd on relief – ADOS enquiring. Instructed to demand dial sights to complete to one spare per Bty, to be held by DADOS. (previous instructions, 1 per gun only, – now in possession). Reinforcement arrived. Visited Salvage dumps with ADOS. Sending separate bulk indents for Arty. & other units.	
— " —	2/10/16		No truck with stores. 10 tents received. Visited shops.	
— " —	3/10/16		Div. HQ moving to adv. quarters. Saw G.O.C. who requires rifle protectors, & suggested breech covers & muzzle covers. Demanded 3000 breech covers. Q. had no instructions later re muzzle covers, but asked for long covers. Two trucks cleared. Winter clothing issues proceeding – vests, drawers, jerkins & bands. Drawers to Baths. Demanded more mule shoes with cogs, forward area.	
— " —	4/10/16		Armies re covers. 3 trucks. Visited shops. Asked for more fatigue men.	
— " —	5/10/16		Bought rope (for mule packs); & sample long rifle cover – instructed to buy 6000. ADOS re box respirators, no instructions yet in this Army, asked Q. for copy of pamphlet issued. Units do not all require body bands – ADMS agrees that issue need not be made in such cases.	
— " —	6/10/16		No car until 11 or later during present position of adv. HQ. – Armourers refurnishing steel helmets. Ordered 6000 long rifle covers on Div. instructions. Saw ADOS. Truck late. Issued 50 sets packsaddlery to D.A.C. for Arty – special supply angle on bad roads.	
— " —	7/10/16		15th DOO states Div. relieving 23rd tomorrow – no information yet at HQ.	
— " —	8/10/16		To Q. at adv. HQ. re blankets. GOC decides blankets for infantry (on loan from Corps) shall not be drawn, nor others for other units demanded. GOC considers some units not well turned out as regards clothing. I pointed out that demands were always met, & were above the average. The appearance of a unit is mainly dependent on its own management. Q.Ms. may keep a small stock, but transport is a difficulty. I do not keep stocks, except when units are coming out of line & have to be equipped during short rest – the present move is apparently to be out of the Corps, & quickly, so best refitting place will be final back area – Units will not draw during moves. Baths & laundry schemes difficult here – Q. unable to make really good arrangements owing to local conditions.	
— " —	9/10/16		Div. moved to Montigny. No car until 4 pm. Dump remaining & units drawing slowly – no shortage. "Baths" also issuing – all demands met. Underclothing demanded already – extra socks demanded for new area.	

(2)

Army Form C. 2118.

Instructions regarding War Diaries and Intelligence Summaries are contained in F. S. Regs., Part II. and the Staff Manual respectively. Title pages will be prepared in manuscript.

WAR DIARY

~~or~~

~~INTELLIGENCE SUMMARY.~~

~~(Erase heading not required.)~~

Place	Date	Hour	Summary of Events and Information	Remarks and references to Appendices
Albert road E.7.a	10/10/16		Artillery moves uncertain as usual – R.A. orders say all Bdes likely to be out of line on 9th. H.Q. give 11th as date of next H.Q. move, & 13/14 for move north. ~~Cancelled~~ Wired Bases not to send trucks to arrive 13th 14th or 15th. To Albert to arrange for trucks to move Baths clothing & any stores, & to Franvillers re tube helmets. Saw 15th D.O.O. re transfer of stores.	
— " —	11/10/16	—	Div. H.Q. not moving until 12th. A few issues only made, units not calling during moves. Albert R.T.O. cancelled trucks, owing to troop movements. O.C. Baths will therefore send clothing later direct to northern area. Arranged for trucks at Méricourt & despatched stores with convoy, also helmets from Franvillers. Orders reducing reserve to 5000 arrived too late to prevent loading. Informed by Q that lorries will go north with us – good; also that R.A. will not move north with us yet. Saw I.O.M. re guns in shops.	
— " — & Ailly le Haut Clocher	12/10/16		Saw A.D.O.S. for instructions re artillery – he will wire me. Moved to Ailly le Haut Clocher with Div. H.Q. A.D.O.S. wired to move artillery to 15th Div & send lorry & Bgr. staff.	
— " — & St Riquier	13/10/16		Lorry & staff to 15th Div for artillery units. Wired I.O.M. & R.A. Remaining truck notified at Vignacourt – lorry will collect artillery stores en route. Very slack day here – all moving. Moved to St Riquier with Div. H.Q.	
— " —	14/10/16		Sent S/C [illegible] & one lorry north to find dump &c – no information yet as to destination. One lorry to railhead to ~~[illegible]~~ collect further artillery stores & take to 15. Div. also to bring back rifle covers from Amiens. New railhead will be Hopoutre, & probably we take over from II Aus. Div. Wired Calais for trucks on 17th. Transferred 1 C.of.T. Train to 15th Div.	
& Bailleul	15/10/16		Sent lorries to new area, to report T.M. Bailleul. Went Bailleul with 70th Brigadier. On to Hopoutre & found that dump will be Poperinghe (Convent). Lorries arrived Bailleul – sent them on to Poperinghe, 11pm.	
Poperinghe	16/10/16		All our staff here, except Ar. S. Sgt with trucks – no trucks yet. Visited 2nd Aus. D.O. – will take over his dump in a few days. Very awkward moving without sole use of car. Notified Base prepared to receive winter clothing.	
— " —	17/10/16		To Corps re blankets, Army having wired Div in last area as to numbers in possession – nil. No stock for Div. here – wired to complete to 1 per man. Informed Army prepared to receive box respirators – Q instruct me to issue directly received. No trucks yet – borrowed gas helmets, respirators & steel helmets from other Divs, & collected from Salvage, for urgent issues.	

Instructions regarding War Diaries and Intelligence Summaries are contained in F. S. Regs., Part II. and the Staff Manual respectively. Title pages will be prepared in manuscript.

WAR DIARY

~~or~~

~~INTELLIGENCE SUMMARY.~~

~~(Erase heading not required.)~~

(3)

Army Form C. 2118.

Place	Date	Hour	Summary of Events and Information	Remarks and references to Appendices
Poperinghe	18/10/16		Eleven trucks at railhead cleared – all trucks notified now in except blankets notified from Paris (boots remaining). Issued to Units – plenty of S.D. clothing available, & helmets. Saw G.O.C. re capes mackintosh – also Second Army; 3500 only will be issued to Divn. 500 horse rugs received without demand! – only 10% horses to be covered in this Divn.	
— " —	19/10/16		Demanded 4000 capes allotted to Divn. – Informed by 15th DOO that 1000 have already been issued to detached artillery. To Bailleul for printing frame glass. Q. re blankets, now notified as on rail, & respirators also notified: fine not required when respirators are issued. Wired Abbeville re blanket truck advised but not in. No socks or shirts yet received off hastened demands – hastened again. 5 trucks	
— " —	20/10/16		ADOS re system. 8 trucks to clear. Blankets arriving, still no socks &c. 70th Bgde H.Q. re stores &c.	
— " —	21/10/16		Hundreds up in quantities – also box respirators. 5 trucks. No trace of boot truck & blanket truck from last area – wired again.	
— " —	22/10/16		ADOS re trench stores: always difficult to discover situation re trench & billet stores. DADOS coming in should know scales, numbers out & due in his area – this is seldom forthcoming – scales appear to vary, also procedure. Bailleul re glass & lamps. 68th Bgde re stores &c. Baths building burnt out.	
— " —	23/10/16		Baths re clothing – laundry will run as before, – baths will reopen soon. Plenty of clothing in hand. Blankets still coming in. Boot truck still untraced. Visited 47th DOO	
— " —	24/10/16		Arranged for trench helmets & blankets to Reinfct. Camp. Visited Gas Officers dump. Saw Town Major re billet & stores & office. Took over stores from 2nd Anzac Div. – but retain dump here.	
— " —	25/10/16		No car until 3. Visited Corps – changing with X Corps tomorrow – ADOS states area 'stores' controlled by Q. Wired for a few trench stores in replacement. Saw RTO at Wippenhoek railhead & collected ground sheets for making into bags for sinks – clear issue to Divisions. Arranging variation of bulk accounting system.	
	26/10/16		No car until afternoon. Chief Clerk will go on leave 27th. Leave question difficult – Div H.Q. appears to be very badly off – Bgde H.Q. staffs frequently go.	
— " —	27/10/16		O.C. on leave, S/C Stone acting. Visited Steaps re trial of fitter & for iron for fire buckets. To ADOS X Corps re trench stores – asked Base what are due for this Div. front	
— " —	28/10/16		Visited all Inf Bgde. H.Q. Changed position of office. Saw Baths in Ypres. Drew lamps & gum boots from X Corps.	

2353 Wt. W2544/1454 700,000 5/15 D. D. & L. A.D.S.S./Forms/C. 2118.

Instructions regarding War Diaries and Intelligence Summaries are contained in F. S. Regs., Part II. and the Staff Manual respectively. Title pages will be prepared in manuscript.

WAR DIARY

or

~~INTELLIGENCE SUMMARY.~~

~~(Erase heading not required.)~~

(4)

Army Form C. 2118.

Place	Date	Hour	Summary of Events and Information	Remarks and references to Appendices
Poperinghe	29/10/16		Bailleul for stores. Also railhead for ground sheets (for sock bags). Truck (despatched from Albert 11/10/16 arrived today with boots & one Lewis gun – had demanded another gun on previous day. Warned by ADOS of possible move from Poperinghe area as dangerous.	
—"—	30/10/16		No truck. Examined abandoned 2nd Anzac Dump & arranged for making up road in event of move there being ordered: "institutions" remaining & troops allowed to pass through Poperinghe. Trench stores coming up.	
—"—	31/10/16		No car until afternoon. Saw Q. re trench stores, gum boot repairs, & good continuous Primus and lamps – these are frequently required by HQ. for offices, baths &c – service types not available or suitable at the time. Inspected Salvage dump.	
			[signature] Capt. DADOS 23 Div	

2353 Wt. W2544/1454 700,000 5/15 D. D. & L. A.D.S.S./Forms/C. 2118.

23rd.Division
No. A. 802.

D.A.G.
BASE.

Reference this Office A/802 dated 7-12-16.

Herewith War Diary of D.A.D.OsS. of this Division for November 1916.

C.F. Haig 2Lieut.,
for Major General,
Commandg.23rd.Division.

19-12-16.

23

Confidential

~~Duplicate~~

War Diary of

Capt. J. B. Oldenham

D.A.D.O.S.

23 Divn.

~~1-31 Oct. 1916~~

1-30. Nov. 1916

Instructions regarding War Diaries and Intelligence Summaries are contained in F. S. Regs., Part II. and the Staff Manual respectively. Title pages will be prepared in manuscript.

(1)

Army Form C. 2118.

WAR DIARY
or
~~INTELLIGENCE SUMMARY.~~

~~(Erase heading not required.)~~

Place	Date	Hour	Summary of Events and Information	Remarks and references to Appendices
Poperinghe	1/11/16		Visited field cashier – also Baillieul re dummy funds. Conference with ADOS re Ord. establishment – present establishment good plus cook & batman & fatigue men. Reported trench & billet store situation at 1–2 Nov	
– " –	2/11/16		Visited Army Sniping School re procedure re telescope rifle issues & repairs. Inspected old Anzac dump with a view to take over if ordered from here.	
– " –	3/11/16		To 2nd Army Shops – inspected stores made there on R.E. indents. Collected rubble for Anzac dump road – lorry failed, road bad. Q order to move, – replied road unfit at present. ADOS visited dump & office.	
– " –	4/11/16		To ADOS re trench area & billet stores – no lists available & no information as to numbers due from Base for me. Demanded 50 tents in replacement.	
– " –	5/11/16		To Sniping School. Visited 41st & 47th Divns. Q taking up dump road question with Corps. 2 more Lewis guns per Bn (to 10) received.	
– " –	6/11/16		To Armourer for rifle covers & Primus stove parts. Notified that capes mack. may be drawn from Army (25 4000). 10 Soyer stoves & 10 Primus received.	
– " –	7/11/16		50 tents received from Base. G re area stores	
– " –	8/11/16		Visited Shops, Supply Col., & railhead. Found sheets for bag making, also re fire boilers for kitchens – Base supply nil for 3 months. To Ypres, visited Baths.	
– " –	9/11/16		To 8th Corps Troops Ord. Arranged to supply him with 50 tin helmets	
– " –	10/11/16 to 21/11/16		On leave. During this period Div completed with bomb carts (trench & Lewis gun). Boilers without taps supply resumed. Shortage in brass brooms & torch refills. Artillery still detached with 15 Div. 2 3" Stokes mortars issued for instruction purposes.	

Cont'd.

2353 Wt. W2544/1454 700,000 5/15 D. D. & L. A.D.S.S./Forms/C. 2118.

Instructions regarding War Diaries and Intelligence Summaries are contained in F. S. Regs., Part II. and the Staff Manual respectively. Title pages will be prepared in manuscript.

(2)

WAR DIARY

~~or~~

~~INTELLIGENCE SUMMARY.~~

~~(Erase heading not required.)~~

Army Form C. 2118.

Place	Date	Hour	Summary of Events and Information	Remarks and references to Appendices
Poperinghe	22/11		Returned from leave. Everything satisfactory.	
— " —	23/11		No visits, owing to bad cold & throat. A.D.O.S on leave.	
— " —	24/11		Look over papers &c. & examined transactions of past week.	
— " —	25/11		Visited Shops, X Corps, Cashier, Winnipeg camp, & Div. H.Q. Purchased paint & brushes. Wired for C.S.C. tents to replace damaged. Divn. now complete with 12 Lewis gun carts per Bn. — also with T.M. carts.	
— " —	26/11		No car available.	
— " —	27/11		Visited Train, & Salvage dump: — arranged for ups blankets for dugouts &c.	
— " —	28/11		Collected Traverser mats (10 issued to 70th Bge for special work) Visited Shops & cleaners — also Cashier & O.C. Corps Troops who has invented a gum boot sandal.	
— " —	29/11		Visited Baths at Ypres. Also 23 Div School of Instruction. Bought brushes.	
— " —	30/11		To Bailleul for brushes. Div. H.Q. re lamps, flags, &c.	

[signature] Capt.
D.A.D.O.S
23 Divn
30/11/16

2353 Wt. W2544/1454 700,000 5/15 D. D. & L. A.D.S.S./Forms/C. 2118.

Vol 15

Confidential

War Diary of

Capt. J. B. Oxenham

D.A.D.O.S. 23. Divn.

1st to 31st Decr, 1916.

Confidential

Instructions regarding War Diaries and Intelligence Summaries are contained in F. S. Regs., Part II. and the Staff Manual respectively. Title pages will be prepared in manuscript.

(1)

WAR DIARY

~~or~~

~~INTELLIGENCE SUMMARY.~~

~~(Erase heading not required.)~~

Army Form C. 2118.

Place	Date	Hour	Summary of Events and Information	Remarks and references to Appendices
Poperinghe	Dec 1		Cashier for 1500 frs. Visited railhead. To Q. re move of dump & suggest office & men's billets remain here, dump only being moved – agreed.	
— " —	" 2		Visited railheads. Moved dump to old Anzac site, after morning issues. HQ agree to leave office & armoury here – men will return here with lorries at 1 pm daily after issues, as at Croix du Bac last year. Asked 15th Div for position of incoming artillery in regard to blankets &c.	
— " —	" 3		No car available all day. Inspected dump arrangements. Flags (on tin) being painted in Armr's shop, for Ambulances.	
— " —	" 4		Visited area comdt re stores – also Bailleul on purchases, & 36th Divn. O.O.	
— " —	" 5		Bailleul for stores urgently required. Purchased & took stores to 70th Bde at 7 pm.	
— " —	" 6		To Dunkirk for sample bags to carry rations to line. GOCs conference – no special points raised, except that Bde. reports of stores in possession are often very inaccurate.	
— " —	" 7		To shops for cleaners required. ADOS inspected books & system of accounts, issues & imprest. – Satisfactory.	
— " —	" 8		No car in morning. 21 Lewis guns from Base, to complete to 12 per Bn (less 1 Bn, – one Bn being already in possession of 12). To Cashier, & Sniping School for telescopic rifles. Bailleul on purchases.	
— " —	" 9		Demanded 16 wagons L.G.S. to complete Inf. to new scale, one Bde. being in possession. Visited shops, – also Hazebrouck for bag material.	
— " —	" 10		To Estaires for sample niff bags for rations. Conference at ADOS's office re local purchase, area stores, special tools. Raised question of additional wagon equipment for M.G. Cos. – procedure to obtain. Div now complete to 12 Lewis guns per Bn, exc. Pioneers (8).	
— " —	" 11		No morning car. Collected stores from O.O. Corps Troops, (baskets for Heavy T.M. by.) To Armentieres for material for ration bags large.	
— " —	" 12		Estaires & Merville on purchases. Procured sample cloth for bags. Wired Base prepared to receive Art'y stores 17th: – submitted indents for artillery requirements.	

2353 Wt. W2544/1454 700,000 5/15 D. D. & L. A.D.S.S./Forms/C. 2118.

(2)

Instructions regarding War Diaries and Intelligence Summaries are contained in F. S. Regs., Part II. and the Staff Manual respectively. Title pages will be prepared in manuscript.

WAR DIARY
or
~~INTELLIGENCE SUMMARY.~~
(Erase heading not required.)

Army Form C. 2118.

Place	Date	Hour	Summary of Events and Information	Remarks and references to Appendices
Poperinghe	Dec 13	—	Visited Shops, 70th Field Amb. & Supply Column. [O.O. Corps Troops.] Unconsigned truck of Art. Stores arrived.	
— " —	" 14		Merville for sample large ration of bags. W/P. bags from Dunkirk are too light for heavy rations.	
— " —	" 15		Hazebrouck & asked R.O.O. to retain surplus Art. stores being returned by 41 Arty (on reorganisation) for issue to 23 Art on arrival to re-equip. Visited Salvage Dump.	
— "	" 16		To Wulverghem & Steenvoorde to see Art. moving up. Sgt. & 2 men moving up with the column — lorry containing stores had been taken by R.A. for baggage & some stores had been issued by them. Army query demand for 16 limb. wagons for Inf. The indent was submitted on Q information — Bdes. were contradictory, some state 5, 7 - 9 in possession. Q. complaining.	
— " —	" 17		Visited Shops, Salvage, Gas officer. Saw 69 Bde. re limb. wagons — all Bdes. now in possession of 9 limb. wagons. Cancelled indent.	
— " —	" 18		No car in morning. Visited Baths at Ypres. Arranged to fix up ground sheets in stores as covers for ration trolleys. Saw Q re limbered G.S. wagon demand cancelled yesterday — Corps asking for explanation.	
— " —	" 19		A.D.O.S. re bomb buckets & tarpaulins required by Div. Also re medical classification of A.O.C. as A or B — ADMS has no detail of classification. Issued box respirators for large reinfts. New area Comdt. re stores. Sent explanation to Corps re demand for 16 wagons. Saw O.C. Pioneers re truck covers.	
— " —	" 20		No ~~morning~~ car all day. Saw representatives of H.Q. Cl Train, & Mob. Vet. Sec. re stores required on return to Div. Demanded caps & mineshafts for arty units.	
— " —	" 21		To Bailleul re local purchases. Inspected Ord. clothing store at Bailleul. Ground sheets being made up into covers for trucks. Collected blankets from 41 Div — for reinfts.	
— " —	" 22		A.D.O.S. re recovery of payment by Bde. for stores purchased. Ar. Sgt. joined staff from 70th Bde.	
— " —	" 23		Arranged for med. examination of staff for A & B classification. Camp Comdt & Q. re indents. Visited shops. Collected 40 sets tent bottoms rejected.	
— " —	" 24		No car all day. Inspected arrangements for water, latrines, & cooking for dump guard. Trucks etc. Blankets & tin boxes for magazines up.	

T2134. Wt. W708—776. 500000. 4/15. Sir J. C. & S.

(3)

Instructions regarding War Diaries and Intelligence Summaries are contained in F. S. Regs., Part II. and the Staff Manual respectively. Title pages will be prepared in manuscript.

WAR DIARY

~~or~~

~~INTELLIGENCE SUMMARY.~~

~~(Erase heading not required.)~~

Army Form C. 2118.

Place	Date	Hour	Summary of Events and Information	Remarks and references to Appendices
Poperinghe	Dec	25	Train delayed. Four trucks received, including 50 sets tent bottoms delivered to area Comdt. Work completed 7 pm.	
— " —	"	26	Visited RA HQ. One Bge Art? (transferred to Calais, 25/12) moved back 20 Shops & Salvage. Solution for gum boot repairs urgently required. Collected quantities from M.T units & delivered to 7 amb. in Ypres	
— " —	"	27	To Cassel for traversor mats. Visited railhead. Bulk system altered – published D.R.O re alteration of dates.	
— " —	"	28	No morning car. Q. want 10 bells for gas alarms in dug outs. To Hazebrouck & Bailleul for bells. Visited shops.	
— " —	"	29	Bailleul for bells. Train coming in later now – difficult to sort & issue same morning.	
— " —	"	30	HQ offices. HQ Train, & area Comdt. re stores for him. Blankets overdue from Base	
— " —	"	31	To Dunkirk for bells & material for ration bags. 2 Lewis guns up, one for KOYLI, & 1 for Div School.	

[signature] Capt
DADOS
23. Div

T2134. Wt. W708–776. 500000. 4/15. Sir J. C. & S.

Vol 16

Confidential

War Diary of

Capt. J. B. Oxenham

D.A.D.O.S

23. Divn.

1st to 31st Jany 1917

Confidential

Instructions regarding War Diaries and Intelligence Summaries are contained in F. S. Regs., Part II. and the Staff Manual respectively. Title pages will be prepared in manuscript.

WAR DIARY

~~or~~

~~INTELLIGENCE SUMMARY.~~

~~(Erase heading not required.)~~

(1)

Army Form C. 2118.

Place	Date	Hour	Summary of Events and Information	Remarks and references to Appendices
Poperinghe	Jan 1	1917	Trucks late – no morning car. Collected trench mechanisms & repaired binoculars from shops. To A.D.O.S with sample cleaners – defective pattern. Q decide not to proceed further with ration bag question.	
— " —	" 2	–	To Bailleul for aeroplane signal strips – also bells & brushes. Medal brooches required by H.Q. – (new years list). 11 chaff cutting machines arrived.	
— " —	" 3	–	Visited Salvage, area comdt. & H.Q. Made up medal ribbons for New year presentations – noted self included for M.C. Bought lamps.	
— " —	" 4	–	No morning car. 1500 blankets arrived. Bought signal strips & issued to O/C Signals	
— " —	" 5	–	Corps Ordnance dump to see mangles – too small. Visited shops.	
— " —	" 6	–	Hazebrouck & St. Omer for rifle covers – ordered samples.	
— " —	" 7	–	No morning car. Looking around for mangles for Baths: bought cord. Bge. demanding "kukris" – cannot obtain.	
— " —	" 8	–	To Dunkirk for mangles & flue brushes – former must be ordered from Paris. 500 blankets up.	
— " —	" 9	–	No truck. To Steenvoorde re r.o. springs. Hazebrouck for samples of rifle covers. Ordered 2 mangles & bought [illegible]	
— " —	" 10	–	No morning car. 69th Bge. H.Q. re rifle covers & bells for dugouts. Lorry shelled 2–3 pm: moved lorries from danger area to dump. To A.D.O.S re vehicles for Lewis guns, & re Brigade stores [illegible] by 70 Bge. [illegible] ask for refund.	
— " —	" 11		To Steenvoorde for spare part for Lorry. Bailleul for brushes & stoves. Q re Brigade stores &c. Arty want white sheets for positions in snow.	
— " —	" 12	–	No car. Train late, no trucks. Sewing machine for converting sheets into capes not yet received – Q. will not withdraw tailors for this work. Bought snow sheets for Arty at Hazebrouck.	
— " —	" 13		No car all day. Demands coming in for blankets – collected 500 from 41 Div & wired Base. Issued snow sheets to Divns. in Corps & own Arty units. A.D.O.S called. Obtained prices for bass brooms.	
— " —	" 14		No car until 5 pm. New floor [illegible] for altering defective H. lamps. To Q. re distribution of sundry stores.	

T2134. Wt. W708—776. 500000. 4/15. Sir J. C. & S.

Instructions regarding War Diaries and Intelligence Summaries are contained in F. S. Regs., Part II. and the Staff Manual respectively. Title pages will be prepared in manuscript.

(2)

WAR DIARY
or
~~INTELLIGENCE SUMMARY.~~
~~(Erase heading not required.)~~

Army Form C. 2118.

Place	Date	Hour	Summary of Events and Information	Remarks and references to Appendices
Poperinghe	Jan: 15		To Hazebrouck for mangles & brooms. Visited 104 Bde, up from training & awaiting transfer to Army Troops. Shops for trench mortar mechanisms.	
— " —	" 16		No morning car. With 47th DADOS to Hazebrouck re mangles. Conference ADOS re thaw road orders, & Baths clothing pools & system. Suggested clothing indents other than for exchange or replacement of M/S at Baths, should be sent to & passed to Baths for issue if clear, & after enquiry into losses.	
— " —	" 17		White clothing – 100 sets for snow use, required at once. Bought material designed & made clothing, ready for issue 5pm. Collected repaired mangle & trench mechs. from Shops & arranged for them to make fire bars for Baths boilers.	
— " —	" 18		No morning car. Visited Area Comdt. re stores. Collected blocks ~~for~~ for altering F.S. lamps.	
— " —	" 19		Bailleul for purchases. Salvage officer re issue made by him direct.	
— " —	" 20		Visited Supply Column & Shops for trench mortar mechs, & mangles repaired. Collected stores from Bailleul.	
— " —	" 21		To Hazebrouck for sewing machine & chains. ADOS re sundry matters. RSO re parking lorries at dump in event of thaw – SSO re rations. 20 tents arrived.	
— " —	22		Purchasing chain & hooks, eyes & buttons for altering ground sheets. Conference at Div. HQ. GOC asked if clothing was short – no. Also re inf. patches now to be supplied by AOD – no indents yet. Art. HQ re demands for "snow" sheets.	
— " —	23		3 tailors arrived to open Div. Shop for altering ground sheets. No car this morning. ADOS arranging to send some clipping knives specially to Base for sharpening & return same day.	
~~— " —~~	~~24~~		~~No morning car~~ No truck. Collected repairs from Shops. Visited Steenvoorde, Godewaersvelde & Hazebrouck with O.C. Baths re farming out laundry work. Also purchased white cotton &c. Demanded 18pr. gun & eqpt. &c.	
— " —	24		ADOS re cancelling Lewis gun cart demands, & on supply of hooks & buttons from Base. Area Comdt. re stores. Div. School re demands. Train late. Demanded clothing for Baths.	
— " —	25		No morning car. Bought soda & brushes for Div. Baths. 18pr. gun & eqp. arrived. ~~for~~ Train late.	
— " —	26		Train late. Arranged to send out stores for railway Co. at H. Camp. Purchased chains at Hazebrouck.	

T2134. Wt. W708—776. 500000. 4/15. Sir J. C. & S.

Instructions regarding War Diaries and Intelligence Summaries are contained in F. S. Regs., Part II. and the Staff Manual respectively. Title pages will be prepared in manuscript.

(3)

WAR DIARY
or
~~INTELLIGENCE SUMMARY.~~
~~(Erase heading not required.)~~

Army Form C. 2118.

Place	Date	Hour	Summary of Events and Information	Remarks and references to Appendices
Poperinghe	27/1/17		Special stores issued to Mob. Vet. Sec. for dealing with mange. No truck. Baths still frozen out – no bathing of units for 3 days. Visited shops. Claims officer & 47th D.O.O. re tailors shops. Shop turning out 60 cape shirts a day.	
— " —	28/1/17		No car. Train late. Demanded stores for isolation & veterinary camp. Tailors shops turned on to corps work temporarily – gun covers.	
— " —	29/1/17		Gun covers finished for Corps. Bought soda for Baths – Base supplies now irregular & uncertain in many instances.	
— " —	30/1/17		Conference at H.Q. re mange. To Hazebrouck for stores required. Saw A.D.V.S re isolation camp.	
— " —	31/1/17		No morning car. Bought bass brooms. Saw A.D.O.S re sewing machine required. To Hazebrouck for cordage, soda &c.	

[signature]
D.A.D.O.S.
23rd Div.

Confidential

Vol 17

War Diary of

Capt. J. B. Oxenham

D.A.D.O.S. 23rd Division

1 – 28 Feby 1917

Confidential.

Instructions regarding War Diaries and Intelligence Summaries are contained in F. S. Regs., Part II. and the Staff Manual respectively. Title pages will be prepared in manuscript.

WAR DIARY

or

~~INTELLIGENCE SUMMARY.~~

~~(Erase heading not required.)~~

(1)

Army Form C. 2118.

Place	Date	Hour	Summary of Events and Information	Remarks and references to Appendices
Poperinghe	Feb. 1		No truck. Bought stores for Vet^y Isolation Camp. Collected pistols from railhead. Saw Area Comdt re stores. A.D.O.S. re indents not completed by Base. Collected stores from Hazebrouck.	
"	2		Truck very late – horse rugs not received.	
"	3		No truck. Saw R.T.O. Hazebrouck re my truck – no sign. Bought brushes & cordage for Mob. Vet. Sec. Bailleul – also cloth for patches, & soda, Hazebrouck.	
"	4		No cars. Conference Div H.Q. – shortage of horse brushes considered – asked Corps to expedite. Horse rugs due but not received.	
"	5		Visited Bath & Bgn in Ypres. 68 Bgn state triplex goggles for tanks not received – gave details of issue. Horse rugs arrive. Bought brushes & irons in Hazebrouck.	
"	6		No ~~morning~~ car. Bought emery for clipping machines. Div require date for arrival of horse brushes – A.D.O.S. states Base have no indent – 'phoned details of indent. Indented again for 400.	
"	7		Bought brushes. Bought irons – took samples of "operation" brassards to Q. & purchased soda. No ropes of safety [?]. Visited Area Comdt, Train, A.D.V.S. & 41st D.O.O.	
"	8		Visited Isolation Mange Camp with stores. Ordered "operation" brassards & bought cord & horse brushes. Visited Salvage Dump. Wheels only on train.	
"	9		No morning car. Trucks still late. 24 Lewis guns – to 14 per Bn – arrive. Base send dandy brushes in lieu of horse brushes – wired for confirmation "not available." Bought soda & cloth for patches. Visited Mange Camp. No nosebags received.	
"	10		To Bailleul & Hazebrouck for soap, soda & nosebags – none available with Base. Visited H.Q. & A.D.O.S. Capt. Brammall [?] took over, he acts during my leave 11–21 Feb.	
"	11 to ~~21~~ 24		On leave. During this period nosebags, soap & soda were deficient from Base & local purchases were made. Armbands for ~~of~~ operations (carrying parties, etc) were bought – also cloth for infantry distinguishing patches. Visits paid to A.D.O.S., Schools, Shops & Mange Camp.	

T2134. Wt. W708–776. 500000. 4/15. Sir J. C. & S.

Instructions regarding War Diaries and Intelligence Summaries are contained in F. S. Regs., Part II. and the Staff Manual respectively. Title pages will be prepared in manuscript.

(2)

WAR DIARY

~~or~~

~~INTELLIGENCE~~ SUMMARY.

~~(Erase heading not required.)~~

Army Form C. 2118.

Place	Date	Hour	Summary of Events and Information	Remarks and references to Appendices
Poperinghe	25/2/17		Division to move to backward area. No stores received after this date at this railhead.	
— " —	26/2/17		Stores sent to new dump at Watten, by road. Collected stores from Bailleul — boards, palliasses &c.	
— " — & Watten	27/2/17		Moved to Watten. Retaining tailors & armourers shops. Issued to 70th Bde in new area.	
— " —	28/2/17		To Bailleul for cloth &c. No trucks yet – railhead opens 1st March. Visited DDOS & H.Q. Hastened dummy drill cartridges.	

[signature] Capt.
DADOS
23 Div.

T2134. Wt. W708—776. 500000. 4/15. Sir J. C. & S.

Vol 8

~~Confidential~~

War Diary of

Capt. J. B. Oxenham

DADOS 23rd Div

1st - 31st March 1917

Confidential

(1)

WAR DIARY
or
~~INTELLIGENCE SUMMARY.~~
(Erase heading not required.)

Army Form C. 2118.

Instructions regarding War Diaries and Intelligence Summaries are contained in F. S. Regs., Part II. and the Staff Manual respectively. Title pages will be prepared in manuscript.

Place	Date	Hour	Summary of Events and Information	Remarks and references to Appendices
Watten	Mar. 1		To Cassel – Army HQ. for [illegible] [illegible]. Brilliant for balance of cloth to Baths is being fixed up, underclothing still issued through Baths. Units asking for camp stores – wired Base. 2 trucks.	
"	" 2		Two trucks. Issuing 69 Bgde direct. Arranged dump for 68th Bgde group. No car until afternoon. Bought lamps in St Omer. Visited Train re dumps & HQ. re any area stores required – Q. will ask Army.	
"	" 3		No car. Trucks up. Units demanding to complete to clothing equipment – several units appear to have worked on one shirt & 2 pr socks during winter months when Baths are running regularly. Asked Corps to [illegible] pistols & [illegible]. Q. suggest purchase of leather – asked Corps.	
"	" 4		To Brilliant for irons & to pay bills. Oil truck up, 2 days late. To Cashier S.S.O. & HQ. No I.O.M. in this district.	
"	" 5		Usual trucks. Saw Q. re area stores – none to be issued here. VIII Corps states leather should not be bought. Purchased cloth & [illegible] material – also needles.	
"	" 6		No car today. No truck. Armourers Shop now fitted with machine for sharpening clipper blades. Tailors still altering ground sheets – about 80 a day. Bns. not yet complete with new identity discs stamped – stamps still circulating.	
"	7		24 Lewis guns up, completing Bns. to 16 each (Pioneers 8). Extra limbered wagons not yet up. Saw G. re grenade rifles – present scale, 34 per Bn – ~~[illegible]~~ mostly long rifles. Bayonets not to be issued for long grenade rifles.	
"	" 8		Bought aeroplane signal strips, also [illegible]. Saw G. re grenade rifles & suggested Bns should make themselves up to 34 short rifles for grenades – G would stamp them if required but would not remove magazines or sights. Long rifles to be returned if not required.	
"	" 9		Two trucks advised not received. Bought flat irons & [illegible]. Visited railhead, – all stores returned.	
"	" 10		Clothing not received in full – nearly 2000 ~~sets~~ suits demanded. No car available. Asked Base when patch cloth would be supplied – local purchase is difficult. Absence of any Ord Shop within reach becoming inconvenient – units have repairs carried out locally.	
"	" 11		HQ. re Bgde. requests for tug of war ropes & [illegible] gloves. Latter not allowed – R.E. will lend ropes. Saw CRE & visited Div. Train.	
"	" 12		To HQ. & Calais re outstanding stores. Bought patch cloth. Notified that art'y detail stores will be supplied by Havre from 14/15.	

WAR DIARY
~~or~~
~~INTELLIGENCE SUMMARY.~~
~~(Erase heading not required.)~~

Army Form C. 2118.

(2)

Instructions regarding War Diaries and Intelligence Summaries are contained in F. S. Regs., Part II. and the Staff Manual respectively. Title pages will be prepared in manuscript.

Place	Date	Hour	Summary of Events and Information	Remarks and references to Appendices
Watten	Mar. 13		To St Omer ROO for bayonets. Received ~~hundreds~~ from Base, after completing from R.E. slips – Some slips re return of carts not required. Brought irons. Collected Lewis gun from 39 Div – property of Div School – presumably I shall have to transport this gun. Saw ADOS XIII Corps re returns.	
— " —	" 14		G. issue instructions to Bdes to mark grenade rifles "RG" – 64 per Bn, & 16 "G": the latter to be used for instruction – the GOC wants the 64 to be efficient rifles, as SAA may have to be fired as well as grenades. Asked Base if grenade rifles are stocked. Asked Havre when 11 limbered wagons for Lewis guns will be delivered – & ADOS for instruction re transport for new Signal Sub Sections. No ans.	
— " —	15		Army require return of 12 clipping machines lent to Div. ADVS returns 7 to me, 5 he returned to 39 Div in last area (subsequently adjusted [illegible]) 3 are remaining, 1 in substitution of an indent, & 2 are for 10 Corps Troops: balance to Base (4).	
— " —	16		Two trucks – only part distributed today, lorries filled. Clothing still short – wired Base for balance, but Base reply not available. Division to move, no details.	
— " —	17		Moving 20th ~~21~~. Cancelled trucks for 19 & 20. Q. & Train in movements. My stores must be at Esquelbecq – far from railhead, Proven, changing on 20th. Car not available for inspection of new area – left details of my requirements with Camp Commdt.	
— " —	18		Stores issued – no issues 19 & 20. To new area & inspected accommodation for offices, 2 shops, dump, billets & WOs & mens messes. All fairly good, but Esquelbecq is far from railhead. Visited HQ.	
— " —	" 19		Part stores moved to new area. Arranged procedure in new area. One lorry will go to ~~railhead or~~ forward area with our Bde. group's stores & this lorry will remain in that area on non-truck days, at railhead, & draw with other lorries on truck days.	
— " — & Esquelbecq	" 20		Moved to new area – Stores &c at Esquelbecq with Div. HQ. Arranged accommodation for stores shops & billets. No trucks. Notified of further forward move of 1 Bde.	
— " —	" 21		Cleared 2 trucks (4 lorries) & brought stores back to dump. Visited forward area & ADOS VIII Corps: agreed to remain here, issuing 2 forward groups at supply refilling points. This is possible at supply refilling points only when interval of 2–3 hours occurs between arrival of train & issues from dump; supplies are often issued within an hour, which does not leave time for sorting Ordnance. However supply transport may not suffice for all Ordnance stores. Alternatives are to take stores to units, or to form special ordnance dumps. Discussed with ADOS formation of Div. Boot	

(3)

WAR DIARY

~~or~~

~~INTELLIGENCE SUMMARY.~~

~~(Erase heading not required.)~~

Army Form C. 2118.

Instructions regarding War Diaries and Intelligence Summaries are contained in F. S. Regs., Part II. and the Staff Manual respectively. Title pages will be prepared in manuscript.

Place	Date	Hour	Summary of Events and Information	Remarks and references to Appendices
Esquelbecq	Mar.		– repairing shops. Advantages appear to be repair of boots of HQ. & small units, & possible special repairs not possible by units' shoemakers. Unless supply of leather is abundant there would not cause reduction in number of boots sent to Base. Q not inclined to take any action, at any rate while Division is being continually moved. Similarly as regards increase in number of armourers in Div. Shop. ADOS suggested increase from 3 to 7 but Div. prefers majority to be with units. Arranged for 194 M.G. Co. to send in guns for overhaul. Visited X Corps shops & 38th Div. Baths & dump.	
"	22		Issuing 2 Bdes forward, & one here. No trucks today. Saw Q re Train re times of supplies refilling.	
"	23		Two trucks at railhead early – attended at railhead. Stores distributed into Bde. groups at railhead, a new departure that worked well. Two groups issued forward. Visited VIII Corps shops, & O.O. Corps Troops. Detail of 3 months clothing issues to 60 Divisions received from Army, – 23rd good re boots & bad re trousers; Art. units away during 2 of these months.	
"	24		70th Bde. group drawing here – no trucks. Decided that when railhead is any distance from central dump, best plan is to split stores at railhead into Bde. groups & issue at convenient dumps, not at supplies refilling times. The latter are usually too early for proper sorting of Ord. stores, transport is insufficient, & issues take longer, thereby blocking refilling points (especially bad if in railhead itself) & delaying convoys. A separate place should be chosen & time about an hour later, any units that can use their supply wagons will send them on for Ordnance after drawing rations.	
"	25		Trucks late but stores issued. Bde. drawing here usually collect most of their stores on day following.	
"	26		No truck. Took S.Sgt. (on probation) – to 47th Div. to which he has been appointed. Collected [illegible] from Army Troops, to replace Pte Sykes evacuated sick.	
"	27		No car available. No truck. HQ. Train re use of light railway for Ord stores – Div. agree to carrying on of lorry system, saving double handling. Lorries must go full [illegible] in any event.	
"	28		HQ 69 Bde. re boots – strongly oppose Div. Shops as against Unit shops. Visited railhead Ord. & VIII Corps Troops re gum boots. Train late – no mineral oil. no ~~[illegible]~~ [illegible]	
"	29		O.C. requires detail of clothing due to 69 & 70 Bdes – sent statement. No car. Changed [illegible] Bde. Armourers, [illegible] under two [illegible]. Saw Q re clothing of 8 Yorks, who had not indented	
"	30		Army re boots 8 Yorks. Also ADOS, & 68 & 69 Bdes. Bdes. do not favour Div. Shops as only means of boot repairing.	
"	31		Bailleul, re furniture. Asked to find Italian medal ribbon! 69 Bde. re 8 Yorks clothing. Visited 47th DOO – & Cashier.	

[signature] Capt.
D.A.D.O.S. 23 Div.

T2134. Wt. W708–776. 500000. 4/15. Sir J. C. & S.

Instructions regarding War Diaries and Intelligence Summaries are contained in F. S. Regs., Part II. and the Staff Manual respectively. Title pages will be prepared in manuscript.

WAR DIARY
or
~~INTELLIGENCE SUMMARY.~~
~~(Erase heading not required.)~~

Army Form C. 2118.

23

Copy DADOS 23 D
Vol 19

Place	Date	Hour	Summary of Events and Information	Remarks and references to Appendices
April 1917.				
Esquelbecq	Apr. 1		To forward area. ADOS & OO Corps Troops. HQ Train re bicycles. HQ RA & T.M. Batteries re indents generally. Q re winter clothing withdrawals.	
— " —	" 2		DOC re indents for clothing 8 Yorks. QM had not resubmitted bulk indents for clothing & boots – also saw DDOS re skins. Selected dump near Bolthe for returned [illegible] – returns [illegible] [illegible] owing to weather. T.M. Poperinghe re dumps when we rejoin X Corps. Visited OO 38 & 55 Divns – also saw ADOS XIII & X Corps. Q informs me I take over 39th dump in new area.	
— " —	" 3		No touch. Move arrangements issued. Made arrangements for supplying in new locations. Saw DOC again re 8 Yorks QM – not a bad sort from QM point of view – his unit alone can say whether he is efficient in equipping his Bn with clothing.	
— " —	" 4		Visited QMS Stores 9 York & Lancs. ADOS X Corps re dump. – I am to take over from 39th. To 39th DOO to arrange transfer.	
— " —	" 5		"Q" re bulk clothing issues. Units being sent in returns of outstanding stores – Form outstanding bulk indents being cancelled weekly. 68 Bde Group issued at Bollezeele. Heavy bulk – boots & clothing.	
— " —	" 6		69 Bde moving. 68 issues at back area. 70 at railhead. Saw 69 & 70 Bde Staffs re locations & arranged for future issues also RA. Visited 39 Dump & arranged for taking stores over.	
— " —	" 7		S/Cond. Gray left for commission – am now 1 W.O. short of establishment. Instructed to exchange my Sergt Clerk for an A/Sergt of 55 Div to act as W.O. Still new [illegible] men – distribution of old [illegible] men very [illegible] – I have never had one of Bde W.O. – other Divisions have them. Issued 69 Bde forward & 68 back. Sent reserve stores on to new dump.	
— " —	" 8		Hqrs Divn move. Orders re dumps change [illegible]. Issues at road dumps today. 39 DOO cannot move tomorrow – arranged to stay here another day. Men from Corps to call in & replaced MK I Vickers barrels & cups. Collected 68 M.Gun Coy at back area & sent to 39 Dump. Other M.Gun Coys unable to send there. 69 have returned theirs to Railhead. 70 sent in 194 Coy – in line not available.	
— " —	" 9		Light truck only. Moved some stores to new dump. No car.	
— " —	" 10		Moved to new (old) dump & relieved 39. No car available. Dump improved by 39 DOO who had all personnel staff & offices here.	

(2)

Army Form C. 2118.

Instructions regarding War Diaries and Intelligence Summaries are contained in F. S. Regs., Part II. and the Staff Manual respectively. Title pages will be prepared in manuscript.

WAR DIARY
or
~~INTELLIGENCE SUMMARY.~~

(Erase heading not required.)

Place	Date	Hour	Summary of Events and Information	Remarks and references to Appendices
Nr Poperinghe ~~April~~	April 11		ADOS & Corps [illegible] re Gum Boots etc. – Div Conference – shortage of Pistols discussed no other Ordnance questions.	
"	" 12		Hazebrouck for chairs, visited Reinforcement Camp & HQs. – ADOS & Proven R'head re 3 mortars returned by a unit without instructions. Demanded to replace.	
"	" 13		8 Yorks [illegible] portion of timber signed for by them last [illegible] but not removed by them from railhead, apparently taken by another unit. RSO re test at Railhead for returned winter clothing.	
	" 14		[illegible] completed issue of Packsaddlery for [illegible]. New WO & [illegible] [illegible] replacing Sergt George & S Cond [illegible]. Visited shops also HQ 102 & 103 RFA at Ypres also 8 Staffs. Blankets required for dug outs as gas protection – arranged supply through Baths. Personnel tested with Box Respirators.	
	" 15		Visited all Bns of [illegible] Bde with Brigadier. Brigade has lost several machine guns – hastened indents for all stores to replace. Drafted circular for issue by G' again explaining indent system.	
	" 16		[illegible] circular issued by G to Bdes & HQrs must be sent to all units. Saw RSO re [illegible] requirements. Returned MG barrels & cups to Base. Pitched store tent at Railhead for winter clothing (return suspended on account of weather).	
	" 17		[illegible] [illegible] Ridge [illegible] broken – [illegible] struck & Reps at railhead – weather still very bad. [illegible] for lost Lewis Guns coming in. Also 18 pdr damaged & amn. wagon.	
	" 18		[illegible] [illegible] stores short again or not supply. ADOS wired Base for [illegible] were also asked to supply deficiencies early. GOC's conference – RE [illegible] & [illegible] wanted for Bde schools. Bought stores in Bailleul. Sundry units attached from 39 Div.	
	" 19		Salvage Dump & Railhead for [illegible] etc required by Bde Schools. ADOS [illegible] for gun limber. Instructions for demanding guns are confusing as are all attempts to define too exactly the form of any [illegible] – special cases arise & cause additional demands for explanations.	
	" 20		Bulk stores continue short 600 [illegible] [illegible] [illegible].	
	" 21		Hazebrouck & Bailleul for stores. Visited all RE Coys. also 18 Bde HQrs.	
	" 22		Visited Bde Schools. 65 [illegible] 70 all correct. Bought [illegible] for Health Detachments.	

T2134. Wt. W708–776. 500000. 4/15. Sir J. C. & S.

Instructions regarding War Diaries and Intelligence Summaries are contained in F. S. Regs., Part II. and the Staff Manual respectively. Title pages will be prepared in manuscript.

WAR DIARY
or
INTELLIGENCE SUMMARY.
(Erase heading not required.)

Army Form C. 2118.

(3)

Place	Date	Hour	Summary of Events and Information	Remarks and references to Appendices
Nr Poperinghe	23-4-17		To Dunkerque – bought soap & [illegible] for RA.	
"	24-4-17		Bought [illegible] for Health Ex. also brushes & nosebags authorised by Army. FGO requires man Steenvoorde [illegible] bathside. Rum received for 8/102 & sent to shops.	
"	25-4-17		Soft soap & bayonets received in part. New Zealand periscopes received for local FGC's conference.	
"	26-4-17		Visited Div Bomb School & 68 Bde School. Nosebags received from Local Purchase.	
"	27-4-17		Reported re procedure in event of advance – no ordnance alterations necessary. Nosebags received in full from Base. MT covers short. Demanded Steenvoorde Hotel.	
"	28-4-17		Arranged to issue truck covers to DSC pending supply of lorry covers [illegible]. Bought brooms in Hazebrouck	
"	29-4-17		Orders to move back. Arranged for return of winter clothing at once. 19 DOO will take over here – we go to new area Steenvoorde. No area available. Camp Comdt billeting. Armourers due to be transferred to 19 Div.	
"	30-4-17		To Steenvoorde re new dump. Found dump – not a good one but will do for a few days – until moving. Shall receive truck on 2nd, reconsigning of [illegible] issue. Left some stores [illegible].	

[signature] Captain

D. A. D. O. S.
23rd DIVISION.

T2134. Wt. W708—776. 500000. 4/15. Sir J. C. & S.

Confidential

Vol 20

War Diary of

Capt. J. B. Oxenham

D.A.D.O.S. 23rd Div.

1 – 31 May 1917.

Confidential

(1)

Instructions regarding War Diaries and Intelligence Summaries are contained in F. S. Regs., Part II. and the Staff Manual respectively. Title pages will be prepared in manuscript.

WAR DIARY

~~or~~

~~INTELLIGENCE SUMMARY.~~

~~(Erase heading not required.)~~

Army Form C. 2118.

Place	Date	Hour	Summary of Events and Information	Remarks and references to Appendices
May	1917.			
Nr Poperinghe G 14 b cen.	May 1		19th Div. sending over stores – portion of mine taken to new dump Steenvoorde. Arranged billets re Steenvoorde. No news of further orders yet – Units instructed to clear all stores early.	
— " — & Steenvoorde	" 2		Moved to new dump – usual [illegible] of owners to remove carts from sheds. Pitched tent for men – no accommodation for Armourers Shop. Truck [illegible] – Units all to draw from this [illegible] dump 3/5/17 & onwards. Saw DOC re clothing & equipment – must expect big indents.	
— " —	" 3		Visited Wippenhoek – winter clothing still coming in. Also 19th D.O.O. re stores transferred & 47th D.O.O. Saw 10 RA re gun [illegible], & wire for [illegible] tanks. Issued [illegible] for [illegible] to DGO. Saw Q re 25% [illegible] authorised in the army – 9. [illegible] [illegible] should be kept up. [illegible] 900 – [illegible] being still short.	
— " —	" 4		To Hazebrouck for machine parts & other stores. Stationery dept any [illegible] for map marking [illegible] AOD supply – bought supply [illegible] to correct. Found place for Armourers Shop. Clothing up in full – [illegible] now good.	
— " —	" 5		Moved Armourers to new shop [illegible] truck. Winter clothing still coming in. Machine guns – one [illegible] Co. called in for examination.	
— " —	" 6		No car available. 69 Bge. [illegible] to supply working parties. Issued to their units at railhead.	
— " —	" 7		Detail truck [illegible] packs [illegible]. Visited ADOS, Wippenhoek, other DOOs & bought [illegible] brushes	
— " —	" 8		Rain: sufficient [illegible] left for winter clothing at railhead – much [illegible] during the 10 days fine weather. Bought brushes Hazebrouck – enquired re soda prices.	
— " —	" 9		68 Bge moving; no issues to them. 69 Bge. drawing at railhead. Soda received.	
— " —	" 10		Box respirator [illegible] received & issued to Units – 68 Bge stores of 9/5/17 issued at railhead.	
— " —	" 11		Bought tools at St Omer. Singer machine parts not yet ready at Hazebrouck. Moving stores back to old dump, taking over again from 19th at G14 b cen. Issues from there today & onward. Notified of 5 trucks [illegible] tents &c., also saddlery, [illegible] for 2 [illegible] Doc wired for the [illegible] fire [illegible] last night. Early [illegible] clearing of railhead. Q [illegible] & take over from 47th on 13th – Arranged another move! Arrange to take tents &c. direct to their dump.	
G 14 b cen.	" 12		Moved back to G 14 b cen. Two trucks [illegible] not received. Stacked tents at 47th Dump. Issued [illegible] &c. to Doc & called for statement of requirements or surpluses. Saw RA re guns & [illegible]. 6 trucks due tomorrow – Div. want to borrow lorry 7 am. [illegible]. Saw 47 D.O.O. re taking over, probably on 14th. ADOS re scheme for issue of [illegible] gun parts from park.	
— " —	" 13		Clearing dump for 47th Div. site. Winter clothing nearly all in & Wippenhoek siding being cleared slowly.	
— " — & G. 27 b. 5. 8.	" 14		Took over dump from 47th DOO [illegible] take over from me. DOCs conference. Wire cutters, mats, gloves [illegible] [illegible] pistols to be kept with Div. – letter to be sent by DOC. ~~[illegible]~~ m. guns, [illegible] & spares – available at park. Drafted letter.	
— " —	" 15		Saw ADOS re Div requirements & m. gun & parts from proposed park – scheme not yet finally approved. Hazebrouck [illegible] for [illegible] [illegible] implement for converting cartridges to blanks.	

T2134. Wt. W708—776. 500000. 4/15. Sir J. C. & S.

(2)

Instructions regarding War Diaries and Intelligence Summaries are contained in F. S. Regs., Part II. and the Staff Manual respectively. Title pages will be prepared in manuscript.

Army Form C. 2118.

WAR DIARY
or
~~INTELLIGENCE SUMMARY.~~
(Erase heading not required.)

Place	Date	Hour	Summary of Events and Information	Remarks and references to Appendices
May 1917 Reninghelst G.27.b.5.8	May	16	Truck load of wheels. Two machine guns demanded. ADOS inspected dump. No car available. Demanded mg gun parts for Armr's Shop. Picketing gear short.	
— " —	"	17	No car. Lorries now often out on loan & corps stone jobs. One to Canal for wire cutters &, one at Wippenhoek, winter clothing. Put Sgt Scott in charge of personnel details. Agreed to running of a [illegible].	
— " —	"	18	To Bailleul for demands & hatchets. Back up in full – some surpluses. DMG officer very keen on collecting mg barrels – wrote ADOS re this – also for authority for extra stakes winter beds.	
— " —	"	19	No morning car. 69 Bde ask for wire cutters in very different proportions from those authorised by the Bde at conference. Sent to Hazebrouck for AA mountings & Lewis gun tripods mountings RE Shop. Div Train also requires fitting for attaching petrol tins to limbered wagons (for water).	
— " —	"	20	No trucks – delayed. Drew camp stores for Div. Hastened R.O. springs for DAC. Second Army offensive scheme received – note Q has circulated Ordnance notes sent to [illegible] in – just marked for information only. Visited DSC re timber, stencils & tanks.	
— " —	"	21	To Bailleul for bolts for fixing water carrier straps to wagons – also RE Shops Hazebrouck re fitting of same. Also stores still coming in from Corps & out of Units. HQ anxious to [illegible] for coming operations – stakes, ammn. carriers, baskets, wire cutters &c – am making up small numbers & obtaining spares for Armr's Shop. Units instructed to keep up mob. stores.	
— " —		22	Bought buttons, tape, brushes & paint. Wheels still arriving – a second 50 today.	
— " —		23	ADOS re special stores asked for by Div. Also Q & RA re camp equipment. DOCs conference – enquiries re numbers of cutters likely to be issued. 1st blankets to be returned early. Rope required for pukka packs. No car.	
— " —		24	A Wed. truck received today. Also 1 4.5" piece. Drawing of pack saddlery & pukka packs. Bought stores for Baths. Also taps for water carriers.	
— " —		25	No trucks. Wippenhoek railhead re return of 1st blankets a week before the programme – all clear. Q re issue of wire cutters &c. & ADMS re drag ropes for trench trucks. Received instructions for gun park procedure.	
— " —		26	Visited line with DADMS re drag ropes for trench tramways. Bought rope & rings. MG gun parts coming up well. Trucks usually a day late now.	
— " —		27	No trucks. RE shops re [illegible] & straps for carrying water tins on limbers. 14 water carts allotted to Div.	
— " —		28	Several vehicles up – & Sunday's truck. Most of the special stores now up & issued – pack saddles, pukka packs, [illegible] &c. DMS demands to Gun Park – first supplies coming.	

WAR DIARY

or

INTELLIGENCE SUMMARY.

(Erase heading not required.)

(3)

Army Form C. 2118.

Instructions regarding War Diaries and Intelligence Summaries are contained in F. S. Regs., Part II. and the Staff Manual respectively. Title pages will be prepared in manuscript.

Place	Date	Hour	Summary of Events and Information	Remarks and references to Appendices
	1917			
[illegible] G.27 c.5.8	May 29		4.5" & sights complete demanded from Gun Park. Visited Gun Park. Also 69 Bde HQ & Bailleul for special flags required.	
— " —	" 30		Trucks still late – one day usually. Buck gun parts received from Park – all being issued through armourers shops.	
— " —	31		DOS conference. All Div. demands for special stores e.g. wirecutters met in full except [illegible] – no increase yet approved. Several M.G. barrels issued from armament spares to Coys. that will probably require most spares, Nos 194 & 68. 12 2" mortars & some spares received – [illegible] replace possible [illegible] – a curiously large issue – An issue of Lewis guns, or Stokes mortars would have been useful. Instruments wanted for bayonet sharpening – will buy files.	

[signature] Capt.
D.A.D.O.S.
23 Div.

1/6/17.

T2134. Wt. W708—776. 500000. 4/15. Sir J. C. & S.

Vol 21

Confidential

War Diary of

Capt J B OXENHAM

D.A.D.O.S.

23 Div.

June 1917.

WAR DIARY

~~or~~

~~INTELLIGENCE SUMMARY.~~

(Erase heading not required.)

Army Form C. 2118.

(1)

Confidential

Instructions regarding War Diaries and Intelligence Summaries are contained in F. S. Regs., Part II. and the Staff Manual respectively. Title pages will be prepared in manuscript.

Place	Date	Hour	Summary of Events and Information	Remarks and references to Appendices
	1917			
Reninghelst G.27.b.5.8	June	1.	To Bailleul for French medal ribbons for brooches required by noon. Bought wire & nails for special stretcher fitting & flags for Inf Bge. "mopping up". Visited Gun Park re 4.5" demanded — also Shops re R.O. springs &c, & D.S.C. re making fittings for stretchers. Wippenhoek railhead, where winter clothing receipts are practically completed. Asked Bges. for distribution of surplus cutters & grenade carriers held by me.	
— " —	"	2	Bought torches — also files for bayonets. Saw ADOS re 4.5 not yet received from Gun Pk. Arr. 2 Sgt returned to 8 KOYLI for duty. One Bge. ask for 5000 yds cordage for hanging boots! 4.5 R.O springs slow — Second Corps.	
— " —	"	3	No morning car. Visited Salvage dump, — almost clear. Bought tape for 69 Bge. Collected special signalling [illegible] from R.E. shops.	
— " —	"	4	To Walou — 17 D.S.C. for clamps required for ambulances. Also ADOS re guns. No arrangement in this Army as on the Somme for Div RA to keep a battery or more in reserve to replace at once guns sent in to Shops for examination: RA therefore is continually agitating for new guns — if possible before defective guns are taken out. Somme scheme worked well last year.	
— " —	"	5	Two Lewis guns lost on bolted mules. Also one Vickers destroyed. Collected new from Park by lorry. To R.E. Shops for rifle grenade cups & signalling flares. Also Q. re proposal to cut down by phone — scheme altered & phone to remain; it is my main medium for sending wires. Received ~~[illegible]~~ 9.45 Hrs. — Dump becoming a small Gun Park.	
— " —	"	6	Two Lewis guns knocked out. Div. HQ [illegible] move up — all quiet before tomorrow's attack. This dump not shelled this year — nearest half a mile away. Poperinghe shelled but not railhead. Collected telescope from Bailleul ROO for Div HQ, who had demanded 3 to replace only a day or two ago & kept hustling. Corps asked Base for early supply without result. Otherwise all stores — including 30 m.g. barrels are out in time for "push" tonight.	
— " —	"	7	M. Guns due not received from Park — sent lorry for them. Removed forty from Wippenhoek railhead, winter clothing being completed. Heard Hill 60 go up 3.10 this morning — offensive reported successful to date. Visited Baths. Everything very quiet behind the line today. Yesterday's truck arrived today, — late, 6 pm.	
— " —	"	8	2 telescopes received for HQ. No truck yet. To Adv HQ with new QA & QMG who took up [illegible] cartridges obtained with difficulty from ammn railhead. Still very quiet & few demands. Have anticipated demands for more tins & water bottles.	
— " —	"	9	3 Vickers & 1 Lewis gun collected from Park on today's demands. No morning car. Bought stores, — visited back Salvage dump where no stores had been received from forward dumps.	

Instructions regarding War Diaries and Intelligence Summaries are contained in F. S. Regs., Part II. and the Staff Manual respectively. Title pages will be prepared in manuscript.

(2)

WAR DIARY

~~or~~

~~INTELLIGENCE SUMMARY.~~

~~(Erase heading not required.)~~

Army Form C. 2118.

Place	Date	Hour	Summary of Events and Information	Remarks and references to Appendices
	1917			
Reninghelst G27.b.5.8	June 10		Demand through Q. for 7 Lewis guns complete & also 4 spares, 12 D.A.L. Wired, & sent lorry to collect. Gun Park is not supplying parts very readily: lorry calls about once a day, & delivers a few small springs – many stores are outstanding. Hastened spoke poles & wheels.	
— " —	" 11		~~Six~~ Four wagons arrived to replace destroyed. Twelve more Lewis guns demanded. Notified Div. moving on 13th. Agreed with Q. to issue clothing in new area – not to make special demands before bath day – 3 days time.	
— " —	" 12		To new area, Bertlen, & found site for dump. Moved part stores down. Four Lewis guns demanded.	
Pitbinck R.21.c.5.0	" 13		Moved to new area. Saw HQ Co. re refilling artillery & sundry units still left in front area. No news about attached units. Move machinery is still slow, units being without stores for some days owing to absence of information of old or new formations.	
— " —	" 14		No trucks in morning – 2 in afternoon. Moved 2" mortars from old dump to Gun Pk (why not consigned there in first place?). To old area re baths clothing. Officer i/c Baths does not now move with Div. – an officer is ~~very~~ essential in back area where laundries must be improvised, otherwise much new issue & an endless accumulation of dirty clothing. RA & RE still in front area, with 24 Div. – no information of refilling point.	
— " —	" 15		Now settled. Issued RA & RE at their own lines forward. With Inspecting Armourer (now attached for a few days) to Salvage dump in Ypres – nearly clear there, nothing to bring back. Visited Baths.	
— " —	" 16		Baillieul or purchase. Gun Park re non-supply of wheels & poles. Following truck arrived, but 2 trucks with special clothing notified, not yet received.	
— " —	" 17 / 18		No car available at all during these 2 days. Trucks are now running regularly at Caestre. S.D. clothing issued in quantities to Inf. who still require time to refit before battle wear, special demand wired. Underclothing issued from Baths – no laundry running: demands not very heavy.	
— " —	19		Trophies received from 69 Bge. M guns to be returned to Base – mortars to be kept for army use. To ADOS re Q's proposal that all returned ordnance stores go to DADOS not to railhead direct. Best to have Salvage Coy. always running & close to dump, using Ord. lorries for railhead work. Visited 24th dump – which we may be taking over.	
— " —	20		Corps 3 for. Visited Train, & 70th Bges re water carts. A.I.A. also with me visited units armourers' shops.	

Instructions regarding War Diaries and Intelligence Summaries are contained in F. S. Regs., Part II. and the Staff Manual respectively. Title pages will be prepared in manuscript.

WAR DIARY

or

~~INTELLIGENCE SUMMARY.~~

(*Erase heading not required.*)

Army Form C. 2118.

(3)

Place	Date	Hour	Summary of Events and Information	Remarks and references to Appendices
1917				
Poperinghe ~~G.29.b~~ R 21.c 5.0	June 21		On purchases at Bailleul: Q. Stores with telescopes defective. ADOS re new type of brush for Lewis gun. Stops re cap for Horse float. Also X C.T. maps at this depot. AIA visited Units. My CC left for leave.	
"	"	22	Balance of clothing received, except trousers in certain sizes. Stops re mat for Horse float. Also Corps re moves.	
"	"	23	Q. state Very pistols & box periscopes short in 70 Bge. Wired Bge. Pistols received yesterday – wired Base for periscopes. Units showed [illegible] demand earlier but repeated orders are neglected in this respect. Hazebrouck RE stops for cart wheel, & Ord. Stops for mat. Visited 24, 41 & 47 DOS re moves.	
"	"	24	No trucks – 3 advised not received, including urgent clothing for Baths.	
"	"	25	Sunday bulk truck received – one day late. Q ask for 290 medal ribbons at once. No car. Attached infantry men medically examined.	
"	"	26	Interpreter [struck through] to buy fans for trenches – none found. Got some from Dunkirk. Visited Corps stops, & 24 & 41 Div re taking over dump &c.	
"	"	27	41 DOS is taking over here on 1/7/17 – inspected dump. No truck. Moved part stores to new dump – now 24th Div. Issued special stores – e.g. periscopes, to 70 Bge from new dump. Not a good dump – all canvas & surrounded by ammunition.	
"	"	28.	Arranged for issues during moves on 29 & 30. Truck one day late as usual.	
"	"	29	Bailleul purchasing. ~~Z~~ New dump also. Found W.O. & 7 men left by 24 Div – apparently leaving their artillery staff; no rations for these men, & no notice of move until afternoon. ADOS confirms move, though it will apparently only be required for a few days. I think a "move" should not be made for less than a 10 day separation if Units are within say 30 miles: – adjustments of bulk & stores in transit occupy several days at ~~each~~ each end of the period.	
N.12.2.1	"	30	Moved to new area, vacated by 24 Div. Fridays truck arrived. Issued R.a. at back refilling point, & others Units draw here. Arranged with W.O. 24th Div. re issues to his Units. Separate bulk indents sent to Base & from PK. for 23 & 24 Units.	

[signature]
DDOS
23 Div.

T2134. Wt. W708–776. 500000. 4/15. Sir J. C. & S.

Vol 22

Confidential

War Diary of

Capt. J. B. Oxenham A.O.D.

D.A.D.O.S. 23rd Div.

July 1917

Confidential

Instructions regarding War Diaries and Intelligence Summaries are contained in F. S. Regs., Part II. and the Staff Manual respectively. Title pages will be prepared in manuscript.

WAR DIARY

~~or~~

~~INTELLIGENCE SUMMARY.~~

(Erase heading not required.)

(1)

Army Form C. 2118.

Place	Date	Hour	Summary of Events and Information	Remarks and references to Appendices
	1917			
N.1.b.2.1 & Reningshelst	July 1		24th Dump not good – ammunition refilling on single track movement, & RA want to return to Ord. ground. 47th are not taking over 41 Dump Reningshelst & as Corps & Div. agree I move in. No truck. Collected 24 A.A. mountings for m. guns from RE shops.	
"	" 2		Transferred 24 RA back to Divn. Gun & eye demanded for 102 Bye. Returned to gun park 5 9.45 & 2 2" T.MS from 24th Div RA.	
"	3 - 13		On leave. Transferred to II Corps 4/7/17, temporarily. Expect to be again in X Corps about 20th. This move entails alterations of bulk drafts & transfer of Gun Pk indents to Base, as II Corps in Fifth Army. Gun Park later transferred to Fifth Army & indents again transferred. Temporary change also causing some confusion in special stores, pack saddlery, Yukon packs &c not being transferred from one Army. Demanded to complete this Divn. but may have to hand over to 41st on relief. Transferred all gas stores to D.G.O. for storage & issue. Water carts & tanks issued for last offensive returned to 10M except 2 awaiting replacement from Base. One RE Co. 24th Div. attached for Ord. services: transfers for short periods not satisfactory – it is better for Divns. to endeavour to supply their own units if detachment is only for a few days. By Q orders all Ord returned stores now come to me & I sort it with assistance of 6 men from Employt Co. when available: this return, & the checking of returned clothing against issues, will be working for next month – at present units are not returning clothing in numbers. All my attached men, tailors, loaders &c. now come from Div Employment Co. – an improvement.	
"	14		Trucks still one day late. Saw Div. re Camp equipment required – none available with Corps, issued my stock.	
"	15		To ADOS II & X Corps re special stores, moves, & dumps. Present dump is in X Corps area & must be retained when Div. goes into that Corps.	
"	16		Bought cutch, tools & pins at Dunkirk. 24 DOO called re dumps. No truck 7th. 2nd Anzac Artillery arrived & transferred to me.	
"	17		Trucks arrived afternoon. 1 Vickers & 1 Lewis gun condemned. Visited DDOS re return of stores & 68 Bye re spare gun parts & telescopic rifles. Baths re underclothing required – quantity demanded.	

(2)

Army Form C. 2118.

Instructions regarding War Diaries and Intelligence Summaries are contained in F. S. Regs., Part II. and the Staff Manual respectively. Title pages will be prepared in manuscript.

WAR DIARY
or
INTELLIGENCE SUMMARY.
(Erase heading not required.)

Place	Date	Hour	Summary of Events and Information	Remarks and references to Appendices
1917				
Reningshelst	July 18		Packsaddles specially issued now being returned esp. by Arty who stay in line. Visited ADOS & shops. Bought stores Bailleul. Demanded ammn carriers for 24 Div. RA. Visited Gun Park re outstanding stores. Moves altered – my dump will probably be Meteren with Div HQ – units going back to Berthen area, 10 Bde moving today.	
— " —	" 19		Bns inform HQ 201 magnetic compasses required to complete establishment! As all were instructed to complete 3 months ago & Base has been supplying, this figure is obviously wrong – a call for confirmation of any figures given by Units always results in wide differences appearing. To Meteren re dump for next move, selected site, but HQ state move now altered. 2 guns demanded	
— " —	" 20		Batty no stocks. 24 D.O.O. called re transfer to him of my Arty & 2 Anzac Arty. No truck. No car all day.	
— " —	" 21		Truck in 2 days late – railhead changed. Today truck not advised yet. To Meris & Meteren re dumps. Saw 24 D.O.O. re transfers &	
— " —	" 22		No truck. Transferred 2nd Bns. Div RA to 24 Div – also our own RA Pioneers, & Ordnance for these will remain at this dump, 24 Div. dump adjacent.	
— " — & Meteren	" 23		Moved to Meteren – Div. at Meris. Truck cleared to new dump, RA stores to old dump. Saw ADOS II & X Corps: also Med. & Light Shops. Div. (exc RA) now in X Corps, Second Army again. Gun Pk incidents, Inf. cancelled, & old truck dates restored.	
— " —	" 24		No truck – clothing overdue & Units hastening. DOCs conference. Raised question of cutting down trousers to shorts. This is authorised in case of old trousers only but Units will do it uniformly & new garments are cut, & trousers not kept up to strength. Agreed that one month be allowed for Units to re-equip with trousers. Also raised establishment of clipping machines – Q. to see if scale can be increased. Compasses to be tabulated. & More [illegible] frocks required.	
— " —	" 25		Still no truck. Visited ADOS re more frocks & supply of emblems. Shops for dismantling – taken to 194 M.G.Co. who go into line. Conference at AA+QMG. Suggested stock of L.G. spares be kept in Arms Shops – Bdes to say what parts most necessary.	
— " —	" 26		All trucks received – 6 loads. Clothing being issued. Two loads to RA detached with 24th Div. 69 Bde. informing [illegible] back – clothing to be sent to them tomorrow. One L.G. [illegible].	

T2134. Wt. W708—776. 500000. 4/15. Sir J. C. & S.

(3)

Army Form C. 2118.

Instructions regarding War Diaries and Intelligence Summaries are contained in F. S. Regs., Part II. and the Staff Manual respectively. Title pages will be prepared in manuscript.

WAR DIARY
or
INTELLIGENCE SUMMARY.
(Erase heading not required.)

Place	Date	Hour	Summary of Events and Information	Remarks and references to Appendices
	1917			
Meteren	July 27		Issued 69 Bge Units at backward area — 3½ hrs by lorry.	
"	28		68 Bge to move back — only one Inf. Bge now in HQ area. Returned clothing coming in; not yet complete with attached men for salvage, only 2 at present. Arranged for disinfection of lorries taking clothing to [illegible].	
"	29		ADOS visited dump — states Army not quite happy about my dealing with returned stores — I suggested experiment should continue. Collected tins(?) from shops. Pte Britt left to join an Inf Bn. Issued 69 Bge stores in back area.	
"	30		No car until 6 pm. To Q. re covers for helmets — Div to be equipped again with these. Also re Yukon packs establishment & for instructions for issue of balance of packsaddlery.	
"	31		Issued 69 & 68 Bge, back areas. To 55 DOO(?) re helmet covers; demanded 4500 from Base. Brought paint & brushes.	

[signature] Capt.
DADOS
23 Div.

T2134. Wt. W708—776. 500000. 4/15. Sir J. C. & S.

Vol 23

Confidential

War Diary of

Capt. J. B. Oxenham AOD

D.A.D.O.S. 23rd Divn.

Aug. 1917.

Confidential

Instructions regarding War Diaries and Intelligence Summaries are contained in F. S. Regs., Part II. and the Staff Manual respectively. Title pages will be prepared in manuscript.

WAR DIARY

or

~~INTELLIGENCE SUMMARY.~~

(Erase heading not required.)

(1)

Army Form C. 2118.

Place	Date	Hour	Summary of Events and Information	Remarks and references to Appendices
1917.				
Aug:	1		No truck. Armourers returning to their Units in turn to inspect rifles.	
Meteren	2		Truck received – also 4 water carts. Issued direct to back Bdes. Visited 68 & 69 Bdes. Took sample of bag for pack rations – demanded 400 sacks to make up these bags.	
—"—	3		ADOS again re hastening breech covers. Wired Base for covers, & helmet covers additional; supply short at Base. Visited 24 & 25 DAC; also Shops re water carts & vehicles for repair.	
—"—	4		Div HQ is to be move back. As railhead does not alter & one Bde remains here I am stopping if possible. Issuing balance of packsaddlery & Jerkin packs. Truck on duty late. Lorry broke down – part stores only delivered.	
—"—	5		No truck today – issuing balance of stores to back Bdes. 70th Bde also to move to back area, – no instructions re any movements. Hastened supply of ration sacks.	
—"—	6		Railhead will not alter until 9th – I am to remain here until 7th or 8th. Visited Div. area Wizernes. Informed that Div. is not remaining there. I am to remain at Meteren until further orders.	
—"—	7		Div. to move to Locke area 9th. Visited ADOS who told me Corps require me to move from here. Arranged for billets with T.M. Locke. Orders for Locke cancelled. To Div., who are now to move to Eperlecques area – instructed to move part stores there tomorrow, completing 9th, when railhead changes. No lorries available tomorrow but I can demand extra ones for 9th.	
—"— Eperlecques	8		Arranging to move to Eperlecques but no car sent from Div. yet – 10.30 – communication with Div. difficult. To Eperlecques & inspected dump & – ...ward office to move in. Div. Conference – question re shortage of ...	
—"—	9		Div. moved to Eperlecques. Artillery still detached. Armourers making a specimen sight for A.A. use, Lewis & Vickers guns.	
—"—	10		Units drawing from dump, except 70 Bde, moved forward. To Calais re helmet covers, breech covers, black blocks & material for distinguishing marks; also web equipment, & revolvers. Armbands will be used on shoulder straps as desired – blue material secured for signallers. Bought parrot & ...	
—"—	11		To forward area, – 70th Bde & detachment with 24 Div. ... Visited Shops & Train Coy. Conference ADOS XVIII Corps & arranged with him & afterwards with ADOS X Corps that packsaddlery should not be called in but 23 & 39 Divs should keep their own or transfer to other armies – XVIII Corps making up deficiencies of 39th Div.	

T2134. Wt. W708—776. 500000. 4/15. Sir J. C. & S.

(2)

Army Form C. 2118.

Instructions regarding War Diaries and Intelligence Summaries are contained in F. S. Regs., Part II. and the Staff Manual respectively. Title pages will be prepared in manuscript.

WAR DIARY

~~or~~

~~INTELLIGENCE SUMMARY.~~

~~(Erase heading not required.)~~

Place	Date	Hour	Summary of Events and Information	Remarks and references to Appendices
1917	Aug.			
[illegible]	12		Am now receiving paper from 2 armies & 3 corps. Fifth Army require statement of position in regard to equipment. Such statements difficult to render if at regular periods, when Units cannot take stock. In any system of visits & returns of indents an O.O. is really dependent on information from Units. Monthly return of certain important items by Units might be useful: conferences better for general items. Salvage staff of 4 now complete.	
— " —	13		To Calais with DAQMG & Staff Capt. of Bgde. Visited stores & Workshops. Issued forward Bge stores – lorry failed to find R.E. Co.	
— " —	14		Two lorries running forward. [illegible] by M.G. Co. ask for 95% [illegible] allowed – another issue of [illegible] to complete after losses. Many orders published from Div. re this.	
— " —	15		Visited 48 D.O.O. & arranged transfer in case of move up. Also A.D.O.S. Bought stores in Poperinghe & tried to have some special AA sights made in Heavy Shops. Visited forward dump & 24 D.O.O. who administers artillery still.	
— " —	16		Q. re wagon loads. Helmet covers arrived to complete infantry – no rifle covers yet, wired A.D.O.S. to hasten. Failed to buy rings for water carriers in St Omer. Instructed to withdraw 3 Lewis guns for use of R.A. Arranged to continue same system of issue to R.A. through 24 Div, though R.A. have moved towards our new area.	
— " —	17		To Calais for rings to complete carriers. Also bought tools for Employment Co. Calais Depot & shops. A/S-C Dakin killed by bomb at Art. dump (24 Div area).	
— " —	18		A.D.O.S. XVIII Corps re carriers now ready & R.A. administration to continue as now, & A.D.O.S. will visit Staff Capt. To Reninghelst dump & 24 D.O.O. Attended funeral of S/C Dakin, & an Arm. Sgt. killed at same time in sleeping hut at dump. Traced field kitchens at Workshops – unit hastening.	
— " —	19		Visited A.D.O.S. X Corps in his place. Lorry sent to forward area broken down – another sent up to replace – forward refilling over 30 miles run. Have 1600 [illegible] tin dixies – 3 loads. Armourers [illegible] with AA sights.	
— " —	20		Forward area with DAQMG – to arrange equipment of reinforcement camp, (afterwards cancelled through move). Visited 70 Bgde, & 48 D.O.O. Div. now to move to II Corps.	
— " —	21		Lorry to Calais for stores. M. Guns being altered for A.A. sights. Q. inspected dump & Salvage. Trucks [illegible] in to date.	
— " —	22		Visited II Corps & 56 Div, which we relieve. Inspected detached artillery A.O.C. personnel & dump. Stopped trucks until 25th. Arranged to keep our pack saddlery & [illegible] packs, drawing equivalent from II Corps & handing to XVIII.	

T2134. Wt. W708—776. 500000. 4/15. Sir J. C. & S.

Instructions regarding War Diaries and Intelligence Summaries are contained in F. S. Regs., Part II. and the Staff Manual respectively. Title pages will be prepared in manuscript.

(3)

WAR DIARY
~~or~~
~~INTELLIGENCE~~ SUMMARY.
~~(Erase heading not required.)~~

Army Form C. 2118.

Place	Date	Hour	Summary of Events and Information	Remarks and references to Appendices
1917				
Steenvoorde	Aug.	23.	No truck. Moved part stores to new area Reninghelst. Attended tests of new Base AA sights & sights made in shops. Latter simpler & quite good. ADOS V Corps inspected dump.	
—"— & Reninghelst	"	24	Moved to Reninghelst & took over a very dirty & dilapidated dump. 56 Div. Art'y now attached to me — 23rd Art'y moved from 24th Div. to 48th Div. Sgt. Donald reported for duty as W.O. vice S-C. Dakin, killed.	
—"—	"	25	No truck – railhead changes. One Bde moving up to line. Arranged for drawal of packsaddlery & Yukon packs from II C.T. to issue to XVIII Corps to replace those taken out by Units on transfer. ADOS visited dump. Sandbag shelters required here – bombing frequent. No car today.	
—"—	"	26	Q. re stores left by 14 Div. Visited 14 DOO & Corps Salvage.	
—"—	"	27	48 Div. Ord. & RA re 3 Lewis guns lent to RA when in XVIII Corps. Bought material in Poperinghe. II Corps ADOS re helmet covers, Base having recently supplied 11000 & now declining to replace [illegible].	
—"—	"	28	New railhead Dickebusch. To [illegible] Owner for stores – also bought kit for [illegible] Bde. Visited HQ – am now detached there, all Div. having moved to advanced HQ.	
—"—	"	29	R.O.O. re cookers issued at railhead to wrong Unit – adjusted. CRE re Yukon packs & HQ re buckets & stoves required. Also visited II C.T. Train Co., Mob. Vet. Sec. Drew 500 blankets for Amb., also Watson fans for Inf.	
—"—	"	30	Now 3 Div. Art. Units attached to me, I Aus. 14 Div. & 56 Div. — mine now with 58th. ADOS & [illegible] re revolvers due. Bought Primus stoves for HQ issue to line.	
—"—	"	31	Two 18pr guns completely demolished, also 2 carriages. On RA condemnation Army always wires for information re condemnation, as this is not shown on [illegible] forms. [illegible] this [illegible] is cut down ~~[illegible]~~ so much, that [illegible] wires are always being sent at Army's request. Bought tins & ladles for [illegible] soup kitchens.	

[signature]
DADOS
23 Div.
31/8/17

Confidential

Vol 24

War Diary of

Capt. J. B. Oxenham
AOD

DADOS. 23 Divn

1 - 30 Sept. 1917

Instructions regarding War Diaries and Intelligence Summaries are contained in F. S. Regs., Part II. and the Staff Manual respectively. Title pages will be prepared in manuscript.

WAR DIARY

~~or~~

~~INTELLIGENCE SUMMARY.~~

~~(Erase heading not required.)~~

(1)

Army Form C. 2118.

Place	Date	Hour	Summary of Events and Information	Remarks and references to Appendices
Reninghelst G34 d 28	Sept. 1		No car. Position of AA mountings not quite clear – sights apparently returned but no mountings yet – ADOS enquiring.	
— " —	2		Div. at Steenvoorde for 2 days only. Visited Lederzeele area for billets, to avoid a one day stay at Steenvoorde. Much bombing, 24 Div. store nearly burned.	
— " —	" 3		No car. Moved part stores & office – 2 journeys. Handed over to 25 Div. & stayed with them pending car. More bombing.	
— " — & Lederzeele	4		Moved over afternoon. No stores for 23 Div. at old railhead. Cleared balance of stores. Wired Calais prepared to receive trucks.	
— " —	5		Visited 70 Bde. Units. Now in 10 Corps & Second Army. From P.K. indents cancelled & demands sent to Base.	
— " —	6		Second Army re windows. Two trucks received, St. Omer. 10 Corps re battle stores – ADOS will obtain.	
— " —	7		To Calais for flag material, lamps & lettering urgently required. Visited groups re special ration bags, dixie ups(?), &c.	
— " —	8		Bulk days again altered, necessitating special addition to demands. Visited 68 Bde. H.Q., ADOS & Div. Art.(?) which is now rejoining Div.	
— " —	9		Alteration of m guns for AA sights completing. ADOS & [illegible] inspected dump, shops & salvage. Units return of w/s clothing improving. Chief Clerk left on special leave. Div. Conference re revolvers still wanted.	
— " —	10		Div. to move forward 13th. Informed ADOS no trucks required at St. Omer after. Called for defence by QM. of 9 Y&L for court martial; not called by Court. To forward area with AA Sqdg.(?) Saw ADOS who states I may go into old dump at Reninghelst by stealth(?). Saw DADOS 24th re taking stores from him – am not to take his old dump.	
— " —	" 11		Moved part stores to new area – Reninghelst. Overdue stores for R.A. received from 58 Div. & issued.	
— " —	" 12		To Calais for special stores required – screws for armourers, collars for wheels, [illegible] &c. More stores moved to Reninghelst dump. 2 Trucks	
— " —	" 13		No truck. Moved rest of stores to Reninghelst dump, – office moves tomorrow with Div. Reported that 41 Div. also sending stores to same dump – spoke ADOS – to remain at dump.	
& Reninghelst G34.d cen.	" 14		Moved up. No car until 2 pm. Saw ADOS re battle stores being drawn from Army & Corps Troops O.O.s. Confirmed that I remain here, 41st taking over old 24th Dump.	
— " —	" 15		No trucks. No car. Issuing battle stores. Sent tents to 41 Div. O.O.	

T2134. Wt. W708—776. 500000. 4/15. Sir J. C. & S.

Instructions regarding War Diaries and Intelligence Summaries are contained in F. S. Regs., Part II. and the Staff Manual respectively. Title pages will be prepared in manuscript.

WAR DIARY
or
INTELLIGENCE SUMMARY.
(Erase heading not required.)

Army Form C. 2118.

(2)

Place	Date	Hour	Summary of Events and Information	Remarks and references to Appendices
1917				
Reninghelst & 34 d Div	Sept 16		Special stores - packsaddlery (300), Yukon packs, water carriers & bottles, illuminating Vickers barrels, food containers, all issued as received. Am trying to get extra packs & food containers. Visited 70 Bde in the line & forward dumps. Also ADOS, Lifton officer (re special mountings), Shops, & DSC.	
"	" 17		Soyers & Primus stoves, ladles & mugs issued for forward kitchens. Still awaiting extra oil tins & torches; also extra ration bags, & additional stretchers & blankets. Base query indent for horse float - procedure in this article uncertain & wheels difficult to obtain. Saw 10 M & RA. re pool scheme for guns. Machine gun store working. 4 trucks	
"	" 18		One truck - no special stores. Collected 60 extra Yukon packs & 46 lamps. Am buying additional lamps for forward tunnels & ARP. Withholding clothing issues to infantry; issue boots & demand reserve.	
"	19		Ordnance train system starts - arrival 3pm, dep 10am. Train oil & torches arrive for operations - also 40 extra food containers; all other battle stores out. Bought iron & drills for armourers who are making special pole mountings for Vickers & Lewis guns, A.A. - as Base supply is slow. Visited ADOS re gun pool scheme. RA late in settling details. Collected dixie sights from Heavy Shop.	
"	" 20		Zero day. RA not yet arranged gun pool. Arranged with Staff Capt., one Bde to form pool.	
"	21		Inspected salvage arrangements. Forward dumps empty, - rear dumps filled. Very little good for immediate reissue.	
"	22		Moves notified. After arrangements with 33 Div. to remain in same dumps on exchange of Divns; Corps decided that dumps must be changed also & 33rd will move there. No indents yet from RA pool to replace issues - wired to hasten. Apparently the mobile pool has been rushed up to replace casualties but very few condemnations necessary.	
"	" 23		Certain battle stores being returned by Units, - packsaddlery to be retained at present. Visited 33 DOO re move. These stores could remain as they are, but Corps say they must all change round. Brought stores. Move probable tomorrow & 25th.	

T2134. Wt. W708—776. 500000. 4/15. Sir J. C. & S.

Instructions regarding War Diaries and Intelligence Summaries are contained in F. S. Regs., Part II. and the Staff Manual respectively. Title pages will be prepared in manuscript.

WAR DIARY
or
~~INTELLIGENCE SUMMARY.~~
(Erase heading not required.)

(3)

Army Form C. 2118.

Place	Date	Hour	Summary of Events and Information	Remarks and references to Appendices
	1917			
Reninghelst G 34 a. cen.	Sept	24	To Bailleul for [illegible] – Army still making a [illegible] [illegible] AA [illegible]. Shops re working of Pool for guns. Westoutre is more [illegible] – 33rd DOO [illegible] & small space for starting my first loads.	
Westoutre	"	25	Moved. No [illegible] until now. RA [illegible] to settle some points re gun pool. Two marquees required at Westoutre in addition to shed accommodation. The idea that 2 marquees will provide a store, office, shops & billets is absurd. Conference Q & Staff Capts, on recent operations 20th. Ordnance all [illegible] [illegible] stores taken out [illegible], asked for late by Div, arrived too late.	
— " —		26	RA re running of pool. All clear now. Arranged with RCO to warn units & repeat till [illegible] when vehicles come up. Drew AA sights from Army – visited Corps. 10 pm informed Div. would relieve 33rd at once; wired DOO re taking over stores – received indents for re-equipment & urged early supply.	
—	—	27	Visited Bgs re equipment, also 33 & 39 DOO & ADOS for battle stores. Sent lorry to Calais & Hazebrouck. Special stores issued.	
— " — Reninghelst G 34 d cen.	—	28	Moved back to old dump. Collecting special stores, eg packs, water bottles, oil tins, food containers, wire cutters, gloves, torches. Ordnance train late as usual – 3 trucks up.	
— " —	"	29	Units drawing to re-equip – many stores up. Clothing being withheld from Inf pro tem. Clearing 33rd special stores dump at H.29 cen. for Corps: stores there are not required by me – I move for Corps only & keep stocks here. No more battle stores to be issued.	
— " —	"	30	Battle stores recalled. 5 Div. will take over from me & will take on my RA & gun pool. RA [illegible] drawn guns [illegible] for [illegible] at [illegible]; the [illegible] notice of arrival was not [illegible] by RCO – saw RCO & [illegible] future action. [illegible] for new dump & billets. Div goes to Bailleul but dump there now given to Reinforcement Camp – supplying latter with camp stores. Usual stores up. On move back am going to supply [illegible]. 41st RA moved to 7th Div.	

[signature] Capt
DADOS
23 Div.

Vol 35

Confidential.

War Diary of

Capt J. B. Oxenham

DADOS. 23. Div.

Oct. 1917

(1)

Instructions regarding War Diaries and Intelligence Summaries are contained in F. S. Regs., Part II. and the Staff Manual respectively. Title pages will be prepared in manuscript.

WAR DIARY

or

~~INTELLIGENCE SUMMARY.~~

(*Erase heading not required.*)

Army Form C. 2118.

Place	Date	Hour	Summary of Events and Information	Remarks and references to Appendices
	1917			
Reningelst G.34.d.cen	Oct	1.	No truck. Moving park stores to Melten. To Melten re billet. Also RA re [illegible] Army RA transferred to 5 Div. & 41st to 7th.	
Melten	"	2	Moved to Melten. No truck. Visited ADOS & 5th DOO re Corps stores taken over. Bought tools for Reinft Camp	
—"—	"	3	Truck late. Issuing accumulated clothing to infantry. To St Omer for machine parts.	
—"—	"	4	Bgde. under 2 hrs. notice to move up. Arranged for issue from old dump by 5 Div. of battle stores – eg. cutters, oil tins, water bottles, food containers. Saw 5 D.O.O. re guns issued – also I.O.M. Div. Adm. Conference – no special Ordnance points. Saw S. Capt. re short issue of special stores.	
—"—	"	5	To St Omer for stores for baths & laundry. Visited 68 & 69 Bgdes. Several Bns. moving up for working parties – all stores remain here.	
—"—	"	6	Truck of clothing 2 days late. Estimates of clothing good except in case of 10 NF & 12 DLI who ask for double average of other Bns. DLI demands "kits" – boots & caps are now required in half the numbers. ADOS for trench lines for conference: more [illegible] wanted: Units state equipment almost complete.	
—"—		7	Visited laundry. Clothing truck arrived 2 days late. 12 DLI want me to hold clothing for them – will do so for 2 days, cannot accommodate longer. ADOS re [illegible] & Poperinghe re [illegible]	
—"—		8	Bought stores at Dunkirk. Div anxious about [illegible] clipping arrangements – Corps scheme late in operating & Army stopping demands for rugs & machines meantime. Demanded some from Base, as an urgent matter.	
—"—		9	Warned of move – wired 7 DOO for dump location. Blankets not yet up – some [illegible]. 7th DOO reports the dump not good – suggests I find another	
—"—		10	Moving tomorrow. To new forward area. Corps give me [illegible] Camp for dump – no accommodation & no road. Div. agree that I move to 7th Div. dump at DHQ. Some blankets arrived & issued.	
H.30.c. (28)		11	Only 2 extra lorries (of 6) arrive for move. Many stores left at Melten. Four trucks up at Bulliant – impossible to clear all.	
—"—		12	No extra lorries until afternoon – need of lorries is very pressing; still not cleared at railhead or Melten, & 4 trucks advised for 13th. Horse rugs notified. Cleared railhead. Visited Ordnance A, 7th DOO, who wants clothing 5th DOO re blankets & rugs for any RA attached. Shops with [illegible] for repairs. Reinft. Camp re stores required, & Melten dump, being cleared.	

T.2134. Wt. W708–776. 500000. 4/15. Sir J. C. & S.

Instructions regarding War Diaries and Intelligence Summaries are contained in F. S. Regs., Part II. and the Staff Manual respectively. Title pages will be prepared in manuscript.

WAR DIARY

~~or~~

~~INTELLIGENCE~~ SUMMARY.

(*Erase heading not required.*)

(2)

Army Form C. 2118.

Place	Date	Hour	Summary of Events and Information	Remarks and references to Appendices
Sheet 28	1917			
H.30.c Anzac Camp	Oct. 13		Railhead changed to Ouderdom A. Cleared Mulvien dump. Collected clipping machines & A.A. sights from Army Troops. Stores from Corps Troops. No train in — 4 borrowed lorries only partly used. Visited Mickmar & Bailleul	
— " —	" 14		Issued stores for new clipping dump. Collected clipping machines for dump & issued. One truck underclothing only arrived this morning — others later but 3 still due. D.A.C. clearing horse rugs to clipping dump. Ouderdom A arrangement bad — trains late & extra lorries kept all day. Made & issued 100 waterproof bags for socks to Baths. Demanded 1000 gum boots & 100 food containers. Dump crowded though occupying a store tent 3 marquees & 2 huts. When units are moving daily there is bound to be an accumulation — in any event the 2 marquees laid down are undoubtedly inadequate. Properly prepared dumps, with in & out roads, half way between front line & first back areas, would enable a Division to supply quicker & eliminate continual short moves of many stores.	
— " —	" 15		1000 gum boots drawn. Visited Corps, Shops, Army Troops (for clipping machine blades) Clipping camp, & R.E. shops Hazebrouck for A.A. sights.	
— " —	16		Trucks nearly normal. A reg truck & one of underclothing still out. Demanded 8 Lewis guns for 9 KOYLI attached. M.G. stores deficient of parts, guns sufficient. Ordnance stores except guns & vehicles to come up to supply railheads — Ouderdom A scheme fails. Corps [illegible] food containers & rail covers for dumps. R.A. [illegible] Trench mortar [illegible]. 33rd Wing Reinfct. Camp to be ordnanced by me.	
— " —	17		Drew AA mountings from Corps Troops. Telescopic sights from Second Army School. Demanded muzzle covers for rifles — previously not required by Div. Shall probably move to Esquelbecq area — D.A.D.O.S. will find dump tomorrow.	
— " —	" 18		Area altered — are to move to Wizernes 20th–23rd. Packsaddles & Yukon packs to be retained. R.E. Cos. & S. Staffs to be moved to 21 Div, also 23 & 33 Reinforcement wings. R.A. remains with 5 Div, plus Sub Park & HQ Train Co. 21 Div are dump & stores he will take over.	
— " —	19		Decided packsaddlery & Yukon packs must be ~~to~~ returned — arrange to receive & hand over to 21st Div railhead. To new area — am going to commandeer Ordnance billets, tents for stores, no other cover available.	
— " —	" 20		Transfer R.E. & Pioneers to 21 Div. R.A. remain with 5th. Horse rugs returned to clipping depot. To Bailleul for stores.	

T2134. Wt. W708—776. 500000. 4/15. Sir J. C. & S.

Instructions regarding War Diaries and Intelligence Summaries are contained in F. S. Regs., Part II. and the Staff Manual respectively. Title pages will be prepared in manuscript.

WAR DIARY or ~~INTELLIGENCE SUMMARY.~~

(Erase heading not required.)

(3)

Army Form C. 2118.

Place	Date	Hour	Summary of Events and Information	Remarks and references to Appendices
1917	Oct.			
~~Chipagon~~ Anzac Camp H. 30. C Sh. 28	21		Moved part stores to new area. 6 extra lorries allowed. Cleared salvage to railhead. Visited shops, only one vehicle under repair, a water cart. Collected Lewis gun from M.G. stores. 21 D.O.O. came over re handing over stores.	
— " — or Wizernes	22		Moved to Wizernes. Div. HQ not moving until 23rd. Camp fixed up — 1 store tent & 3 marquees.	
— " —	23		Div. moved. Saw QMs of several Units re equipment — not so much wanted this time — clothing averaging 100–150 suits a Bn. Visited 11 Sherwoods.	
— " —	24		With DA & QMG visiting Units	
— " —	25		All tentage blown down by gale — arranged fresh site for store tent. Visited Units with DA & QMG	
— " —	26		Further visits to Units with DA & QMG. Q arranged trip of QMs to Calais to see stores & shops — DADOS in charge. Q allotting [illegible] time for most of 4 days during that week. Requirement [illegible] — not much required.	
— " —	27		To Calais for stores — fortunately clipping plates, Lewis guns & magazines. Also bought stores. Re equipment proceeding — Visited 11 W. Yorks.	
— " —	28		To RA in forward area re clipping machines. Heads are filed down at Base in at fingers, cut too low, or plates are badly shaped. Sample brought back for Armourer to improve by raising fingers. Saw 5th DOS re RA Units who are likely to be transferred back to 23rd — guns nearly complete. Warned of move by train — all stores to be [illegible] up. Asking clothing this in hand. Wired 5th DOS re winter clothing situation in RA Units. Spoke to Army re move — will MT Units move?	
— " —	29 30 31		Div. to be equipped for transfer to another front. Preference being given by Base for [illegible]. Saw Army re equipment. Getting 10 extra lorries daily to clear rush of trucks. All bulk indents & special demands wired daily. Late indents sent Base by lorry daily & stores cleared direct. All winter clothing & 2nd blanket being issued. Reinforcements coming in with defective clothing — one batch without steel helmets. Asking for 3 trucks to clear Ord stores stocks re to new area — exclusive of blankets. RA Units being equipped by 5th Div. Pioneers by 14th Div. & RE by 21st, except for winter clothing & blankets which I send out to forward area — Fleetes, Westoutre &c.	

[signature]
DADOS
23 Div.

T2134. Wt. W708—776. 500000. 4/15. Sir J. C. & S.

23RD DIVISION

ASST DIR. VETY SERVICES

AUG 1915 — 1917 OCT

TO ITALY

A.D.S. 23rd Div.
Vols: 1, 2, 3, 4, 5.

121/7931

Aug '15
Mar '19

August. 1915.

War Diary of A.D.V.S. 23rd Division

Instructions regarding War Diaries and Intelligence Summaries are contained in F. S. Regs., Part II. and the Staff Manual respectively. Title pages will be prepared in manuscript.

WAR DIARY or INTELLIGENCE SUMMARY. 1

(Erase heading not required.)

Army Form C. 2118.

Place	Date	Hour	Summary of Events and Information	Remarks and references to Appendices
Bordon	24/8		Left Bordon with Hd Qrs Horses and Military Police Horses for Southampton	
Southampton	"		Detrained, watered horses and embarked on S.S. Archimedes	
"	"		2 Horses taken by V.O. for Hospital, 2 Remounts collected.	
"	"		Sailed at 5 pm.	
Havre	25/8		Disembarked, 5 horses evacuated for injuries.	
"	"	7 pm	Entrained	
"	26/8		Arrived at Mont ——, watered horses	
"	"	8 am	Arrived at Abbeville, watered and fed horses	
Tilques	"	1-45 pm	Arrived at St Omer, detrained and marched to ~~St O~~ Tilques	
"	27/8		Fixed office. Rode around district	
"	28/8		Rode to R.A. Hd Qrs to see horses, also saw Divl horses	
	"		Saw site alloted to 35 Mobile Veterinary Section	
"	29/8		Rode to St Omer to meet M.V.S. and took them to their destination	
"	30/8		Motored to Kuminghem, Polincore, Journchem and Bonninghue to see 4 Bdes. R.A.	
"	31/8		Motored to Hd Qrs of 3 Inf Bdes, alloted district to Vet Officers	

Frank D. [illegible]
MAJOR,
A.D.V.S. 23RD DIVISION.

2353 Wt. W2544/1454 700,000 5/15 D. D & L. A.D.S.S./Forms/C. 2118.

September. 1915.

War Diary of A.D.V.S. 23rd Division.

Instructions regarding War Diaries and Intelligence Summaries are contained in F. S. Regs., Part II. and the Staff Manual respectively. Title pages will be prepared in manuscript.

WAR DIARY or INTELLIGENCE SUMMARY.

(Erase heading not required.)

2

Army Form C. 2118.

Place	Date	Hour	Summary of Events and Information	Remarks and references to Appendices
Tilques	1/9/15		Route march of Division in morning, called and inspected Yeomanry horses also where they were watered.	
"	2/9		Motored to Lombres to see A.D.V.S. Guards Division and then to Artillery Brigades and Divl Ammn Column.	
"	3/9		Went to 35. M.V.S. in morning. The D.V.S. wired for V.Os names and appointments. Rode over to Divl Train. Hd Qrs.	
"	4/9		Inspected 3 Remounts for No 1 Signal Co. Motored out to see Artillery horses and back to 35. M.V.S.	
"	"		Received orders at midnight to prepare to leave on Monday	
"	5/9		Went to 35. M.V.S. and then to D.L.O. Yeomanry lines to see a horse with fractured Radius. Went with O.C 35 M.V.S. to St Omer to arrange with R.T.O. about trucks for 8 horses evacuated that evening	
"	6/9		Went to 35. M.V.S., saw Division marched through Tilques, had man posted in road with flag to direct to M.V.S. Arrived at Renescure	
Renescure	6/9	4 pm	4 pm and billeted, sent messages to all Hd Qrs for returns of horses	

2353 Wt. W2544/1454 700,000 5/15 D. D. & L. A.D.S.S./Forms/C. 2118.

Instructions regarding War Diaries and Intelligence Summaries are contained in F. S. Regs., Part II. and the Staff Manual respectively. Title pages will be prepared in manuscript.

WAR DIARY
or
INTELLIGENCE SUMMARY.
(*Erase heading not required.*)

2

Army Form C. 2118.

Place	Date	Hour	Summary of Events and Information	Remarks and references to Appendices
Renescure	6/9		left on line of march	
"	7/9	8.30am	Left Renescure and rode 16 miles to Merris	
Merris	7/9	2.15pm	Arrived at Merris. The D.D.V.S. 1st Army came to see me	
"	8/9		Fixed for an office. Went through Divl Hd Qrs lines and then to 35 M.V.S. Two Batteries of 102nd 104th and 105th Brigades R.A. went on to Steinwerck. V.O. went with them. A.A. & Q.M.G. recalled them.	
"	9/9		Rode round the district to see various Units, Lieut Starkey reported his return.	
"	10/9		9 Sergeants A.V.C. arrived. Motored to D.A.C and 102nd Bde R.F.A. Lieut Shipley A.V.C. on sick list	
"	11/9		D.D.V.S. 1st Army came out and met V.Os. of 23rd Division. Lieuts Shipley and Allinson absent. Instructions given to these Officers by D.D.V.S. as to their duties. Lieut Starkey sent to Steinwerck to take Vety charge of the Artillery horses of this Division	

2353 Wt. W2544/1454 700,000 5/15 D. D. & L. A.D.S.S./Forms/C. 2118.

Instructions regarding War Diaries and Intelligence Summaries are contained in F. S. Regs., Part II. and the Staff Manual respectively. Title pages will be prepared in manuscript.

WAR DIARY 2
or
INTELLIGENCE SUMMARY.
(*Erase heading not required.*)

Army Form C. 2118.

Place	Date	Hour	Summary of Events and Information	Remarks and references to Appendices
~~Renescure~~ Sierres	11/9		A number of mules in South Stafford Regt required Shoeing, this had to be done at night	
"	12/9		Went to Yeomanry lines. horse killed during night by Sentry's Bayonet. Board held. Went to Divl Train Hd Qs. List received of 14 Sergeants A.V.C from D.V.S. office	
"	13/9		Motored round to the D.A.C and Artillery Brigades. Gave O.C 35 M.V.S. orders to detail 1 N.C.O. and 3 men to proceed to Croix du Bac to establish a Dressing station.	
"	14/9		Capt Bosley. A.D.V.S. 24th Division called to see me Motored to Croix du Bac with Lieut Percy. A.V.C and saw A.D.V.S. 27th Division and M.V.S. attached 27th Division.	
"	15/9		Rode over to see Batteries 104th I.A. then to 35 M.V.S., In afternoon Went to Divl Train.	
"	16/9		Moved off at 8 am to Croix du Bac	

2353 Wt. W2544/1454 700,000 5/15 D. D. & L. A.D.S.S./Forms/C. 2118.

Army Form C. 2118

WAR DIARY 2
or
INTELLIGENCE SUMMARY.
(Erase heading not required.)

Instructions regarding War Diaries and Intelligence Summaries are contained in F. S. Regs., Part II. and the Staff Manual respectively. Title pages will be prepared in manuscript.

Place	Date	Hour	Summary of Events and Information	Remarks and references to Appendices
Croix du Bac	16/9		Arrived at Croix du Bac, 20 Horses taken over from M.V.S. 24th Division and evacuated by 35 M.V.S.	
"	17/9		Conference with V.Os. of Division in morning, went around Hd Qrs lines	
"	18/9		Motored to Armentieres and Steenwerck. Rode to D.A.C. in afternoon	
"	19/9		Looked through Mobile Section horses then to D.L.O.Y. lines. Went to Bac St Maur to see 118th Heavy Artillery Bty attached to 24th Division. Called on Major Harris A.D.V.S. 8th Division	
"	20/9		Went round Hd Qrs horses, Sent Weekly report to D.D.V.S. 1st Army	
"	21/9		Rode out with Lieut Hamilton A.V.C. to 103rd Batteries and Ammn Column Motored to Hd Qrs 103rd Bde R.F.A. in afternoon and went to Steenwerck after tea	
"	22/9		Motored with Lieut Starkey A.V.C. to see his Brigade (105th) D.D.V.S. 1st Army came out before lunch, Sent report to A A & Q M G 23rd Division recommending clipping	

2353 Wt. W2544/1454 700,000 5/15 D. D. & L. A.D.S.S./Forms/C. 2118.

Instructions regarding War Diaries and Intelligence Summaries are contained in F. S. Regs., Part II. and the Staff Manual respectively. Title pages will be prepared in manuscript.

WAR DIARY 2
or
INTELLIGENCE SUMMARY.
(*Erase heading not required.*)

Army Form C. 2118.

Place	Date	Hour	Summary of Events and Information	Remarks and references to Appendices
Croix du Bac	23/9		Rode with Capt Allinson A.V.C. to see his Units. Rode to Erquingham in afternoon to select site for Advanced Dressing Station. Drew up defence Scheme, approved by Col Blair	
"	24/9		Lieut Percy. O.C. removed 35. M.V.S. to another site. V.Os. brought in A 2000 forms in afternoon and instructions were given about active operations.	
"	25/9		Went to Wagon lines and Dressing posts, afterwards to 35. M.V.S.	
"	26/9		Rode to 102nd Bde Ammn Col and wagon lines at Erquingham. 1 Horse sent to 35 M.V.S. with shrapnel wounds, 68th Inf Bde left to join 20th Division.	
"	27/9		Rode out with Capt Allinson to see D.L.O. Yeomanry lines and Divl Train Cos. 68th Inf Bde returned from 20th Division, walked to 35. M.V.S. in evening	

2353 Wt. W2544/1454 700,000 5/15 D. D. & L. A.D.S.S./Forms/C. 2118.

Army Form C. 2118.

Instructions regarding War Diaries and Intelligence Summaries are contained in F. S. Regs., Part II. and the Staff Manual respectively. Title pages will be prepared in manuscript.

WAR DIARY
or
INTELLIGENCE SUMMARY.
(Erase heading not required.)

2

Place	Date	Hour	Summary of Events and Information	Remarks and references to Appendices
Croix du Bac	28/9		68th Inf Bde again left 23rd Division for the 20th with 71st Field Ambulance and 1 Coy Divl Train. D.D.V.S. 1st Army came out. Inspected 14th and 118th Batteries Heavy Artillery. attached 23rd Division	
"	29/9		Attended Genl Babington's conference at 9 am. Went to see 102nd Bde R.F.A. horses and 70th Infantry transport	
"	30/9		Sergt Dunbar A.V.C. arrived posted to 105th Bde R.F.A. Establishment for this Divn complete, sent him to 35 M.V.S. Inspected horses in 68th Inf Bde and called at M.V.S.	

Frank D. [illegible] MAJOR,
A. D. V. S. 23RD DIVISION.

2353 Wt. W2544/1454 700,000 5/15 D. D. & L. A.D.S.S./Forms/C. 2118.

October. 1915.

War Diary of A.D.V.S. 23rd Division.

Army Form C. 2118.

Instructions regarding War Diaries and Intelligence Summaries are contained in F. S. Regs., Part II. and the Staff Manual respectively. Title pages will be prepared in manuscript.

WAR DIARY or INTELLIGENCE SUMMARY. 3

(Erase heading not required.)

Place	Date	Hour	Summary of Events and Information	Remarks and references to Appendices
Croix du Bac	1/10/15		Motored to Petit Sec Bois to see a horse which was left behind by 105th Bde. R.F.A.	
	2/10/15		Inspected horses and lines of 105th Bde. R.F.A. with Lieut Starkey V.O. i/c. Examined horses at 35. M.V.S.	
	3/10/15		Inspected horses of D.A.C. In afternoon motored to Merris to see a horse left behind by 20th Division.	
	4/10/15		Sent to collect horse at Merris. went to Erquinghem in afternoon	
	5/10/15		Inspected Hd Qrs Group and C Bty and Ammn Col. 104th Bde. R.F.A. Sent to Base for drugs	
	6/10/15		Attended General's conference at 9 am. went to 35 M.V.S., 69th Inf Bde Transport lines, and B Battery 104th Bde. R.F.A., D.D.V.S. 1st Army came out but did not see him	
	7/10/15		Visited 70th Inf Bde transport, South Staffs, 2 Batteries 104th Bde R.F.A. and Heavy Bty attached 23rd Division, V.Os. came to office at 5 pm	

2353 Wt. W2544/1454 700,000 5/15 D. D. & L. A.D.S.S./Forms/C. 2118.

Instructions regarding War Diaries and Intelligence Summaries are contained in F. S. Regs., Part II. and the Staff Manual respectively. Title pages will be prepared in manuscript.

WAR DIARY
or
INTELLIGENCE SUMMARY.

(Erase heading not required.)

3

Army Form C. 2118.

Place	Date	Hour	Summary of Events and Information	Remarks and references to Appendices
Croix du Bac	7/10/15		with Weekly reports. A 2000 forms., Wrote re watering horses for insertion in D. R. O.	
	8/10/15		Rode to Ammn Col. 103rd Bde R.F.A. and remainder of morning with D.A.C. Went to 35. M.V.S. in afternoon.	
	9/10/15		Lieut Shipley A.V.C. on sick leave. Wired to D.D.V.S. 1st Army Saw D.L.O.Y. horses also machine gun section. Wrote a report on Horse rugs	
	10/10/15		Motored to Renescure to see 2 mules left by 23rd D.A.C. visited 35 M.V.S. in afternoon.	
	11/10/15		Inspected Hd Qrs horses and Divl Train. In office in afternoon	
	12/10/15		D.D.V.S. 1st Army came out, went to 68th and 70th Inf Brigades also D.A.C., Rode to Divl Train after tea.	
	13/10/15		Attended General's conference at 9 am, went through horses of	

2353 Wt. W2544/1454 700,000 5/15 D. D. & L. A.D.S.S./Forms/C. 2118.

Instructions regarding War Diaries and Intelligence Summaries are contained in F. S. Regs., Part II. and the Staff Manual respectively. Title pages will be prepared in manuscript.

WAR DIARY
or
INTELLIGENCE SUMMARY.
(Erase heading not required.)

3

Army Form C. 2118.

Place	Date	Hour	Summary of Events and Information	Remarks and references to Appendices
Croix du Bac	13/10/15		signal Co and then to Divl Train.	
	14/10/15		Motored to "Bac" to see 2 horses left behind by 27th Division Lieut Shipley A.V.C returned to duty. V.Os. came in for a conference	
	15/10/15		Went to 35 M.V.S., 2 Field Ambulance Cos and D.A.C	
	16/10/15		Corp Martin A.V.C. (Clerk) sent to hospital, went to 35 M.V.S. stayed in office in afternoon	
	17/10/15		Inspected horses at 35 M.V.S., then went to Ammn Col 104th Bde R.F.A. and D.A.C. Wrote out number of suggestions for R.A. Brigade Orders.	
	18/10/15		Called on General Tasson R.A. Inspected 2 Batteries 103rd Bde and 2 Batteries 105th Bde. F.A.	
	19/10/15		Went to 35 M.V.S. to see 2 N.C.Os. and 6 Privates which arrived in exchange for same number sent away. Inspected 68th Inf Brigade transport	

2353 Wt. W2544/1454 700,000 5/15 D. D. & L. A.D.S.S./Forms/C. 2118.

Instructions regarding War Diaries and Intelligence Summaries are contained in F. S. Regs., Part II. and the Staff Manual respectively. Title pages will be prepared in manuscript.

WAR DIARY
or
INTELLIGENCE SUMMARY.
(*Erase heading not required.*)

3

Army Form C. 2118.

Place	Date	Hour	Summary of Events and Information	Remarks and references to Appendices
Croise du Bac	20/10/15		Attended General's conference at 9 am, brought up the question of clipping horses which was turned down. 70th Inf Bde left for the 8th Division. Sherwood Foresters, Worcesters and 2nd Northants Regt from 24th Division joined 23rd Division. Visited D.A.C. in afternoon	
"	21/10/15		Called at 35 M.V.S. in morning, then to D.L.O. Yeomanry. V.Os. came to office at 5 pm.	
"	22/10/15		Made up weekly returns. D.D.V.S. 1st Army called, went to see Major Watsons mare. Visited 35 M.V.S. in afternoon.	
"	23/10/15		Sent weekly returns to D.D.V.S. Rode to Steinwerck, Hd Qrs, 24th Brigade then to D.L.O.Y. Called on Lieut Hamilton on sick list.	
"	24/10/15		Rode to Batteries 102nd Bde. R.F.A. in office afterwards.	
"	25/10/15		Sergt Dunbar. A.V.C. posted to Div. Ammn. Column to replace Sergt. Price who was sent to No 3 Vet Hospital. visited 35 M.V.S. and 68th Inf Bde	
"	26/10/15		Visited 3 Inf Brigades and 35 M.V.S.	

2353 Wt. W2544/1454 700,000 5/15 D. D. & L. A.D.S.S./Forms/C. 2118.

Army Form C. 2118.

Instructions regarding War Diaries and Intelligence Summaries are contained in F. S. Regs., Part II. and the Staff Manual respectively. Title pages will be prepared in manuscript.

WAR DIARY
or
INTELLIGENCE SUMMARY. 3

(Erase heading not required.)

Place	Date	Hour	Summary of Events and Information	Remarks and references to Appendices
Croix du Bac	27/10/15		Attended General's conference, then to D.A.C. Went to Erquinghem in afternoon	
"	28/10/15		Miserable weather. Rode to 35 M.V.S. in morning. V.Os. met at my office in afternoon.	
"	29/10/15		Corp Marlin (clerk) returned to duty. Looked through horses 104th Bde. R.F.A. visited 35 M.V.S. in afternoon.	
"	30/10/15		Called at 35 M.V.S. in morning, attended conference of A.Ds.V.S. at Locon in afternoon. D.D.V.S. 1st Army presided	
"	31/10/15		Rode to Steenwerck in morning, then to D.A.C. Wrote a report on number of injuries from kicks and rope galls & sent to Divl. Hd. Qrs.	

Frank W. McElhinnish
MAJOR,
A.D.V.S. 23RD DIVISION,

2353 Wt. W2544/1454 700,000 5/15 D. D. & L. A.D.S.S./Forms/C. 2118.

November 1915

War Diary of A.D.V.S. 23rd Division.

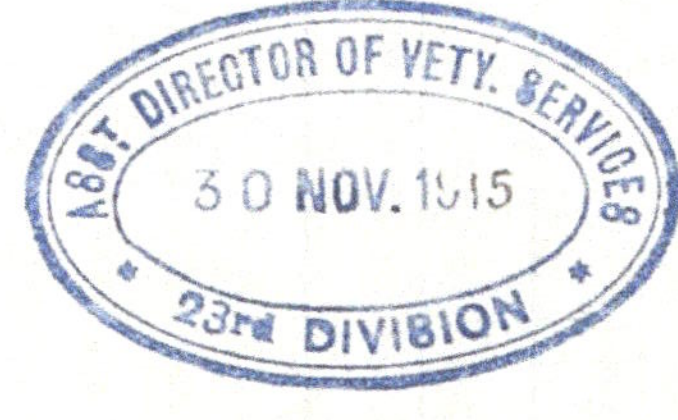

Instructions regarding War Diaries and Intelligence Summaries are contained in F. S. Regs., Part II. and the Staff Manual respectively. Title pages will be prepared in manuscript.

WAR DIARY 4
or
INTELLIGENCE SUMMARY.
(Erase heading not required.)

Army Form C. 2118.

Place	Date	Hour	Summary of Events and Information	Remarks and references to Appendices
Croix du Bac	1/11/15		Visited 35 M.V.S. in morning, visited 2 Field Ambulance Cos and 2 Batteries and Ammn Col of 105th Bde R.F.A.	
	2/11/15		Weather still bad, Lines in wretched condition, went to 103rd Bde Ammn Column lines, shelters not making much headway, attended administrative conference at A.A. & M.G.s office	
	3/11/15		Attended General's conference, called at 35 M.V.S., Rode to Erquinghem in afternoon.	
	4/11/15		Motored to Erquinghem and saw 3 Engr Cos and other Units, Capt Postal Remount Officer came out, Evacuated 6 Horses and 6 mules, 40 Remounts arrived at Steinwerck. V.Os. came to office in afternoon.	
	5/11/15		Lieut Hamilton sent to Steinwerck Hospital, went to 35 M.V.S., then saw Hd Qrs horses	
	6/11/15		Visited 35 M.V.S., then to Ammn Col: 103rd Bde R.F.A. ~~Bridging Train~~ Aux Transport In afternoon motored to La Motte to inspect roads where timber is fetched	
	7/11/15		Visited 35 M.V.S., 8 Horses evacuated, rode to Cable Section & Bridging Train	

2353 Wt. W2544/1454 700,000 5/15 D. D. & L. A.D.S.S./Forms/C. 2118.

Army Form C. 2118

WAR DIARY 4
or
INTELLIGENCE SUMMARY.
(Erase heading not required.)

Instructions regarding War Diaries and Intelligence Summaries are contained in F. S. Regs., Part II. and the Staff Manual respectively. Title pages will be prepared in manuscript.

Place	Date	Hour	Summary of Events and Information	Remarks and references to Appendices
Croix du Bac	8/11/15		Called on Lieut Hamilton in Hospital, then to D.A.C and Aux Transport. Attended conference at A.A. & Q.M.G's office.	
"	9/11		Called at 35 M.V.S. in morning, then to Erquinghem. Horse lines in a muddy condition everywhere	
"	10/11		Attended Genls' conference. D.D.V.S. 1st Army came out; went to 35 M.V.S, then to Signal lines and M.M.P. horses.	
"	11/11		V.Os came in to conference with weekly returns A 2000 forms. Lieut Lowe. A.V.C reported himself as V.O. 4th Heavy Bde. R.G.A.	
"	12/11		Went to 35 M.V.S and Ammn Col: 103rd Bde. R.F.A	
"	13/11		Met V.Os. at 35 M.V.S; the D.D.V.S. came out and gave practical demonstration on the Mallein eye test. After lunch went with D.D.R to Divl Ammn Col: and evacuated several animals	
"	14/11		Went with Capt Allinson A.V.C. to 4 Co's Divl Train and the Auxiliary Horse Transport lines. Col Newsome. A.V.C came out in afternoon with the new D.D.V.S 1st Army	

2353 Wt. W2544/1454 700,000 5/15 D. D. & L. A.D.S.S./Forms/C. 2118.

Instructions regarding War Diaries and Intelligence Summaries are contained in F. S. Regs., Part II. and the Staff Manual respectively. Title pages will be prepared in manuscript.

WAR DIARY
or
INTELLIGENCE SUMMARY.
(*Erase heading not required.*)

4

Army Form C. 2118.

Place	Date	Hour	Summary of Events and Information	Remarks and references to Appendices
Croix du Bac	15/11/15		Went to 35. M.V.S. 68th Inf Bde and attended conference at A.A. & M.G. office	
"	16/11		Went to Erquinghem to see 9th Btn S Staffs Regt, A Battery 104th Bde R.F.A 128th Field Co R.E., went to 35. M.V.S. in afternoon, called on G.O.C. R.A. re. debilitated animals	
"	17/11		Attended Genls conference, Inspected D.L.O.Y. horses also Bridging Train	
"	18/11		Inspected horses of 4th Heavy Bde R.G.A. with Lieut Lowe A.V.C., evacuated 6 horses. One horse 69th Inf Bde killed by shrapnel. V.Os. came to office at 4 o'clock and brought weekly returns	
"	19/11		Went to 35. M.V.S., then to Ammn Col. 105th Bde R.F.A. and 71st Field Ambulance	
"	20/11		Inspected animals of 24th and 68th Inf Bdes	
"	21/11		Inspected horses with G.O.C., R.A. of 103rd and 104th Bdes R.F.A.	
"	22/11		Inspected horses with G.O.C., R.A. of 102nd and 105th Bdes R.F.A., sent away 31. Attended Conference at A.A. & M.G. office	
"	23/11		Called at 35. M.V.S. in morning and arranged for evacuating debility	

2353 Wt. W2544/1454 700,000 5/15 D. D. & L. A.D.S.S./Forms/C. 2118.

Army Form C. 2118.

Instructions regarding War Diaries and Intelligence Summaries are contained in F. S. Regs., Part II. and the Staff Manual respectively. Title pages will be prepared in manuscript.

WAR DIARY 4
or
INTELLIGENCE SUMMARY.
(Erase heading not required.)

Place	Date	Hour	Summary of Events and Information	Remarks and references to Appendices
Croix du Bac	23/11/15		Cases. Went to 69th Inf Bdex.	
"	24/11/15		Attended Genl's conference, went to La Motte to see condition of animals hauling timber. Major Love D.L.O.Y. lectured in wagon lines of 104th Bde. R.F.A.	
"	25/11/15		Walked to 35. M.V.S., went with Major Love D.L.O.Y. to Erquingham. V.Os. came in with weekly Returns. Lieut Macdougall A.V.C. reported arrival	
"	26/11/15		Lieut Macdougall posted to 103rd Bde. R.F.A. to replace Lieut Hamilton A.V.C. D.D.V.S. 1st Army came out, went to 35. M.V.S. with him. Attended lecture in afternoon.	
"	27/11		Called at 35. M.V.S., then to Ammn Col: 103rd Bde. R.F.A., went to Divl Ammn Col: in afternoon	
"	28/11		Went to 35. M.V.S and 69th Inf Bde, then to Station to see 13 animals evacuated. Lecture in afternoon	
"	29/11		Visited D.A.C, Misc Horse Transport: Bridging Train and attended Lecture in afternoon	
"	30/11		D.D.V.S. came out and inspected 35 cases at M.V.S. In afternoon inspected Debility cases in R.A. 41 to be sent away. Attended conference at A.A. & M.G. office	

Frank W. [illegible]
MAJOR,
A.D.V.S. 23RD DIVISION.

2353 Wt. W2544/1454 700,000 5/15 D. D. & L. A.D.S.S./Forms/C. 2118.

December. 1915.

War Diary of A.D.V.S. 23rd Division.

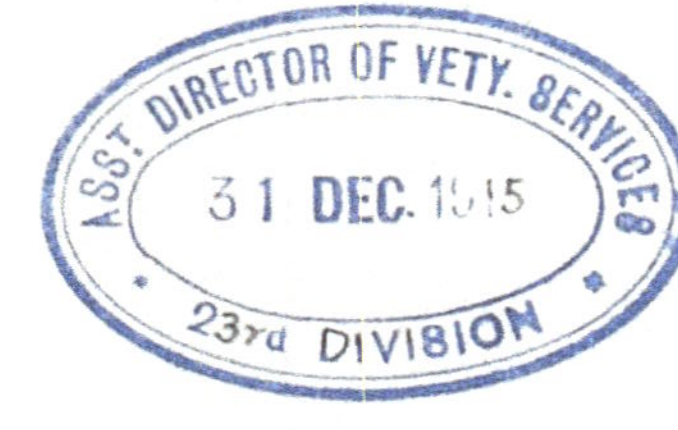

Instructions regarding War Diaries and Intelligence Summaries are contained in F. S. Regs., Part II. and the Staff Manual respectively. Title pages will be prepared in manuscript.

WAR DIARY 5
or
INTELLIGENCE SUMMARY.
(Erase heading not required.)

Army Form C. 2118.

Place	Date	Hour	Summary of Events and Information	Remarks and references to Appendices
Croix du Bac	1/12/15		Attended Genl's conference, then to 35. M.V.S. and Railhead, 43 Animals evacuated	
"	2/12		Went to 35. M.V.S., then to Railhead, 53 animals evacuated. V.Os. came in with weekly Returns. Inspected horses Ammn Col. 104th Bde. R.F.A. at Steinwerck	
"	3/12		Went to 35. M.V.S. and then to 24th Inf Bde. D.D.V.S. could not come out. his car broken down.	
"	4/12		Went to see horses in Signal Co and then to Divl Ammn Col. 2 horses 68th Inf Bde killed by shrapnel	
"	5/12		Called at 35. M.V.S. and then to Railhead. 7 horses evacuated. Visited Ammn Col: 102nd Bde. R.F.A.	
"	6/12		Went to 35 M.V.S. and then went with Lieut O'Brien. A.V.C. to see Battery horses of 104th Bde. R.F.A. Major-General Babington sent for me in afternoon re report from D.D.V.S. 1st Army. Attended conference at Q Branch. Lieut Starkey. A.V.C. went on leave.	
"	7/12		Drove round with D.A.Q.M.G. and S.S.O. to look for Chaff cutters at various farms	

2353 Wt. W2544/1454 700,000 5/15 D. D. & L. A.D.S.S./Forms/C. 2118.

Instructions regarding War Diaries and Intelligence Summaries are contained in F. S. Regs., Part II. and the Staff Manual respectively. Title pages will be prepared in manuscript.

WAR DIARY 5
or
INTELLIGENCE SUMMARY.
(Erase heading not required.)

Army Form C. 2118.

Place	Date	Hour	Summary of Events and Information	Remarks and references to Appendices
Croix du Bac	8/12/15		Attended General's conference. Went to Railhead to see 8 horses evacuated, then to Erquingham to make a post-mortem examination of Horse from 105th Bde. R.F.A. Tuberculosis	
"	9/12		Sent routine Stable Orders to G.O.C. Went with interpreter to Estaires to find out about a mule from 23rd Division left with inhabitant on Oct 18th	
"	10/12		Discovered a Clinical case of Glanders in 41st Field Ambulance at Steinwerck Sent wire to D.D.V.S., reported to A.D.M.S. and O.C. Sanitary Section	
"	11/12		Reported case of Glanders to G.O.C. Inspected all horses of the Field Ambulance. Found another Clinical case. D.D.V.S. came out in afternoon	
"	12/12		Went with Capt Allinson to 4 companies Divl Train. Field Ambulance horses tested with Mallein	
"	13/12		Inspected Field Ambulance horses. 1 mule reacted. D.L.O.Y. horses tested D.D.V.S. came out, no conference in evening	
"	14/12		Called at 35 M.V.S., then went with Lieut Shipley A.V.C. to Batteries 102nd Bde. R.F.A.	

Instructions regarding War Diaries and Intelligence Summaries are contained in F. S. Regs., Part II. and the Staff Manual respectively. Title pages will be prepared in manuscript.

WAR DIARY
or
INTELLIGENCE SUMMARY.
(Erase heading not required.)

5

Army Form C. 2118.

Place	Date	Hour	Summary of Events and Information	Remarks and references to Appendices
Croix du Bac	15/12/15		Attended General's conference, went to 35 M.V.S., Railhead and D.A.C. Lieut Starkey A.V.C. returned from leave	
"	16/12		Lieut Shipley A.V.C went on leave. Visited 68th Inf Bde and Hd Qrs 103rd Bde R.F.A. After lunch made a P.M. examination on mule of 71st Field Ambulance. V.Os. came in at 4 o'clock	
"	17/12		Had a parade of horses and mules of D.A.C. about 80 were evacuated, reported to G.O.C. After lunch inspected 110 Heavy Bde at Estaires with Lieut Lowe A.V.C	
"	18/12		Called at 35 M.V.S., then to Aux horse transport to see a horse which had reacted to the mallein test. Called at A Battery 103rd Bde R.F.A.	
"	19/12		Met V.Os. at Aux horse transport lines, made P.M. Exam. on horse which had reacted after mallein test. lungs badly affected. Afternoon went to 190 Co. Divl Train to see another reactor	
"	20/12		Inspected horses in Signal Co. then to 190 Co Divl Train. Destroyed reactor and	

Army Form C. 2118

Instructions regarding War Diaries and Intelligence Summaries are contained in F. S. Regs., Part II. and the Staff Manual respectively. Title pages will be prepared in manuscript.

WAR DIARY 5
or
INTELLIGENCE SUMMARY.
(Erase heading not required.)

Place	Date	Hour	Summary of Events and Information	Remarks and references to Appendices
Croix du Bac	20/12/15		made P.M. Exam. No conference in evening.	
"	21/12		Visited Ammn Col: 103rd Bde. R.F.A. in morning and called 35. M.V.S. in afternoon.	
"	22/12		Attended General's conference. D.D.R and D.D.V.S. came and inspected animals of D.A.C., about 20 evacuated.	
"	23/12		Called at 35 M.V.S. in morning. Inspected horses 4th Heavy Bde. R.G.A (attached) with Lieut Lowe A.V.C. also 101st and 102nd Co's. R.E.	
"	24/12		Went to Estaires, then to Bridging Train, 2 horses reacted also visited 191st Co Divl Train. Visited Ammn Col 102nd Bde. R.F.A. with Capt Allinson. A.V.C	
"	25/12		Went to 35. M.V.S. and inspected Yeomanry horses after.	
"	26/12		Lieut Shipley A.V.C. returned from leave. Called at D.A.C. and back to 35. M.V.S.	
"	27/12		D.D.V.S. came out and went to Bridging Train, then to Divl Train. In afternoon Capt Allinson and I made P.M. Exam. on 2 reactors, both Glandered and one was also Tuberculosis.	

2353 Wt. W2544/1454 700,000 5/15 D. D. & L. A.D.S.S./Forms/C. 2118.

Instructions regarding War Diaries and Intelligence Summaries are contained in F. S. Regs., Part II. and the Staff Manual respectively. Title pages will be prepared in manuscript.

WAR DIARY or INTELLIGENCE SUMMARY.

(Erase heading not required.)

5

Army Form C. 2118.

Place	Date	Hour	Summary of Events and Information	Remarks and references to Appendices
Croix du Bac	28/12/15		Went with S.S.O. to see chaff cutting machine. Inspected horses for evacuation at 35 M.V.S.	
"	29/12		Attended Generals conference. called at 35 M.V.S. Inspected animals of Ammn Col. 104th Bde. R.F.A. at Steenwerck. Saw evacuated animals trucked at Bac St Maur	
"	30/12		Inspected horses in Ammn Col. 103rd Bde. R.F.A. Visited 35. M.V.S., 69th Inf Bde and 24th Inf Bde.	
"	31/12		Lieut Percy A.V.C. went on leave. Capt Allenson A.V.C. acting O.C. 35 M.V.S. 1 Bay mare of Bridging Train reacted to second Mallein Test.	

Frank W. McElmurch[?] MAJOR,
A.D.V.S. 23RD DIVISION.

2353 Wt. W2544/1454 700,000 5/15 D. D. & L. A.D.S.S./Forms/C. 2118.

A.D.S. 23rd Div:
Vol: 6

Instructions regarding War Diaries and Intelligence Summaries are contained in F. S. Regs., Part II, and the Staff Manual respectively. Title pages will be prepared in manuscript.

WAR DIARY
or
INTELLIGENCE SUMMARY.
(Erase heading not required.)

January
A.D.V.S.
23rd Division.

Army Form C. 2118.

Place	Date	~~Hour~~	Summary of Events and Information	Remarks and references to Appendices
Croix du Bac	1/1/16		Went to 35 Mobile Vety Section & 68th Inf Bde in morning. after lunch to Bridging Train. One horse reacted to Mallein Test	
"	2/1/16		Went to 35 M.V.S. & then to Erquinghem, inspected Pioneer transport animals. Steenwerck in afternoon to see D.L.O. Yeomanry horses	
"	3/1/16		Went to wagon lines of 103rd Bde. R.F.A. Amm Col: & 2 Batteries, inspected reaction in Bridging Train	
"	4/1/16		Went to 35 M.V.S. 13 animals evacuated, called at 69th Inf Bde. horse lines	
"	5/1/16		Attended Genl's Conference, rode to 35 M.V.S. Signal Co. M.M.P. stables, inspected Div Amm. Col.	
"	6/1/16		Went to 35 M.V.S. Div: Amm: Col, and 101st Co R.E., 3 doubtful cases of mange at the latter place made Post-Mortem exam on horse at Bridging Train lines, Glanders.	
"	7/1/16		Visited transport lines of 68th Inf Bde & inspected with Capt Haddon, went to Amm Col 105th Bde R.F.A. in afternoon	
"	8/1/16		Went to 35 M.V.S. inspected 100 mules from Remount Depot at Div: Amm: Col:, 1 horse in Div: Amm: Col: reacted to Mallein Test	
"	9/1/16		Lieut Percy A.V.C. returned from leave, went to 35 M.V.S., visited Div Amm: Col: in afternoon made Post-Mortem Exam: on horse which reacted, Glanders, then went to D.L.O. Yeomanry.	
"	10/1/16		Capt Allinson A.V.C. went for leave. The S.S.O. saw me about reduction of Hay ration called at M.M.P. stables. Lectured at Div: Amm: Col: in evening	

2353 Wt. W2514/1454 700,000 5/15 D. D. & L. A.D.S.S./Forms/C. 2118.

Army Form C. 2118.

Instructions regarding War Diaries and Intelligence Summaries are contained in F. S. Regs., Part II. and the Staff Manual respectively. Title pages will be prepared in manuscript.

WAR DIARY
or
INTELLIGENCE SUMMARY.
(Erase heading not required.)

Place	Date	~~Hour~~	Summary of Events and Information	Remarks and references to Appendices
Croix du Bac	11/1/16		went to 35 M.V.S. signal Coy and M.M.P. Lectured at Div: Amm: Col: in evening	
"	12/1/16		Attended Genl's conference. went to 35 M.V.S. and M.M.P. visited signal Co and D.L.O. Yeomanry in afternoon. Lectured at Div: Amm: Col: in evening	
"	13/1/16		went to 35 M.V.S., M.M.P. and signal Co. Lieut Percy A.V.C. lectured to Div: Amm: Col: on shoeing	
"	14/1/16		went to 35 M.V.S., M.M.P., A & B Btys 103rd Bde. R.F.A., sent mallein return to D.D.V.S. 1st Army, Report asked for, whether 1 M.V.S. would do for the Corps, instead of 1 each Division	
"	15/1/16		Corp Martin (Clerk) went on leave, visited horse lines of 68th, 69th and 24th Inf Bdes	
"	16/1/16		went to 35 M.V.S., B Bty. 104th Bde R.F.A., Amm: Col: 103rd Bde R.F.A., Signal Co and M.M.P.	
"	17/1/16		Went to 35 M.V.S., D.L.O. Yeomanry and Div: Amm: Col:	
"	18/1/16		Lieut Lowe A.V.C. (attached) gone on leave. called on 101st Co. R.E. at Erquinghem. saw animals at 35 M.V.S.	
"	19/1/16		Attended Genl's conference. went to 35 M.V.S. and to 9th S Staffs at Erquinghem, & 2 Btes of 104th Bde R.F.A.	
"	20/1/16		Lieut O'Brien A.V.C. went on leave. visited 35 M.V.S., 102nd Bde R.F.A. amm: Col:, D.L.O. Yeomanry and Div: Ammn: Col:	
"	21/1/16		Went to Div: Amm: Col: with Lieut Macdougall A.V.C. who is acting for Lieut O'Brien A.V.C. called to see Aux Transport horses and Bridging Train	
"	22/1/16		Rode to 24th and 68th Inf Bdes transport lines. motored to Erquinghem, saw 1 Bty 103rd Bde. R.F.A. 2 Btes 104th Bde. R.F.A., 1 Bty 102nd Bde. R.F.A. also 9th S Staffs Regt	

2353 Wt. W2544/1454 700,000 5/15 D. D. & L. A.D.S.S./Forms/C. 2118.

Instructions regarding War Diaries and Intelligence Summaries are contained in F. S. Regs., Part II. and the Staff Manual respectively. Title pages will be prepared in manuscript.

WAR DIARY
or
INTELLIGENCE SUMMARY.
(Erase heading not required.)

Army Form C. 2118.

Place	Date	~~Hour~~	Summary of Events and Information	Remarks and references to Appendices
Croix du Bac	23/1/16		went to 35. M.V.S., 69th and 71st Field Ambulance, also Amm: Col: 105th Bde. R.F.A.	
"	24/1/16		went to 35 M.V.S., inspected 3 Field Co's R.E. also 4th How Bde. R.G.A. (attached)	
"	25/1/16		went to 4 Co's A.S.C., Corpl Martin (clerk) returned from leave, visited 35 M.V.S. also 101st & 102nd Field Co's. R.E. in afternoon.	
"	26/1/16		Attended Genls conference, visited 35 M.V.S., D.L.O. Yeomanry, and Div: Ammn: Col.	
"	27/1/16		Inspected 69th Inf Bde transport animals, 2 Btns Inf from 34th Div attached, Lieut: O'Brien A.V.C. granted extension of leave on medical certificate.	
"	28/1/16		Went to Nieppe to see A.D.V.S. 9th Division, called on D.L.O. Yeomanry and Div Amm: Col: in afternoon	
"	29/1/16		Went to 35 M.V.S. then to Erquinghem to see 2 Co's R.E. and 103rd Inf Bde (attached) from 34th Div	
"	30/1/16		Left France on 8 days leave.	

Frank W. [illegible]

MAJOR,
A. D. V. S. 23RD DIVISION.

2353 Wt. W2514/1454 700,000 5/15 D. D. & L. A.D.S.S./Forms/C. 2118.

[illegible] 23 [illegible]

vol 7

February

Army Form C. 2118.

Instructions regarding War Diaries and Intelligence Summaries are contained in F. S. Regs., Part II. and the Staff Manual respectively. Title pages will be prepared in manuscript.

WAR DIARY
or
INTELLIGENCE SUMMARY.
(Erase heading not required.)

Place	Date	~~Hour~~	Summary of Events and Information	Remarks and references to Appendices
Croix du Bac	8/2/16		Returned from leave, went to 35 Mobile Vety Section, D.L.O. Yeomanry and M.M.P.	
〃	9/2/16		attended Genl's conference, went to 35 M.V.S. inspected horses 2 Co's R.E., 9th Btn S Staffs and 2 Btes 102nd Bde R.F.A. at Erquinghem	
〃	10/2/16		went to 35 M.V.S., 103rd Bde Infantry (attached) 102nd Bde R.F.A. amm: Col: and Div: Amm: Col:	
〃	11/2/16		Went to 68th and 69th Inf Bdes transport lines, went to 35 M.V.S. in afternoon.	
〃	12/2/16		went to 35 M.V.S., 102nd Bde R.F.A. amm: Col:, D.L.O. Yeomanry and Div: Amm: Col:	
〃	13/2/16		Went in car to Blaringhem to see A.D.V.S. 34th Div.	
〃	14/2/16		went to 35 M.V.S., 68th Inf Bde and 4th Hvy Bde. R.G.A.	
〃	15/2/16		A.D.V.S. 34th Div: came over, showed him 35 M.V.S. etc. made a Post-Mortem exam: on Major Watson's charger which died suddenly	
〃	16/2/16		went to 35 M.V.S. and D.L.O. Yeomanry also Div Amm Col and 9th S Staffs. attended conference at 6 pm	
〃	17/2/16		Capt R C Allinson A.V.C. took over command 35 M.V.S. from Lieut H W Percy A.V.C. who returned to England. visited 24th and 68th Inf Bdes also 102nd Co. R.E.	
〃	18/2/16		Capt R C Allinson A.V.C. left with 35 M.V.S. for Steenbecque to take over from 34th Div	
〃	19/2/16		Lieut Bambridge A.V.C. arrived with 44 M.V.S. visited Div: Amm: Col:, 23rd Div Train. Aux horse transport and Bridging train	
〃	20/2/16		Went to 68th Inf Bde, then to 4th Hvy Bde R.G.A., called on Signal Co in afternoon	
〃	21/2/16		Went in car to Blaringhem, called on 35 M.V.S.	

Army Form C. 2118.

Instructions regarding War Diaries and Intelligence Summaries are contained in F. S. Regs., Part II. and the Staff Manual respectively. Title pages will be prepared in manuscript.

WAR DIARY
or
INTELLIGENCE SUMMARY.
(Erase heading not required.)

Place	Date	~~Hour~~	Summary of Events and Information	Remarks and references to Appendices
Croix du Bac	22/2/16		Went to 68th Inf Bde horse lines, sent 2 horses and 1 mule to 44 M. V. S., then to Signal Co. and Cable section	
"	23/2/16		Lieut Simons A. V. C. reported arrival and was attached to 23rd Div Train. Looked through Aux Transport horses, 20th Co. R. E. and Bridging Train.	
Estaires	24/2/16		Div Hd Qrs left Croix du Bac for Estaires, hunted around for an Office + billet	
"	25/2/16		Went in car to Steinbecque to 35 M. V. S.	
Blaringhem	26/2/16		Left Estaires for Blaringhem, arrived after dark.	
"	27/2/16		Went in car to Vieux Berquin	
"	28/2/16		Rode round to find out where some of the Hd Qrs horses were stabled	
Bruay	29/2/16		Left Blaringhem at 11 am for Bruay. Capt Allenson A. V. C. arrived about 6.30 pm with 35 M. V. S.	

Frank W. [illegible]
MAJOR,
A. D. V. S. 23RD DIVISION.

2353 Wt. W2544/1454 700,000 5/15 D. D. & L. A.D.S.S./Forms/C. 2118.

A D V S
23rd D

Vol 8

War Diary March. 1916.

1

Army Form C. 2118.

Instructions regarding War Diaries and Intelligence Summaries are contained in F. S. Regs., Part II. and the Staff Manual respectively. Title pages will be prepared in manuscript.

ASST. DIRECTOR OF VETY. SERVICES
1 APR. 1916
23rd DIVISION

WAR DIARY or INTELLIGENCE SUMMARY.

(Erase heading not required.)

March, 1916.

Place	Date	Hour	Summary of Events and Information	Remarks and references to Appendices
Bruay	Mar 1		Rode with Capt Allinson A.V.C. to find suitable site for 35 M.V.S. Message received in evening to go to 69th Bde. to see Brigadier's Horse.	
	" 2		Visited 69th Bde transport lines, then to 35 M.V.S.	
	" 3		Rode to 35 Mobile Vety Section, 23rd Signal Co. and Hd Qrs 24th Inf Bde	
	" 4		Attended General's conference, went with Interpreter to Bruay Station to arrange with Station master about trucks for evacuating animals. Attended lecture in afternoon by Corps Commander.	
	" 5		Eight horses evacuated from 35 M.V.S. Too slippery for riding.	
	" 6		Went with O.C. 35 M.V.S. to Xerwin to look for site for 35 M.V.S. and billets for men	
	" 7		Went with Interpreter to Caucourt, arranged a site for 35 M.V.S. and billets.	
	" 8		Eight horses evacuated. Left Bruay for Caucourt. On arrival looked round for office.	
Caucourt	" 9		Rode round several Units and looked through horses.	
	" 10		Rode to Div Hd Qrs at Chateau de la Haie.	
	" 11		D.D.V.S. came out; went to 35 M.V.S. with him and also some of the horse lines	
	" 12		Rode to Div Hd Qrs and inspected horses also horses of 3 Cos R.E.	
	" 13		Rode to Reserve area at Frevilliers, gave instructions for one horse to be left at Farm, visited D.A.C.	

2353 Wt. W2544/1454 700,000 5/15 D. D. & L. A.D.S.S./Forms/C. 2118.

7

Army Form C. 2118.

WAR DIARY
or
INTELLIGENCE SUMMARY.
(*Erase heading not required.*)

Instructions regarding War Diaries and Intelligence Summaries are contained in F. S. Regs., Part II. and the Staff Manual respectively. Title pages will be prepared in manuscript.

Place	Date	Hour	Summary of Events and Information	Remarks and references to Appendices
Caucourt	March 14		Rode to Div Hd Qrs and inspected horses. One horse left with Farmer (belonging to C.R.E.) Saw Lieut O'Brien A.V.C. and inspected horses of Div: Amm: Col:	
	" 15		Eight horses evacuated. Rode to Div Hd Qrs. In the afternoon A.D.V.S. 47th Div came over	
	" 16		Left Caucourt at 10 am for Bruay. Took another office	
Bruay	" 17		Rode to Ruitz in morning. Saw C.R.E. re his horse. Capt R C Allinson A.V.C. away collecting left horses	
	" 18		Inspected 2 Btes 104th Bde + Amm: Col: of 103rd Bde R.F.A. Lieut Simons A.V.C admitted to Hospital.	
	" 19		Went to 35 M.V.S. Twenty horses evacuated also 7 evacuated from 47th Div Looked through Signal Co horses	
	" 20		Went with S.S.O. to refilling point and then to Sains en Gohelle. Called on A.D.V.S. 2nd Div	
	" 21		A.D.V.S. 2nd Div. came over to see M.V.S. etc. Looked through Hd Qrs horses + Sig Co	
	" 22		Left Bruay for Sains en Gohelle. In afternoon rode to 35 M.V.S. at Barlin attended Generals conference in evening	
Sains en Gohelle	" 23		Rode to 35 M.V.S. Looked round district re horse shelters and watering places	

2353 Wt. W2514/1454 700,000 5/15 D. D. & L. A.D.S.S./Forms/C. 2118.

3

Army Form C. 2118.

Instructions regarding War Diaries and Intelligence Summaries are contained in F. S. Regs., Part II. and the Staff Manual respectively. Title pages will be prepared in manuscript.

WAR DIARY
or
INTELLIGENCE SUMMARY.
(Erase heading not required.)

Place	Date	Hour	Summary of Events and Information	Remarks and references to Appendices
Sains-en-Gohelle	March 24		Rode to Bully Grenay in morning and Barlin in afternoon	
	" 25		Went to 35 M.V.S., then to Reserve Park and D.L.O. Yeomanry. Lieut J.A. Carroll. A.V.C. reported for duty. Sent him to Hd Qrs 23rd Div Train	
	" 26		Rode to 35 M.V.S. in morning and then to Div: Amm: Col.	
	" 27		One horse killed and one destroyed of Signal Co. through a wall in stable collapsing. Went to D.A.C. to look through horses with O.C. re HD class	
	" 28		Inspected horses Amm: Col: 102nd Bde R.F.A. and 101 Co R.E. then to 35 M.V.S	
	" 29		Rode to Barlin, inspected the watering of horses. then to 35 M.V.S. attended Brig: Genl Oxley's conference in evening	
	" 30		Inspected transport horses of 68th Inf Bde and then went to see a practical demonstration of the Flamenwerfer. Went to 35 M.V.S. in afternoon.	
	" 31		Went to 35 M.V.S. and D.A.C. In afternoon called on R.E. Officer at Compingay re the proposed sinking of wells for supplying water for horses	

Frank W. McElhinish
MAJOR,
A.D.V.S. 23rd DIVISION.

2353 Wt. W2544/1454 700,000 5/15 D. D. & L. A.D.S.S./Forms/C. 2118.

ADVS 23 Div
Vol 9

Army Form C. 2118.

A.D.V.S. 23rd Division

WAR DIARY
or
INTELLIGENCE SUMMARY.
(Erase heading not required.)

Instructions regarding War Diaries and Intelligence Summaries are contained in F. S. Regs., Part II, and the Staff Manual respectively. Title pages will be prepared in manuscript.

Place	Date	Hour	Summary of Events and Information	Remarks and references to Appendices
Sains-en-Gohelle	1/4/1916		Rode to 35 Mobile Vety Section at Barlin and then to Bruay to see A.D.V.S. 2nd Div. Went to 191 Co. A.S.C. Div Train in afternoon.	
"	2/4/16		Inspected Divl Hd Qrs horses in morning and went to Barlin after lunch	
"	3/4/16		Went with Lieut Starkey A.V.C. and inspected horses of 105th Bde R.F.A. at Hersin. Office work in afternoon.	
"	4/4/16		Rode to 35 M.V.S. in Barlin. Wrote a report on watering of horses. Inspected horses of 23rd Signal Co and 101st Field Co. R.E.	
"	5/4/16		Inspected horses of A Bty and Amm: Col: of 102nd Bde R.F.A. at Coupigny. then horses of D.L.O. Yeomanry and No 1 section 2nd Reserve Park. Attended G.O.C. conference in evening	
"	6/4/16		Rode to 35 M.V.S. and Divl Amm: Col: . Went to see horses of D.L.O. Yeomanry.	
"	7/4/16		One horse killed and two wounded by shell fire in Hersin. Inspected horses of Amm: Col: 104th Bde R.F.A.	
"	8/4/16		Rode with Lieut Macdougall A.V.C. to A Bty 103rd Bde R.F.A., 101st and 102nd Field Cos R.E. also 70th Field Ambulance	

2353 Wt. W2544/1454 700,000 5/15 D. D. & L. A.D.S.S./Forms/C. 2118.

Army Form C. 2118.

Instructions regarding War Diaries and Intelligence Summaries are contained in F. S. Regs., Part II. and the Staff Manual respectively. Title pages will be prepared in manuscript.

WAR DIARY
or
INTELLIGENCE SUMMARY.
(*Erase heading not required.*)

Place	Date	Hour	Summary of Events and Information	Remarks and references to Appendices
Sains-en-Gohelle	9/4/1916		Went to Amm: Col: 103rd Bde R.F.A. then to 35 M.V.S.	
	10/4/16		Rode with Lieut Shipley A.V.C. to see horses of 68th and 69th Inf: Bdes. also to Hd Qrs R.A.	
"	11/4/16		D.D.V.S. 1st Army inspected animals of 23rd Divl Train also most of Artillery Horses.	
"	12/4/16		Met D.D.V.S and D.D.R. 1st Army at Hersin and inspected D.L.O. Yeomanry horses etc.	
"	13/4/16		Office in morning. Rode to 35 M.V.S. in afternoon and Bouvigny after tea.	
"	14/4/16		Inspected horses of 23rd Signal Co, 101st Field Co R.E. and A Bty 103rd Bde R.F.A.	
"	15/4/16		Called to see horse of 68th Inf Bde badly wounded by shell fire. then to 35 M.V.S. Went to see horses of D.L.O. Yeomanry.	
"	16/4/16		Called for A.D.V.S. 2nd Division at Bruay and drove to Aire to attend conference by D.D.V.S. 1st Army.	
"	17/4/16		Inspected horses of D.L.O. Yeomanry who are joining 1st Cav: Div. Went to 35 M.V.S.	
"	18/4/16		Placed horse standings of 101st Field Co R.E. out of bounds for suspected mange. went to 35 M.V.S. Inspected horse lines of E Anglian and 126th Field Co R.E. at Fosse 10.	
"	19/4/16		Left Sains-en-Gohelle for Bruay. took over M.V.S. site from 2nd Division.	
Bruay	20/4/16		Rode to 35 M.V.S. and then to Ruitz and inspected R.E. and 9th Btn S Staffs Regt horses	

2353 Wt. W2544/1454 700,000 5/15 D. D. & L. A.D.S.S./Forms/C. 2118.

Instructions regarding War Diaries and Intelligence Summaries are contained in F. S. Regs., Part II. and the Staff Manual respectively. Title pages will be prepared in manuscript.

WAR DIARY
or
INTELLIGENCE SUMMARY.
(Erase heading not required.)

Army Form C. 2118.

Place	Date	Hour	Summary of Events and Information	Remarks and references to Appendices
Bruay	21/4/16		Went to Houdain to see 2 horses of 4th Labour Btn R Fusiliers (attached), then to 35 M. V. S.	
"	22/4/16		Rode to Barlin and inspected horses of 23rd D.A.C. also part of 23rd Divl Train horses	
"	23/4/16		Went to 35 M. V. S. and to 23rd Signal Co. then to 70th Field Ambulance and to Ruitz to see horses of R. E. Cos and 9th Btn S. Staffs Regt.	
"	24/4/16		Drove to Manoeuvring Area to see horses of 69th Inf Bde also called to see 191 Co. A.S.C. Div: Train	
"	25/4/16		Rode to Barlin and then to Ruitz. Office work in afternoon. 45 horses evacuated from M.V.S.	
"	26/4/16		Went to 35 M.V.S. Mule from D.A.C. dropped dead in street. Motored to La Thieuloye in afternoon, saw horses of 104th Bde R.F.A. also horses of Amm: Col: 103rd Bde R.F.A.	
"	27/4/16		Went to 35 M.V.S. in morning, held conference with V.Os. in afternoon.	
"	28/4/16		Rode to D.A.C. and then to Ruitz, called at 35 M.V.S. in afternoon	
"	29/4/16		Rode to R.A. Hd Qrs, then to 68th Inf Bde, Office in afternoon	
"	30/4/16		Rode to Houdain and then to M.V.S., inspected horses of Div: Hd. Qrs.	

Frank W. Mitchell
MAJOR,
A. D. V. S. 23RD DIVISION.

2353 Wt. W2544/1454 700,000 5/15 D. D. & L. A.D.S.S./Forms/C. 2118.

Instructions regarding War Diaries and Intelligence Summaries are contained in F. S. Regs., Part II. and the Staff Manual respectively. Title pages will be prepared in manuscript.

Army Form C. 2118.

Vol 10

WAR DIARY or INTELLIGENCE SUMMARY. A.D.V.S. 23rd Division.

(Erase heading not required.)

Place	Date	~~Hour~~	Summary of Events and Information	Remarks and references to Appendices
Bruay	May 1st/16		Went in Car to manouvre area at Matringham and inspected horses of 24th Inf Bde. 191 Co. A.S.C. and section of 70th Field Ambulance	
	" 2		Went to No 35 Mobile Vety Section and then inspected Div: Train horses.	
	" 3		Went in Car with D.A.Q.M.G. 23rd Div: to Matringhem to inquire into issue of mouldy Oats to 24th Inf: Bde. looked through their horses.	
	" 4		Inspected Div: Signal Co horses and then to 35 M.V.S. Conference of V.Os in afternoon After tea rode to 68th Inf Bde.	
	" 5		Went to 35 M.V.S. and then to Bethune. Inspected Div: Hd Qrs horses after tea.	
	" 6		Inspected horses of 24th Inf Bde in Hersin, took particulars of five for casting.	
	" 7		Attended conference of A.Ds.V.S. in Aire.	
	" 8		Office work in morning. Attended General's conference in afternoon.	
	" 9		D.D.V.S. and D.D.R. 1st Army came out to D.A.C. and drafted out a number of Animals as this Unit is to be demobilized.	
	" 10		Motored to manouvre area, inspected horses of 68th Inf Bde. 1 horse of 70th Field Ambulance to be left at Farm in Laires.	
	" 11		Rode to 35 M.V.S. and D.A.C., Had conference with V.Os. in afternoon	

Army Form C. 2118.

Instructions regarding War Diaries and Intelligence Summaries are contained in F. S. Regs., Part II. and the Staff Manual respectively. Title pages will be prepared in manuscript.

WAR DIARY
or
INTELLIGENCE SUMMARY.

(Erase heading not required.)

Place	Date	Hour	Summary of Events and Information	Remarks and references to Appendices
Bruay	May 12		Went to Hd Qrs R.A. and then to Houdain to inspect horses of 33rd Labour Btn R Fusiliers. In afternoon met Lieut Starkey A.V.C. and inspected horses of 105th Bde R.F.A.	
	" 13		Left Bruay for Sains en Gohelle. Inspected horses of 3 Co's. R.E.	
Sains en Gohelle	" 14		Rode to Aix Noulette and Fosse 10. Saw 2 Infantry Bdes	
	" 15		Rode to 35 M.V.S. in Barlin, then to Div: Train stables. In office in afternoon.	
	" 16		Went to R.A. Hd Qrs, then inspected horses of a Bty in 102nd Bde R.F.A. Went to 35 M.V.S. In afternoon motored to manouvre area to see horses of 68th Inf: Bde	
	" 17		Inspected Div: Hd Qrs horses and A Bty 103rd Bde R.F.A. Inspected D.A.C. horses.	
	" 18		Inspected 3 Btys of 102nd Bde R.F.A. also 71st Field Ambulance. Went to 35 M.V.S. in afternoon. Lieut Shipley A.V.C. proceeded on leave.	
	" 19		Rode with Lieut Macdougall A.V.C. and inspected horses of R.E. Cos and 69th Inf: Bde Went to Hersin and Barlin in afternoon.	
	" 20		Went to 35 M.V.S., inspected Signal Co horses and A Bty 103rd Bde R.F.A. A civilians horse in Hersin was injured by a Motor Lorry.	
	" 21		Had civilians horse sent to 35 M.V.S. Went to D.A.C. and Div Train	

2353 Wt. W2544/1454 700,000 5/15 D. D. & L. A.D.S.S./Forms/C. 2118.

Instructions regarding War Diaries and Intelligence Summaries are contained in F. S. Regs., Part II. and the Staff Manual respectively. Title pages will be prepared in manuscript.

WAR DIARY
or
INTELLIGENCE SUMMARY.
(Erase heading not required.)

Army Form C. 2118.

Place	Date	~~Hour~~	Summary of Events and Information	~~Remarks and references to Appendices~~
Sains en Gohelle	May 22		Rode to Hersin and Coupigny. Motored to La Thieuloye to see 104th Bde R.F.A.	
	" 23		Went to Hd Qrs 24th Inf: Bde to see General's Charger. then to 35 M.V.S.. Motored to Saines in afternoon to see horse left by 70th Field Ambulance.	
	" 24		Sains en Gohelle was fairly heavily shelled. Had to leave Office and Billet. Took Office and Billet in Barlin. Attended General's conference in evening.	
Barlin	" 25		Rode over to Div: Hd Qrs. Inspected horses in 1st Siege Battery, 10 wounded. V.Os. conference in afternoon.	
	" 26		Rode to Sains en Gohelle. Went to Hd Qrs. 104th Bde R.F.A. in afternoon.	
	" 27		Lieut W Shipley. A.V.C. back from leave. Visited D.A.C. and 103rd Bde R.F.A. in Hersin	
	" 28		Went to 2nd Reserve Park, 9th Btn S Staffs Regt, and 69th Field Ambulance.	
	" 29		Q Branch 23rd Div came to Barlin owing to heavy shelling at Sains en Gohelle. All horses brought in	
	" 30		Capt R.C. Allinson A.V.C. gone on leave. D.D.R. 1st Army inspected some horses for casting	
	" 31		Major Abson. A.D.V.S. 47th Div: came over to see me. Went to different sections of D.A.C. Attended General's conference.	

[illegible] MAJOR,
A. D. V. S. 23RD DIVISION.

2353 Wt. W2544/1454 700,000 5/15 D. D. & L. A.D.S.S./Forms/C. 2118.

A.D.V.S. 23rd Division.

WAR DIARY or INTELLIGENCE SUMMARY.

(Erase heading not required.)

June. 1916.

Army Form C. 2118.

ADVS 23 Div Vol 11

Instructions regarding War Diaries and Intelligence Summaries are contained in F. S. Regs., Part II. and the Staff Manual respectively. Title pages will be prepared in manuscript.

Place	Date	Hour	Summary of Events and Information	Remarks and references to Appendices
Barlin	June 1/16		DDVS and DDR 1st Army came to inspect Horses of 68th Inf Bde at Hersin. V.Os conference in afternoon. Capt Hodge A.V.C. reported, being in charge of Heavy Artillery attached	June
"	2		Went to D.A.C. in morning. Inspected Train Co's in afternoon.	
"	3		Rode over to Hd Qrs, Naval Bde in morning and then inspected Animals of Inf Bde. Called at 71st Field Ambulance.	
"	4		Payed N.C.Os and men at 35 Mobile Vety Section. Attended D.D.V.S. conference at Aire.	
"	5		Inspected cases at Mobile Vety Section for evacuation. Went with Lieut Shipsley A.V.C. to see horses of 102nd Bde. R.F.A.	
"	6		Major F. J. Taylor A.V.C., A.D.V.S. 62nd Division arrived from England for 3 days duty. Took him to see D.A.C. and Div: Train horses.	
"	7		Rode to Hd Qrs, Sains-en-Gohelle. Saw transport Animals. A Bty 103rd Bde R.F.A. and 101st Field Co. R.E., attended Generals conference in evening.	
"	8		Went to Sains-en-Gohelle in morning. D.D.V.S. came out to see Major Taylor. V.Os. conference in afternoon	
"	9		Major Taylor returned to England. Rode round with Lieut Carroll A.V.C. & inspected his Units	
"	10		Capt Allinson A.V.C. returned from leave. Inspected horses of 104th Bde. R.F.A. and 70th Field Ambulance	
"	11		Rode to Div Hd Qrs, Inspect A Bty 103 Bde R.F.A., Sent 6 cases suspected mange to 35 Mobile Veterinary Section.	

2353 Wt. W2534/1454 700,000 5/15 D. D. & L. A.D.S.S./Forms/C. 2118.

Instructions regarding War Diaries and Intelligence Summaries are contained in F. S. Regs., Part II. and the Staff Manual respectively. Title pages will be prepared in manuscript.

WAR DIARY
or
INTELLIGENCE SUMMARY.
(Erase heading not required.)

Army Form C. 2118.

Place	Date	Hour	Summary of Events and Information	Remarks and references to Appendices
Barlin	June 12/16		Rode to Hersin Coupigny in morning and saw 24th Inf: Bde. Went to Bruay in afternoon	
"	13		Rode to Sains-en-Gohelle. A horse in 35 Mobile Vety Section got cast and fractured tibia	
"	14		Left Barlin for Bruay. Went to 35 Mobile Vety Section.	
Bruay	15		Inspected Div: Hd Qrs horses, 23rd Div Signal Co and then went to 35 Mobile Vety Section	
"	16		Motored with Cols Watson and Wilkinson to Borny. found site for 35 Mobile Vety Section also office and billet	
"	17		Walked to 35 M.V.S., inspected Div: Hd Qrs and M.M.P. horses. Attended Generals conference	
"	18		Went to see transport animals of 68th Inf Bde. Motored to RA to see suspected case of mange. D.D.V.S and D.D.R. 1st Army came out later	
"	19		Rode to Matringham in morning, saw 9th Btn S Staffs horses also 3 Co's R.E. Motored to Roquetoire in afternoon to see horse left at a farm	
"	20		Evacuated horses from Aire. Rode to M.G. Co. of 24th Inf: Bde	
"	21		Rode to Hd Qrs R.A. and then rode with Lieut Shipley A.V.C. and saw horses 102 Bde R.F.A.	
"	22		Went to 35 M.V.S. and then to inspect horses of 23rd Div: Train.	
"	23		Motored to Aire, saw D.D.V.S. 1st Army, then saw horses trucked for evacuation	
"	24		Left in car 7.am. for Berguette, entrained for Longeau and then rode 8 miles to Vaux-en-Amienoise	

2353 Wt. W2544/1454 700,000 5/15 D. D. & L. A.D.S.S./Forms/C. 2118.

Army Form C. 2118.

Instructions regarding War Diaries and Intelligence Summaries are contained in F. S. Regs., Part II. and the Staff Manual respectively. Title pages will be prepared in manuscript.

WAR DIARY
or
INTELLIGENCE SUMMARY.
(Erase heading not required.)

Place	Date	Hour	Summary of Events and Information	Remarks and references to Appendices
Vaux-en-Amienoise	June 25		Rode to the village and inspected sites for 35 Mobile Vety Section. 35 M.V.S. arrived 6 pm	
	26		Went to 35 M.V.S. Horse collected for the 30th Division. Motored to see horses of 105 Bde R.F.A.	
"	27		D.D.V.S. 4th Army. Lt Col Hunt came out and inspected 35 M.V.S. Went to D.A.C in afternoon	
"	28		Capt Allinson A.V.C. O.C. 35 M.V.S. sent over to engage trucks for evacuations. Stayed in office	
"	29		Motored to 3 Cos R.E. saw horses also Artillery horses	
"	30		Rode to Breilly to inspect 23rd Div: Train horses also 69th Field Ambulance horses	

Frank W. McKinnish

MAJOR,
A.D.V.S. 23RD DIVISION.

2353 Wt. W2544/1454 700,000 5/15 D. D. & L. A.D.S.S./Forms/C. 2118.

Army Form C. 2118.

Jelly

A.D.V.S. 23 DW

Vol 12

A.D.V.S.

Instructions regarding War Diaries and Intelligence Summaries are contained in F. S. Regs., Part II. and the Staff Manual respectively. Title pages will be prepared in manuscript.

23rd Division

WAR DIARY or INTELLIGENCE SUMMARY.

(Erase heading not required.)

29 July 1916.

Place	Date	Hour	Summary of Events and Information	Remarks and references to Appendices
Baizieux	July 1/16		Orders came to shift 35 Mob: Vet: Section to ALLONVILLE. Div Hd Qrs moved to BAIZIEUX at 7.30 pm 35 Mob: Vet: Section moved from ALLONVILLE with Div: Amm: Col. to ST GRATIEN	
"	" 2		Inspected Div Hd Qrs horses, called at 35 Mob: Vet: Section of 8th Division. In afternoon went to ST GRATIEN	
"	" 3		Motored to ST GRATIEN in morning. Rode to HENENCOURT to see A.D.V.S. 12th Division in afternoon.	
"	" 4		A.D.V.S. 34th Division came to see me. Div Hd Qrs moved to DERNANCOURT in afternoon	
Dernancourt	" 5		Rode to 44 Mob: Vet: Section and collecting post at DERNANCOURT. Motored to ST GRATIEN Inspected horses of 9th S Staffs. 35 Mob: Vet: Section moved from ST GRATIEN to DERNANCOURT	
"	" 6		Capt Maconochie A.V.C in charge of Hoy Art: attached for administrative purposes Several horses of 9th S Staffs killed by shell fire. Went to ST GRATIEN to see 2 horses left behind by 35 Mob: Vet: Section. Arranged with Town Major about their disposal	
"	" 7			
"	" 8		Rode to Div Hd Qrs, 23rd Signal Co and 70th Field Ambul: in morning. 35 M.V.S. in afternoon	
"	" 9		Rode with Capt Starkey A.V.C to see horses of 9th S Staffs and 69th Inf Transport	
"	" 10		Rode to Div Hd Qrs and Art: lines. Went to see D.L.O. Yeomanry horses in afternoon	
"	" 11		23rd Division relieved by 1st Division. 23rd Division moved back to St GRATIEN	
St Gratien	" 12		Rode to 4th Army Hd Qrs to see D.D.V.S., 35 Mob: Vet: Section remained at DERNANCOURT Inspected horses in 34th Reserve Park	

Army Form C. 2118.

Instructions regarding War Diaries and Intelligence Summaries are contained in F. S. Regs., Part II. and the Staff Manual respectively. Title pages will be prepared in manuscript.

WAR DIARY
or
INTELLIGENCE SUMMARY.
(Erase heading not required.)

Place	Date	Hour	Summary of Events and Information	Remarks and references to Appendices
St Gratien	July 13/16		Motored to Dernancourt to 35 Mob: Vet: Section. Inspected Div: Amm: Col: animals.	
"	" 14		Rode to 69th Inf Bde, 192nd A.S.C. Co and 101st Field Co. R.E. at Molliens au Bois.	
"	" 15		Motored to LONGUEAU Station to see Animals of 24th Inf: Bde entrain. In afternoon went to ALBERT to see animals of 68th Inf: Bde	
"	" 16		Inspected 69th Bde transport horses, 2 Cos A.S.C and 9th S. Staffs., 70th Inf Bde arrived	
"	" 17		Wired to Lt Macdougall A.V.C. 103rd Bde R.F.A. to proceed to MOLLIENS AU BOIS and take over Vet: charge of 69th and 70th Inf Bdes. Lt Carroll A.V.C. to look after 103rd Bde R.F.A. horses	
"	" 18		Motored to DERNANCOURT to 35 Mob: Vet: Section. In afternoon inspected animals of Div: Hd Qrs and 70th Inf: Bde transport	
"	" 19		Rode round to 2 Bdes with Lt Macdougall A.V.C. After lunch motored to DERNANCOURT saw 69th and 71st Field Ambul, 102nd, 128th Field Cos R.E. and Hd Qrs 23rd Div Train.	
"	" 20		Inspected horses of 192 and 193 Cos A.S.C. In afternoon went to FRANVILLERS and inspected horses of 68th Inf Bde	
"	" 21		M.M.P. horse destroyed for Tetanus. Town Major arranged burial. Div Hd Qrs moved to Henencourt	
Henencourt	" 22		Inspected horses of Div Hd Qrs, 23rd Div Signals, 101st and 102nd Field Cos R.E. In afternoon rode to BAIZIEUX to see 70th Inf Bde and 9th S Staffs animals	

2353 Wt. W2544/1454 700,000 5/15 D. D. & L. A.D.S.S./Forms/C. 2118.

Instructions regarding War Diaries and Intelligence Summaries are contained in F. S. Regs., Part II. and the Staff Manual respectively. Title pages will be prepared in manuscript.

WAR DIARY
or
INTELLIGENCE SUMMARY.

(Erase heading not required.)

Army Form C. 2118.

Place	Date	Hour	Summary of Events and Information	Remarks and references to Appendices
Henencourt	July 23/16		Inspected 69th Inf: Bde horses. went to 35 Mob: Vet: Section at DERNANCOURT	
"	" 24		Inspected horses of 69th Field Ambul:, 101st, 102nd Field Cos R.E. and 23rd Div: Signal Co	
"	" 25		Motored to Artillery lines and 35 Mob: Vet: Section at DERNANCOURT	
"	" 26		23rd Div: moved to ALBERT. Inspected horses of 71st Field Ambul: in BECOURT WOOD	
			Saw Div: Amm: Col: animals in afternoon	
Albert	" 27		Rode over to 35 Mob: Vet: Section. Shifted billets and office to 23rd Div Train.	
"	" 28		Rode to FRICOURT and BECOURT WOOD. Went through Artillery wagon lines.	
"	" 29		Inspected animals of 101st Field Co. R.E., 69th Inf: Bde and 9th S Staffs, Mob: Vet: Sec: in afternoon	
"	" 30		Inspected Div: Amm: Col: animals and then over to Div: Hd Qrs and 23rd Div Signal Co	
"	" 31		Went to see M.M.P. and D.L.O. Yeomanry horses also Div Hd Qrs and 23rd Div Signal Co	
			Wrote report on watering of animals.	

Frank W. McElhinish
MAJOR.
A. D. V. S. 23RD DIVISION.

2353 Wt. W2544/1454 700,000 5/15 D. D. & L. A.D.S.S./Forms/C. 2118.

Army Form C. 2118.

A.D.V.S. Vol 13

Instructions regarding War Diaries and Intelligence Summaries are contained in F. S. Regs., Part II. and the Staff Manual respectively. Title pages will be prepared in manuscript.

WAR DIARY
or
INTELLIGENCE SUMMARY.
(Erase heading not required.)

Place	Date	Hour	Summary of Events and Information	Remarks and references to Appendices
Albert	Aug 1.		Inspected D.A.C. Horses and mules and rode to M.V.S. In afternoon called to see 2 wounded horses of 68th Infantry Brigade. – 8 Draft Horses of same brigade killed in Albert.	
	2		Went to Headquarters and Signal Horse lines; afternoon saw the South Staffords and 101 Coy. R.E. and M.V.S.	
	3		Inspected 69th and 70th Infantry transport with Macdougall. Office work in afternoon.	
	4		Forwarded a letter of Macdougall's opened by Censor to D.D.V.S. Inspected Headquarter's horses, M.M.P., Signals and Yeomanry	
	5		Visited Mobile Veterinary Section and 104th Bde. R.F.A., – Saw Headquarter's horses after lunch.	
	6		Inspected transport animals 68th Infantry Brigade and some suspicious skin cases of D.A.C.	
	7		A.D.V.S. 15th Division came to see me. Took him to our M.V.S. and collecting post. Inspected Artillery Horses of 102nd and 103rd Brigades with V.O.'s attached.	
Baizieux	8		On Headquarters move to Baizieux, M.V.S. remained behind. Looked through Hd. Qrs. Horses on arrival.	
Querrieu and St Gratian	9		Went to Querrieu and St Gratian – inspected horses of 192 Coy. A.S.C. – office work in afternoon.	
	10		Looked through Hd. Qrs transport and riding horses – they moved off at 1.30 for new area.	
Ailly le Haut	11		Left Baizieux for Frechencourt, waited 6 hrs for train – reached Longpre 8.30 – rode to Ailly le Haut. Glocher.	
	12		Went to see 3 companies of train, 128 Coy R.E. – Left one horse of 68th Infantry Brigade behind with a wound on stifle.	
Fletre	13		Left Ailly for Bailleul, arrived 7 p.m. – rode to Fletre.	
	14		Now out of 4th Army Area and in 2nd. D.D.V.S. came out to see me. – Went with him to M.V.S. at Nieppe.	
	15		Went to Steenwerck with O.C. Train to see some horses in 192 Coy. – Saw Headquarter's Horses and 70th Field Ambulance.	
	16		One horse from Div. Headquarters and one from 192 Coy. Train have to be left at Fletre. – went to Steenwerck in afternoon to arrange about sick horses left at 51 M.V.S.	
Steenwerck	17		Went to Coq de Paille to see billeting site for our M.V.S. – after lunch Div. Hd Qrs shifted to Steenwerck	
	18		Motored to Coq de Paille to see M.V.S. which arrived 5 a.m., then on to inspect horses which had to be left behind.	
	19		Looked through Hd Qrs horses and 71st Field Ambulance. – sent one horse to be evacuated – Office work in afternoon – Capt. Allinson arrived with M.V.S.	

Frank W. McClimish
MAJOR,
A.D.V.S. 23rd DIVISION.

2353 Wt. W2544/1454 700,000 5/15 D. D. & L. A.D.S.S./Forms/C. 2118.

Army Form C. 2118.

WAR DIARY
or
INTELLIGENCE SUMMARY.
(Erase heading not required.)

Instructions regarding War Diaries and Intelligence Summaries are contained in F. S. Regs., Part II. and the Staff Manual respectively. Title pages will be prepared in manuscript.

Place	Date	Hour	Summary of Events and Information	Remarks and references to Appendices
Steenwerck	Aug 20		A.D.V.S. 41st Division called to see me - went with him to our M.V.S., then on to Div Train horses	
	21		Inspected 70th Infantry Transport and then to M.V.S. Lt Macdougall placed under arrest. Attended General's Conference in afternoon.	
	22		Went to see Lt. Macdougall's horse lines - afterwards met D.D.R. at Hd. Qrs D.A.C. - 10 animals cast.	
	23		Rode to Wagon lines of various batteries. Met D.D.R. at D.A.C. - Lt Shipley A.V.C. reported sick with Tonsilitis	
	24		Capt. Allinson and I rode round horse lines of train companies - Inspected watering troughs at different places. Met A.D.V.S. 36th Division - went to Bailleul and Caestre in afternoon to see horses in 70th Field Ambulance.	
	25		Lt. Shipley A.V.C. back for duty - Went to M.V.S. and 101 Coy. R.E. Lt. Macdougall was paraded before G.O.C. and severely reprimanded for coding letter to Canada. Went with Capt. Hadden to see horses in his train company.	
	26		Met D.D.R. at Steenwerck Station, 84 Remounts arrived. - at 2.30. G.O.C. inspected 70th Infantry Brigade Transport.	
	27		Went through Hd. Qrs. Horses with Camp Commandant. D.D.V.S. came out to see Lt Macdougall - office all the afternoon.	
	28		Lt. Macdougall A.V.C. left for 22nd Base Veterinary Hospital at Abbeville. Lt Bourke A.V.C. arrived to replace him. Visited wagon lines of Artillery Batteries and M.V.S.	
Bailleul	29		Div. Hd Qrs moved to Bailleul. - Private Littlefair reported for duty as Clerk. - very wet day. Had all Hd. Qrs Horses put under cover.	
	30		D.D.V.S. came to see me - Inspected horses of Hd. Qrs in various stables - saw 70th Field Ambulance.	
	31		Saw 69th and 70th Infantry Brigade transport animals with Lt. Bourke A.V.C. - Sent a mule from 70th Field Ambulance to Abattoir for destruction - received 90 francs for carcase.	

Frank W. McEchrnish [signature]
MAJOR,
A.D.V.S. 23RD DIVISION.

2353 Wt. W2544/1454 700,000 5/15 D. D. & L. A.D.S.S./Forms/C. 2118.

Instructions regarding War Diaries and Intelligence Summaries are contained in F. S. Regs., Part II. and the Staff Manual respectively. Title Pages will be prepared in manuscript.

WAR DIARY
or
INTELLIGENCE SUMMARY

(Erase heading not required.)

Army Form C. 2118.

Place	Date	Hour	Summary of Events and Information	Remarks and references to Appendices
Ribemont	1.8.16		Admitted (3) Horses (1) Mule 23 Div	
"	2.8.16		Admitted (7) Horses (1) Mule " "	
"	3.		Admitted (10) Horses (2) Mule (6) other Divs (6) 23 Div Evacuated (20) Horses (7) Mules } (1) Destroyed	
"	4		Admitted (8) Horses (1) Mule (3) other Divs (6) 23 Div	
"	5		Admitted (3) Horses 23 Div	
"	6		Admitted (8) Horses (1) Mule (2) other Div (7) 23 Div Evacuated (13) Horses (2) Mules } (1) Destroyed	
"	7		Admitted (9) Horses 23 Div.	
"	8		Admitted (4) Horses (3) other Div (1) 23 Div	
"	9		Admitted (3) Horses (2) 23 Div (1) other Div Evacuated (18) Horses (2) Destroyed	
"	10		Admitted (7) Horses (3) Mules 23 Div.	
"	11		Admitted (7) Horses 23 Div (2) Picked up Evacuated (11) Horses (3) Mules (1) Reissued (1) Died	
"	12		Admitted (4) Mules (2) 23 Div (2) Picked	
"	13		Admitted (5) Horses 23 Div 14.8.16 Evacuated (6) Horses (2) Mules Handed over (2) Horses (2) Mules 15 R. V. S.	
Nieppe	19		Admitted (31) Horses (4) Mules other Divs	
"	20		Admitted (4) Horses (2) 23 Div (2) other Div. Evacuated (21) Horses (4) Mules	
"	21		Admitted (4) Horses (3) 23 Div. (1) other Div	
"	22		Admitted (5) Horses (1) Mule 23 Div Evacuated (12) Horses	

R C Allman
Capt A V C

35th MOBILE VETERINARY SECTION
No. 9
Date 8/16
A. V. C.

2449 Wt. W14957/M90 750,000 1/16 J.B.C. & A. Forms/C.2118/12.

Army Form C. 2118.

Instructions regarding War Diaries and Intelligence Summaries are contained in F. S. Regs., Part II. and the Staff Manual respectively. Title Pages will be prepared in manuscript.

WAR DIARY
or
INTELLIGENCE SUMMARY
(Erase heading not required.)

Place	Date	Hour	Summary of Events and Information	Remarks and references to Appendices
Nieppe	23.8.16		admitted (1) Horse 23 Div	
"	24.8.16		admitted (1) Horse 23 Div	
"	25		admitted (3) Horses 23 Div.	
"	26		admitted (25) Horses (14) Mules 23 Div. (11) Cast D.D.R.	
"	27		admitted (2) Horses 23 Div. Evacuated (34) Horses (14) Mules	
"	29		admitted (3) Horses 23 Div Evacuated (6) Horses (1) Mule.	
"	30		admitted (2) Horses 23 Div.	
"	31		admitted (2) Horses (1) Mule 23 Div.	

R. C. Allinson
Capt A.V.C.

35th MOBILE VETERINARY SECTION
No. 9
Date 8/16
A. V. C.

2449 Wt. W14957/M90 750,000 1/16 J.B.C. & A. Forms/C.2118/12.

Army Form C. 2118.

ADVS 23 D
VOO 14

Instructions regarding War Diaries and Intelligence Summaries are contained in F. S. Regs., Part II. and the Staff Manual respectively. Title pages will be prepared in manuscript.

WAR DIARY
or
INTELLIGENCE SUMMARY.
(Erase heading not required.)

Place	Date 1916	Hour	Summary of Events and Information	Remarks and references to Appendices
Bailleul.	Sept 1		Inspected train horses with O.C. Div. Train; then to 70th Field Ambulance	
	2		Sold a mule with injured hock to local butcher for 90 frs. Sent off report to DDVS on reorganisation of R.F.A.	
	3		Corp. Martin (Clerk) sent to M.V.S. – Private Littlefair A.S.C. took his place. Inspected Hd. Qrs horses in various stables.	
	4		Went with G.O.C. R.A. to inspect horses for debility. 40 horses sent to M.V.S. Called for Lt. Bourke A.V.C. and went to Hd. Qrs 69th Bde. ADVS. 19th Division called on me in the afternoon.	
Tilques	5		Div. Hd Qrs horses and transport left for TILQUE. Had orders to vacate M.V.S. tomorrow. Went over in car to see O.C.	
	6		Lorries packed at 8.30 a.m. Went to TILQUE after lunch.	
	7		Capt. Allinson arrived with M.V.S. at 3 o'clock. Went with Camp Commandant and selected a site in TILQUE.	
	8		Went in car to 3 companies of Train, 69th and 70th Fd. Ambulances. In afternoon went to Hd. Qrs. 70th Infantry Bde at LOMBRES.	
	9		Left TILQUE for AMIENS.	
Allonville	10		Went to ALLONVILLE – found billet, office and M.V.S. site.	
	11		M.V.S. arrived at 5 a.m. Inspected horses of 101 and 102 Co. R.E., Div. Signals, and South Staffords. Wire received from DDVS. about Supernumary A.V.C. Sergeants.	
Baizieux	12		Left ALLONVILLE 9 a.m. for BAIZIEUX. In afternoon inspected Hd. Qrs. horses and Signals. M.V.S. sent to St. GRATIEN.	
	13		102 Bde R.F.A. left for the 47th Division. 103 Bde R.F.A. left for the 15th Division. Attended G.O.C's Conference at 5 p.m.	
	14		Attended Conference of A.D's.V.S. at Hd. Qrs. 4th Army. Went to M.V.S. at St GRATIEN and Hd. Qrs. R.A. in afternoon.	

Frank W. Mellows [illegible]
MAJOR,
A.D.V.S. 23rd DIVISION.

2353 Wt. W2544/1454 700,000 5/15 D. D. & L. A.D.S.S./Forms/C. 2118.

Instructions regarding War Diaries and Intelligence Summaries are contained in F. S. Regs., Part II. and the Staff Manual respectively. Title pages will be prepared in manuscript.

WAR DIARY
or
INTELLIGENCE SUMMARY.
(Erase heading not required.)

Army Form C. 2118.

Place	Date	Hour	Summary of Events and Information	Remarks and references to Appendices
Baizieux	15		Sent amended roll of A.V.C. Sergeants to Records. In afternoon went to see D.D.V.S., 69th Fd. Ambulance and M.V.S.	
	16		Rode to BRESLE – inspected horses 102 Coy. A.S.C. and 101 Coy. R.E.	
	17		Went in car to Army Hd. Qrs. then to 69th Fd. Ambulance, 104 Bde R.F.A. and M.V.S.	
	18		Raining in torrents – stayed in office.	
Millencourt – Albert road.	19		Left BAIZIEUX for camp near Albert. – took over from 15th Division. Capt Allinson called to see me about moving the M.V.S.	
	20		M.V.S. took over site occupied by 15th Division; also Advanced Collecting Post. Inspected both places.	
	21		Went to M.V.S. in morning. Lt. Bourke A.V.C. sent to 50th Div. Rest Station. Inspected horses and mules of 68th Infantry Bde.	
	22		Inspected 1st line transport of 70th Inf. Bde; then to Advanced Collecting Post and M.V.S.	
	23		Went to BAIZIEUX to see Lt. Bourke in 50th Div Rest Station. Saw Train horses in afternoon.	
	24		Went in car to MAMETZ to see 102 and part of 104 Brigades R.F.A.	
	25		Inspected animals of 68 and 69th Infantry Bdes and South Staffords. After tea rode over to MILLENCOURT to see Artillery horses attached to the Division	
	26		Rode to M.V.S and Adv. Collecting Post. Looked through animals of 68th Inf. Bde and South Staffords.	
	27		Went to Becourt Wood to 71st Fd. Ambulance; then inspected 1st line transport 70th Inf. Bde.	
	28		Capt. Shipley A.V.C. gone on 7 days leave. Capt. O'Brien looking after his artillery and Lt. Bourke the 68th Inf. Bde. In afternoon inspected D.A.C.	
	29		Went to M.V.S. and then to Adv. Collecting Post. Inspected a remount at Hd. Qrs. of Train which arrived with Pioneers.	
	30		Rode to Becourt – saw 69th + 70th Inf. Bdes, 101 Coy. R.E. and 71st Fd. Ambulance. Went to M.V.S in afternoon.	

Frank W. Mellhuish
Major,
A.D.V.S. 23rd Division.

2353 Wt. W2544/1454 700,000 5/15 D. D. & L. A.D.S.S./Forms/C. 2118.

1

Instructions regarding War Diaries and Intelligence Summaries are contained in F. S. Regs., Part II. and the Staff Manual respectively. Title pages will be prepared in manuscript.

WAR DIARY
or
INTELLIGENCE SUMMARY.

(Erase heading not required.)

A. D. V. S. Oct. Army Form C. 2118.

VOL 15

Place	Date 1916. Oct.	Hour	Summary of Events and Information	Remarks and references to Appendices
ALBERT	1		Inspected D.A.C. in morning. Visited M.V.S. in afternoon and 12 horses and 3 mules evacuated.	
	2.		Inspected animals of 70th Fd. Ambulance in Becourt Wood and then to 101 Coy. R.E. Office work in afternoon.	
	3		"2" branch moved to Shelter Wood. Went to M.V.S. and then saw 3 companies Div. Train.	
	4		A.D.V.S. 15th Division called - rode around with him and went to M.V.S. 1 Truckload of horses sent away	
	5		Inspected 104 Bde R.F.A. and part of 102 Bde. D.A.R. came out to inspect some horses for casting	
	6		Went with Lt. Carroll A.V.C. to inspect horses of 103 Bde R.F.A. Picked out about 50 for evacuation (Debility)	
	7		A.D.V.S. 15th Division called to see me about taking over. Went to Albert Station 2.30 p.m. to see to the distribution of 58 Remounts.	
	8		Inspected transport of 69th + 70th Infantry Bdes.	
MONTIGNY	9		Orders for M.V.S. to move with D.A.C. Went to 50th Division M.V.S. and arranged for them to take 18 of our animals for evacuation. Left for MONTIGNY - M.V.S. to ST. GRATIEN	
	10		Rode to M.V.S. and inspected horses of 102 Bde. R.F.A. Picked out over 50 for Debility. In afternoon went to R.A. Hd.Qrs. and then to D.D.V.S.	
	11		Rode to see D.D.V.S. and D.D.R. about supplying Remounts to replace debility cases. One transport left at 1.30 p.m.	
AILLY le HAUT CLOCHER	12		Left MONTIGNY for AILLY LE HAUT CLOCHER. Inspected Hd. Qrs., Div Signals and D.L.I. on arrival.	
ST RIQUER	13		Left for ST RIQUER. In afternoon inspected Signals and 128 Coy. R.E.	
	14		Motored over to ST GRATIEN with O.C. Train - saw 1 Coy and M.V.S.	
	15		Saw Hd. Qrs. horses and 101 Coy. R.E.	
POPERINGHE	16		Left CONTEVILLE at 6.30 a.m. for POPERINGHE. Arrived 1.30 rode out to camp.	

2353 Wt. W2544/1454 700,000 5/15 D. D. & L. A.D.S.S./Forms/C. 2118.

2

Army Form C. 2118.

WAR DIARY
or
INTELLIGENCE SUMMARY.
(Erase heading not required.)

Instructions regarding War Diaries and Intelligence Summaries are contained in F. S. Regs., Part II. and the Staff Manual respectively. Title pages will be prepared in manuscript.

Place	Date 1916 Oct.	Hour	Summary of Events and Information	Remarks and references to Appendices
POPERINGHE	17		Inspected Hd. Qrs. Horses and 69th Infantry Transport.	
	18		Went over to see A.D.V.S. 2nd Australian Division at RENINGHELST. In afternoon went to HAZEBRUCK to see D.D.V.S. Second Army.	
	19		Looked through horses of Divisional Train. Raining hard all day.	
RENINGHELST	20		The Division took over from 2nd Australian Division at RENINGHELST. Lt. Caroll A.V.C. wrote saying leave had been given him by O.C. 103 Bde R.F.A. Rode over to 68th Infantry Transport.	
	21		Visited horse lines of 71st Fd. Ambulance, 101st, 102nd, 128th Coys. R.E. D.D.V.S. called in afternoon.	
	22		Went with O.C. Train to inspect 1st line Transport of 68th Inf. Bde - saw M.G.C. of 70th Bde.	
	23		Rode to 70th Fd. Ambulance and transport lines of 8th and 9th Yorks.	
	24		D.D.V.S. came out in morning. In afternoon went to train companies, West Riding lines and M.G.C. of 69th.	
	25		D.D.V.S. came out and inspected transport lines of 70th Bde., 3 Coy R.E. and 3 Corps. Train.	
	26		Had a parade of Hd. Qrs. horses with the Camp Commandant. In afternoon went to 2nd Canadian Reserve Park and 2nd Entrenching Battalion.	
	27		Rode to 9th S. Staffs - evacuated 2 animals and then to 3 Corps. R.E.	
	28		Rode over to A.D.V.S. 47th Division to see about evacuating from his M.V.S. and saw the site of 35 M.V.S. Went over to Train in the afternoon	
	29		Inspected transport lines of 68th Inf. Bde. Called at Canadian Reserve Park in afternoon.	
	30		Saw animals of 71st Fd. Ambulance and back to the Train companies.	
	31		Lt. Caroll back from leave. Went to 12th and 13th D.L.I., 2nd Canadian Reserve Park and 2nd Entrenching Battalion.	

Frank G. Mellwish

MAJOR. A.D.V.S. 23RD DIVISION.

2353 Wt. W2514/1454 700,000 5/15 D. D. & L. A.D.S.S./Forms/C. 2118.

Army Form C. 2118.

ADVS 23D Vol 16

Instructions regarding War Diaries and Intelligence Summaries are contained in F. S. Regs., Part II. and the Staff Manual respectively. Title Pages will be prepared in manuscript.

WAR DIARY
or
INTELLIGENCE SUMMARY
(Erase heading not required.)

Place	Date 1916 Nov	Hour	Summary of Events and Information	Remarks and references to Appendices
RENINGHELST	1.		Went to 71st Fd. Ambulance. Lt. Page A.V.C. arrived to replace Capt. Ripley. Inspected 9th S. Staffs and 3 Corps R.E.	
	2.		Inspected transport lines of 69th Inf. Bde in the morning and Canadian Reserve Park in afternoon.	
	3.		D.D.V.S. came out at 11 o'clock. Went with him to inspect horses and lines of 180 Bde R.F.A. and wrote report on same.	
	4.		Inspected 3 Corps of Train and 70th Fd. Ambulance	
	5.		Went to see M.V.S. Site and then to 71st Fd. Ambulance. Capt. Starkey gone on leave	
	6.		Rode over to see A.D.V.S. 47th Division. Inspected horses of Hd. Qrs., M.M.P., and Signals.	
	7.		Very rough and wet day - remained in office.	
	8.		Inspected transport lines of 70th Inf. Bde in morning. Rode over to Train after lunch.	
	9.		Rode to 10th + 11th N.F. lines and afterwards to 11th W. Ridings.	
	10.		Rode round with Lt. Page to 9th S. Staffs., 3 Corps R.E., 2nd Entrenching Bn. + Canadian Reserve Park.	
	11.		Went to 70th Fd. Ambulance and 3 corps of Train.	
	12.		Inspected Hd. Qrs and Signal horses, then to 70th + 71st Fd. Ambulances.	
	13		Inspected transport animals of 70th Inf. Bde, less the M.G.C.	
	14		Went in car to 70th and 71st Fd. Ambulances and then to 69th at STEENVOORDE, then back to 9th S. Staffs.	

2449 Wt. W14957/M90 750,000 1/16 J.B.C. & A. Forms/C.2118/12.

Army Form C. 2118.

Instructions regarding War Diaries and Intelligence Summaries are contained in F. S. Regs., Part II. and the Staff Manual respectively. Title Pages will be prepared in manuscript.

WAR DIARY
or
INTELLIGENCE SUMMARY

(Erase heading not required.)

Place	1916 Date Nov.	Hour	Summary of Events and Information	Remarks and references to Appendices
RENING HELST	15		Feeling seedy after inoculation last evening.	
	16		Inspected transport lines of 9th Yorks, 11th W. Ridings, 8th Yorks & Lancs, & 8th Yorks.	
	17		Rode to 3 coys of R. E's, and Canadian Reserve Park.	
	18		Inspected 70th Fd Ambulance and 3 coys. of Train.	
	19		Looked through Signal Horses, then over to M. V. S. and on to 71st Fd Ambulance. Office work in afternoon.	
	20		Rode to 9th S. Staffs. Met Lt BOURKE A.V.C. and went with him to transport lines of 9th Yorks, 11th W. Ridings, and 8th Yorks & Lancs.	
	21		Called on A.D.V.S. 41st Division. Afterwards went to 70th Fd Ambulance and the Train Coys.	
	22		Inspected 11th Yorks Lines, 71st Fd Ambulance and M. G. Section 70th Bde.	
	23		Inspected Train in the morning. After lunch I went to POPERINGHE to inspect remounts for division on arrival.	
	24		Met D.D.R. who came over to inspect animals for casting for other than Veterinary reasons. Looked through Hd. Qrs. horses in afternoon.	
	25		Rode to 9th S. Staffs and Engineer coys. After lunch went in car with A.D.M.S. to STEENVOORDE to see 69th Fd. Ambulance.	
	26		Stayed in my hut; had 2nd inoculation last evening.	

2449 Wt. W14957/M90 750,000 1/16 J.B.C. & A. Forms/C.2118/12.

Instructions regarding War Diaries and Intelligence Summaries are contained in F. S. Regs., Part II. and the Staff Manual respectively. Title Pages will be prepared in manuscript.

WAR DIARY
or
INTELLIGENCE SUMMARY

(Erase heading not required.)

Army Form C. 2118.

Place	1916 Date Nov	Hour	Summary of Events and Information	Remarks and references to Appendices
RENINGHELST	27		Rode to 70th and 71st Fd. Ambulances and then to Div. Train.	
	28		Went round Hd. Qrs, Signals and R.E's. Arranged about tin plates for shoes to prevent picking up nails.	
	29		Suffering from TONSILITIS. Stayed in office.	
	30		Throat worse. Did not go out.	

Frank W. Mellhuish MAJOR,
A.D.V.S. 23RD DIVISION.
A.L.

2449 Wt. W14957/M90 750,000 1/16 J.B.C. & A. Forms/C.2118/12.

Army Form C. 2118

ADVS 23 D

Vol 17

WAR DIARY
or
INTELLIGENCE SUMMARY

(Erase heading not required.)

Instructions regarding War Diaries and Intelligence Summaries are contained in F. S. Regs., Part II. and the Staff Manual respectively. Title Pages will be prepared in manuscript.

Place	Date 1916	Hour	Summary of Events and Information	Remarks and references to Appendices
RENINGHELST	Dec 1.		Suffering from Tonsilitis and was sent to Hospital.	
	" 8		Discharged from Hospital and was granted ten days leave.	
	" 18		Returned from England.	
	" 19		Arrived in RENINGHELST. Inspected Head Quarter horses.	
	" 20		Inspected debility cases in R.A. with General Fasson at STEENVOORDE. Fifty one picked out for evacuation.	
	" 21		Went to STEENVOORDE. Called at M.V.S, met Capt Shipley A.V.C. - went to No 1 Section D.A.C. and then to Hd 2ns Coy of Train. Motor car got stuck in a ditch and could not get it out until evening.	
	" 22		Went to see a civilian's horse at CASSEL which had been injured by one of our motor cars. Then inspected 2 battery lines of 103 Bde and some of 102 Brigade.	
	" 23		Saw horse lines of Div. Signals and then to STEENVOORDE to see remainder of 102 Bde.	
	" 24		Went to STEENVOORDE to see M.V.S. and on to D.A.C; from there to CASSEL.	
	" 25		Xmas Day. Went to Div. Train.	
	" 26		Visited 69th Fd Ambulance and No 2 Section D.A.C. Went to Canadian Reserve Park and 2nd Entrenching Battalion in afternoon.	
	" 27		No 35 M.V.S. moved from STEENVOORDE to RENINGHELST ROAD. Went with Capt. Allenson A.V.C. to 192 Coy of Train. Inspected transport of South Staffords and 3 comps. R.E. lines.	

2449 Wt. W14957/M90 750,000 1/16 J.B.C. & A. Forms/C.2118/12.

Army Form C. 2118.

Instructions regarding War Diaries and Intelligence Summaries are contained in F. S. Regs., Part II. and the Staff Manual respectively. Title Pages will be prepared in manuscript.

WAR DIARY
or
INTELLIGENCE SUMMARY
(Erase heading not required.)

Place	Date 1916	Hour	Summary of Events and Information	Remarks and references to Appendices
RENINGHELST	Dec 28		Met Lt. Bourke A.V.C. and saw the 1st line transport of 69th Infantry Bde.	
	" 29		Went with A.D.V.S. 41st Division to inspect shoeing with steel plates at 191 Coy of Train. Then to 194 M.G.C. and South Staffords.	
	" 30		Rode to Engineer Corps, West Ridings and back to M.V.S. After lunch saw 2 Sections of D.A.C.	
	" 31		Rode to 'D' Battery 102 Brigade and then to 103 Brigade. In afternoon saw horses at M.V.S. and inspected No 4 Section D.A.C.	

Frank W. McElhinist
MAJOR,
A.V.C. 23rd D[illegible]

2449 Wt. W14957/M90 750,000 1/16 J.B.C. & A. Forms/C.2118/12.

Instructions regarding War Diaries and Intelligence Summaries are contained in F. S. Regs., Part II. and the Staff Manual respectively. Title Pages will be prepared in manuscript.

WAR DIARY
or
INTELLIGENCE SUMMARY

(Erase heading not required.)

Army Form C. 2118.

ADVS 23 Div
Vol 18

Place	1917. Date	Hour	Summary of Events and Information	Remarks and references to Appendices
RENINGHELST	Jany. 1		Went to M.V.S. Then to Div. Train and 8th Yorks & Lanc. In afternoon went with Staff Captain R.A. to POPERINGHE to inspect 72 remounts which arrived.	
	2		Rode to M.V.S. and then to 3 Section D.A.C. - picked out a number of mange cases to isolate and clip. Went to R.E. companies and South Staffords in afternoon.	
	3		Inspected 'C' Battery 102 Bde. Capt Shipley A.V.C. on sick list. Looked through Wagon lines of 103 Bde.	
	4.		Rode to M.V.S. Inspected Signal and Div. Hd. Qrs horse lines. Wrote a report on preventative measures against mange.	
	5.		Went to CASSEL to see an injured civilian's horse. Came back to 194 M.G.Co, South Staffs and 3 Corps R.E.	
	6.		Inspected cases for evacuation at M.V.S. Then to Div. Train, 8th Yorks & Lancs, and 8th & 9th Yorks. Saw C.R.A acting G.O.C. re clipping horses.	
	7.		Visited M.V.S. and on to the D.A.C., 69th Fd. Amb., 8th Yorks and 'A' Battery 102 Bde.	
	8.		Inspected 103 Bde R.F.A, 'C' Battery 102 Bde and Sherwood Foresters. M.V.S. in afternoon.	
	9.		Inspected 68th Inf. Bde with Sgt. Brooks A.V.C. After lunch saw 194 M.G.C. S. Staffs and M.V.S.	
	10		Had a parade of Suspected Mange cases at No 3 D.A.C. Went to M.V.S.; then had an inspection of cases in 103 Bde. Saw Gen. Fasson about clipping.	
	11		Saw S. Staffs, 68 + 69 M.G.C. 8th Yorks and 192 Co. Train. In afternoon to M.V.S. and Nos 1 + 4 Sect. D.A.C.	
	12		Had an inspection of cases picked out from D.A.C. Then to M.V.S., 69th Fd. Amb., and saw horses paraded in 103 Wagon lines.	
	13		Met Lt. Bourke A.V.C. and saw transport animals of 69th Inf. Bde and 194 M.G.C. M.V.S. in afternoon.	

2449 Wt. W14957/M90 750,000 1/16 J.B.C. & A. Forms/C.2118/12.

Army Form C. 2118.

Instructions regarding War Diaries and Intelligence Summaries are contained in F. S. Regs., Part II. and the Staff Manual respectively. Title Pages will be prepared in manuscript.

WAR DIARY
or
INTELLIGENCE SUMMARY

(Erase heading not required.)

Place	1917 Date Jany	Hour	Summary of Events and Information	Remarks and references to Appendices
RENINGHE-LST	14		Too slippery to ride. Walked to No 3 Section D.A.C. and on to M.V.S. Looked through Signals and Div. Hd. Qrs in afternoon.	
	15		Went in car to STEENVOORDE to inspect horses of 104 Bde R.F.A. Saw a number of Mange cases.	
	16		Went to M.V.S. in morning and then to 'A' & 'B' Batteries 102 Bde. D.D.V.S. came out in the afternoon to inspect M.V.S. We then went to 191 Co. Train to see shoeing with steel plates.	
	17		Attended Conference at BAILLEUL. Inspected D.H.Q and Signals in afternoon.	
	18		Inspected 78 remounts at RENINGHELST Siding. Went with A.D.R. to M.V.S. Saw 'D' Battery 102 Bde Wagon lines.	
	19		Rode 'A', 'B', 'D' Batteries 102 Bde. Horses from 104 Bde evacuated from STEENVOORDE. Saw M.V.S. No 1 and 4 Sections D.A.C. in afternoon.	
	20		Conference of A.D's V.S at X Corps Hd. Qrs. Went on to HAZEBROUCK to see D.D.V.S. Saw 69th Fd Amb and M.V.S. in afternoon.	
	21		Received message to go to Corps H.Q. Waited all the morning to see Gen. Leslie who questioned me as to the ages of men in M.V.S. and A.V.C. Sergeants. Met the Town Major of BOESCHEPE and looked out for an isolation camp.	
	22		Rode to Div. Train and 1 and 4 Sections D.A.C. In afternoon saw batteries of 103 Bde. Attended conference.	
	23		Inspected 78 remounts which arrived at RENINGHELST Siding. Then to No 3 Section D.A.C. Capt. Shipley A.V.C. demobilized. Capt. O'Brien A.V.C. left division with 104 Bde R.F.A.	
	24		Visited M.V.S. and then went with Area Commandant to see some empty wagon lines at G.15.d.5.2. which was allotted as an Isolation Mange Camp. Went over in the afternoon with the Sanitary Officer.	

2449 Wt. W14957/M90 750,000 1/16 J.B.C. & A. Forms/C.2118/12.

Army Form C. 2118.

WAR DIARY
or
INTELLIGENCE SUMMARY
(Erase heading not required.)

Instructions regarding War Diaries and Intelligence Summaries are contained in F. S. Regs., Part II. and the Staff Manual respectively. Title Pages will be prepared in manuscript.

Place	1917 Date Jany	Hour	Summary of Events and Information	Remarks and references to Appendices
RENING HELST.	25		Inspected Wagon lines of 3 batteries 102 Bde and looked through cases at M.V.S.	
	26		Rode to Mange Camp and M.V.S. afterwards to South Staffords. Conference with V.O's in afternoon.	
	27		Rode to No 17 Hospital to have a tooth extracted. After lunch went with DAQMG to see C.R.A. who arranged for an officer and N.C.O. to take charge of Isolation Camp	
	28		Had a parade of Signal horses - six selected for clipping. Went to M.V.S. and Hd Qrs Co of Train. Saw 103 Bde lines in afternoon.	
	29		G.O.C. sent for me at 9 a.m. All mange cases to be sent at once to Isolation Camp. Went with D.A.Q.M.G. to inspect camp. Afterwards to M.V.S. After lunch to 2nd Entrenching Bn lines to see horse with Laminitis. At 6 p.m. had a discussion on Mange at 'Q' branch.	
	30		Attended at Q with DADOS and Staff Capt R.A. about disinfecting measures. Went with Claims Officer to secure a field close to camp. 72 horses sent in for treatment.	
	31		Spent the day at Isolation Camp with Capt Allinson A.V.C. who has Veterinary charge.	

Frank W. Mellwick
MAJOR,
A.D.V.S. 23rd DIVISION.

2449 Wt. W14957/M90 750,000 1/16 J.B.C. & A. Forms/C.2118/12.

Army Form C. 2118.

ADVS 23 D

Vol 19

Instructions regarding War Diaries and Intelligence Summaries are contained in F. S. Regs., Part II. and the Staff Manual respectively. Title Pages will be prepared in manuscript.

WAR DIARY
or
INTELLIGENCE SUMMARY

(Erase heading not required.)

Place	Date	Hour	Summary of Events and Information	Remarks and references to Appendices
DIEPPE	Jan. 30		Received orders from D.V.S. by telephone at 7.45 p.m. to proceed at once to 23rd Division as A.D.V.S.	
	31		Left DIEPPE 1.30 p.m. by motor.	
RENINGHELST	Feby 1		Arrived 23rd Div. H.Q. at 6 p.m.	
	2		Visited Mange Isolation Camp with Major Melhuish. Not satisfied with it. Many very bad cases of mange and some not affected. Organization and administration of it leaves much to be desired. Telephoned to D.D.V.S. asking him for permission to evacuate about 70 cases or to come over and see the camp.	
	3		Had conference with the Div. V.O's; after which I sorted the cases in the camp (273) and placed them in 3 classes viz (A) Badly affected needing evacuation, (B) Slightly affected, (C) Very slightly affected or not at all. Impossible to say how matters stand as very few animals clipped. Accompanied D.D.V.S. 2nd Army to Mange Isolation Camp. He gave instructions as to what he wanted done and ordered all slight cases or those which were apparently alright to be returned to their units after dipping and clipping – to be worked in isolation. Afterwards returned with D.D.V.S. to see G.O.C. and C.R.A. 12 Clipping machines arrived from X Corps. Obtained permission to retain Sgt Owens A.V.C. for temporary duty at Mange Isolation Camp.	
	4		Went to see dipping at ST. JANS. CAPPEL of Mange Isolation Camp cases. All animals put through except very bad cases. Lt. CARROLL in charge of it. 220 animals dipped. Conference of V.O's at Mange Isolation Camp – gave instructions as to what I wanted done re mange.	

2449 Wt. W14957/M90 750,000 1/16 J.B.C. & A. Forms/C.2118/12.

Army Form C. 2118.

WAR DIARY
or
INTELLIGENCE SUMMARY

(Erase heading not required.)

Instructions regarding War Diaries and Intelligence Summaries are contained in F. S. Regs., Part II. and the Staff Manual respectively. Title Pages will be prepared in manuscript.

Place	Date	Hour	Summary of Events and Information	Remarks and references to Appendices
RENINGHELST	Feby. 4		Inspected M.V.S. - very satisfactory. Animals in very good condition and no signs of skin disease amongst the horses belonging to the unit. Inspected Div Train animals - in very good condition and free from skin disease. Attended conference at Div. H.Q. Explained D.D.V.S. plan to C.R.E. for spraying douche to be put up in Mange Isolation Camp. Sgt Owens A.V.C. to be retained for temporary duty.	
	5		Major Melhuish A.V.C. left for No 3 Base Remount Depot, Dieppe.	
			Inspected 'C' Battery 103 Bde R.F.A. - animals looking fairly well.	
			" 'B' " " " - Very few clipped.	
			" 'A' " " " } Animals not looking well	
			" 'D' " " " } Very few clipped	
			All cases of Mange or any suspected of having it are in the Mange Isolation Camp.	
			Inspected 'C' Battery 102 Bde R.F.A. - The animals on the whole are looking well.	
			" 'A' " " " - All animals clipped, but most of them are itchy and condition bad.	
			Ordered all animals to be washed twice weekly with Calcium Sulphide.	
			Gave orders re dipping at 8th Corps Bath. Practically all animals under cover.	
	6.		Inspected 'D' Battery 102 Bde - animals in fair condition. Dipped Mange Camp animals at POPERINGHE.	
	7.		Inspected D.A.C. No 1 Section - in good condition but very itchy - advised all to be clipped.	
			- 2 — - good	
			- 3 — - very good	
			Inspected 70th Fd. Ambulance - very good.	

Army Form C. 2118.

WAR DIARY
or
INTELLIGENCE SUMMARY

(Erase heading not required.)

*Instructions regarding War Diaries and Intelligence Summaries are contained in F. S. Regs., Part II. and the Staff Manual respectively. Title Pages will be prepared in manuscript.

Place	Date	Hour	Summary of Events and Information	Remarks and references to Appendices
RENINGHELST	Feby 8		Inspected 68th Inf. Bde 10th N.F. in good condition. 11th — very good. 12th Durham very good. 13th — very good. Inspected 70th Inf. Bde 11th S + D's good. 9th Yorks L. very good. 10th W. Ridings very good.	
			A.D.V.S. arrived and gave instructions re feeding and protecting Mange Isolation Camp; also spoke about baths and dressings. 71st. Fd Ambulance very good. Clipping and Mange Precautions Orders issued to Division by G.O.C.	
	9		Inspected 8th Yorks, 8th Yorks & Lancs, 68th + 69th Machine Gun Co – All very good. Conference with V.O's at 3 p.m. – gave orders to them re drawing Linseed and Bran for poor cases from M.V.S.	
	10		Proceeded to BAILLEUL to purchase hose tubing for spray. Inspected D.H.Q. – very good. D.D.V.S. at Mange Camp in afternoon. Visited No 1 Section D.A.C. to see horses clipped out – many cases of mange.	
	11		Telegram from D.D.V.S. to evacuate 59 mange cases.	
	12		Thawing. Inspected 3 Fd Coys R.E. – Animals in very good condition.	
	13		Inspected A.S.C. units – animals in good condition. then Div. Signals – animals in very good condition.	
	14		Inspected 8th K.O.Y.L.I. and Signal Coy – animals in very condition. Received remounts 11 a.m. RENINGHELST Siding – in good condition. Inspected Fd Ambulance near POPERINGHE – animals in very good condition.	
	15		Inspected 8th + 9th K.O.Y.L.I. – animals in very good condition. Douche in Mange Camp in working order.	
	16		Conference of V.O's at my office – general matters discussed.	

2449 Wt. W14957/M90 750,000 1/16 J.B.C. & A. Forms/C.2118/12.

Army Form C. 2118.

*Instructions regarding War Diaries and Intelligence Summaries are contained in F. S. Regs., Part II. and the Staff Manual respectively. Title Pages will be prepared in manuscript.

WAR DIARY
or
INTELLIGENCE SUMMARY
(Erase heading not required.)

Place	Date	Hour	Summary of Events and Information	Remarks and references to Appendices
RENINGHELST	Feby 17		Visited Dipping at 8th Corps Bath – Put through 'A' Battery 102 Bde 174 animals, Section 1 DAC. 124 animals, and Section 3 D.A.C. 70 animals and all equipment of each unit.	
	18		Gave the Artillery Bdes full use of douche for washing dipped animals	
	19		Inspected 'A' 102 Bde – many poor horses, then 194 M.G.C. – mules in good condition Inspected 9th S. Staffords – conditions of animals good except for 6 mange cases.	
	20		Inspected 'A' 103 Bde R.F.A. – half battery fair, half good 'B' do – animals looking well 'C' do – do Lt. M.M. McLeod arrived and took over 102 Bde R.F.A.	
	21		Arranged with A.D.V.S. 39th Division to take over Mange Camp on 24th. Clipping at 'B' 102 Bde R.F.A. where all the machines are, very unsatisfactory. Asked to have the Veterinary Sergeant placed in charge of it. Inspected 'C' and 'D' 102 Bde R.F.A. – animals in fair condition. Met remounts on arrival.	
	22		Arranged about winding up the Mange Camp. D.D.R. inspected surplus horses at noon at Div. H.Q. All clipping proceeding very slowly.	
	23		12 Clipping machines recalled by D.A.D.O.S.	
	24		Inspected 10th West Yorks – animals looking well. Mange Camp closed.	
	25		Met remounts on arrival – in good condition.	

2449 Wt. W14957/M90 750,000 1/16 J.B.C. & A. Forms/C.2118/12.

Army Form C. 2118.

Instructions regarding War Diaries and Intelligence Summaries are contained in F. S. Regs., Part II. and the Staff Manual respectively. Title Pages will be prepared in manuscript.

WAR DIARY
or
INTELLIGENCE SUMMARY
(Erase heading not required.)

Place	Date Feby.	Hour	Summary of Events and Information	Remarks and references to Appendices
RENINGHELST	26		Office work	
ST. OMER	27		Division moved back to ST. OMER.	
	28		Visited area.	

Summary of Mange Camp.

Opened Jany. 30th 1917.
Closed Feby. 24th 1917.

Unit	Admitted	Cured or found not to be affected	Evacuated	Died or Destroyed
'A'. 102 Bde R.F.A.	48	33	10	5
'B'	14	7	7	–
'C'	29	23	6	–
'D'	16	9	5	2
'A' 103 Bde R.F.A.	42	25	15	2
'B'	45	19	22	4
'C'	11	8	3	–
'D'	12	7	4	1
Sect. 1. D.A.C.	44	15	26	3
2.	18	7	10	1
3.	8	7	1	–
23rd D.HQ.	2	2	–	–
101 Fd Co. R.E.	10	8	2	–
Totals	299	170	111	18

J. J. Hilliard

MAJOR
A.D.V.S. 23rd DIVISION

2449 Wt. W14957/M90 750,000 1/16 J.B.C. & A. Forms/C.2118/12.

Army Form C. 2118.

Instructions regarding War Diaries and Intelligence Summaries are contained in F. S. Regs., Part II. and the Staff Manual respectively. Title Pages will be prepared in manuscript.

WAR DIARY or INTELLIGENCE SUMMARY

(Erase heading not required.)

ADVS 3rd D Vol 20

Place	Date 1917 March	Hour	Summary of Events and Information	Remarks and references to Appendices
ST. OMER	1		Saw 69th & 70th Infantry Bdes on the march – transport animals in splendid condition.	
	2		Inspected D.A.C. No 1 Section – mange seems well in hand – all horses clipped – ordered 2 debility cases to Hospital – remainder of horses in fair working condition. No 2 Section – animals in fair condition – few clipped. No 3 Section – All mules in splendid condition.	
	3		Saw Artillery Brigades on the march passing WATTEN. 'A' Batt. 102 Bde – Horses in fair condition – some bad 'B' " " " " " " " 'C' " " " " " few " 'D' " " " " " " " 'A' Batt 103 Bde – Horses in good condition – some debility cases. 'B' " " " " " not many debility cases. 'C' " " " very fair " " " " 'D' " " " good " some debility cases. All unclipped horses sweating freely, though the day was cold. Visited M.V.S. at HOULLE – All correct after their march.	
	4		Inspected Artillery Bdes. Selected following horses to be evacuated. H.Q. 102 Bde Debility 2 cases; A 103 Bde Debility 8 cases Lame 4 cases A " " 9 "; B " " 5 " B " " 9 " Blind 2 cases; C " " 4 " C " " 2 " " 1 "; D " " 6 " D " " 3 " Mange 1 " There does not appear to be many more mange cases amongst the units.	

2449 Wt. W14957/M90 750,000 1/16 J.B.C. & A. Forms/C.2118/12.

Instructions regarding War Diaries and Intelligence Summaries are contained in F. S. Regs., Part II. and the Staff Manual respectively. Title Pages will be prepared in manuscript.

WAR DIARY
or
INTELLIGENCE SUMMARY
(Erase heading not required.)

Army Form C. 2118.

Place	Date 1917 March	Hour	Summary of Events and Information	Remarks and references to Appendices
ST. OMER	4	Contd	Advised C.R.A. to go very easy with his horses, as it will pull them to pieces doing fast or very hard work on account of so many not being clipped and the horses not getting a lot of work in last billets, but to gradually take them on. All the horses now left with the Brigades are in good workable condition. All are standing in the open and the lines are very soft.	
			Telephoned and wrote to D.D.V.S. 2nd Army asking him for permission to crush oats for a quarter of the number of horses. in R.A. units	
			Capt. ALLINSON A.V.C. went on leave.	
	5		Spent day at M.V.S. getting horses ready for evacuation. Evacuated 25 to No 23 Vety Hospital, ST. OMER.	
			Transferred Lt. B. OURKE A.V.C. from 68th Inf. Bde to 70th Inf. Bde.	
	6		Capt. STARKEY A.V.C. placed i/c 68th Inf. Bde in addition to his other duties.	
			Recommended horses of R.A. to be placed on full rations. Got 35 horses ready at M.V.S. for evacuation.	
	7		Letter from D.D.V.S. to collect horse at A.23.c.0.5. Sheet 27. Letter No H.C.113 d/- 5.3.17.	
			Went out to see R.A. – left tooth rasps for Capt. CARROLL, A.V.C. and Lieut. M.M. McLEOD, A.V.C.	
			Asked D.A.D.O.S. if division can retain borrowed clipping machines.	
			Inspected Div. H.Q and Signals – animals all well.	
	8		Snowing. Visited M.V.S. – sent 2 Quittors that were collected by float and 2 Mange Cases to Vety. Hospital.	
	9		Visited M.V.S. Inspected D.A.C. – Mange appears to be under control – cases of it doing well.	
			Ordered all clipping machines which were useless to be sent to M.V.S.	

Army Form C. 2118.

3

Instructions regarding War Diaries and Intelligence Summaries are contained in F. S. Regs., Part II. and the Staff Manual respectively. Title Pages will be prepared in manuscript.

WAR DIARY
or
INTELLIGENCE SUMMARY

(Erase heading not required.)

Place	Date 1917 March	Hour	Summary of Events and Information	Remarks and references to Appendices
ST. OMER	9	Contd	Visited 23 Vety Hospital – met D.V.S. – conducted him to G.O.C. 23rd Division Charger arrived from No 3 Base R. Depot.	
	10		Visited M.V.S. Went to inspect 103 Bde R.F.A. All officers away at a conference – walked round lines with V.O. i/c – lines very muddy.	
	11		Visited M.V.S. and sent personnel to 23 Vety Hospital for baths. Inspected 9th S. Staffs at GANSPETTE – mange well under control – no fresh cases for some time – the old ones appear to be doing well. Accompanied G.O.C. to 23 Veterinary Hospital.	
	12		Inspected 103 Bde R.F.A at POLINCOVE – mange appears to be under control – still experiencing trouble with clipping machines. Animals on the whole looking pretty well. 2 horses not doing well – recommended O.C. to evacuate. Inspected 71st Fd Ambulance at NORDASQUES – horses in splendid condition. Met arrival of Remounts at WATTEN for R.A. Mules in excellent condition and horses in very good.	
	13		Visited M.V.S. Sergt. Spice A.V.C. returned to M.V.S. Visited M.V.S. Visited area over which artillery are training. Inspected 102 Bde R.F.A. 'A' Batt. show a considerable falling off in condition since I saw it last – all horses are clipped – 18 evacuation cases of debility. 'B' Batt – clipped horses not looking well – 9 cases of debility for evacuation – no change in unclipped horses. 'C' and 'D' Batteries on the whole looking well – the clipped horses of these batteries do not show falling off in condition. Reported result of my inspection to G.O.C. and D.D.V.S. by telephone. Was accompanied on my inspection by C.R.A and O.C. Bde.	

2449 Wt. W14957/M90 750,000 1/16 J.B.C. & A. Forms/C.2118/12.

Instructions regarding War Diaries and Intelligence Summaries are contained in F. S. Regs., Part II. and the Staff Manual respectively. Title Pages will be prepared in manuscript.

WAR DIARY
or
INTELLIGENCE SUMMARY
(Erase heading not required.)

Army Form C. 2118.

Place	1917 Date March	Hour	Summary of Events and Information	Remarks and references to Appendices
ST. OMER	14		Visited M.V.S. - collected 34 horses for evacuation; most Debility. Saw O.C. 102 Bde R.F.A - advised him to put more rugs on the horses of 'A' 102 Bde R.F.A. Letter from D.A.D.O.S. to return clipping machines which we have on loan.	
	15		Received orders for Sergt. King A.V.C. to proceed to No 7 V.H. Visited M.V.S. Accompanied D.D.R. 2nd Army to inspect 102 Bde R.F.A. - informed us that we could draw 40 remounts from No 23 V.H. - he said 'A' 102 Bde should be in better condition. Inspected 69th Fd Ambulance - animals looking well.	
	16		Visited M.V.S. Sergt. King A.V.C. left for No 7 V.H. Inspected thin horses of 102 Bde and evacuated the debility ones. The thin horses which are stabled in 'A' 102 Bde are doing well. Capt. Allinson A.V.C. returned from leave.	
	17		Inspected thin and skin disease animals of D.A.C. - ordered some for evacuation. Telegram received that a case suspicious of having Glanders was at H.Q., 70th Inf. Bde - proceeded at once and applied Mallein Test.	
	18		No reaction to mule at H.Q. 70th Bde. Visited 103 Bde R.F.A - selected 9 animals for evacuation for debility and skin disease.	
	19		Most units moving - fine weather.	
ESQUELBECQ	20		Changed D.H.Q. to ESQUELBECQ.	
	21		Very cold and wet. Saw 103 Bde R.F.A arrive - very few poor horses " 102 " " " " " " " 70th Inf. Bde - animals in very good condition.	

2449 Wt. W14957/M90 750,000 1/16 J.B.C. & A. Forms/C.2118/12.

Instructions regarding War Diaries and Intelligence Summaries are contained in F. S. Regs., Part II. and the Staff Manual respectively. Title Pages will be prepared in manuscript.

WAR DIARY
or
INTELLIGENCE SUMMARY
(Erase heading not required.)

Army Form C. 2118.

5

Place	1917 Date March	Hour	Summary of Events and Information	Remarks and references to Appendices
ESQUELBECQ	22		Cold, wet and snowy. Saw D.A.C. arrive – all No 3 Section mules looking in good condition – No 2 Section – some poor horses – remainder looking well – mules very good – No 1 Section – some poor horses – remainder looking well – mules looking well.	
			One case of Stomatitis Contagiosa occurred in 194 M.G. Coy – all precautions taken. The horse has been away from the company for some time and has only recently rejoined.	
			Some changes with V.O's necessary owing to dispositions of units. Lt. Bourke i/c 69th and 70th Inf. Bdes, Lt. McLeod i/c 102 Bde R.F.A and Div. Train, Capt Carroll i/c 103 Bde R.F.A and 68th Inf. Bde.	
			Location of 35 M.V.S. at HERZEELE – arrived today at 3 p.m.	
	23		Cold, wet and snowy. Inspected Div Train – animals mostly in very good condition – none of them poor. Saw nose bag designed by Capt Hadden A.S.C. – appears to me to be a very serviceable one for transport animals – too heavy to carry on saddle.	
			Visited 102 Bde R.F.A. to arrange about inspecting their horses ~~today~~ tomorrow	
	24		Cold. Inspected 102 Bde R.F.A. – condition of animals remaining stationary or improving – all batteries on standings	
			" 'A' 103 Bde R.F.A – " " " " " "	
	25		Fine. Inspected 103 Bde R.F.A. – some horses show a falling off in condition; about 20. The condition of remainder is stationary.	
	26		Visited M.V.S., Div Signals and 9th S. Staffs.	
	27		Inspected No 1 Sect. D.A.C. – horses and mules in good condition	
			" " 2 " " " " " "	
			" 102 Fd Coy R.E – Animals in very good condition	

2449 Wt. W14957/M90 750,000 1/16 J.B.C. & A. Forms/C.2118/12.

Army Form C. 2118.

Instructions regarding War Diaries and Intelligence Summaries are contained in F. S. Regs., Part II. and the Staff Manual respectively. Title Pages will be prepared in manuscript.

WAR DIARY
or
INTELLIGENCE SUMMARY
(Erase heading not required.)

6

Place	1917 Date March	Hour	Summary of Events and Information	Remarks and references to Appendices
EGQUELBECQ	27	Contd	Took over 113 Inf. Bde in lieu of 68 Inf. Bde. Capt Allinson A.V.C. placed i/c	
	28		Cold, wet and windy. Inspected 69th Inf. Bde – animals on the whole in splendid condition.	
	29		Cold, wet and windy. Judged transport class in 70th Inf. Bde competitions – all animals in splendid condition.	
	30		Cold, wet and windy. Visited M.V.S., 9th S. Staffs and 194 M.G. Coy – no further cases of Stomatitis in latter unit.	
	31		Inspected 103 Bde R.F.A – the horses are falling away in condition. Evacuated for debility – 'A' Batt 3, 'B' 4, 'C' 6, 'D' 8. Visited No 23 Veterinary Hospital. I ascribe the falling off in condition to the severe weather which we have had recently, acting on horses short of rations to sustain them. 9lbs Oats and 12lbs Hay or Straw is, in my opinion, not sufficient to keep horses, which are not in first class condition, up to the mark when they are standing in the open. These remarks apply only to the Brigades of R.F.A. The horses of the D.A.C. appear to hold their own, speaking generally. The remainder of the Divisional units (Inf. Bdes, Signal Coy, R.E. Coys, Div. Train, M.V.S., and M.G. Coys) have their animals in splendid condition, as are all the mules. Mange appears well under control.	

J. J. Hilliard
MAJOR,
A.D.V.S. 23RD DIVISION.

2449 Wt. W14957/M90 750,000 1/16 J.B.C. & A. Forms/C.2118/12.

Army Form C. 2118.

Instructions regarding War Diaries and Intelligence Summaries are contained in F. S. Regs., Part II. and the Staff Manual respectively. Title Pages will be prepared in manuscript.

WAR DIARY
or
INTELLIGENCE SUMMARY

(Erase heading not required.)

ADVS 23 D

Vol. 21

Place	Date 1917 April	Hour	Summary of Events and Information	Remarks and references to Appendices
ESQUELBECQ	1		Inspected 102 Bde R.F.A. – evacuated for Debility 'A' Batt 10, 'B' 7, 'C' 2, 'D' 4. All the horses appear to be falling away in condition, except 'C' Battery, which is the best in the Division.	
	2		Visited M.V.S. to see horses for evacuation – stopped several cases of Debility. 103 Bde R.F.A. sent no rugs with their 27 Debility cases – sent telegram to them at 9.45 a.m. to send rugs at once to M.V.S. These rugs did not arrive until 8.30 p.m. when they were sent on to the Sick Horse Halt. Bitterly cold day with very heavy snowstorm; a similar snowstorm during the night. Saw Staff Capt R.A. and Adj. 103 Bde as well as C.O's Batteries, who stated that the rugs were on their way. Sent report to D.D.V.S. on condition of horses of R.A. units – advised wind screens.	
	3		Snowy. Inspected Signals and went to POPERINGHE to see horse in Signals there.	
	4		Inspected D.A.C. No 1 Section – few poor horses and mules – the remainder seem to have improved a little – wind screen all round the camp. No 2 Section – All animals looking well and they have improved in condition – wind screens all round the camp. No 3 Section – all in splendid condition. Authority received from D.D.O.S. by D.D.V.S. for 800 yds of Canvas for windscreens. Horse wastage through Debility – permission for full rations obtained for all horses debilitated – Authority 2nd Army Q/2029/26 of 2.4.17. Telephoned D.D.V.S. re condition of R.A. horses – he wants all thin horses that are put on full rations to be placed together, so that progress can be watched.	

2449 Wt. W14957/M90 750,000 1/16 J.B.C. & A. Forms/C.2118/12.

Army Form C. 2118.

Instructions regarding War Diaries and Intelligence Summaries are contained in F. S. Regs., Part II. and the Staff Manual respectively. Title Pages will be prepared in manuscript.

WAR DIARY
or
INTELLIGENCE SUMMARY

(Erase heading not required.)

Place	1917 Date April	Hour	Summary of Events and Information	Remarks and references to Appendices
ESQUELBECQ	5		Inspected 102 Bde R.F.A. – severe weather during week has caught hold of the thin horses to some extent. In compliance with G.R.O 1399, recommended that horses to the following number be placed on extra rations. 'A' Battery 28, 'B' 16, 'C' 18, 'D' 4. Judged at Transport Competition 69th Inf. Bde – all animals in splendid condition.	
	6		Inspected 103 Bde R.F.A. and recommend that the following animals be placed on full rations 'A' Battery 22 horses, 'B' 30 horses, 'C' 21 horses, 'D' 18 horses.	
	7		Inspected poor horses in No 1 Section D.A.C. – recommended to D.D.V.S. that 7 of them be placed on full rations. Visited M.V.S.	
BUSSEBOOM	8		Changed area to Busseboom. Orders received to send Sgt. Lenham A.V.C. to England.	
	9		Very wet and cold. Instructed Capt Starkey to take over Veterinary charge of 68th Inf. Bde. Saw 103 Bde R.F.A arrive about 2 p.m. – 9 horses killed by shell fire. Saw A.D.V.S. 39th Div re change of 35 M.V.S. with 39th Div. mobile Section.	
	10		Very wet and cold. No 7683 Sgt Lenham A.V.C. att. 'A' Batt 103 Bde R.F.A. left for England with a view to qualifying for a commission R.F.A. M.V.S. arrived at G.14.b.2.6 Sheet 28.	
	11		Very wet and cold – snowing. Judged in 68th Inf Transport Competitions.	

2449 Wt. W14957/M90 750,000 1/16 J.B.C. & A. Forms/C.2118/12.

Instructions regarding War Diaries and Intelligence Summaries are contained in F. S. Regs., Part II. and the Staff Manual respectively. Title Pages will be prepared in manuscript.

WAR DIARY
or
INTELLIGENCE SUMMARY

(Erase heading not required.)

Army Form C. 2118.

Place	Date 1917 April	Hour	Summary of Events and Information	Remarks and references to Appendices
BUSSEBOOM	12		Wet and cold. Went round 102 Bde Wagon lines – they are very bad in most places; particularly in 'A' 102 Bde. Rang up A.D.V.S. re extra forage for the thin horses.	
	13		Wet and cold – Inspected 103 Bde R.F.A. – all pretty fair except 'B' Battery. Inspected R.E. companies – all in good order.	
	14		Windy. Inspected 102 Bde R.F.A. – 'A' Battery show a falling off in condition – 'B', 'C' + 'D' stationary – fair in condition except for a certain amount of poor horses.	
	15		Very cold and wet	
	16		Inspected 69th Inf. Bde – animals in very satisfactory condition.	
	17		Very cold and snowing. Inspected 103 Bde R.F.A – little change from previous week – B/103 still bad.	
	18		Inspected 102 Bde R.F.A. Very wet and cold. Attended conference of G.O.C.	
	19		Inspected 68th Inf. Bde. A.D.V.S. proceeded on 10 days leave to England – Capt R.C. Allinson A.V.C., O.C. 35 M.V.S. deputising	

2449 Wt. W14957/M90 750,000 1/16 J.B.C. & A. Forms/C.2118/12.

Army Form C. 2118.

Instructions regarding War Diaries and Intelligence Summaries are contained in F. S. Regs., Part II. and the Staff Manual respectively. Title Pages will be prepared in manuscript.

WAR DIARY
or
INTELLIGENCE SUMMARY

(Erase heading not required.)

Place	Date 1917 April	Hour	Summary of Events and Information	Remarks and references to Appendices
BUSSEBOOM	20		Evacuated from M.V.S. 12 animals including one in foal and one for vic. One N.C.O. and 3 men sent from M.V.S. to X Corps, BOESCHEPE at 6 p.m. – Cpl Jones, Ptes Bird, Neal + Choupard – to form Corps M.V.S. under command of Capt Dennis A.V.C.	
	22		189 Army Field Artillery Bde temporily attached to 23rd Div. Artillery – V.O. reported personally.	
	27		Inspected farm at H.8.b.8.3. Sheet 27 – found it suitable for "Advanced Collecting Post" – reported this to A.A.+Q.M.G., Division.	

J. J. Hilliard

MAJOR,
A.D.V.S. 23rd DIVISION.

2449 Wt. W14957/M90 750,000 1/16 J.B.C. & A. Forms/C.2118/12.

Army Form C. 2118.

Instructions regarding War Diaries and Intelligence Summaries are contained in F. S. Regs., Part II. and the Staff Manual respectively. Title Pages will be prepared in manuscript.

WAR DIARY
or
INTELLIGENCE SUMMARY

(Erase heading not required.)

ADVS 23D
Vol 22

Place	Date 1917 May	Hour	Summary of Events and Information	Remarks and references to Appendices
BUSSEBOOM	1		Fine. Returned to D.H.Q. from leave.	
WINNEZEELE	2		Fine. Changed area to WINNEZEELE.	
	3		Inspected 102 Bde R.F.A. – 'A' Battery looking better than when I saw them last, but still leaves much to be desired – 'B' Battery steady improvement – 'D' Battery steady improvement. I find that there are many cases of Lice amongst the unclipped horses; as the weather is now so fine, I recommend that they be clipped as there is no chance of getting rid of the nits otherwise. Also re horses under treatment for Mange – advised washing and sweating whilst the days are warm and to stop putting on oil for the present.	
	4		Visited Field Remount Section, 2nd Army Judged Transport and inspected 71st Fd Ambulance – animals in splendid condition. G.O.C. inspected M.V.S.	
	5		Inspected 103 Bde R.F.A. – considerable improvement noted – many cases of Lice – advised clipping all lousy horses. The following horses are suffering from Debility:- 'B' Batt. 4, 'C' Batt. 5, 'D' Batt. 9.	
	6		Visited M.V.S.	

Army Form C. 2118.

Instructions regarding War Diaries and Intelligence Summaries are contained in F. S. Regs., Part II. and the Staff Manual respectively. Title Pages will be prepared in manuscript.

WAR DIARY
or
INTELLIGENCE SUMMARY

(Erase heading not required.)

Place	1917 Date May	Hour	Summary of Events and Information	Remarks and references to Appendices
WINNEZEELE	7		Visited 36th Division Horse Show.	
	8		Visited 102 + 103 Bdes R.F.A, D.A.C., & M.V.S. with Gas Officer to instruct units in the fitting of Anti-gas masks; also the 68th Inf. Bde.	
	9		D.D.V.S. Inspection – he inspected, accompanied by C.R.A., Artillery units. 102 Bde R.F.A. – horses only fair; 103 Bde – horses a little better; D.A.C. – satisfactory. Also inspected 70th Inf. Bde – in splendid condition; Signals – good. Sent an order to 'Q' Branch about animals in the Division not being properly branded, and asked that a certificate be sent by C.O.s that all animals under their charge, have been done, if necessary.	
	10		Picked out Debility cases from 102 Bde R.F.A. for evacuation	
	11		Division moving	
BUSSEBOOM	12		Division moved to BUSSEBOOM – Mobile Vety Section to G. 27 a. 5. 9. Sheet 28.	
	13		Capt Walker V.O. i/c 189 Army Fd Art. Bde called – made appointment to meet him 9.30 Wednesday to inspect the animals under his charge.	
	14		Inspected 102 Bde R.F.A.	
	15		Inspected 103 Bde R.F.A.	

2449 Wt. W14957/M90 750,000 1/16 J.B.C. & A. Forms/C.2118/12.

Army Form C. 2118.

Instructions regarding War Diaries and Intelligence Summaries are contained in F. S. Regs., Part II. and the Staff Manual respectively. Title Pages will be prepared in manuscript.

WAR DIARY
or
INTELLIGENCE SUMMARY

(Erase heading not required.)

Place	1917 Date May	Hour	Summary of Events and Information	Remarks and references to Appendices
BUSSEBOOM	15		Placed Sergt. Shoesmith A.V.C. att. C/103 Bde on 14 days trial as his C.O. and V.O. state he is not satisfactory.	
			Report sent to D.D.V.S. re mule shoes:-	
			"There does not seem to be much necessity for a mule shoe size 15½; at least, very few mules in this Division require more than a size 15. A size 14½ would be very useful if made from heavier material than that at present used with size 14.	
			Many mules have to be shod 3 times a month and at least 60% twice a month, owing to the softness of the metal. Another very weak point is the clips, which has been badly drawn".	
	16		189 A.F.A. Bde transferred to 24th Division.	
			Inspected Nos 1 and 2 Sections D.A.C.	
			Reported to A.D.M.S. that a cow in wagon lines of 12th Durham L.I. appears to me to be suffering from Tubercle.	
			Inspected 12th D.L.I. Transport - very good.	
	17		X Corps Orders state Dip at ST. JANS, CAPPEL available for 90 horses on Friday - made arrangements for all mange cases of D.A.C. to go.	
			Inspected 190 Coy. A.S.C. - all animals in grand condition. Also inspected 10th North. Fus. - animals in good condition.	
			Telegram from X Corps states Dip available for 100 horses on Saturday.	

2449 Wt. W14957/M90 750,000 1/16 J.B.C. & A. Forms/C.2118/12.

Army Form C. 2118.

Instructions regarding War Diaries and Intelligence Summaries are contained in F. S. Regs., Part II. and the Staff Manual respectively. Title Pages will be prepared in manuscript.

WAR DIARY
or
INTELLIGENCE SUMMARY
(Erase heading not required.)

Place	1917 Date May	Hour	Summary of Events and Information	Remarks and references to Appendices
BUSSEBOOM	18		90 horses from D.A.C. dipped at IX Corps Bath. Arranged for new site for M.V.S.	
			Saw D.A.D.O.S. re fixing Horse Ambulance which has gone on its axle.	
			Inspected 11th North. Fus. – animals in splendid condition.	
			" 101st + 102nd Fd Coys. R.E. – animals in good condition.	
			" C/102 Bde R.F.A. – animals in good condition	
			All Batteries working very hard every night taking up ammunition to Front line – practically every animal has to go out.	
			Inspected 191 Coy. A.S.C. – animals in splendid condition.	
	19		X Corps wire states cancel dipping arrangements.	
			Inspected 192 Coy A.S.C. – animals in excellent condition.	
			Inspected 103 Bde R.F.A. – great decrease in mange – animals appear to be holding their own.	
			Selected site for Collection Post for 35 M.V.S.	
			Lieut. J. J. Bourke A.V.C. proceeded on 10 days leave to England.	
			O.C. M.V.S. indented for new Horse Float.	
	20		Inspected D/102 Bde – Animals holding their own – the horses with blistered skins are slow to heal.	
	21		Inspected 194 M.G. Coy – This unit is not good – gave orders as to what is to be done.	

2449 Wt. W14957/M90 750,000 1/16 J.B.C. & A. Forms/C.2118/12.

Army Form C. 2118.

Instructions regarding War Diaries and Intelligence Summaries are contained in F. S. Regs., Part II. and the Staff Manual respectively. Title Pages will be prepared in manuscript.

WAR DIARY
or
INTELLIGENCE SUMMARY
(Erase heading not required.)

Place	Date 1917 May	Hour	Summary of Events and Information	Remarks and references to Appendices
BUSSEBOOM	21	Contd	Inspected A/102 Bde R.F.A. – many horses falling off in condition – 8 Debility cases evacuated. Inspected B/102 Bde – a few debility horses that were in fair condition are holding their own with the hard work. Wrote following report to C.R.A.:- "As the horses of A/102 Bde are still falling away in condition owing to the work they are doing at present, I would suggest, if it is possible, that some other unit do their work. I advised that 8 horses be evacuated today for Debility from this battery". Inspected 189 Army Fd. Art. Bde. 'A' Batt – very satisfactory, 'B' – moderate, 'C' – satisfactory, 'D' – not good. All animals were clipped during December and very little mange appeared. Inspected No 3 Sect. DAC – mules in very good condition. Received D.D.V.S. report on inspection 8/5/17. 102 Bde R.F.A. 'A' Batt – looking very poor; tired. 'B' " – In moderate condition. 'C' " – Poor. 'D' " – In the best condition in the Brigade.	

Army Form C. 2118.

Instructions regarding War Diaries and Intelligence Summaries are contained in F. S. Regs., Part II. and the Staff Manual respectively. Title Pages will be prepared in manuscript.

WAR DIARY
or
INTELLIGENCE SUMMARY
(Erase heading not required.)

Place	1917 Date May	Hour	Summary of Events and Information	Remarks and references to Appendices
BUSSEBOOM	21		103 Bde R.F.A. 'A' Batt. – In fair condition 'B' " – In moderate condition. 'C' " – The best in the Brigade – condition quite satisfactory. 'D' " – Condition quite satisfactory. D.A.C No1 Sect – In good condition considering everything – well groomed. 2 " – Condition very good – many only half clipped. 3 " – Mules in excellent condition – well groomed and cared for. 70th Inf. Bde Group. All the animals were well groomed, fit and well cared for; especially those of the 8th Y&Lancs Regt – those of the 11th Sherwood Foresters and 9th Yorks & Lancs were very good. The 102nd Coy R.E. is the best R.E. Coy I have seen for a long time. The animals considering their size were in very good condition.	
	22		Made arrangements for dipping Inspected several skin cases in R.A. units.	

2449 Wt. W14957/M90 750,000 1/16 J.B.C. & A. Forms/C.2118/12.

Army Form C. 2118.

Instructions regarding War Diaries and Intelligence Summaries are contained in F. S. Regs., Part II. and the Staff Manual respectively. Title Pages will be prepared in manuscript.

WAR DIARY
or
INTELLIGENCE SUMMARY

(Erase heading not required.)

Place	1917 Date May	Hour	Summary of Events and Information	Remarks and references to Appendices
BUSSEBOOM	23		Inspected 69th Inf Bde – 69th M.G. Coy very good – 8th + 9th Yorks and 10th W. Ridings – horses and mules in excellent condition – 11th West Yorks horses good; mules good.	
			Saw V.O. i/c 315 A.F.A. Bde – just arrived in Division	
			Saw V.O's i/c 102 + 103 Bdes R.F.A. re skin cases.	
			Attended conference of G.O.C. division	
			Made arrangements for dipping at IX Corps Dip.	
	24		Inspected 103 Bde R.F.A – some few cases of Debility and Mange sent to M.V.S. – horses on the whole stand the very hard work well.	
			Inspected A, B + C. Batteries 102 Bde R.F.A. – some horses falling away in condition – sent some Debility and Mange cases to M.V.S.	
			Inspected 315 A.F.A. Bde – animals on the whole looking well but nearly every one affected with lice – ordered some horses to be sent to M.V.S. as mange.	
	25		Asked for a qualified knacker who is in the 10th L.F. to be attached to the M.V.S. for temporary duty.	
			Inspected Nos 1 + 2 Sections D.A.C. – animals on the whole looking very well.	
			Inspected 71st Fd Ambulance – animals in splendid condition.	

2449 Wt. W14957/M90 750,000 1/16 J.B.C. & A. Forms/C.2118/12.

Army Form C. 2118.

Instructions regarding War Diaries and Intelligence Summaries are contained in F. S. Regs., Part II. and the Staff Manual respectively. Title Pages will be prepared in manuscript.

WAR DIARY
or
INTELLIGENCE SUMMARY
(Erase heading not required.)

Place	1917 Date May	Hour	Summary of Events and Information	Remarks and references to Appendices
BUSSEBOOM	25		Orders to remove M.V.S. from mud Camp	
			Inspected 191 Coy A.S.C. – animals in very satisfactory condition.	
			Conference of V.O's at my office.	
	26		Inspected A/119 A.F.A. Bde – this is the best conditioned battery that I have seen in France.	
			Also inspected A, B + C Batteries 298 A.F.A. Bde – satisfactory and no skin disease.	
			Skinning demonstration at the M.V.S. for Wagon Line and Transport Officers; Vety Sergts and Sergts.	
	27		Inspected D/102 Bde R.F.A. – no change – dipping going on well.	
			M.V.S. moved to G.27.a.4.9. Sheet 28.	
	28		Inspected A.B+C. 102 Bde R.FA. – no change in animals' condition.	
			Casualties: Killed 9, wounded 11, Gassed 2.	
	29		Arrangements made for general dipping R.A. units.	
			Casualties: Killed 6, wounded 11, missing 7.	
	30		Inspected 103 Bde R.F.A. – no change in condition of animals.	
			Visited Dipping at 8th Corps Bath and visited Mobile Vety. Section.	

2449 Wt. W14957/M90 750,000 1/16 J.B.C. & A. Forms/C.2118/12.

Army Form C. 2118.

Instructions regarding War Diaries and Intelligence Summaries are contained in F. S. Regs., Part II. and the Staff Manual respectively. Title Pages will be prepared in manuscript.

WAR DIARY
or
INTELLIGENCE SUMMARY

(Erase heading not required.)

Place	Date 1917 May	Hour	Summary of Events and Information	Remarks and references to Appendices
BUSSEBOOM	30	Contd	Casualties: Killed 33, wounded 32, missing 9.	
	31		Visited various units	
			Reported a large percentage of punctured wounds - picked up nails - occuring at Refilling Point.	
			Met D.D.V.S. 2nd Army.	
			All units on full rations since 1st May - general condition of all animals greatly improved.	
			Casualties: Killed 2, wounded 9. missing 3.	
			J. J. Hilliard Major A. D. V. S. 23RD DIVISION.	

2449 Wt. W14957/M90 750,000 1/16 J.B.C. & A. Forms/C.2118/12.

Instructions regarding War Diaries and Intelligence Summaries are contained in F. S. Regs., Part II. and the Staff Manual respectively. Title Pages will be prepared in manuscript.

WAR DIARY
or
INTELLIGENCE SUMMARY
(Erase heading not required.)

Army Form C. 2118.

ADVS 23 D
Vol 23

Place	1917 Date June	Hour	Summary of Events and Information	Remarks and references to Appendices
BUSSEBOOM	1		Visited various units to see casualties.	
			Gave instructions re dipping at 8th Corps Dip – many units sending sections down.	
			2 men returned from X Corps M.V.S.	
			Casualties 3 wounded, 1 missing.	
	2		Visited various units:	
			Inspected 9th S. Staffs – animals in splendid condition.	
			Casualties 3 Killed, 2 wounded, 4 missing.	
	3		Visited various units.	
			Casualties 3 Killed, 2 wounded.	
	4		75 Remounts for R.A. arrived in good condition	
			Received Q.C. 257 23rd Division marked "confidential".	
			Inspected 193 Coy A.S.C. – very good.	
			Casualties 19 Killed, 13 wounded, 29 missing, 70 Gassed.	
			Anti gas masks most satisfactory.	
	5		Saw all gassed cases; 2 died and 1 destroyed.	
			Visited each Art. Bde – casualties very small.	
			Visited M.V.S. at WIPPENHOEK.	
			Inspected A/102 Bde R.F.A. – a great improvement noticed	
			Casualties 3 Killed, 3 wounded, 5 missing, 12 Gassed.	

2449 Wt. W14957/M90 750,000 1/16 J.B.C. & A. Forms/C.2118/12.

Army Form C. 2118.

Instructions regarding War Diaries and Intelligence Summaries are contained in F. S. Regs., Part II. and the Staff Manual respectively. Title Pages will be prepared in manuscript.

WAR DIARY
or
INTELLIGENCE SUMMARY

(Erase heading not required.)

Place	1917 Date June	Hour	Summary of Events and Information	Remarks and references to Appendices
BUSSEBOOM	6		Inspected 'B', 'C' + 'D' Batts 103 Bde - satisfactory - great improvement in 'B' Battery.	
			Advanced post for M.V.S. established at H.13.d.8.4. under Sergt Fairbrother and 3 men.	
			Gassed horses all doing very well.	
			Casualties 4 Killed, 5 missing, 1 Gassed.	
	7		Visited all Art. Bdes.	
			Inspected 189 Bde A.F.A. - horses in fair condition considering the work they are doing - B.A.C. - very good.	
			Made arrangements for evacuation from M.V.S.	
			Casualties 3 missing.	
	8		Visited all Art Bdes.	
			Inspected 'C' + 'D' 102 Bde R.F.A. - great improvement.	
			Conference of V.O's.	
			Visited Battle Hd Qrs.	
			Casualties 5 Killed, 7 Wounded, 1 missing.	
	9		Inspected 315 A.F.A. - all batteries except 'A' are holding their condition	
			Inspected No 2 Section D.A.C. - very good.	
			169 remounts arrived in good condition	
			Casualties 1 Killed, 1 Wounded.	

2449 Wt. W14957/M90 750,000 1/16 J.B.C. & A. Forms/C.2118/12.

Army Form C. 2118.

WAR DIARY
or
INTELLIGENCE SUMMARY
(Erase heading not required.)

Instructions regarding War Diaries and Intelligence Summaries are contained in F. S. Regs., Part II. and the Staff Manual respectively. Title Pages will be prepared in manuscript.

Place	Date 1917 June	Hour	Summary of Events and Information	Remarks and references to Appendices
BUSSEBOOM	10		Inspected 70th Inf. Bde – all animals in very good condition – 11th Sherwoods are not so good as the others, besides which the animals want trimming.	
			Advanced Mobile Vety Detachment withdrawn.	
			Casualties 7 Killed, 13 Wounded.	
	11		Visited various units – also No 2 Adv. Remount Squadron.	
			Casualties 1 Killed, 11 Wounded, 3 Missing, 17 Gassed.	
	12		Visited various units	
			Met D.D.V.S. in M.V.S.	
			Inspected 11th West Yorks – very good – also 69th M.G. Coy. – very good.	
			Casualties 2 Killed, 2 Wounded.	
BERTHEN	13		Changed area to BERTHEN – 35 M.V.S. to R.21.b.1.3. Sheet 27.	
			All R.A. Units, R.E.s and Pioneers left behind and handed over to 24th Division.	
	14		Inspected transport of 11th N.F., 12th D.L.I., 13th D.L.I., 8th Yorks, 9th Yorks, 10th W.R., and 11th W. Yorks – all in very good condition	
	15		Visited 102 Bde R.F.A. – improvement maintained in all Batteries	
			Visited Nos 1 + 3 Sections D.A.C. – No 3 Section very good and No 1 Section great improvement.	
	16		Visited 69th, 70th, 71st Fd Ambulances – all satisfactory	

2449 Wt. W14957/M90 750,000 1/16 J.B.C. & A. Forms/C.2118/12.

Army Form C. 2118.

Instructions regarding War Diaries and Intelligence Summaries are contained in F. S. Regs., Part II. and the Staff Manual respectively. Title Pages will be prepared in manuscript.

WAR DIARY
or
INTELLIGENCE SUMMARY

(Erase heading not required.)

Place	Date 1917 June	Hour	Summary of Events and Information	Remarks and references to Appendices
BERTHEN	17		Horse Show meeting	
	18		Visited 103 Bde R.F.A. – 'C' Battery not holding its own.	
	19		Visited various units	
			Judged at 69th Inf. Bde Horse Show	
	20		Attended conference of D.V.S. at ST. OMER.	
	21		Judged at Inter Field Ambulance Horse Show.	
	22		Ordinary routine work	
	23		Visited by D.D.V.S., Second Army.	
	24		Routine work	
	25		Divisional Horse Show	
	26		Inspected 102 Bde R.F.A. – steady improvement maintained.	
			Inspected No 1 Sect. D.A.C. – saw mange cases – all under strict isolation and 2 sent to M.V.S. – remainder are very slight.	
			Arrangements are made to dip all the Section on 30th at IX Corps Dip.	
	27		Visited No 2 Adv. Remount Section.	
			Accompanied G.O.C. round 102 Bde R.F.A.	

Instructions regarding War Diaries and Intelligence Summaries are contained in F. S. Regs., Part II. and the Staff Manual respectively. Title Pages will be prepared in manuscript.

WAR DIARY
or
INTELLIGENCE SUMMARY

(Erase heading not required.)

Army Form C. 2118.

Place	1917 Date June	Hour	Summary of Events and Information	Remarks and references to Appendices
BERTHEN	28		Inspected 10th NF and 12th D.L.I. - very satisfactory	
			Visited A.D.V.S. X Corps to arrange about dipping No1 Sect. D.A.C.	
			Sent following letter to C.R.A. Division.	
			"Will you kindly arrange the transfer of Sgt Shoesmith A.V.C. att. C/103 Bde R.F.A. to No 2 Section D.A.C. and that of Sergt. Hebditch A.V.C. att No 2 Section D.A.C. to C/103 Bde R.F.A."	
	29		Inspected 103 Bde. R.F.A. – C/103 Bde not gaining in condition.	
ZEVECOTEN	30		Changed area to Zevecoten.	
			Outbreak of Stomatitis reported in C/103 Bde — Capt Allenson A.V.C. and Lieut Macleod A.V.C. discovered 5 cases and put 12 aside as suspicious of having the disease – informed A.D.V.S. X Corps by telegram.	
			Sergt. Shoesmith A.V.C. transferred to No 2 Section D.A.C. from C/103 Bde R.F.A.	

J. J. Hilliard
MAJOR,
D. A. D. V. S. 23RD DIVISION.

2449 Wt. W14957/M90 750,000 1/16 J.B.C. & A. Forms/C.2118/12.

Instructions regarding War Diaries and Intelligence Summaries are contained in F. S. Regs., Part II. and the Staff Manual respectively. Title pages will be prepared in manuscript.

WAR DIARY
or
INTELLIGENCE SUMMARY.
(Erase heading not required.)

Army Form C. 2118.

DADVS 23 D
Vol 24

Place	Date 1917 July	Hour	Summary of Events and Information	Remarks and references to Appendices
ZEVECOTEN	1		Visited A.D.V.S. X Corps. Inspected all 103 Bde R.F.A. – contagious stomatitis is apparently confined to 'C' Batt – isolated affected cases and gave orders about watering etc. Reported the disease to the G.O.C. Div., C.R.A., O.C. 103 Bde and D.A.Q.M.G. Div. Directed V.O. i/c 102 Bde R.F.A. to inspect all horses under his charge and O.C. M.V.S. to daily inspect C/103 Bde.	
	2		Visited various units in area. Made arrangements for C/103 Bde to have separate watering places	
	3		Many more cases of Stomatitis reported in C/103 Bde – this unit is moving one section today and one tomorrow – strict instructions given not to use any water-trough other than their own. Reported personally to A.D.V.S. X Corps and D.D.V.S. 2nd Army what had been done. Reported personally to A.D.V.S. II Corps. Inspected 68th and 69th Inf Bdes; also 69th M.G. Coy. and 11th Sherwoods	
	4		Selected position for Adv. M.V.S. at H.33.b.7.6. Sheet 28. Visited C/103 Bde with A.D.V.S. II Corps. Reported to A.A. + Q.M.G. that the water troughs properly marked were not yet in position. 57 cases have been segregated, but most of these are cured cases with the ulcers healed up.	
	5		Inspected the 57 cases segregated and placed 20 aside for A.D.V.S. inspection – A.D.V.S. pronounced cases slight. – 20 cases as suffering and 47 cases suspicious segregated Inspected 191 Coy A.S.C. – good.	

2353 Wt. W2514/1454 700,000 5/15 D. D. & L. A.D.S.S./Forms/C. 2118.

Army Form C. 2118.

Instructions regarding War Diaries and Intelligence Summaries are contained in F. S. Regs., Part II. and the Staff Manual respectively. Title Pages will be prepared in manuscript.

WAR DIARY
or
INTELLIGENCE SUMMARY
(Erase heading not required.)

Place	Date July 1917	Hour	Summary of Events and Information	Remarks and references to Appendices
ZEVECOTEN	6		Proceeded to C/103 Bde with D.D.V.S. 5th Army and A.D.V.S. II Corps to see Stomatitis cases. They pronounced the cases to be very slight but that no precautions were to be relaxed.	
			Inspected No 2 Section D.A.C. – very good.	
	7		Inspected A/102 Bde – still improving very much; B/102 – very fair, no mange; C/102 – very fair, some mange; D/102 – very fair, some mange. A/103 Bde – Very good; B/103 – Very good; D/103 – Good } All are improving	
			Inspected No 1 Section D.A.C. – Very good; 3 do – Splendid	
			Many complaints from practically every battery about the quantity of water – it is very hard to get – reported fact to "Q".	
	8		Visited various units	
	9		D.V.S., D.D.V.S., 5th Army and A.D.V.S. II Corps visited C/103 Bde – stomatitis cases doing well	
	10		A.D.V.S. II Corps inspection of R.A. cancelled	
	11		Inspected 101, 102, 128 Fd Coys R.E. – all in excellent condition	
			Also No 2 Sect. D.A.C. – in very good condition.	
			Inspected 298 Bde A.F.A. – in fairly good condition	

2449 Wt. W14957/M90 750,000 1/16 J.B.C. & A. Forms/C.2118/12.

Army Form C. 2118.

Instructions regarding War Diaries and Intelligence Summaries are contained in F. S. Regs., Part II. and the Staff Manual respectively. Title Pages will be prepared in manuscript.

WAR DIARY
or
INTELLIGENCE SUMMARY
(Erase heading not required.)

Place	1917 Date July	Hour	Summary of Events and Information	Remarks and references to Appendices
ZEVECOTEN	11	Contd	Lt. J.J. Bourke A.V.C. transferred to No 13 Veterinary Hospital Received D.V.S. letter that Cables to England regarding leave are not sent at the Public Expense.	
	12		Saw 70th Inf. Bde. march out – very good order Inspected mange cases in 102 Bde R.F.A. Have no doubt that Calcium Sulphide (as it is put on in lines) is absolutely useless for the cure of mange. The mixture composed of Whale Oil, Sulphur, Soap and Calcium Sulphide appears to be an excellent dressing, and after a few applications the irritation due to the Acarus, disappears. Inspected 52nd Bde A.F.A. – B.A.C. and 'C' Batt very good – 'D' and 'B' Fair – 'A' Batt splendid and is the best battery that I have ever seen as regards the condition of their horses.	
	13		Inspected No 3 Section D.A.C. – animals in splendid condition. A.D.V.S. II Corps inspected 102 Bde R.F.A. and 'A' and 'B' Batts 103 Bde R.F.A. He is not satisfied with the condition of 102 Bde – mange cases all doing well.	
	14		Attended conference of A.D.V.S. at II Corps. Inspected 193 Coy A.S.C. – very good.	

2449 Wt. W14957/M90 750,000 1/16 J.B.C. & A. Forms/C.2118/12.

Army Form C. 2118.

WAR DIARY
or
INTELLIGENCE SUMMARY

(Erase heading not required.)

Instructions regarding War Diaries and Intelligence Summaries are contained in F. S. Regs., Part II. and the Staff Manual respectively. Title Pages will be prepared in manuscript.

Place	Date 1917 July	Hour	Summary of Events and Information	Remarks and references to Appendices
ZEVECOTEN	14	Contd	Inspected 8th K.O.Y.L.I. – there are 4 cases of mange.	
	15		Casualties reported up-to-date this time in the line. Killed 14, wounded 27, missing 24, Gassed 1.	
	16		Inspected 191 + 192 Corps A.H. – animals in splendid condition	
			Visited II Corps M.V.S.; also A.D.V.S. II Corps.	
			Visited C/103 Bde and asked A.D.V.S. re the 57 isolated cases of Stomatitis – he said that they might be sent back to their lines. This leaves 11 cases still isolated	
			Casualties Killed 2, wounded 5, missing 1	
	17		S. Sergt Fairbrother A.V.C. transferred to 23 M.V.S.	
			Inspected 12th D.L.I., 11th W. Yorks, 68th, 69th + 70th M. G. Coys, 8th Yorks, 9th Yorks and 10th W. Ridings	
			Visited 8th K.O.Y.L.I. to see 4 mange cases – ordered one to the M.V.S. for treatment	
			Although dip allotted for 120 horses, none were put through as some other unit was also allotted.	
			Casualties Killed 12, wounded 4, Gassed 8	
	18		Inspected 10th N.F., 11th N.F., 13th D.L.I. and 70th Fd Ambulance – all are very good	
			Mange cases returned from II Corps M.V.D. to 35 M.V.S.	
			No casualties reported today.	

2449 Wt. W14957/M90 750,000 1/16 J.B.C. & A. Forms/C.2118/12.

Instructions regarding War Diaries and Intelligence Summaries are contained in F. S. Regs., Part II. and the Staff Manual respectively. Title Pages will be prepared in manuscript.

WAR DIARY
or
INTELLIGENCE SUMMARY
(Erase heading not required.)

Army Form C. 2118.

Place	1917 Date July	Hour	Summary of Events and Information	Remarks and references to Appendices
ZEVECOTEN	19		Inspected D/102 + D/103 Bde R.F.A. – both fair. The artillery for the past fortnight have been working very hard.	
			No 1 Sect. D.A.C. – very good – as is 71st Fd. Ambulance	
			Struck off all Stomatitis cases in C/103, except 5 which have not quite healed up.	
			56 Remounts arrived yesterday for R.A. – they are in good condition.	
			Casualties wounded 2.	
			Divisional weekly State:- In last return 159, Admitted since 156, Total 315, Cured 104, Evacuated 33, Died 30, Destroyed 7, Remaining under treatment 141, Strength of Formation 6,056 animals.	
	20		Again disappointed over the II Corps Horse Dip.	
			Inspected some skin cases – all doing well.	
			Casualties Killed 4, wounded 4, missing 1.	
	21		Attended conference at A.D.V.S. II Corps HQ.	
			C/103 Bde declared free from Stomatitis.	
			Casualties Killed 1, wounded 1, missing 2.	
	22		Water very short at 102 Bde; also at No 2 Section D.A.C. – reported fact to D.A.Q.M.G.	
			D.D.V.S. 5th Army inspected the M.V.S.	
			Visited various units.	
			Casualties Killed 1, wounded 17	

2449 Wt. W14957/M90 750,000 1/16 J.B.C. & A. Forms/C.2118/12.

Instructions regarding War Diaries and Intelligence Summaries are contained in F. S. Regs., Part II. and the Staff Manual respectively. Title Pages will be prepared in manuscript.

WAR DIARY
or
INTELLIGENCE SUMMARY
(Erase heading not required.)

Army Form C. 2118.

Place	1917 Date July	Hour	Summary of Events and Information	Remarks and references to Appendices
MERRIS	23		Changed area to Merris.	
	24		Letter sent to DADOS re great shortage of Shoes No 9 Hind, 9 Fore, 10 Hind, 10 Fore and 7 Hind Wheeler. Warned him that serious consequences would arise if indents were not quickly completed.	
			Inspected 70th Inf. Bde. – all transport very satisfactory.	
			Accompanied X Corps Horsemastership Officer to select brood mares.	
	25		Visited M.V.S.	
			Accompanied X Corps Horsemastership Officer to select mares suitable for breeding.	
	26		Inspected 68th Inf. Bde — the 10th North. Fusiliers are not so good as the others.	
			Accompanied X Corps Horsemastership Officer to select mares suitable for breeding.	
	27		Visited various units.	
	28		Went to see ADVS X Corps and then to 102 Bde R.F.A.	
	29		Proceeded on 5 days leave in France.	

J J Hilliard
MAJOR,
D. A. D. V. S. 23rd DIVISION.

2449 Wt. W14957/M90 750,000 1/16 J.B.C. & A. Forms/C.2118/12.

DADVS 26 Army Form C. 2118.

Vol 25

Instructions regarding War Diaries and Intelligence Summaries are contained in F. S. Regs., Part II. and the Staff Manual respectively. Title Pages will be prepared in manuscript.

WAR DIARY
or
INTELLIGENCE SUMMARY
(Erase heading not required.)

Place	1917 Date Aug	Hour	Summary of Events and Information	Remarks and references to Appendices
MERRIS	2		Returned from leave.	
	3		Visited M.V.S and other units.	
	4		Visited R.A. in the line – in spite of the very bad weather the horses have fallen away very little.	
	5		Visited 8th + 9th Yorks + Lancs.	
WIZERNES	6		Changed area to WIZERNES.	
	7		Visited various units. Inspected 13th D.L.I. and 11th N.F. Reported that 194 M.G. Coy are not good and have fallen off lately.	
	8		Visited M.V.S.	
			Inspected remounts and 192 Coy. A.S.C.	
			Conference of G.O.C.	
EPERLECQUES	9		Changed area to EPERLECQUES	
			Inspected remounts and 191 Coy A.S.C.	
			Changed to V Corps Area.	
	10		Inspected 70th Inf: Bde on the march. As usual the breechings do not fit properly owing to carelessness in putting harness together after cleaning. Showed errors to all Transport Officers.	

2449 Wt. W14957/M90 750,000 1/16 J.B.C. & A. Forms/C.2118/12.

Army Form C. 2118.

WAR DIARY
or
INTELLIGENCE SUMMARY
(Erase heading not required.)

Instructions regarding War Diaries and Intelligence Summaries are contained in F. S. Regs., Part II. and the Staff Manual respectively. Title Pages will be prepared in manuscript.

Place	1917 Date Aug.	Hour	Summary of Events and Information	Remarks and references to Appendices
EPERLECQUES	10		Visited 10th N.F.	
	11		Visited 10th N.F. – animals on the whole not quite satisfactory – informed the C.O.	
			" 12 DLI. – animals are in splendid order.	
			Visited A.D.V.S. V Corps.	
	12		Inspected 194 M.G. Coy. – they are not as good as the other M.G. Corps. – reported the Transport Sergeant to C.M.G.O. Div and his C.O. as not being a good man.	
	13		Inspected 9th Yorks, 10th W. Ridings, 11th W. Yorks and 8th Yorks – they are all very good except 8th Yorks which are not so good.	
			Inspected 192 Coy A.S.C. – satisfactory; also 69th Fd Ambulance – good.	
			Visited 9th R. Scots, 7th Argyll + Suth H. and extra M.G. Coy of 154 Inf. Bde now in my charge; also visited Staff Capt of same brigade.	
	14		Inspected 68th M.G. Coy – satisfactory; also 191 Coy A.S.C. – very good.	
			Lt McLeod A.V.C. evacuated to Hospital for Fractured Femur.	
	15		Placed Lt. McLeod's Vety equipment in charge of Vety Sergt 68th Bde.	
			Inspected 69th M.G. Coy and visited various units	
			Reported Lt. McLeod's casualty to D.D.V.S. 5th Army repeated A.D.V.S. 5th Corps	
			Asked opinion re Chaff Cutters 5th Army Q/865/319 – advised all units be supplied where more than 70 animals.	

2449 Wt. W14957/M90 750,000 1/16 J.B.C. & A. Forms/C.2118/12.

Army Form C. 2118.

Instructions regarding War Diaries and Intelligence Summaries are contained in F. S. Regs., Part II. and the Staff Manual respectively. Title Pages will be prepared in manuscript.

WAR DIARY
or
INTELLIGENCE SUMMARY
(Erase heading not required.)

Place	1917 Date Aug	Hour	Summary of Events and Information	Remarks and references to Appendices
EPERLECQUES	15		Took over charge of 68th + 69th Inf. Bdes.	
	16		Inspected 68th Inf. Bde	
	17		Visited various units	
			Vety. Sergt. Hebditch att C/103 Bde R.F.A. wounded and evacuated.	
	18		Visited various units and 69th Inf. Bde.	
			Received wire from 'A' Division that Capt. H. Jewell AVC. was being sent vice Lt. McLeod AVC.	
	19		Capt. H. Jewell AVC. arrived - posted to 13th D.L.I.	
			Recommended SE. 8485 R/A/Cpl Jones R and SE. 14972 Pte. Hutson E. be promoted to rank of Sergeant.	
	20		Visited various units in 68th and 69th Inf Bdes with V.O i/c	
	21		Visited 102 Bde R.F.A. and 103 Bde R.F.A. - both have improved since I saw them last.	
			Also saw DAC. - very good.	
	22		Inspected mares for repatriation with V Corps Horsemastership Officer	
			All requests for Wheel Clipping Machines which have been put in up to the present have been refused.	
			Informed 'Q' that there is a great deal of carelessness in the way the lids of the ration boxes are placed on the wagons, causing thereby a scattering of nails along the roads.	
	23		Routine Duties	
			Inspected 194 M.G. Coy - improving - Transport Sergeant is useless.	

2449 Wt. W14957/M90 750,000 1/16 J.B.C. & A. Forms/C.2118/12.

Army Form C. 2118.

Instructions regarding War Diaries and Intelligence Summaries are contained in F. S. Regs., Part II. and the Staff Manual respectively. Title pages will be prepared in manuscript.

WAR DIARY
or
INTELLIGENCE SUMMARY.
(Erase heading not required.)

Place	Date 1917 Aug.	Hour	Summary of Events and Information	Remarks and references to Appendices
RENINGHELST	24		Changed area to RENINGHELST.	
	25		No 5888 Sgt Taylor A.V.C. attached D/102 Bde placed under arrest for "creating a disturbance in camp and being out of bounds". Reported to me by V.O. i/c D.A.C.	
DICKEBUSCH	26		Changed area to DICKEBUSCH.	
			Attended II Corps A.D.V.S. conference.	
			Sent order to O.C. M.V.S. to have men of Section classified by A.D.M.S. at WIPPENHOEK	
			9 a.m. 27.8.17. Asked A.D.V.S. II Corps to have men on attachment Corps M.V.D examined.	
	27		Selected site for Advanced Detachment of M.V.S. in case the Division should go into action.	
			R/A/Sgt Parker W. No SE 15830 arrived for duty with C/103 Bde R.F.A.	
			Orders sent to all V.O.'s (see attached)	
	28		Inspected animals in M.V.S. for evacuation	
	29		Inspected 9th S. Staffs - very good	
			" 101, 102 + 128 Fd Coys R.E. - very good.	
	30		Duties in M.V.S. - interview with A.D.V.S. II Corps.	
	31		Selected horses for evacuation	
			One bomb dropped in 128 Coy R.E. lines — Killed 5, wounded 18.	
			Conference of V.O.'s at my office.	

2353 Wt. W2544/1454 700,000 5/15 D. D. & L. A.D.S.S./Forms/C. 2118.

MAJOR,
D. A. D. V. S. 23RD DIVISION.

A.D.V.S.
23rd DIVISION.
No.
Date.

23RD DIVISION.

ORDERS FOR VETERINARY OFFICERS WHILST ATTACHED TO THIS DIVISION.

1. CONFERENCE at 10.30 a.m. Fridays.
2. DAILY CASUALTY REPORT showing any casualties that have occurred from the following causes :- Shells, Gas, Bombs and Picked-up Nails, each to be specified; also if the injuries happened in the Wagon Lines or elsewhere, and by day or night.
3. OPHTHALMIA. The class of horse affected must be ~~down~~ shown on the A.F. A.2000, whether Colonial or home-bred.
4. Horses incurably injured must be destroyed forthwith, also old debilitated horses which have no chance of ever being fit for re-issue.
5. Horses for evacuation to the M.V.S. must have a halter or head-collar and nose-bag, and be properly shod.
6. Care to be used in the differentiation of Contusion, Bruised Sole, and Wound Punctured picked-up-nail.
7. Bad cases of Cellulitis which have resisted treatment are to be destroyed.
8. The practice of poulticing foot cases whilst the animal is on muddy standings is to cease.
9. Any unusual occurrences, or exceptional outbreaks of disease will be reported at once.

(Signed) J.J.HILLIARD,
Major,
D.A.D.V.S., 23rd Division.

27th August 1917.

Instructions regarding War Diaries and Intelligence Summaries are contained in F. S. Regs., Part II. and the Staff Manual respectively. Title pages will be prepared in manuscript.

WAR DIARY
or
INTELLIGENCE SUMMARY.
(*Erase heading not required.*)

Army Form C. 2118.

DADVS 23 D
Vol 26

Place	1917 Date Sept.	Hour	Summary of Events and Information	Remarks and references to Appendices
DICKEBUSCH	1.		Made arrangements to move M.V.S.	
STEENVOORDE	2.		Changed to X Corps. Moved to Steenvoorde. M.V.S. to K.31. b o 2. Sheet 27	
			Killed by bomb at 101 Fd Coy R.E. 29 animals, wounded 20 animals.	
	3		Routine Duties	
LEDERZEELE	4		Moved to Lederzeele. M.V.S. in same village.	
	5		Accompanied O.C. Div Train and inspected 69th Inf. Bde - everything satisfactory except the 11th W. Yorks and the 8th Yorks who are not good	
	6		Capt Jewell AVC. proceeded on 10 days leave.	
			Accompanied O.C. Div. Train and inspected 70th Inf. Bde. All units very good except Sherwood Foresters whose transport on the whole is bad. 8th Yorks & Lancs easily best	
	7		Sergt Webb AVC att. DAC evacuated to Hospital for Eczema	
			Accompanied O.C. Div. Train and inspected the 68th Inf. Bde. All transport very good - great improvement in the 10th North Fusiliers.	
			Also inspected 69th, 70th, 71st Fd. Ambulances - all very good. Also 194 M.G. Coy - shows some improvement. 191 Coy A.S.C. - very good	
	8		Accompanied O.C. Div. Train and inspected 3 Corps R.E. - all in good condition. Also 9th S. Staffs (P)	

A6945 Wt. W11422/M1160 350,000 12/16 D. D. & L. Forms/C./2118/14.

Army Form C. 2118.

Instructions regarding War Diaries and Intelligence Summaries are contained in F. S. Regs., Part II. and the Staff Manual respectively. Title pages will be prepared in manuscript.

WAR DIARY
or
INTELLIGENCE SUMMARY.
(Erase heading not required.)

Place	Date 1917 Sept	Hour	Summary of Events and Information	Remarks and references to Appendices
LEDERZEELE	9		Routine Duties	
	10		Routine Duties.	
			Telegram sent to ADVS 1st Anzac Corps to return 4 men of 35 M.V.S.	
			Visited 10th W. Riding	
	11		Sergt. Goodley A.V.C. 70th Bde proceeded on leave. During his absence Sergt Daniels A.V.C.	
			35 M.V.S. is placed with Brigade	
	12		Arranged Veterinary Duties for Offensive with AA & QMG	
			Accompanied O.C. Div. Train to inspect 8th Yorks transport which shows improvement	
			Also 11th W. Yorks – no improvement.	
			Second Army Order. "All clipping under Central Clipping Scheme"	
			F.Q.M.S. Ross A. R.H. and R.F.A transferred to A.V.C. from 11th inst with substantive rank of	
			Staff Sergeant. Posted to D/102 Bde R.F.A. and gave orders for SE/5888 Sergt. Taylor J. A.V.C.	
			to be sent to No 2 Vety Hospital, HAVRE to await reposting	
	13		M.V.S. moved to Steenvoorde	
LACLYTTE CAMP	14		Changed area to M.6.d.5.8. Sheet 28 and M.V.S. arrived at M.6.b.4.4. Sheet 28.	
M.6.d.5.8. Sheet 28.			Horse Float wheel broken – reported it at once to DADOS.	

A6945 Wt. W11422/M1160 350,000 12/16 D. D. & L. Forms/C./2118/14.

Army Form C. 2118.

Instructions regarding War Diaries and Intelligence Summaries are contained in F. S. Regs., Part II. and the Staff Manual respectively. Title pages will be prepared in manuscript.

WAR DIARY
or
INTELLIGENCE SUMMARY.
(Erase heading not required.)

Place	1917. Date Sept.	Hour	Summary of Events and Information	Remarks and references to Appendices
LA CLYTTE CAMP M.6.d.5.8 Sheet 28	15		Attended conference by AA+QMG.	
			Showed Float to DADOS.	
			Inspected 103 Bde R.F.A. and No 2 Sect. DAC. – all fairly good	
	16		Inspected 'A' and 'D' Batteries 102 Bde R.F.A.	
	17		Visited ADVS. X Corps to discuss dipping, and informed G.O.C. Div and C.R.A.	
			of D.D.V.S., 2nd Army Scheme.	
			Inspected 'B' and 'C' Batteries 102 Bde R.F.A.	
			Visited Advanced Vety Detachment.	
	18		Visited units of 69th Inf Bde except ASC and Fd Ambulance.	
			Inspected 66 horses for evacuation.	
	19		Inspected No 1 Sect. D.A.C. – satisfactory	
			There is a great deal of Ophthalmia in various units	
			Ordered Sgt Daniels AVC to be sent to X Corps Mobile Vety. Detachment on his	
			return from 70th Inf. Bde at 9 a.m. 20.9.17.	
			Inspected 194 M.G. Coy. – no improvement.	
	20		Sent ophthalmia treatment by Iodine to all V.O's.	

A6945 Wt. W11422/M1160 350,000 12/16 D. D. & L. Forms/C./2118/14.

Army Form C. 2118.

Instructions regarding War Diaries and Intelligence Summaries are contained in F. S. Regs., Part II. and the Staff Manual respectively. Title pages will be prepared in manuscript.

WAR DIARY
or
INTELLIGENCE SUMMARY.
(Erase heading not required.)

Place	1917 Date Sept	Hour	Summary of Events and Information	Remarks and references to Appendices
LA CLYTTE CAMP M.6.d. 5.8. Sheet 28.	20	Contd	Inspected 190 Coy A.S.C. - animals in splendid condition.	
			Visited Advanced M.V.S. - very little to report and I doubt if there is any use in having one.	
			Sent Sgt Daniels to X Corps M.V.D.	
	21		Inspected 192 Coy A.S.C. - animals showing great improvement. Also inspected 11th Sherwoods - some improvement noticed.	
	22		Attended conference of A.D.V.S. X Corps.	
			Withdrew Advanced Section. Borrowed float from M.V.S. 33rd Division.	
			Visited units bombed last night - Casualties Killed 9, wounded 28 - 37.	
			Advised AA + QMG that a sandbagged wall 2 feet high round standings would save a good many casualties.	
	23		Visited 190 Coy A.S.C.	
			Inspected class "B" cases at M.V.S. for evacuation.	
			Visited 69th and 71st Fd Ambulances - condition of animals satisfactory.	
	24		Branded mares for repatriation after the war.	
			Inspected No 3 Sect. D.A.C. - animals in splendid condition.	

A6945 Wt. W11422/M1160 350,000 12/16 D. D. & L. Forms/C./2118/14.

Instructions regarding War Diaries and Intelligence Summaries are contained in F. S. Regs., Part II. and the Staff Manual respectively. Title pages will be prepared in manuscript.

WAR DIARY
or
INTELLIGENCE SUMMARY.
(Erase heading not required.)

Army Form C. 2118.

Place	Date 1917 Sept.	Hour	Summary of Events and Information	Remarks and references to Appendices
WESTOUTRE	25		Changed area to Westoutre.	
			Capt. R.C. Allinson A.V.C. proceeded on 10 days leave.	
			Evacuated 58 animals to Base by road. Branded more mares.	
	26		Commenced treatment of eye cases by Lugol's Solution.	
	~~26~~		Inspected 10th h.T. - great improvement in condition of animals.	
			Visited 128 Coy R.E.	
	27		A.A. & Q.M.G. instructs me to get in touch with D.A.D.V.S. 33rd Div and arrange for	
			35 M.V.S. to go into billet occupied by theirs.	
			Visited D.A.D.V.S. but he was out.	
			Visited 191, 192, 193 Coys A.S.C.; also 10th W. Ridings.	
LA CLYTTE CAMP.			Injected all eye cases with Lugol's Solution in units under Capt. Allinson not done.	
M. 6. d. 5. 8.	28		Wire from D.A.D.V.S. 33rd Division that he leaves M.V.S. lines on 29.9.17 at 8 a.m.	
			Visited various units	
			Changed area to La Clytte	
	29		M.V.S. moved to La Clytte.	
			Only 1 Sergt and 1 man left behind with 57 sick horses. Wired to D.A.D.V.S. 33rd Divn	

A6945 Wt. W11422/M1160 350,000 12/16 D. D. & L. Forms/C./2118/14.

Army Form C. 2118.

WAR DIARY
or
INTELLIGENCE SUMMARY.
(Erase heading not required.)

Instructions regarding War Diaries and Intelligence Summaries are contained in F. S. Regs., Part II. and the Staff Manual respectively. Title pages will be prepared in manuscript.

Place	Date 1917 Sept	Hour	Summary of Events and Information	Remarks and references to Appendices
LA CLYTTE CAMP M.6.d.5.8	29	Contd	to send 5 more men as this was not sufficient	
			Visited various units	
			98 sick in M.V.S.	
	30		Met A.D.V.S. X Corps who gave permission to evacuate 40 Class 'B' cases to	
			Corps M.V. Detachment.	
			J.J. Hilliard	
			MAJOR, D.A.D.V.S. 23rd DIVISION.	

A6945 Wt. W11422/M1160 350,000 12/16 D. D. & L. Forms/C./2118/14.

DADVS 23D Army Form C. 2118.

Vol 27

Instructions regarding War Diaries and Intelligence Summaries are contained in F. S. Regs., Part II. and the Staff Manual respectively. Title pages will be prepared in manuscript.

WAR DIARY
or
INTELLIGENCE SUMMARY.
(Erase heading not required.)

Place	Date 1917 Oct.	Hour	Summary of Events and Information	Remarks and references to Appendices
LA CLYTTE CAMP. M.6.d.5.8.	1		Visited 102 and 103 Bdes R.F.A; also 9th S. Staffs and Trench mortars.	
			Visited 191 Coy A.S.C.	
BERTHEN	2		Changed area to Berthen; also moved M.V.S. to same place as before R.21.b.2.3 Sheet 27.	
			Visited various units and evacuated 77 cases by Road, and left 13 Class 'B' cases.	
	3		Visited 190, 192, 193 Coys A.S.C. Inspected 33 remounts; also 71st Fd Ambulance.	
	4		Visited various units and A.D.V.S. X Corps.	
			Attended conference at A.A. + Q.M.G. office.	
	5		Visited various units	
	6		Visited units and A.D.V.S. X Corps re clipping. Apparently no arrangements made for doing it by the Scheme in the Area - told to do so myself - informed A.A. + Q.M.G.	
			Attended conference by G.O.C.	
			Arranged with 'Q' for staff for Clipping Depot and 5 men to report to D.A.D.O.S. from units for instruction in sharpening and minor repairs to machines (Q wire Q.Q. 692 d/- 6.10.17)	
			A.D.V.S. X Corps informs me that the machines and rugs for the animals are ready for issue.	

D. D. & L., London, E.C. (A8004) Wt. W1771/M2031 750,000 5/17 Sch. 52 Forms/C2118/14

Army Form C. 2118.

WAR DIARY
or
INTELLIGENCE SUMMARY.
(Erase heading not required.)

Instructions regarding War Diaries and Intelligence Summaries are contained in F. S. Regs., Part II. and the Staff Manual respectively. Title pages will be prepared in manuscript.

Place	Date 1917 Oct	Hour	Summary of Events and Information	Remarks and references to Appendices
BERTHEN	7		Selected site for Central Clipping Depot at R.17. a. 0. 3. There is a good stable already there and only needs a shed put up for drying and grooming the animals prior to Clipping. 'Q' informed and they are arranging with the X Corps	
	8		On transfer of F.Q.M.S.'s Jones C.P. and Burrows E. R.H. & R.F.A. to A.V.C., I gave orders for them to be sent to No 2 Veterinary Hospital, HAVRE to await re-posting.	
			Informed a Clipping Depot is in ~~progress~~ process of erection at METEREN – visited it and found stabling nearly completed.	
			No 2383 Sgt. Goodley F. A.V.C. att 70th Inf. Bde reduced to the ranks for inefficiency and to proceed to No 2 Vety. Hospital, HAVRE, on relief.	
			Informed by A.D.V.S. X Corps that 700 horse rugs and 20 sets Stewart's Clipping machines would be issued on indent by D.A.D.O.S. from Army Reserve; the others to be issued on indent from Base – informed D.A.D.O.S. for action.	
			Capt. Allinson A.V.C. back from leave.	
	9		Visited Artillery units and C.R.A.	
			Asked 'Q' for additional personnel for Clipping Depot. 30 men for turning machines 4 " for Sanitary duty.	

D. D. & L., London, E.C. (A8004) Wt. W1771/M2'31 750,000 5/17 Sch. 52 Forms/C2118/14

Army Form C. 2118.

WAR DIARY
or
INTELLIGENCE SUMMARY.

(Erase heading not required.)

Instructions regarding War Diaries and Intelligence Summaries are contained in F. S. Regs., Part II. and the Staff Manual respectively. Title pages will be prepared in manuscript.

Place	Date 1917 Oct.	Hour	Summary of Events and Information	Remarks and references to Appendices
BERTHEN	10		Went to see D.A.D.V.S. 7th Divn but he was not in.	
			Capt. Starkey A.V.C. went on 10 days leave.	
H.30.C.5.8. Sheet 28.	11		Changed area to H.30.C.5.8. Sheet 28.	
			Discussed the Clipping Depot with G.O.C. and C.R.A. The central scheme is impossible to work unless all the Division is together – will make 2 Sections under A.V.C. N.C.O.s	
			F.Q.M.S.s Jones and Burrows left for Base today.	
	12		Made arrangements for Clipping Depot.	
	13		Made arrangements for Clipping Depot – personnel collected at the Depot.	
	14		Machines taken over for Clipping – all is ready to start, but as the horse rugs have not come, the start must be delayed.	
	15		Proceeded on Special leave – Capt Allinson A.V.C. acting in my place.	
			Clipping Instructions issued.	
	17		Clipping started on R.A. Horses.	
	18		Arrived back in France.	
			No SE/451 A/Sgt Gowenlock J. A.V.C. reported for duty with 70th Inf. Bde.	
	19		Arrived back at D.H.Q.	
			Visited Clipping Depot – averaging about 80 horses per day clipped.	

D. D. & L., London, E.C.
(A8004) Wt. W1771/M2931 750,000 5/17 Sch. 52 Forms/C2118/14

Army Form C. 2118.

Instructions regarding War Diaries and Intelligence Summaries are contained in F. S. Regs., Part II. and the Staff Manual respectively. Title pages will be prepared in manuscript.

WAR DIARY
or
INTELLIGENCE SUMMARY.

(Erase heading not required.)

Place	1917 Date Oct.	Hour	Summary of Events and Information	Remarks and references to Appendices
H.30.c.5.8. Sheet 28.	20		The blades in the Clipping Shed are not lasting very long. About 8 animals suffices to make them useless and though re-sharpening is being done by experienced men, they do not stand clipping more than one horse.	
			Visited 'B' and 'D' Batts 102 Bde R.A. - horses are in fair condition	
	21		Visited 'A' and 'C' Batts 102 Bde R.A. – animals in fair condition - evacuated several Debility cases.	
			Visited Clipping Depot accompanied by the C.R.A.	
			Informed D.A.D.O.S., G.O.C. Div. + A.A.+Q.M.G. re the blades.	
			Visited with C.R.A. B/103 Bde R.A. – condition of animals fairly good.	
			No SE/2383 R/A/Sgt Goodley J. A.V.C. reverted to the ranks for inefficiency and despatched to No 2 Vety. Hospital, HAVRE. (Authority A.D.V.S. X Corps V.624 d/8.10.17)	
	22		Inspected 'A', 'C' and 'D' Batts 103 Bde R.A. - animals in good condition - also No 2 Sect. D.A.C.	
			35 M.V.S. moved to EECKE area.	
WIZERNES	23		Changed area to Wizernes. 35 M.V.S. to QUERCAMP.	
	24		Accompanied A.A.+Q.M.G. round Inf. Units - 8th Yorks, 9th Yorks, 10th W. Ridings, 10th North. Fus, 8th K.O.Y.L.I.	
			Reported shortage of Horse Shoes to D.A.D.O.S.	
	25		Inspected 68th Inf. Bde and many units of 70th Inf. Bde with A.A.+Q.M.G.	
			Clipping Depot closed owing to camp being taken over by other units.	

D. D. & L., London, E.C.
(A8004) Wt. W1771/M2-31 750,000 5/17 Sch. 52 Forms/C2118/14

Army Form C. 2118.

Instructions regarding War Diaries and Intelligence Summaries are contained in F. S. Regs., Part II. and the Staff Manual respectively. Title pages will be prepared in manuscript.

WAR DIARY
or
INTELLIGENCE SUMMARY.
(*Erase heading not required.*)

Place	1917 Date Oct.	Hour	Summary of Events and Information	Remarks and references to Appendices
WIZERNES	26		35 M.V.S. moved to Wizernes	
			Accompanied A.A.+Q.M.G. to inspect 68th, 69th + 70th M.G. Coys.	
	27		Inspected 8th Yorks+Lancs and 11th Notts+Derbys.	
	28		Visited C.R.A. and some Artillery units	
			Wired to A.D.V.S. X Corps to return men attached to X Corps M.V.D.	
			Wire received that all personnel including Artillery employed Clipping Depot rejoin their units forthwith. Stores and machines to be returned to D.A.D.O.S.	
	29		Inspected 191 Coy A.S.C., 193 Coy A.S.C., and 71st Fd Ambulance - all satisfactory.	
			Inspected remounts at No 23 Veterinary Hospital.	
	30		Discussed with G.O.C. under the special circumstances in which we are placed whether clipping should be carried out or not.	
			Visited 23 Veterinary Hospital to inspect remounts.	
	31		Visited 9th S. Staffs and R.E. Companies - all animals in splendid condition.	
			Clipping is now being done under unit arrangements	

J.J. Hilleard
MAJOR,
D.A.D.V.S. 23RD DIVISION

D. D. & L., London, E.C.
(A8004) Wt. W1771/M2-31 750,000 5/17 Sch. 52 Forms/C2118/14

www.ingramcontent.com/pod-product-compliance
Lightning Source LLC
Chambersburg PA
CBHW081430300426
44108CB00016BA/2342